Praise for *Chicago's Great Fire*

"*Chicago's Great Fire* is . . . powered by a narrative that moves at the speed of the galloping flames. It unravels the mystery of Mrs. O'Leary and her poor cow, and is also sadly relevant, in revealing the steps and missteps, the generosity and greed, the stupidity and invention that accompanied a great city's recovery from near-total disaster."

—Scott Turow

"Carl Smith has written the definitive work on the Great Chicago Fire— the context, the stories, and the aftermath. He masterfully demonstrates how disaster can unveil forces at work in society."

—Gary T. Johnson, President, Chicago History Museum

"Smith's well-written narrative not only examines the fire itself, but also the rise of the city of Chicago and how it was forced to rebuild after the blaze tore through its neighborhoods. With accessible writing, Smith tells the story of the disaster through various individuals who lived in and around the city . . . Stunningly well-researched, this book fully examines a pivotal moment in Chicago's history. Readers of Smith's other Chicago-based books will find this fascinating. Fans of Erik Larson, American history, and the triumph of the human spirit will also greatly enjoy."

—*Library Journal* (starred review)

"Smith drops readers right into the action, transforming us into virtual citizens caught up in the conflagration and its aftermath of raucous political debates, intense class and ethnic tensions, yellow journalism, and the incredible energy and drive that enabled Chicagoans to rebuild . . . Smith, professor emeritus at Northwestern University, the author of a plethora of books on urban development and crises, and a true master of his craft, sets the historical record straight in advance of the sesquicentennial anniversary of Chicago's 'great fire.' An accessibly dramatic, even gritty factual account of a much-mythologized historic disaster."

—*Booklist* (starred review)

"A definitive retelling of one of America's 'most fabled disasters.'"

—*Publishers Weekly*

CHICAGO'S GREAT FIRE

CHICAGO'S GREAT FIRE

*The Destruction and Resurrection
of an Iconic American City*

Carl Smith

Grove Press
New York

Published simultaneously in Canada
Printed in the United States of America

First Grove Atlantic hardcover edition: October 2020
First Grove Atlantic paperback edition: September 2021

Library of Congress Cataloging-in-Publication data is available for this title.

ISBN 978-0-8021-5912-0
eISBN 978-0-8021-4811-7

Grove Press
an imprint of Grove Atlantic
154 West 14th Street
New York, NY 10011

Distributed by Publishers Group West
groveatlantic.com

21 22 23 24 10 9 8 7 6 5 4 3 2 1

To my family

CONTENTS

It takes all sorts of people to make a great fire.

—Horace White

PREFACE

The spectacular conflagration that struck Chicago on the evening of Sunday, October 8, 1871, is the most well-known urban fire in the history of the United States and one of the nation's most fabled disasters. The flames that started in the West Side barn where Catherine O'Leary tended her milk cows devastated close to three square miles of cityscape, including the heart of the city's kinetic downtown, and left around ninety thousand people homeless. The overmatched fire department was unable to stop it, especially once the roof of the city's new waterworks Pumping Station collapsed onto the machinery below. The relentless fire did not cease until it burned itself out in the early morning of Tuesday, October 10, some thirty hours after it began.

The Great Chicago Fire has had a powerful and enduring imaginative resonance. It immediately drew enormous attention, including a spontaneous outpouring of millions of dollars in charitable contributions from around the nation and the globe. This was because Chicago, which barely existed only forty years earlier, had already assumed a commanding position in the urbanizing and industrializing world's widening transportation and communications network. In its insatiable ferocity and preternatural vigor, the fire was a fitting counterpart to this epic new city. Chicago had burst into being with an explosive force that transformed it in mere decades from a distant dot on the periphery of the American frontier to one of the country's largest and most important cities. It was emblematic of the urban future and the disruptive arrival of modernity itself.

Almost immediately, many Chicagoans paradoxically came to see the heroic destruction of their city as an unexpectedly positive event, a stage in its irresistible upward development rather than a dispiriting setback. They viewed the legendary conflagration as merely the prelude to Chicago's triumphant recovery out of the ashes, a mythic second creation. The most important lesson of the city's apparent destruction, they maintained, was that Chicago was indestructible, since it emerged from this literal trial by fire bigger and stronger than ever. When in the years ahead Chicago looked back on the disaster, as during the World's Columbian Exposition of 1893 and the semicentennial and centennial commemorations of the fire in 1921 and 1971, it chose to remember the devastation mainly in order to celebrate the city's insuperable resilience.

Chicago's Great Fire recounts both the harrowing experience of the fire and the equally extraordinary rebuilding. The reasons why Chicago rebounded so rapidly and convincingly were very similar to why it came into being in the first place. The recovery was both miraculous and inevitable.

At the same time, this book points out how much more complicated— and interesting—the story of Chicago's heroic creation, undoing, and re-creation is. The fire's magnitude and fierceness were unfortunate but unsurprising consequences of the haste and heedlessness with which the city was constructed and the insufficiency of the safeguards put in place to protect it from just such a fate.

The systemic sources of the colossal damage were not something recognized only in retrospect but identified in advance by those who bothered to take an honest look. Fire officials and newspaper editors had repeatedly warned that the carelessness of Chicago's hasty making could precipitate just this kind of abrupt, massive, and fearsome unmaking.

Neither the grave destruction inflicted by the flames nor continued warnings proved enough to get Chicagoans to alter their ways significantly in the Great Fire's aftermath. Rather than having learned their lesson, residents resisted taking meaningful steps to avoid having it happen again. One result was a second serious downtown fire in the summer of 1874. Even after that, reforms came slowly.

Chicago's Great Fire also makes clear how flammable the city was socially as well as physically. Chicago was undeniably a distinctively American urban success story, a gathering of a vast and ever increasing number of people of very different backgrounds and outlooks who joined together to accomplish great things. But inherent in the formation of this sudden city of so many individuals from so many places were sharp economic, ethnic, political, and religious differences.

The multiple crises and challenges posed by the fire brought these differences fully out into the open. In the days that followed the devastation, Chicago's leaders needed to decide how to reestablish order amid the ruins and distribute aid and assistance to the tens of thousands of homeless and hungry people who desperately needed help. In less than a month after the flames ended, voters faced an election in which they would choose a new mayor and Common Council. And all residents would need to pick up the burned and broken pieces of their city and their lives and put them back together again. While Chicagoans confronted all of these crises with impressive success, the ways in which they did so did not melt their differences as much as magnify and harden them.

Chicago's unyielding spirit in the face of the most daunting adversity is an altogether engrossing and inspiring story. The recovery was nonetheless anything but smooth and simple. Trying to fireproof Chicago's volatile social environment proved if anything a more difficult and delicate task than keeping the physical city from blazing up again.

Chicago's rise represented the evolution of modern urban democracy as much as or more than any place else in the United States, perhaps on earth. Taken together, the city's destruction and resurrection indicate the extent to which Chicago was, like modernity itself, an expression of restless energy addicted to change, a profoundly unstable combination of irrefutable strengths and potentially self-destructive flaws, an open-ended work in progress in which the Great Chicago Fire was as compelling for how much it revealed as for how much it destroyed.

A NOTE ON SOURCES

In addition to print and manuscript sources, this book uses digital sources of several kinds. The most frequently cited is the Chicago History Museum's *The Great Chicago Fire and the Web of Memory* (https://www.greatchicagofire.org/), curated and written by the author, in collaboration with CHM and the Media and Technology Innovation division of Northwestern University Information Technologies.

An ever increasing proportion of the historical print resources cited here are available online. Some, like the *Chicago Tribune*, require a paid subscription, but there are also many free online repositories full of documents relevant to the fire and Chicago history. There are also several sites devoted to Chicago and urban history that have been created by knowledgeable individuals.

All italicized quotations are from the original sources.

The following abbreviations are used for frequently cited sources:

Andreas: A. T. Andreas, *History of Chicago*, 3 vols. (Chicago: A. T. Andreas, 1884–86).

Angle: Paul M. Angle, ed., *The Great Chicago Fire* (Chicago: Chicago Historical Society, 1946).

Bales: Richard F. Bales, *The Great Chicago Fire and the Myth of Mrs. O'Leary's Cow* (Jefferson, NC: McFarland, 2002).

CHMCF: Chicago History Museum, Chicago Fire of 1871 Collection.

Colbert and Chamberlin: Elias Colbert and Everett Chamberlin, *Chicago and the Great Conflagration* (Cincinnati: C. F. Vent, 1871).

CRepub: *Chicago Republican*.

CTimes: *Chicago Times*.

CTrib: *Chicago Tribune*.

EC: Chicago History Museum, the Newberry Library, and Northwestern University, *Encyclopedia of Chicago*, http://www.encyclopedia.chicagohistory.org/. Published in 2005, this

A Note on Sources

includes the text of the print edition edited by James
R. Grossman, Ann Durkin Keating, and Janice L. Reiff and
published by the University of Chicago Press in 2004. The
order of editors is reversed in the online edition.

GCFWOM: Chicago History Museum and Northwestern University, *The Great Chicago Fire and the Web of Memory*,
https://www.greatchicagofire.org/. Originally created in 1996,
this was extensively revised in 2011. It is also available as an
Apple iOS app.

ISZ: *Illinois Staats-Zeitung.* The English translations of this
German-language newspaper are accessible through the Newberry Library Foreign Language Press Survey, https://flps
.newberry.org/.

McIlvaine: Mabel McIlvaine, *Reminiscences of Chicago during the
Great Fire* (Chicago: Lakeside, 1915). The contents of this
volume are reprinted, with different pagination and many
excellent illustrations, in David Lowe, ed., *The Great Chicago
Fire* (New York: Dover, 1979).

Musham: H. A. Musham, "The Great Chicago Fire, October 8–10, 1871," in *Papers in Illinois History and Transactions
for the Year 1940* (Springfield: Illinois State Historical Society,
1941): 69–149.

Pierce: Bessie Louise Pierce, *A History of Chicago*, 3 vols. (Chicago:
University of Chicago Press, 1937–57).

Sawislak: Karen Sawislak, *Smoldering City: Chicagoans and the
Great Fire, 1871–1874* (Chicago: University of Chicago Press,
1995).

Skogan: Wesley G. Skogan, ed., *Chicago since 1840: A Time-Series
Data Handbook* (Urbana: University of Illinois Institute of
Government and Public Affairs, 1976).

DOLLAR VALUES AND
STREET NAMES

Costs given are those at the time, not current equivalents. As explained by the website Measuring Worth, calculating equivalents is complicated by the fact that there are different ways of doing so that result in very different equivalents. The simplest is by comparing purchasing power then and now. For example, by that measure the worth of something in 2018 was 21.2 times what it was in 1871. So something that cost $100 in 1871 would cost about $2,100 in 2018. But by other measures (e.g., labor value, income value, economic share) the multiple is much higher. Similarly, there are different multipliers to use in order to compare wealth and income or the cost of a particular project in different times. See https://www.measuringworth.com/index.php for more details, as well as an online calculator. As indicated, some figures cited in this book are estimates, which frequently vary from source to source.

The street names given in the text are those at the time. In the several instances where the name has changed, the current name is indicated in parentheses. Rather than identify street address numbers, the book gives locations, since most Chicago streets affected by the fire had their addresses renumbered early in the twentieth century in order to make them more consistent.

CHICAGO'S GREAT FIRE

- 1 -
"KATE! THE BARN IS AFIRE!"

At seven o'clock on the morning of Sunday, October 8, 1871, Chief Fire Marshal Robert A. Williams decided he could finally take a break. Williams had been up all night battling a horrendous fire that started between ten and eleven o'clock Saturday night in the boiler room of the Lull & Holmes Planing mill. The mill was in a two-story sixty-by-eighty-foot brick building on South Canal Street between Jackson and Van Buren Streets in the West Division, just across the South Branch of the Chicago River from the downtown. Local insurance men dubbed the area in which the building was located the Red Flash.

There was good reason for the gallows humor. Everything in the vicinity was poised to burn. The mill was full of raw wood and sawdust, while next door was a cardboard box factory. The neighborhood was dotted with coal and lumber yards. Two of these yards contained between them more than seven million feet of dry pine, enough to build a small village. Or feed a large fire.

People rushed to the scene to take in the spectacle of sight, sound, and smell—the mesmerizing dance of the flames, the crackle and crash of tumbling beams, the acrid smoke—and thrill at the firemen's battle to contain it all. The "dense fiery glow of the destroying element," which illuminated the area all around it, "made up a panorama of grand but terrible features," the *Chicago Tribune* reported. The fire devastated four city blocks, about sixteen acres, inflicting damages estimated at $750,000. Once the flames burned out on Sunday afternoon, smoldering coal piles continued to glow ominously, like the eyes of a fire-breathing dragon only pretending to sleep.

The Saturday Night Fire was the most serious of more than two dozen conflagrations in Chicago during that past week alone. On September 30 the contents of Burlington Railroad's twenty-two-thousand-square-foot Warehouse A had caught fire. The warehouse was crammed with cases of liquor and stacks of dried cornstalks used for making brooms, all highly combustible. By the time the fire was put out, the building, valued at more than $600,000, was a total loss and a Burlington employee was dead.

Firemen blamed boys smoking for the destruction the following day of a two-family brick residence near the lakefront south of the downtown. That same afternoon a careless roofer set off a blaze in the Chicago and North Western Railway freight office. As the week unfolded, a church, a hotel, a furniture factory, a butcher shop, and several barns and dwellings were hit. The fire department attributed these fires to causes ranging from more worker carelessness and mischievous boys to defective chimneys and outright arson.

While it might seem otherwise, Chicago had been lucky. Almost no rain—less than an inch and a half—had fallen since early July, which had left everything so dry that a wayward spark could prove catastrophic. A persistent October heat wave—reaching eighty degrees by afternoon—and strong prevailing winds out of the southwest put everybody on edge. As the family of seven-year-old A. S. Chapman rode their carriage to church Sunday morning "into the teeth of a withering gale from the southwest," Chapman's father voiced a thought on many minds: "If a fire should start, Chicago will burn up."

Before Chief Williams could slip gratefully into bed, he was summoned to another fire, a small one. Once this was out, he returned home and at last made it to sleep. He awakened at 2:15 p.m., washed his face, and put on clean clothes. Williams, who had missed breakfast, went downstairs to join his wife Harriet, back from church, for lunch. Williams then walked to the nearby station where his driver had the chief marshal's horse and wagon hitched up. He wanted to check on the state of the Saturday Night Fire and the condition of his men and equipment.

Williams learned that the fire had severely weakened the department. At full strength, it consisted of about 190 men serving in seventeen steam fire engine companies, four hook and ladder companies, and six hose companies. Even before the Saturday Night Fire, one of the hose companies was not in service, and one of the fire engines, *Liberty No. 7*, was in the shop. The Saturday Night Fire destroyed the truck used by Pioneer Hook and Ladder Company No. 1, and the *William James Engine No. 3* needed extensive repairs. Hoses and protective gear had also been

Chicago Chief Fire Marshal Robert A. Williams. In his lap is a speaking trumpet, a megaphone through which officers shouted orders during a fire. (Chicago History Museum, ICHi-012924)

damaged. The firefighters were in even worse shape. About one-third of the force was incapacitated by exhaustion and exposure to the smoke, glare, and unrelenting heat. Of the approximately 125 remaining, many could barely open their swollen and bloodshot eyes.

Williams was back home in time for supper, after which he and Harriet planned to visit Mathias Benner, one of his three assistant marshals, and Benner's wife Mary. On the way, the chief received word of yet another fire, which canceled the social call.

It was a false alarm, a common occurrence. On his way home, Williams had trouble keeping his hat on his head because of gusts from the southwest. He had a premonition of more trouble to come. "I felt it in my bones," he remembered, that "we were going to have a 'burn.'" He decided that the best thing to do was get some more sleep.

Williams was back in bed around eight o'clock. Before he lay down, he set out his coat, helmet, and boots, so if need be he could "jump into them." He asked Harriet, who was reading in the parlor, to close the door to the bedroom so the light would not disturb him.

Patrick and Catherine O'Leary lived with their five children—two girls and three boys, ranging from a fifteen-year-old to an infant—about three quarters of a mile south of the Saturday Night Fire, on the north side of DeKoven Street, some two hundred feet east of Jefferson Street. A local reporter described the neighborhood, one of the most densely populated sections of the city, as "a *terra incognita* to respectable Chicagoans," packed with "one-story frame dwellings, cow-stables, corn-cribs, sheds innumerable; every wretched building within four feet of its neighbor, and everything of wood."

Catherine O'Leary was about forty, and Patrick O'Leary a few years older. They were both immigrants from Ireland, he from County Kerry in the southwest and she from adjoining County Cork. They married before departing for America in 1845, at the onset of the potato blight that starved the country and killed or drove out more than 20 percent of the population over the next half dozen years. They had first lived in Harrisburg, Pennsylvania, where Patrick had enlisted to serve in the Union Army.

Patrick was an unskilled laborer, earning perhaps $1.50 to $2.00 a day when he found work. Catherine kept house and conducted a small dairy business in the neighborhood. By this time most milk arrived by train from the surrounding countryside, but it struck no one as unusual that a family, whether wealthy or poor, might keep farm animals well within the city limits. Catherine O'Leary sheltered her four cows, a calf, and the horse that pulled her milk wagon in the barn behind their home. The livestock was an important source of income in which she and Patrick had made a significant investment. She had taken delivery of two tons of timothy hay for the animals the day before. The O'Learys had also recently received and stored in the barn a supply of wood shavings and coal for cooking and to keep them warm in colder days ahead.

A person of generous inclination might call the O'Leary home a cottage, but it was not much more than a ramshackle shanty, sixteen feet wide and about twice that deep. Like thousands of others throughout the city, it consisted of a frame made of two-by-fours covered with bare pine shingles and roofed with tar paper. Houses like this were easy and inexpensive to build because of the availability of standardized milled lumber and machine-made nails. This kind of structure was well suited to circumstances where speed and economy mattered more than solidity.

The seven O'Learys shared two rooms. They enjoyed little natural light since there was only a single small window on each of their home's four sides. The building had no foundation. Instead, wooden supports raised it a few feet above the bare ground. The rough planks that covered the gaps between these supports helped cut the wind but were hardly enough to keep the winter cold from seeping up through the floor. A stove vented with a simple brick chimney provided heat and a

The O'Leary family lived in the rear cottage and rented the front one to their tenants, the McLaughlins. Like most Chicago streets, DeKoven Street was unpaved. Wooden fences and sidewalks, which were commonplace throughout the city, were very flammable. From a stereograph by J. H. Abbott, 1871. (Chicago History Museum, ICHi-002741)

place to cook. Chicago streets were lit by gas, as were better offices, stores, homes, many of which also had indoor plumbing. Chicago working people like the O'Learys relied on the light of lanterns and candles, fetched water from public pumps, and used a privy.

Humble as it was, this dwelling was possibly better than what Catherine and Patrick had known in Ireland. Most important, it was theirs. Many Chicagoans even as poor as the O'Learys owned their homes, spare as those homes might be. In fact, the O'Learys owned two very similar houses, one right behind the other on their twenty-five-by-one-hundred-foot lot, as well as the sixteen-by-twenty-foot back barn. The second house provided rental income. Multiple buildings jammed together like this were commonplace. The O'Learys' current tenants were the McLaughlins, also Irish born and named Catherine and Patrick, and their toddler, Mary Ann.

Virtually all their neighbors were immigrants, mostly from Bohemia as well as Ireland. Timothy and Katie Murray lived in a cottage just to the west, James and Katie Dalton and their five children in one to the east. Murray was a carpenter, and Dalton was an unskilled laborer like Patrick O'Leary. Daniel Sullivan lived across the street with his mother. The twenty-six-year-old Sullivan earned his living driving a dray, a heavy-duty delivery wagon. A gregarious and garrulous man who favored his pipe, Sullivan was an easily recognizable figure on DeKoven Street since he hobbled about on a wooden leg.

The O'Learys turned in about the same time as Chief Fire Marshal Williams. Catherine, who was nursing a sore foot, would have to awaken a little after 4:00 a.m. to milk her cows. Daniel Sullivan came by to chat the O'Learys up, but he left when he discovered they had already gone to bed. As Catherine and Patrick dropped off to sleep, they could hear through the wall quadrilles rising from Patrick McLaughlin's fiddle, to which guests danced in a welcome celebration for a relative just arrived in America.

An hour later, about nine o'clock, Daniel Sullivan's urgent shouting roused Patrick. O'Leary jumped out of bed, opened the door, and looked to the rear of the lot.

"Kate!" Patrick screamed to his wife, "the barn is afire!"

"TO DEPRESS HER RISING CONSEQUENCE WOULD BE LIKE AN ATTEMPT TO QUENCH THE STARS"

In 1673 two Frenchmen, Jesuit missionary Jacques Marquette and explorer Louis Jolliet, became the first white men to visit the marshy area where the Chicago River meets Lake Michigan. The North, South, and Main Branches (the last is also called the Main Stem) of the river together form a sideways T with a very long top that splits Chicago into its North, South, and West Sides, officially called divisions at the time of the fire. The river and the city's almost unrelievedly level terrain are the heritage of the last glacial age, which ended about 13,500 years ago. Since Chicago sits just to the east of a virtually imperceptible subcontinental divide, the North and South Branches flowed into the Main Branch, which emptied into the lake.

The region had long been a vital locus of Native American life and continued to be so even as the French and British fought for dominance in North America. The Seven Years' War—known in the United States as the French and Indian War—ended in 1763 with Britain victorious. By then the estimated Native American population on the western Great Lakes frontier was about thirty thousand Illinois, Kickapoo, Miami, Ojibwa, Odawa, and Sauk.

France and Britain had been less interested in settling the region than continuing the fur trade. The new American nation that soon ousted the British was by contrast bent on integrating this expanse into the rest of the country. In 1803 the US Army arrived to erect Fort Dearborn, named after Henry Dearborn, President Thomas Jefferson's secretary of war, on the south bank of the river where it now crosses Michigan Avenue. Over the next three decades the Americans expelled the indigenous

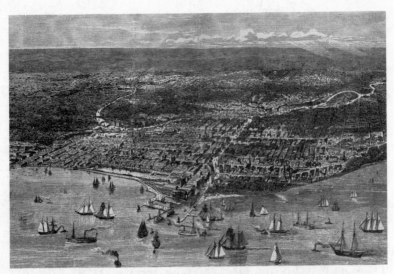

"The City of Chicago as it was before the Great Conflagration of October 8th, 9th, & 10th, 1871." The view is looking west, with Lake Michigan in the foreground. On the eve of the fire, the three divisions comprised around thirty-six square miles—approximately one-sixth of Chicago's present size—with an estimated population of just over 334,000 people. Almost half of Chicagoans lived in the West Division, which included about two-thirds of Chicago's total area. Next in population and size was the South Division, with slightly more than 91,000 people in just over eight square miles, followed by the North Division, with almost 78,000 Chicagoans in four square miles. (Library of Congress, G4104.C6A35 1871 .D3)

population beyond the Mississippi River through treaties backed by armed force.

The most notable resistance in Chicago occurred near the beginning of the War of 1812. Fearing local Native Americans allied with the British, on August 15, 1812, the soldiers and civilians living in Chicago decided to retreat eastward to Fort Wayne. They did not get far. Along the lakeshore near what is now Roosevelt Road, they were attacked by Potawatomi. More than half were killed. The rest were taken captive and eventually ransomed or freed.

The war officially ended late in 1814 with the Treaty of Ghent, which recognized US control over the western Great Lakes. In 1816, soldiers returned to rebuild Fort Dearborn. Between then and 1833, Native Americans ceded almost all of their homelands east of the Mississippi. By 1818 Illinois was a state, though the great majority of its white people were well south and west of Chicago, in places like New Salem on the Sangamon River, where young Abraham Lincoln arrived in 1831 before moving to the state capital in Springfield six years later.

The mercantile imperatives of an ambitious and growing nation conjured the city of Chicago into being. The completion of the Erie Canal in 1825, which connected the Hudson River to the Great Lakes, not only ensured the commercial eminence of New York City by affording it superior access to the riches of the hinterland but also made Chicago, thanks to its position at the southwestern edge of Lake Michigan, the western terminus of a major trade route. The next step was to realize an idea that dated back to Marquette and Jolliet. If a canal could be built from the Chicago River southwest to the Illinois River, which flowed into the Mississippi, it would open up commerce even farther westward and further enhance the value of Chicago's location.

In 1827 the federal government gave the state of Illinois 300,000 acres of land to sell in order to pay for building the canal. This became the funding model for the enormous land grants that financed private railroads in the decades ahead. In 1833, when there were perhaps five hundred people living in the newly established town of Chicago, the federal government cleared a sandbar that blocked the entrance to the river to make it accessible from the lake.

The final Native American attempt to halt settlement in Illinois was the Black Hawk War of the spring and summer of 1832. Black Hawk, a Sauk chief living on the eastern shore of the Mississippi, tried to enlist other Native Americans to join him. Sensing a lost cause, the Potawatomi, the largest Native American presence in the Chicago area, held back. Most of the fighting was in the western part of the state and neighboring portions of the Wisconsin Territory. By August, Black Hawk was defeated. In 1833, six thousand Potawatomi and their allies gathered in Chicago for negotiations in which they exchanged five million acres of land in northeastern Illinois and southeastern Wisconsin for five million west of the Mississippi. By 1835 they were virtually gone.

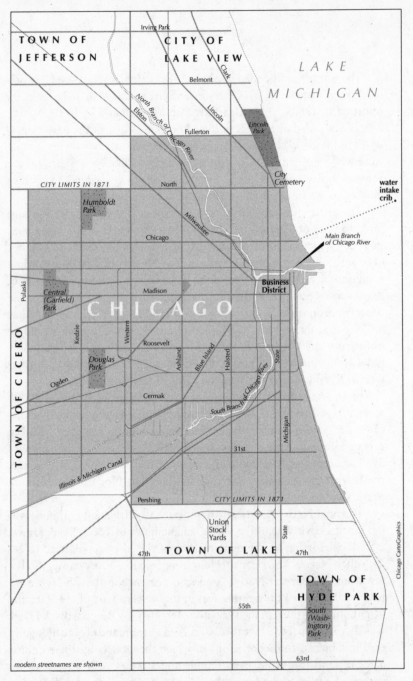

TOWN OF JEFFERSON

CITY OF LAKE VIEW

LAKE MICHIGAN

Irving Park
Belmont
Clark
Lincoln
Elston
North Branch of Chicago River
Fullerton

Lincoln Park

City Cemetery

water intake crib

CITY LIMITS IN 1871

Humboldt Park

North

Milwaukee

Chicago

Main Branch of Chicago River

Pulaski

CHICAGO

Central (Garfield) Park

Madison

Business District

TOWN OF CICERO

Kedzie

Western

Roosevelt

Ashland

Blue Island

Halsted

South Branch of Chicago River

State

Douglas Park

Ogden

Cermak

Michigan

Illinois & Michigan Canal

31st

CITY LIMITS IN 1871

Pershing

Union Stock Yards

State

47th   TOWN OF LAKE   47th

TOWN OF HYDE PARK

55th

South (Washington) Park

63rd

Chicago CartoGraphics

modern streetnames are shown

Chicago and surrounding areas in 1871. As indicated here and on other maps, the street names, some of which have been changed since the time of the fire, are the current ones.

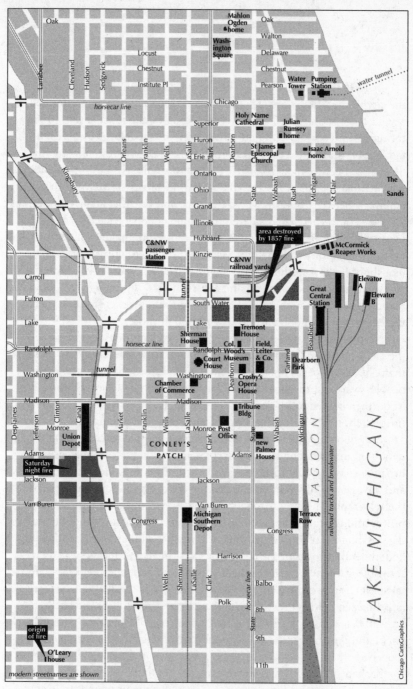

The central portion of the city on the eve of the Great Chicago
Fire. Several of the sites indicated on the map are
discussed in later chapters.

In 1836 work began on the Illinois and Michigan Canal to connect the city to the Mississippi. This accelerated settlement and precipitated a wild land boom. The Panic of 1837—one of the most severe to hit the nineteenth century's up-and-down economy—burst the local real estate bubble and stalled construction on the canal, but it did not stop the flow of settlers to Chicago. The 1840 census counted 4,470 residents, which ranked Chicago as the ninety-second largest settlement in the country—between Beverly, Massachusetts, and Carlisle, Pennsylvania.

Newcomers arrived at a heretofore unimaginable pace. By 1850 the number of Chicagoans was up to thirty thousand, making this scruffy upstart the nation's twenty-fourth largest metropolis, now between Williamsburg (later a section of Brooklyn) and Troy, New York. Chicago's rise was part of a national urbanizing trend. In 1790 the United States had only five cities with more than ten thousand people. By 1870 there were fourteen with populations of 100,000 or more.

No place grew as fast as Chicago. In the twenty-one years between the 1850 census and the fire, its population increased elevenfold, to more than 330,000, a net figure that did not come close to the total number of people swarming through the city on their way elsewhere. Only New York (then limited to Manhattan), Philadelphia, Brooklyn, and St. Louis (just barely, if at all) were bigger than the Chicago that burned.

And no other city so fully embodied the seismic forces behind the nation's transformation from an overwhelmingly rural to an increasingly urban society: immigration and westward migration, industrialization and the mastery of steam power, and the conquest of space and time by the telegraph and the railroad. Situated between the vast productive power and consumer appetite of the eastern United States and the prodigious bounty of the farms, ranches, ranges, timberlands, coalfields, and mineral deposits of the continent's vast interior, Chicago was an irresistible attraction for investment capital and people of entrepreneurial spirit. "See two things in the United States, if nothing else,—Niagara and Chicago," British textile manufacturer and reform statesman Richard Cobden advised in 1867. The falls represented the nation's extraordinary natural wonders, and Chicago the central stage for the enactment of modernity.

Backed by eastern and European investors and an expanding national and international economy that needed a major inland trade and transportation center, local businessmen turned Chicago first into a mercantile wonder and then an industrial colossus. The year 1848, sometimes referred to as the city's annus mirabilis, witnessed the completion of the ninety-six-mile Illinois and Michigan Canal, the opening of the Board of Trade, Chicago's initial telegraphic communication (with Milwaukee, Wisconsin, on January 1), and the maiden journey of its first railroad. By the next decade it was the country's primary corn and wheat market, the center of its lumber trade, its leader in meatpacking, and the midcontinent's transportation hub.

Chicago was also assuming a key role in the international economy. The outbreak of the Crimean War in 1853 caused American wheat exports to double in volume and triple in value. With the development of the grain elevator, the standardization of the grading of commodities, and the thickening of the railroad and telegraph networks, Chicago traders began to sell contracts that promised delivery of an agreed-upon quantity and quality of grain by a specified date. In 1865 the Board of Trade set the first formal rules for this market in futures.

During the 1860s the provisioning needs of the Union Army not only benefited Chicago's commodities and meat merchants but also amplified the output of factories that turned out uniforms, boots, bridles, and saddles. In spite of a postwar lull in the economy, late 1860s Chicago was filling large orders for men's and women's clothing, engines and boilers, iron pipes and stoves, wagons and carriages, bricks and shingles, plows and reapers, and railroad cars and tracks.

The famed Union Stock Yards opened on Christmas Day 1865, five miles south of Chicago's downtown in the adjoining town of Lake. Stretching over almost 350 acres, it was a city in itself, one of the greatest concentrations of capital investment and industrial production in the world. The Union Stock Yards' more than two thousand pens could hold well over 100,000 head of cattle, hogs, and sheep. It contained seven miles of streets and alleys, as well as its own rail network, drainage system, water supply, and hotel.

The canal was of vital importance in connecting Chicago to western Illinois and the Mississippi, while lake traffic made Chicago one of the busiest ports in the country. Lake and canal shipping, however, could not match the rising significance of the railroad. In the key decade of the 1850s, the miles of railroad tracks in the nation jumped from 9,000 to 30,000, with 2,500 miles of this growth in Illinois alone. In the following decade, 22,000 miles were added, almost 2,100 of these in the state.

In the early 1850s the Illinois Central Railroad—in which Senator Stephen Douglas was a major investor and for which attorney Abraham Lincoln did legal work—obtained rights to lay its tracks along a trestle four hundred feet out into the lake in exchange for building a breakwater that would protect the shore against erosion. The railroad was eager to obtain these rights in order to gain prime access to the city: the tracks terminated in the Great Central Station at Randolph Street east of Michigan Avenue. The trestle and the breakwater drew a dark line across the horizon and turned the portion of the lake between the tracks and Michigan Avenue into a basin.

Chicago was the vital nexus through which grain, coal, lumber, livestock, and packed meat traveled east and manufactured goods of every variety moved north, west, and south, with countless people traveling in all directions. Since Chicago was the terminus of all of the railways that served it, neither passengers nor freight could pass through the city without stopping in the city to change lines. The four major train termi-

Great Railway Station at Chicago—Departure of a Train.
From Appleton's Journal, *1870. Note the mixed crowd,
including (right center) a frontiersman and two Plains Indians.*
(Chicago History Museum, ICHi-035823)

nals surrounded the center of the downtown, with freight facilities, and the Union Stock Yards, on the periphery.

A traveler could make it from Chicago to New York in thirty hours without the inconvenience of changing trains. Following the completion of the transcontinental railroad in 1869, it took a little over one hundred hours to get to San Francisco. Eight days before the fire, the Michigan Central Railroad brought to the city its first carloads of bonded European goods, to be opened by local US Customs inspectors, bypassing delays and handling charges of middlemen on the East Coast. By then almost two hundred passenger and 240 freight trains arrived in or departed from Chicago every day.

The constant coming and going of trains, with their black smoke and piercing whistles, intruded everywhere, spurring disputes about right-of-way and posing a significant safety hazard. The Illinois Central tracks disrupted the serenity of anyone hoping to gaze upon Chicago's sole natural wonder, Lake Michigan. A reporter writing in June 1871 asserted that "an intelligent person coming into Chicago" along the

View looking north of Michigan Avenue and the Illinois Central trestle and breakwater in the lake. (Chicago History Museum, ICHi-063068)

Illinois Central tracks "cannot fail to observe the somewhat slovenly appearance of the lake front as contrasted with the palatial elegance of Michigan Avenue in the background." Nor could this passenger avoid "a feeling of contempt for the folly that overlooks an opportunity of creating a beautiful approach to the city out of the miry, ragged-looking space between the railroad track and the avenue."

The city's boosters, whose promotional enthusiasm and rhetoric knew no bounds, dismissed criticisms of Chicago's haphazard and provisional quality. Since tomorrow was sure to be bigger and better, it was foolish to be concerned about today. The present was only a gateway to ever greater accomplishment. "To depress her rising consequence," local attorney Henry Brown declared in 1846 (when there were only fourteen thousand Chicagoans), "would be like an attempt to quench the stars."

Chicago's rapid development was a marvel, but it brought difficult challenges. The city was a socially, economically, and politically divided and contested place. And the manner in which it had been built made it especially vulnerable to fire.

After the Great Fire, some longtime native-born residents would wax nostalgic about the city's early years as a friendlier time, when Chicagoans knew each other much better and shared common interests. This was probably never the case, or certainly not for very long. Chicago's most notable demographic characteristic was how many people, whether prominent or obscure, had come to the city from somewhere else. Much more often than not, that somewhere else was far away. In 1870 almost half of all Chicagoans—48 percent—were, like the O'Learys and their neighbors, immigrants from abroad. A considerably higher percentage had at least one foreign-born parent.

The first immigrants to arrive in significant numbers came from Ireland, many to work on the Illinois and Michigan Canal. The next were people from the German states, many of them Forty-Eighters who emigrated to the United States after the failure of the midcentury democratic revolutions in Europe. Germans soon became the city's biggest ethnic group. By 1870 almost 20 percent of Chicago residents were German born, while over 13 percent were natives of Ireland, with smaller representations from Scandinavia, the rest of Great Britain, and Central Europe, including the O'Learys' Bohemian neighbors. Germans and Irish lived all over the city, but the former were especially concentrated in the northern half of the North Division.

Much of Chicago's minority "American" population, which had begun to arrive before either the Irish or the Germans, had also come a significant distance. While almost two-thirds of US-born Chicagoans living in the city in 1870 were from the Old Northwest (Ohio, Indiana, Illinois, Michigan, Wisconsin, and Minnesota), over 28 percent were from the Middle Atlantic and New England states. No matter where they were born, Chicagoans were overwhelmingly white. The African American population was growing, but in 1870 only about 1.2 percent of the city was black. It was not until 1870 that African Americans could vote in the city, and the public schools would not be integrated until a few years after that. In Chicago, as elsewhere, no woman of any color could cast a ballot for almost another half century. There was virtually no Asian presence in prefire Chicago.

Ethnic ties were neither simple nor straightforward. Chicago's "Americans" and its "foreign" groups, especially the Germans and Irish, were far too large to be monolithic. They were divided by class, particular region of birth, political views (regarding the old country as well as the new one), and, especially in the case of Catholic and Protestant Irish and Germans, by religion.

As a general rule, however, the three categories of ethnicity, class, and religion correlated: the city's richest residents were mainly members of a small group of native-born individuals of British Protestant ancestry. From their ranks came most of the 20 percent of Chicagoans who owned almost all of the city's wealth. The balance of the population, which included virtually all of the city's working people, were preponderantly immigrants and their children. Ethnic prejudice, especially toward Irish Catholics, was a given among native-born Protestants. The wealthy were adamantly opposed to emerging labor unions. In the late 1860s the movement to institute an eight-hour workday—as opposed to the normal ten or twelve hours, six days a week—had failed.

The immigrants who provided so many of Chicago's workers and small tradesmen were loyal American citizens. Many fought in the Civil War to save the Union. Their determination to honor and preserve their heritage could still put them at odds with the Yankee population.

Native-born Chicagoans provided moral and financial support for France in the Franco-Prussian War, holding a rally on February 4, 1871, and a benefit concert a few weeks later. Four months after that, even a downpour could not discourage a much larger group of Germans from cheering their country's victory and unification at a picnic in bosky Lake View, then a separate city bordering Chicago on the north.

Immigrants and working people asserted their presence in Chicago through their houses of worship. There are few better examples than the Holy Family Church, the vision of Dutch-born Jesuit priest Arnold Damen, who persuaded the skeptical local hierarchy to let him build it more than two miles southwest of the center of the city, just west of the intersection of Twelfth Street (Roosevelt Road) and Blue Island Avenue. Few people lived near there at the time, but Damen was confident the church would draw them.

Holy Family was dedicated in 1860. With a seating capacity of two thousand, the Gothic sanctuary was one of the largest in the country. Draw the people it did, assisted by Chicago's rapid growth and expansion: by 1871 it served the largest parish in the city, with a congregation of almost twenty thousand, including Patrick and Catherine O'Leary, who baptized their children there and educated them in the parish schools. For humble people like them, who lived within very narrow margins, the pennies they were able to contribute to Holy Family were more than worth it. The great church provided a sublime retreat of holiness and beauty that was their own, through which they could declare they belonged to Chicago, and it to them.

Local politics, like everything else in prefire Chicago, was continuously shifting and evolving, as the state and the city became much more important nationally. Two Illinois politicians, Abraham Lincoln and Stephen Douglas, were the leading vote-getters in the pivotal 1860 presidential election. The Republicans held their national convention in Chicago that year and again in 1868, while the Democrats convened in the city in 1864 to nominate Lincoln's second-term opponent, General George McClellan.

Chicago's mayor, who served a two-year term, could make certain appointments and did much to set the public agenda, often through force of personality. Through much of the nineteenth century, however, the most powerful branch of government was the unicameral Common Council. At the time of the fire its membership comprised forty aldermen, two from each of twenty wards. They also served two-year terms, with one of the two seats up in the annual election. Independently elected boards administered the police and fire departments and public works.

In the city's early years, native-born Chicagoans ran the city government, and through the middle decades of the century and beyond they held the mayoralty. By 1871, however, immigrants constituted a majority of voters—about 56 percent—and ethnic politicians occupied a comparable percentage of seats on the Common Council. The Irish, who arrived earlier, were a stronger presence in city politics than the Germans even after the latter became the city's largest ethnic group. Spokesmen for the Germans bristled at their underrepresentation. In May 1871 the *Illinois Staats-Zeitung* complained that while seventeen of the city's forty aldermen were born in the United States, and thirteen in Ireland, only eight were from Germany.

Over the previous few decades, government activities, services, and expenses had greatly expanded to such an extent that expenditures for a single day of the 1870–71 fiscal year equaled those of the entire 1847–48 fiscal year. This was due to the city's exponential growth over that period and the accompanying costs of building major infrastructural improvements, maintaining existing public works, operating the police and fire departments, and funding public schools. Aldermen had considerable control of the rising number of government jobs, contracts, and property deals, which created opportunities for the abuse of patronage and outright bribery. Members of the Common Council drew no salary (they kept their other jobs), making such practices all the more tempting.

Native-born business leaders were unhappy with their diminishing influence in the conduct of government just as its powers and costs were expanding. At the time of the fire, the leading English-language dailies, most of which spoke for this constituency, attacked the integrity of ethnic politicians. They singled out Alderman James McCauley, who represented the North Side's Nineteenth Ward. They compared him and his allies, known as McCauley's Nineteen, to the greedy schemers of New York's Democratic political organization known as Tammany Hall, headed by William "Boss" Tweed. The public exposure of Tweed's corruption made national headlines during the summer and fall of 1871. For their part, McCauley and his cohort countered that their critics preferred aldermen who obeyed the privileged few rather than "the people."

Roswell B. Mason. (Chicago History Museum, ICHi-040044)

In the mayoral campaign of 1869, a coalition that included some labor leaders formed what they named the Citizens Party, which nominated Roswell B. Mason for mayor. Central to Mason's appeal was that he had almost no apparent political connections. Born near Utica, New York, in 1805, he was a member of the generation of American civil engineers who received their training on the job, many on the Erie Canal. After taking positions of increasing responsibility on a series of other canals, Mason switched to railroads. In 1851 he resigned his post as engineer and superintendent of the New York and New Haven Railroad to oversee the construction of the Illinois Central, after which he engaged in various businesses in Chicago.

Political and cultural issues constantly intermixed. The temperance cause, so powerful among native-born American Protestants through the nineteenth century, intensified prejudice toward Irish Catholics and alienated much of the city's German population of all religions.

Bohemian, German, and Irish immigrants, even those who did not drink, accurately viewed attempts to prohibit alcohol as a condemnation of their customs and identity and, by extension, their presence in the city. In 1855, Levi Boone, a grandnephew of Daniel Boone and veteran of the Black Hawk War, was elected mayor on the Know-Nothing platform, which opposed immigration and favored abstinence. A few weeks later, Boone's attempt to enforce a Sunday closing law passed a decade earlier touched off the so-called Lager Beer Riot of April 21, 1855, a brief but full-fledged battle between protesters and police backed by local militia.

This aroused such bad feeling that afterward authorities largely ignored the Sunday closing law, though abstainers repeatedly and loudly called for its enforcement. In early June 1871, German residents filled a meeting hall on North Clark Street, where they passed resolutions denouncing the law and those who demanded the police observe it, as infringing upon their "social privileges as citizens." It was "unconstitutional" and "inconsistent with the spirit of our republican institutions," discriminatory in the way it expressed "a direct preference of that religious denomination, which is based upon orthodox Puritanism and intolerant Calvinism." Chicagoans deserved "a more liberal conception of the nature and commands of a Divine Providence."

As inflammatory as might be political, economic, and social conflicts, literal fire was the most persistent clear and present danger in American urban life. In the half century before the Great Chicago Fire, major conflagrations had occurred in Savannah, Georgia (1820); New York City (1835 and 1845); Pittsburgh (1845); San Francisco (1851); and Portland, Maine (1866).

Until shortly before the Civil War, cities heavily relied for protection on a volunteer firefighting force made up of independent companies. Men of spirit, strength, and stamina "ran with the machine," the iron engine on wheels they pulled through the streets as fast as they could, heedless of any vehicles or pedestrians in their way. When they reached the fire, the real effort began. Two or three men on either side of the engine worked its broad pump handles up and down in order to push the water through the hose and out the nozzle that the pipemen trained on burning buildings.

Like those elsewhere, Chicago's volunteer fire crews, which dated from the 1830s, favored stirring, colorful, and patriotic names like Red Jackets and Washington Volunteers. Often organized by neighborhood and nationality, volunteer fire companies were as intent on besting other contingents as on saving property and lives. The struggles between men and flames were a favorite subject of contemporary lithographs, as well as a free and rousing spectacle for city dwellers. Volunteer firemen proudly took part in the multiplicity of civic ceremonies, marching in full uniform alongside their equipment, which they polished as bright as altar pieces. Organized competitions between fire companies were unsubtle demonstrations of virility. In 1848, Chicago's Red Jacket crew proved its mettle by spurting a powerful stream out of its hose higher and farther than all others.

When the city purchased its first steam-powered pumping engine in 1858, the volunteers greeted it as an insult and a threat. The steamer *Long John* was named after six foot six (seven feet, in his top hat) "Long John" Wentworth, Chicago's strong-willed mayor at the time. The weight of such engines, some over four tons, required that they be pulled by teams of as many as four horses. The new engines made hand pumping obsolete. During a tryout conducted at LaSalle Street and the Main Branch, the *Long John* thrust two streams of water seventy feet into the air and a distance of over two hundred feet. Fit and experienced firefighters pumping manually might match this for a short stretch of time, but the *Long John* never tired. As A. T. Andreas, the foremost nineteenth-century historian of Chicago, sympathetically observed, "The boys of the volunteer department saw in its every puff a death blow to their own system."

The new equipment undoubtedly better served the needs of places like Chicago, which as they grew larger, taller, and denser became all the more prone to serious fires. A minor blaze could quickly lead to major harm. On October 19, 1857, Chicago's deadliest fire to date incinerated a four-story brick wholesale store just south of the Main Branch, destroying property worth a half million dollars and killing twenty-three Chicagoans, including three firemen. The entire city felt the pain. The caskets of the deceased rested on biers in the Courthouse, as the combined Chicago City Hall and Cook County administrative building was called, before being borne in a procession to a public funeral service. Twenty thousand Chicagoans, more than one-fifth of the population, paid their respects.

The volunteers' unsatisfactory response to the fire persuaded the Common Council not only to purchase steam-powered equipment but also to create a professional department of trained and organized municipal employees. Its first members were specifically assigned to man the new steam-powered engines, which required technical knowhow rather than brute strength, though firefighting has never been a job for weaklings.

The transition from a volunteer department to full professionalization took about a decade. Many members of the paid department— including future chief marshal Robert A. Williams, a native of Canada who was twenty-one when he came to Chicago in 1849—had begun as volunteers. Salaried firefighters cost tax dollars, but paying men enabled the city to control and discipline them, which was not possible with the volunteer companies.

Firemen and police (the Chicago Police Department dates to 1855), along with a rising number of Americans employed in factories and offices, now found themselves in a top-down hierarchy of coordinated workers who followed set rules and procedures. While fighting a blaze, firemen were outfitted in uniforms consisting of high boots, heavyweight rubber trench coats, and leather hats peaked high in the front to display an identifying badge and with a flared brim at the rear to deflect falling water.

When the flames erupted in the O'Leary barn, Chicago was as up-to-date as any city and ahead of most when it came to firefighting. Since 1865 the fire department had been supervised jointly with the police department by a combined board of commissioners. That year it had installed a state-of-the-art signal system, with 172 alarm boxes distributed throughout the three divisions. To guard against false alarms, the boxes were locked, the keys entrusted to citizens (often storeowners) located nearby, who, when they saw or were notified of a fire, unlocked the box and pulled the switch that signaled the telegraph operator in the fire department's communications center on the third floor of the Courthouse. Once the operator determined the source of the signal, he alerted firemen and residents to the approximate location of the fire by sounding alarms located throughout the city. If the source of the alert was Box 125, for example, he would ring once, then twice, and then five times.

Steam Fire Engine Fred Gund, *No. 14. From City of Chicago,*
Report of the Board of Police, in the Fire Department, 1871–72.
(Chicago History Museum, ICHi-051522)

When the watchman on duty in the cupola of the Courthouse spotted a fire, he reported it through a speaking tube to the operator on the third floor, who set off the bells. In addition, a member of each company stood watch atop its firehouse from nightfall to morning to scan the vicinity. If he saw flames, he alerted another fireman in the station, who would telegraph the operator in the Courthouse. Three assistant marshals each oversaw one of the divisions. During a fire, they and the chief marshal could recruit private citizens to help out if they thought it advisable. There was also a fire warden for each division, who monitored violations of building regulations and fire hazards generally.

Fire engine operators used a device called a tender to maintain steam pressure in the engines' boilers even in the station houses, so that the machines would be ready to start pumping as soon as they arrived at a fire. Once at the scene of a blaze, firemen connected the engines to the nearest pump. They might also try to draw water from the river if it was in reach of their hoses, which came in lengths of several hundred feet that could be attached to each other. The department followed a three-

*Looking northeast along Chicago Avenue toward the Chicago Water
Tower and Pumping Station, with Lake Michigan in the distance.
(Chicago History Museum, ICHi-006859)*

alarm system. The first alarm signaled a small fire that could be handled
by nearby companies. If the marshal or one of his assistants decided that
more help was required, he would order a second alarm. A third alarm
summoned everyone.

While the city's new waterworks, constructed in the 1860s, greatly
raised the cost of public services, it also enabled the Board of Public
Works to expand the number and capacity of hydrants significantly. The
most visibly impressive parts of this system were the "battlemented"
Gothic revival Chicago Water Tower and Pumping Station flanking Pine
Street (Michigan Avenue) at Chicago Avenue, three quarters of a mile
north of the Main Branch. The tower housed a standpipe that regulated
water pressure. At 182 feet, it was one of the highest points in the city.

The waterworks' most remarkable component, one of the century's
many great engineering achievements, was hidden from sight. This was a
two-mile tunnel constructed not into Lake Michigan itself but under the
lakebed. At its far end was a vertical water intake topped by the "crib,"
a pentagonal wooden structure at the lake's surface that was forty feet

high and fifty-eight feet wide on each side. To speed the building of the
tunnel, separate crews laboring twenty-four hours a day dug from both
ends toward the middle.

Since the lake was the source of water used for drinking, cooking,
and sanitation, as well as firefighting and industrial purposes, the hope
was that at this distance river-borne pollutants from the vile Chicago
River would be diluted into harmlessness. The city also set about attacking the threat to its water supply with another mammoth project, the
reversal of the natural flow of the Chicago River away from the lake by
deepening the Illinois and Michigan Canal where it joined the South
Branch. The idea was that gravity, assisted by pumps, would turn the
river around and cleanse it with clean lake water.

The tunnel opened on March 25, 1867, and the Deep Cut, as the
dredging of the river was called, on July 15, 1871, both to grandiloquent
speechifying and joyous fanfare that celebrated them as heroic mile-
stones in the conquest of nature for the purposes of humankind. While
the waterworks was a success, the Deep Cut was not. The river would
not be successfully reversed until the completion of the monumental
project that was the Sanitary and Ship Canal in 1900.

However up to date the fire department was in most respects, it was
small and underequipped. Chief Fire Marshal Williams regularly beseeched the mayor and Common Council for more resources. As he explained, the department needed them desperately because Chicago had
become so large and, more to the point, it was dangerously prone to
fire. In April 1871 Williams reported that the city had suffered 669 fires
during 1870, more than in any year since the establishment of the paid
department. These destroyed almost $2.5 million in property, an in-
crease of more than $1.5 million over 1869.

In 1868 the police and fire board commissioners had described the
city, if not in so many words, as a glorified fuel pile hungry for a match.
Many buildings covered in brick and stone were separated by flammable
pine boards, and also were festooned with wooden cornices and signs. The
tar roofing in common use was another serious hazard. "In very many
cases," the commissioners observed, "ornament is substituted for strength,
and safety is sacrificed for cheapness." While some city streets paved with
tightly packed hardwood proved to be surprisingly fire-resistant, this was
not at all true of Chicago's raised wooden sidewalks, which, like balloon-
frame houses, seemed to be designed for easy lighting and rapid burning.

In their 1870 report, the commissioners lamented the fact that property owners and investors were so selfishly intent on personal profit that they ignored the common good. "Private interests impel men to disregard the rights of the public," they wrote. The worst problem was not poor Chicagoans like the O'Learys, but greedy landlords who wanted to squeeze every penny they could out of their properties. "It will be found on inquiry," the commissioners asserted, "that most of the wooden rookeries in the heart of the city are owned by non-residents, speculators, or non-progressive citizens, of abundant means, who in the greater number of instances obtain large rents for their miserable buildings from gamblers, prostitutes, and kindred characters; such rents as no persons following honest callings could afford to pay." While they did not mention it by name, the commissioners had in mind areas like Conley's Patch, a blighted cluster of hovels, bars, gambling houses, and brothels just a few blocks southwest of the Courthouse. Until everyone realized that improved protection would benefit them, Chicago would suffer "many devastating fires."

The political leadership of the city denied there was a problem. Speaking in 1867, Mayor John B. Rice, admitting that "some complaints have been made of the Fire Department," stated that "after careful inquiry, I am satisfied that the Chicago Fire Department is well managed, is efficient, and in every way entitled to the favorable opinion of all our citizens." One might think that Rice would be attuned to the danger of fire. He was an actor and theater manager from Maryland whose Rice's Theater had burned down in 1850 during a performance of Vincenzo Bellini's opera *La Sonnambula*.

Rice and the Common Council were less concerned with the danger of fire than they were sensitive to the opposition of property owners to higher taxes. If the department was indeed inadequate, Rice reminded the aldermen, "and you desire to supply those wants, of course you know it will require a vast amount of money, and that money is to be obtained by taxation." After his election in 1869, Mayor Roswell Mason hemmed and hawed on the adequacy of the department. He characterized it as "well disciplined, prompt and reliable," stating that it "ju⁻ merits the high appreciation in which it is held by the public." B⁻ Rice, he dodged the question of whether Chicago needed it ⁻ and better equipped.

- 3 -

"A REGULAR NEST
OF FIRE"

The West Division

Blacksmith William Lee lived two lots east of the O'Learys on DeKoven Street in the West Division. His home was the middle of three cottages shoehorned into the lot, along with a rear barn. He shared it with his wife Mary, their toddler Joseph, and Lee's younger brother Mike. When he spotted the flames in the O'Leary barn, Lee did exactly what a responsible citizen was supposed to do: he tried to notify the fire department as quickly as possible.

In Lee's case, this meant a quarter-mile southward sprint to Box 296, at the northwest corner of Twelfth Street (Roosevelt Road) and Canal Street. It was not the nearest signal box but evidently the closest one whose location he knew. Box 296 was mounted on the exterior wall of a two-story building owned by Bruno Goll, who lived on the second floor with his family, above his drugstore. Goll was in the store when Lee arrived. He stepped outside, opened the box with his key, and pulled the lever. Confident that help was on the way, Lee rushed back to DeKoven Street. For whatever reason, the alarm telegraph operator on the third floor of the Courthouse heard nothing.

About ten minutes later, a second man rushed into Goll's store, barefoot and out of breath, screaming, "The fire is spreading very rapidly!" Judging from this person's wild look and disheveled hair, Goll at first thought the man was insane. Goll, who believed that he had already reported the fire successfully, nonetheless stepped outside and peered to the north. Insane or not, the man was correct about the fire's growth. To be doubly sure the fire department knew of the danger, Goll pulled the lever a second time. Again, unbeknownst to him, the system failed.

As soon as William Lee got back to DeKoven Street, he removed his belongings from his home in the hope that they might be spared

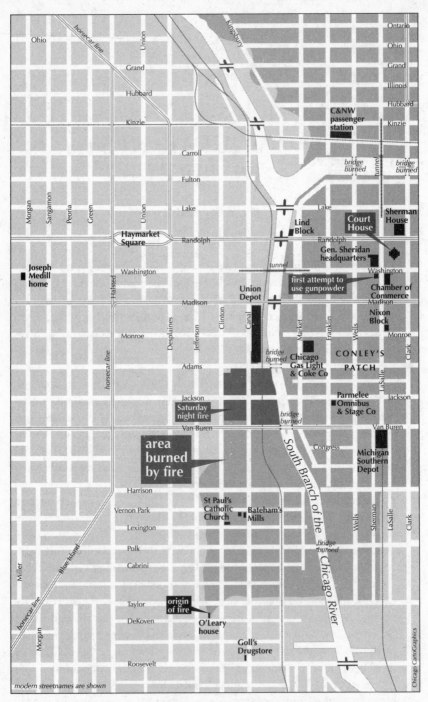

The fire in the West Division and the western portion of the South Division.

even if his cottage was not. Mary Lee took their son Joseph across DeKoven Street to the empty lot next to the house where Daniel Sullivan, who had alerted the O'Learys to the fire in their barn, lived with his mother.

After waking the O'Learys, Sullivan and another neighbor, Dennis Regan, tried to save what they could from the burning barn. Regan hoped to pull Catherine O'Leary's milk wagon out of danger, but the flames were too hot. Sullivan rescued the calf, though not before it was badly singed. Some accounts say he lost his peg leg when it wedged between boards in the barn floor. One way or another, Sullivan managed to lead the calf to the empty lot across the street, where it passed the long and anxious night where Mary and Joseph Lee also found refuge. Back in the barn, the cows and the horse became the fire's first fatalities.

Soon several houses on the north side of DeKoven Street were burning. Residents frantically filled washtubs and buckets from hydrants and threw the water on the flames, to no avail.

Shortly before 9:30, close to a half hour after the fire had begun, telegraph operator William Brown detected it by direct sight from the Courthouse. His window afforded him a view of the brightness a mile and a half to the southwest. In the first of several questionable decisions he made that evening, Brown did not sound an alarm. He wrongly assumed that the source of the glow was a harmless momentary flare-up from coal piles still smoldering in the aftermath of the Saturday Night Fire. When Brown looked again a few moments later, he was startled that the light was now much brighter.

At about the same moment, Mathias Schaefer, the watchman on duty above Brown in the Courthouse cupola, finally spotted the flames. Schaefer raised his watchman's telescope to his eye for a better look, then shouted down the speaking tube to Brown that the fire was near Box 342, located at the corner of Canalport Avenue and Halsted Street. Box 342 was on the same southwest directional line from the Courthouse as the O'Leary barn, but a mile beyond it.

Brown set alarm bells to sound three rings, then four, and then two. When Schaefer caught his own error, he told Brown to change the call to Box 319, still seven blocks southwest of the fire but closer than 342. Brown reportedly refused, contending that the conflicting signals would confuse the firefighters, and that in any event they would find the right location on their way to the wrong one.

Schaefer received signals from three other boxes closer to the fire than Box 342. Believing that they all related to the same fire, he ignored them.

Little Giant Engine Company No. 6 was on its way to DeKoven Street even before the first alarm sounded. The company bore the nickname of the redoubtable Senator Stephen Douglas, whose height had been the only diminutive thing about him. Joseph Lauf, standing watch that evening on the roof of the company firehouse about a half mile south of the O'Leary home, saw the flames and called down to the officer on duty, company foreman and acting captain William Musham. Musham was a relative rarity in the city, an actual native of Chicago.

The Saturday Night Fire had damaged the Little Giant's equipment and injured its men, but it had done nothing to diminish the spirit of those who remained on duty. As the company raced north, Musham heard the 3–4–2 alarm that was incorrectly telling him to go the other way. He decided to trust Lauf's eyes.

The Little Giant reached the fire around 9:30 p.m. Its crew connected several lengths of hose to the hydrant at Jefferson and DeKoven. They sprayed water on the burning houses, barns, and sheds along the alley behind the O'Leary cottage. Because of all the pine buildings, tar roofs, and wood shavings in the neighborhood, fireman Michael Sullivan recalled, "The facility for burning was very good." Musham recruited a few civilian spectators to assist his men in placing a second line of hose in the alley between DeKoven and Taylor Streets. Department practice permitted this kind of extra help, but usually only one of the marshals was authorized to ask for it.

Soon America Hose Company No. 2, which had also disregarded the alarm's instructions, joined the Little Giant Company on the scene. Its men attached hoses to a plug at Clinton and Taylor Streets, a block north and east of the Little Giant's engine, where they tried to halt the progress of the flames. The Tempest Hose Company No. 1 arrived and also hooked up to the hydrant at Clinton and Taylor. Chicago Engine Company No. 5, based at Jefferson and Van Buren, about ten blocks north of DeKoven Street, connected its hoses to a hydrant at Jefferson and Forquer (Arthington) Streets. The Waubansia Company No. 2 set up directly in front of the flames in an attempt to head them off.

Around 9:45 p.m., some forty-five minutes after Daniel Sullivan told the O'Learys that their barn was burning, Chief Fire Marshal Williams, his hopes for a decent night's sleep dashed, reached the scene, which he described as "a regular nest of fire." Adding to the department's logistical difficulties, residents attempting to save their belongings by evacuating them to the street were blocking fire equipment. Knowing he needed all the help he could muster, Williams ordered a second and then a third alarm, which brought out what was left of the fire department after the Saturday Night Fire.

Though it seemed as bright as day, firefighters could only barely discern each other through all the smoke. The high wind dispersed the streams of water from their hoses into an ineffective spray.

To make matters worse, Chicago Engine Company No. 5's hose burst and the engine itself broke down. Musham's civilian recruits abandoned the fight. Waubansia No. 2's engine could not produce sufficient pressure to drive its pump. Other engine companies were running low on the coal they needed to generate steam. In desperation, their crews ripped up wooden sidewalks to use as fuel.

Williams believed there was a chance his men might yet contain the fire, but it had such a substantial head start that they were caught in a futile game of catch-up. He later stated that "the only secret in putting out fires" was "to strike it before it gets the start of you." Chicago had previously dodged wholesale disaster because the fire department had been "right on [its] taps." On this evening, because of the delay in reporting the fire, the department was never going to catch up.

As the fire advanced, it generated convection whirls, also known as fire devils. These can occur when air near the ground becomes very hot. The cool air above rapidly descends, creating the whirls and an accompanying updraft. As the wind continued to roar, not just cinders but whole chunks of burning wood hurtled overhead as the firefighters watched helplessly.

At about ten o'clock, one such chunk lodged in the 140-foot wooden steeple of St. Paul's Catholic Church, on the northeast corner of Clinton and Mather (Lexington) Streets. Williams put three engines on the church, but the extreme heat made it impossible for firefighters to get close enough to do any good. When he saw the steeple fall, Williams admitted to First Assistant Marshal John Schank that the fire "is getting ahead of me in spite of all I can do."

St. Paul's Church was in the Red Flash territory of the West Division. On the same block were the Roelle Furniture Finishing Company, the Frank Mayer Furniture Company, a shingle mill, and a box factory, all housed in two large buildings. The bigger of the two structures was four stories tall, 245 feet long, and sixty feet wide, while the other was only slightly smaller. Both were full of flammable materials, including volatile chemicals. Next to them were a thousand cords of wood stacked twenty-five feet high, 600,000 feet of furniture lumber, and 750,000 shingles. Foreman Leo Myers of the Tempest Hose Company described this spot as "the most combustible place in the city of Chicago."

The owner of the buildings was William Bateham, a onetime fire marshal who was now an alderman from the West Division's Seventh Ward. He lived slightly north and a half dozen blocks west of his commercial properties. Bateham spotted the fire on DeKoven Street from his back parlor shortly after it began. The blaze was at that time still blocks away from his buildings, but he was alarmed by the airborne flaming fragments careering their way. It was time to see if there was anything he could do to protect them.

Bateham did not surrender without a fight. He, his watchman, and a friend he met on the way to his buildings hooked a steam-powered pump to a hydrant in front of the mill. Their idea was to drench the property so it would not burn.

This did nothing to halt the fire. The flames gorged themselves on the Bateham buildings and all the wood near them. The firemen were no longer battling a mere fire, but an inferno.

Williams himself entered one of Bateham's buildings to check on his firefighters, who were working two separate leads of hose. The fire "was coming down thicker than any snowstorm you ever saw, and the yard between the two mills was all filled with shavings, and chunks of fire came in of all sizes, from the length of your arm down to three inches," he recalled. His men followed the only prudent course: they dropped their hoses and ran.

When they asked Williams what they were to do next, he replied, "God only knows."

The fire attracted a large and growing number of onlookers, drawn by the pulse-quickening clamor of the alarms and the brilliance of the flames. Some members of the crowd allegedly enhanced the experience by drinking heavily. At one point Denis Swenie, foreman of Fred Gund Engine Company No. 14, ordered his pipeman to clear the spectators by spraying them with the fire hose. Those knocked down by the force of the water rose up laughing and asked Swenie to give others the same treatment.

Cassius Milton Wicker first viewed the fire looking west through the window of his room in the Tremont House hotel. The Tremont, a block above the Courthouse at Lake and Dearborn, was perhaps the most storied hotel in the city. Stephen Douglas and Abraham Lincoln had spoken outside it on successive nights in 1858 when they were vying for the Senate. Three years later Douglas, then only forty-eight, died in his room at the Tremont of complications relating to typhoid.

The twenty-seven-year-old Wicker was a Mayflower descendant from Vermont and newcomer to the city who had just started work as a freight agent for the Chicago and North Western Railway. The alarm made it impossible for him to sleep. Worried about how far this fire might go, Wicker ascended to the top of the hotel to get a better look. He went back to his room and tried again to go to bed, but he was too agitated. He dressed again and headed downstairs, informed the desk clerk he was going to the fire, and set off to the West Division.

As Wicker got closer, he noted that "sparks were blowing high in the air," some streaking "like huge meteors" toward the other divisions. Another onlooker, prominent attorney Thomas Hoyne, crossed the South Branch via the Polk Street Bridge in time to assist a family of poor Germans fleeing the "cataract of fire" that had engulfed their home. Hoyne was one of the few individuals of Irish Catholic background among the membership of Chicago's elite businessmen's clubs and organizations. At Hoyne's death in 1883 at the age of sixty-six, a Chicago minister no doubt believed he was paying his late friend a high compliment when he remarked, "Mr. Hoyne, though a Catholic in belief, was to a great extent a Protestant in practice."

Twelve-year-old Cora Heffron, who also was in the South Division, resented the fact that her mother made her stay in though she permitted Cora's older sisters Helen, Ida, and Ella to venture out to see the fire. Cora poured her envy into her diary: "My big sisters came back—couldn't get beyond Madison Street bridge—awful sight they said, and they wouldn't let me see it. Mean!"

When Chief Williams's attempt to create a firebreak by having his men knock down a building in the fire's path failed, he pinned his hopes on the larger break created less than twenty-four hours earlier by the Saturday Night Fire. This did help stop the fire's advance directly northward, but the most ominous threat was the eastward thrust of all those burning pieces of the West Division whirling high in the air, since just across the river lay the downtown.

Here were the overwhelming majority of the city's offices, hotels, and local and national government headquarters; its retail establishments, wholesale houses, newspapers, and several of its most important factories, as well as its theaters and most notable saloons and restaurants. Here lived over twenty thousand of Chicago's inhabitants, in some of the city's finest mansions and worst slums.

Awakened by a family member around eleven o'clock, Joseph Medill "jumped up and looked out the window to see the whole heavens to the east and south lighted up as if it were day." Medill lived a mile from the Courthouse in a well-to-do section of the West Division. Like Chief Fire Marshal Robert Williams and blacksmith William Lee, Medill had been born in eastern Canada. He had moved to Ohio and briefly practiced law before turning to journalism. In 1855 he and a group of partners purchased the *Chicago Tribune*, founded eight years earlier. As managing editor, Medill built it into one of the city's most influential voices, though he currently was not actively involved in the daily management of the content of the paper.

Given the direction of the wind, Medill was confident that his home would not be hit, but he was eager for a closer view. He threw on his clothes and joined the throng of onlookers. In order to get a good angle on the spectacle, Medill edged out onto the Randolph Street Bridge, several blocks north of the flames. It was about eleven thirty.

"I stood among a great crowd that filled the bridge to a dangerous extent," he remembered, "and saw the flames jump, with a bound as it were, in sheets" across the South Branch into the South Division, "and ignite frame buildings and sheds, and push their way rapidly to the northeast."

Chief Marshal Williams was near the ruins of the Lull & Holmes Planing mill, fighting a fire that was now three quarters of a mile long and extended over 150 acres, when Long John foreman Alexander McMonagle, who had just glanced across the river, told his commander the last thing Williams wanted to hear:

"Robert, the fire is on the South Side."

"The devil it is," Williams replied.

"You look," McMonagle answered.

Williams looked.

He turned back to McMonagle with fresh orders: "Go for it. I'll be there in a minute."

4

"IT WAS NOTHING BUT EXCITEMENT"

The South Division

Up to now, those who lived, worked, or owned property in the South Division could admire the fire as a marvelous pyrotechnic display. Their sympathy for the unfortunates on the West Side may have tempered their aesthetic enjoyment, but the misfortune was still something happening over there, to other people.

Not anymore.

The South Branch proved to be no obstacle at all. The first building set aflame was not on the near edge of the opposite bank but fully four hundred feet east of the river. It was the three-story brick stable of the Parmelee Omnibus and Stage Company at Franklin and Jackson.

The multitude of passengers passing through Chicago relied on Franklin Parmelee's conveyances to shuttle them from one station to another. If they stayed overnight or longer, Parmelee's fleet could take them to and from their hotel. He had just invested $80,000 in the facility, which he planned to open in the middle of the week. Parmelee's one consolation would be that he had not yet moved in his horses.

Another flying brand lodged on the main works of the Chicago Gas Light and Coke Company, two blocks north and one block west of Parmelee's stable. The destruction of the gasworks cut off the fuel supply to street lamps and to the lighting fixtures in commercial buildings, hotels, and the homes of those who could afford this amenity. The fire that was destroying Chicago was now all that illuminated it.

A little before 12:30 a.m. on Monday, October 9, a large flaming fragment landed in the slum district of Conley's Patch, which burst into flame like the tinder pile it was, sending inhabitants scattering. "Vice and crime had got the first scorching [in the South Division]," Horace White wrote. White was currently editor in chief of the *Chicago Tribune*,

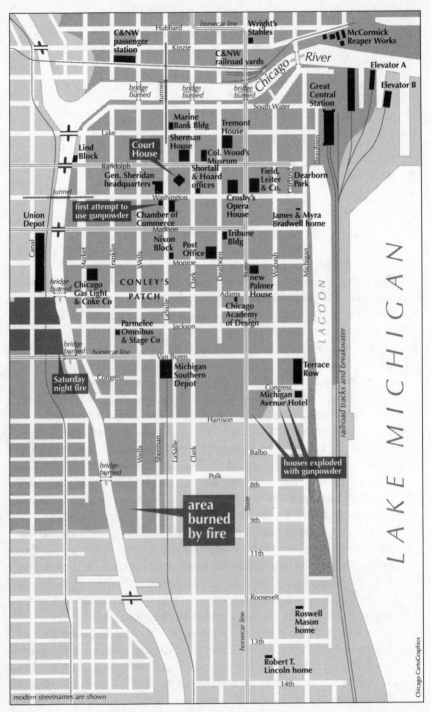

The fire in the South Division.

of which he had been a part owner since 1864. He described those fleeing the Conley's Patch fire disparagingly as "a crowd of blear-eyed,
drunken, and diseased wretches, male and female, half naked, ghastly,
with painted cheeks, cursing and uttering ribald jests as they drifted
along."

In short order the Parmelee, Chicago Gas and Light, and Conley's
Patch fires merged into one titanic mass of flames that advanced directly toward the Courthouse and Chicago's downtown, which comprised about twenty-five blocks at the upper end of the South Division.
The Courthouse was located about a quarter mile below the Main
Branch in the center of the block known as Courthouse Square, bordered
by Randolph, Dearborn, Washington, and Clark Streets. The building
contained almost all municipal and county offices, records, and court-
rooms, and it had a jail in the basement. It had grown along with Chicago: the more recent renovations had added another story and wings
on the east and west, as well as the central cupola, accessible by a spiral
staircase leading to an open balcony. Even expanded, the Courthouse
took up only the middle of the square, leaving room next to it for grass,
trees, and walkways.

For most Chicagoans, the Courthouse's most familiar feature was its
great bell, more than five feet tall and weighing almost eleven thousand pounds. In a memoir published in 1910, journalist Frederick Francis Cook recalled how the resonant tolling of the bell to mark the hours
served as "everybody's monitor and guide" through their daily lives. It
also rang "paeans of victory" following Union battlefield triumphs, and
"its slow, solemn monotone voiced the anguish of all hearts" after Abraham Lincoln's assassination. "And, finally," Cook noted, "how it clanged,
and clanged, and clanged again, on that fearful night of fire, each stroke
heightening the terror that possessed the fleeing multitude, while the
'fiend' that lashed the elements to such boundless fury, compelled it to
sound its own death-knell."

A reporter for the *Chicago Times* vividly wrote, "The twin rioters
of flame and wind, with their appetite sharpened instead of gorged by
the feast among the meaner buildings of the West Division and the river
side, now fell in dire carnival upon the noble edifices of LaSalle Street"
below the Courthouse. As people who lived in the area were driven out
of their homes, they sought safety in the open area of Courthouse Square,
even though the enormous fire was heading that way. To Alexander

The Courthouse shortly before the Great Chicago Fire, complete with the new east and west wings. Refugees from the fire briefly huddled in the park next to the Courthouse until forced to flee the South Division. (Chicago History Museum, ICHi-022314)

Frear, a visiting New York politician who viewed the refugees from the Sherman House hotel opposite the northeast corner of Courthouse Square, they "appeared to be huddled together in a solid mass, helpless and astounded."

Jennie Otis gaped at the fire from her bedroom in her family's home several blocks to its east on Wabash Avenue near Adams Street. Jennie, the middle child and oldest girl of the five Otis siblings, watched spellbound until fascination turned to fear.

She went down the hall and tried to awaken her two older brothers, who were sleeping off their fatigue from being out late the previous night to view the Saturday Night Fire. They refused to budge. Back at her bedroom window, Jennie saw the flames move closer, "leaping and spreading at a terrific rate." She tried and failed again to rouse the boys. Warm as the night was, Jennie realized her teeth were chattering in dread. Not to be denied a third time, she forced her brothers to get up.

Soon the whole household was readying for flight. They headed southward several blocks to Prairie Avenue, where her Uncle Fred lived. When no one answered the doorbell, they threw pebbles at the second story window, stirring Jennie's aunt, who looked out to see them and the flames to the north. "Fred, Fred, wake up!" she cried. "Lydia and her children are down at the door, and the whole city is on fire."

Accompanied by one of his adult sons, Mayor Roswell B. Mason arrived at the Courthouse between eleven o'clock and midnight from his home two miles away, on the west side of Michigan Avenue south of Twelfth Street (Roosevelt Road). Mason realized that he had little time to act. After conferring with Chief Fire Marshal Robert A. Williams, he sent telegrams to other cities across the Upper Midwest, pleading for emergency assistance as quickly as possible.

In this moment of crisis, Mason also reluctantly approved a scheme proposed by James H. Hildreth. During the Civil War Hildreth had joined the artillery company raised by the Board of Trade, where he worked as a grain inspector. He had once served as a city alderman. Perhaps emboldened by his combination of military and political experience, Hildreth insisted to Mason that the best available tactic was to deploy gunpowder to cut off the fire by blasting away buildings in its path. Hildreth had recommended the same strategy earlier in the evening to Chief Williams when the fire reached William Bateham's mills in the West Division.

Williams put Hildreth off, explaining that he himself did not know how to handle gunpowder, and that in any case he had neither the authority to approve such a radical step nor a supply at hand. Hildreth replied that Chief Williams certainly did have the requisite authority. To which Williams answered impatiently, "Get your powder, then."

Williams may have thought he was calling Hildreth's bluff, but Hildreth was not bluffing. He crossed the river to the South Division, commandeered a wagon, drove it to a powder magazine he knew below the Main Branch, and seized the kegs. Hildreth transported the dangerous cargo southward to the Courthouse, where he unloaded it. He then went to look for Williams or any police or fire commissioner he could find to give him the final go-ahead.

Having failed to locate a suitable official on the streets, Hildreth decided he might do better if he returned to the Courthouse. He had no luck at first, but as he was leaving he ran into Mayor Mason, who was just arriving. Hildreth persuaded Mason to sign an order empowering him to detonate the powder, albeit under the direction of the chief fire marshal. With the document in hand, Hildreth searched again for Williams.

Williams was less than a block away to the south, where his men were trying to save the five-story Oriental Building on LaSalle Street, so named because it was owned by the Oriental Lodge of the fraternal order of Masons. Hildreth showed Williams the document signed by the mayor. "That gives you all the power that you want," he declared. Williams, preoccupied with the Oriental Building, demurred. Nothing if not determined, Hildreth hastened back to the mayor. Mayor Mason's city was burning down; he had no better alternative. "Go on and do something," he instructed.

Hildreth recruited a police sergeant and a group of officers to help him transfer the load of powder across the street to the Union Bank at LaSalle and Washington. After kicking open the powder kegs with his boot, Hildreth spread their contents about, and, with considerable difficulty, set the explosive off. He did the same in another building nearby. The blasts did little more than shatter some windows.

The front edge of the flames had now reached the Chamber of Commerce, just south of Courthouse Square at Washington Street and LaSalle Streets, where the organization had moved six years earlier from its quarters among the traders and commission brokers on the south bank of the Main Branch. While the Chamber of Commerce building was technically only two stories, the second floor was forty-five feet high, with stately Romanesque windows that belied the frenzied activity inside. Here was the grand trading hall where brokers determined the price of grain by open outcry. The exterior stonework was the current material of choice, aspirationally named Athens Marble—creamy yellow dolomite limestone quarried southwest of the city in Joliet and Lemont and floated in on barges plying the Illinois and Michigan Canal.

Up in the Courthouse cupola, watchman Mathias Schaefer and telegraph operator William Brown saw that they were face-to-face with the danger that not long ago seemed so remote. Their replacements, Dennis Deneen and George Fuller, had reported for duty at eleven o'clock, but

Schaefer and Brown opted to stay. While city workers were busy trying to extinguish little fires on the roof of the building, a brand sailed
through a broken window on the southwest side of the tower and took
hold. Up in the cupola, Schaefer and Deneen realized that if they stayed
any longer they would burn to death. Since the stairway was ablaze,
they apparently jumped down—though some descriptions have them
sliding along the bannister—and fled the building. Brown and Fuller left
at about the same time.

Meanwhile, fire was eating through the supports of the massive bell
that was ringing the alarm. Shortly after 2:00 a.m., five and a half tons
of scalding metal plummeted through the collapsing building and went
silent.

Boston-born and Harvard University–educated Samuel Sewell Greeley, who ran a busy land survey practice, witnessed the dying throes of
the Courthouse from his home near the lakefront five blocks north of
the Main Branch. "The smoke was stifling, but through it the stars were
looking placidly down from a clear steel blue sky, and the full moon
shed a cold white light, to which the bloody glare of the fire made a
ghastly contrast," he later wrote. It seemed to Greeley that nature was
"pitilessly indifferent to this fury and turmoil, in which a City was being shriveled, and rolled together as a scroll." The bell fell with "a crash
like a broadside of artillery," as "a vast jet of smoke and sparks shot to
heaven." Although he was nearly a mile away, Greeley thought he felt
the earth tremble.

Police captain Michael C. Hickey was in the Courthouse during its
last moments. In a department where political skills and connections
could count as much as merit, Hickey had both. Born in Ireland, he emigrated to Boston in 1844, when he was eighteen. Four years later he
was in Chicago. Hickey joined the police department in 1861 as a pa-
trolman. He was a sergeant in three months, a captain in five years. Along
the way he survived a serious gunshot wound sustained during a bur-
glary. Though not especially handsome, he was said to be "very popular,
especially with the ladies."

Hickey later claimed that he was most concerned about the prisoners held in the Courthouse jail. According to A. T. Andreas, they "ran
to the doors of their cells and shook the iron bars with the strength of
frenzy, uttering fearful yells and imprecations of despair, as a horrid fear
that they were to be burned alive possessed them." Hickey said he told

the keeper of the basement jail to release the prisoners so they would not die helplessly in terrible agony. When the keeper refused to take responsibility, Hickey said that he would. With too many prisoners to herd, Hickey set milder offenders free while he and his men put dangerous felons in handcuffs and led them to a station on the North Side.

Andreas states that the prisoners Hickey liberated, "all bareheaded, many barefooted, rushed into the street, yelling like demons." Spotting a passing truck full of ready-made clothing, they "swarmed upon it, emptied it of its contents and fled to remote alleys and dark passages to don their plunder and disguise themselves."

Sherman House hotel desk clerk John Hickie and a fellow employee saved the life of an ill female guest by breaking into her room, soaking her down with water, and carrying her out of the doomed building. Cassius Milton Wicker assisted other Tremont House guests with their belongings before removing his own from his room, which he placed in a trunk. On his way out, he grabbed a bottle of brandy.

Unable to hail a wagon, Wicker found a very short length of rope that he used as best he could to drag the trunk away. He told his family in Vermont that he "would have given $10 for a rope five feet long— I never knew the value of such a rope until my back was nearly broken and hands so tired I could no longer stir the trunk." Wicker thought his luck had changed when he spotted a horse and wagon, as well as a man who agreed to help him lift the trunk into it, albeit the man had only one hand. Unfortunately the owner of the wagon, or at least "a man stronger than I," insisted the wagon was his. So Wicker hired the one-handed man to assist him in dragging the trunk to Dearborn Park, a rectangular patch of land on the west side of Michigan Avenue between Randolph and Washington Streets.

Dearborn Park was the only downtown green space besides the landscaped portion of Courthouse Square. It was used for social gatherings, political demonstrations, and traveling entertainments. In early August 1871, Old John Robinson's Circus, Menagerie, Museum, and Caravan chose Dearborn Park as the place to pitch its three tents, inside which champion rider Robert Stickney, "child equestrienne" Minnie Marks, Old Emperor the elephant, Billy the trained seal, and Conrad's comical monkeys, as well as "mammoth sea lions," "monster camels," and "educated dogs," performed.

Wicker ran out of energy a block short of his destination. Then appeared an Englishman who was straining to pull a horseless express wagon in which were his ailing wife and their household goods.

A few moments later Wicker's trunk was part of the wagon's burden, and the two of them were tugging it along together. Wicker had enough perspective to view with amusement their resemblance to a team of jackasses. After reaching Dearborn Park, Wicker left to aid a friend in clearing out his art collection and other valuables before they burned. Wicker and his friend had just enough time to "kick the fine pictures from their frames," load two wagons, and get away "amid fire engines, everybody's last team and crowds of departing homeless people."

All through the night and into the next morning, the bottle of brandy "did good service . . . and many a stranger took courage from it."

John G. Shortall rescued not people but vital documents. Shortall was born in Ireland to Protestant parents who emigrated to New York in 1841, three years after his birth. In his early teens he worked for illustrious journalist Horace Greeley on the *New-York Tribune*. Shortall followed Greeley's famous advice to "go west" and "grow up with the country." He was sixteen when he reached Chicago.

Shortall became a wealthy real estate attorney who specialized in preparing abstracts, the legal papers that record the ownership history of individual parcels of real estate and are essential to land sales and transfers. His company, Shortall and Hoard, was in a five-story building, the Larmon Block (as large commercial structures were called), located on the east side of Clark Street above Washington, across the street from Courthouse Square. He hoped to salvage his firm's files in any case, but once he saw the flames from the Courthouse, where official property records were stored, Shortall knew that the importance of the documents had greatly increased.

Shortall first tried to defend the Larmon Block by tearing off its flammable awnings. When he saw that the building was beyond saving, he instructed employees who had joined him to start removing the records while he would attempt to hire a wagon to cart them away. Shortall tried to flag down fifteen different passing drivers, only to find that each was already occupied with saving other refugees' belongings. He told the drivers they could name their price if they came back after they finished with their current loads.

Shortall then spotted James Nye, who worked for the nearby hardware firm of Hibbard and Spencer. Nye agreed to help him secure transportation for the records. Nye took a position on Clark Street, Shortall on Washington. When Shortall spied flames leaping from the Courthouse cupola, he shouted to Nye that they absolutely had to find a wagon in the next five minutes, "or we were utterly lost."

Nye successfully obtained the first wagon that passed by adopting a more aggressive method than calling out to drivers. Seizing the horse's reins with one hand, he drew a revolver from his pocket with the other and pointed it at the driver. But the wagon was far too small to hold the some two hundred volumes of documents. Then another friend of Shortall's, John L. Stockton, unexpectedly appeared with a larger wagon driven by one of the men who had told Shortall he would return.

Shortall handed five dollars to the driver Nye had "hired" and released him. "Meanwhile the flames were roaring and surging all around us," Shortall recalled. He was so intent on the abstracts that he did not notice the collapse of the Courthouse tower and the thunderous descent of the bell. Rumors circulated among the frightened people on the street that an explosive was about to be set off on a building close by, which sent a crowd rushing along Washington Street past Shortall's office and toward the lake.

The new driver swore "that he would not be blown up for us or the whole county," but Shortall managed to cajole him into staying until everything was loaded. Progress was very slow, so the wagon did not arrive at Shortall's home safely below the fire until 3:00 a.m. Shortall claimed he used Nye's gun to "convince" two prisoners let out of the jail in the Courthouse to help. They stood on each side of the wagon to keep the records from falling off. After the abstracts were unloaded into the house, Shortall returned to the fiery fray "to see what aid I could give other sufferers."

Twenty-eight-year-old Robert Todd Lincoln, son of the late president and now a Chicago attorney beginning his career as a corporate lawyer, lived well out of danger on South Wabash Avenue with his wife, two-year-old daughter, and widowed mother, all named Mary. The two younger Marys were out of the city visiting his in-laws, but his mother, Mary Todd Lincoln, was in Chicago. Robert had recently returned from a recuperative trip to the Rocky Mountains following the death in mid-July of eighteen-year-old Tad Lincoln, the third and last of his three brothers. Robert arranged to have Tad interred at Oak Ridge Cemetery in Springfield, along with their father and brothers Eddie, who had died in 1850 shortly before his fourth birthday, and Willie, who was eleven when he passed away in the White House of typhoid fever in 1862.

As dawn arrived, Robert risked going to his downtown office. Once there, he placed his most valuable papers on a tablecloth, whose corners he gathered up to form a sack, which he slung over his shoulder for his getaway. Lincoln walked east to Michigan Avenue and then turned south, stopping at the home of family friend J. Young Scammon. Scammon, who came from Whitefield, Maine, about sixty miles northeast of Portland, had lived in Chicago since 1834, when he turned twenty-two. He had become wealthy in law, real estate, and banking. Lincoln had finished his legal training in Scammon's practice, and his office was in Scammon's Marine Bank Building. Scammon's home was one of the eleven contiguous deluxe townhouses of Terrace Row, which took up

Terrace Row, looking southwest along Michigan Avenue, which
was still unpaved. From a stereograph by Copelin & Melander.
(Chicago History Museum, ICHi-064156)

much of the block between Congress and Van Buren Streets on the west side of Michigan Avenue, about five blocks southeast of the Courthouse. The two of them breakfasted together in Scammon's residence, Lincoln recalled, "with a feeling of perfect security."

Many were able to rescue little or nothing from their offices. Lawyer and notary Jonas Hutchinson, who worked on Washington Street near the Courthouse, wrote to his mother in New Hampshire on Monday, October 9, "I am discouraged & what to do I know not." He had been able to grab a few papers before being forced to retreat. When he exited the building, "the street was full of flames & smoke. I had to run for dear life. $5000 worth of books besides furniture fed the flames & as I went out, not to enter again, leaving all that valuable stuff to be devoured, I could but cry."

People whose homes were in the fire's path faced the heartbreaking task of deciding what, if anything, they could take with them as they fled. Even if their house fell to the flames, they reasoned, they might save something. For most working people, the contents of their homes were all they owned.

"Men, women and children loaded with everything you can conceive were blocking up the sidewalks," divinity student William Gallagher told his sister Isabel in a long letter dated October 17, a week after the fire. "Here comes a woman with all her bed and bedding on her back. Here was a little girl with her arms full of cooking utensils. Here comes a team with a little of everything on it, and curled up on a mattress in a secure position two or three young children. One of the shafts has a tea kettle hanging to it, another a coal-hod. If any pictures were being carried away, they were always the Virgin or Christ crucified. One man was hurrying along with nothing but a flatiron in his hand, another had two or three pieces of old board, and so they went, hurrying, pushing, scrambling, crowding, jostling, shouting, and laughing even."

It was a surreal scene. Arthur M. Kinzie, grandson of pioneer fur trader John Kinzie, spotted one man carrying a rubber tube and piece of a broken lantern, while another had somehow propped a cook stove onto a wheelbarrow. As he pushed his heavy and ungainly burden along, the man bore a large feather bed on his back. Alexander Frear wrote that he saw "a ragamuffin on the Clark-street bridge, who had been killed by a marble slab thrown from a window, with white kid gloves on his hands, and whose pockets were stuffed with gold-plated sleeve-buttons." On the same bridge was "an Irish woman leading a goat that was big with young, while under the other arm she carried a piece of silk."

As Shortall had discovered, the demand for wagons dwarfed the supply. While there were open-spirited drivers who charged regular rates or even nothing at all, plenty of others were ready to exploit the emergency. *Chicago Tribune* editor Horace White located a driver who informed him the charge was twenty dollars. This would have been outrageous at any other time, but White was happy with the terms. He had assumed he would have to pay five times as much or seize a wagon from someone else—"and this was a bad time for a fight."

Whatever the price, it went without question that one had to pay cash. With the downtown banks doomed, no driver would accept anything else, no matter how wealthy or trustworthy the passenger appeared to be. As White observed, "Never was there a community so hastily and completely emancipated from the evils of the credit system."

The highest reported fee was the $1,000 that E. I. Tinkham of the Second National Bank paid an expressman for conveying him and a box containing $600,000 he removed from his firm's vault to a West Side railroad station, where he boarded a train to Milwaukee and deposited the money in a bank there. Given the princely sum at risk and the daring of the man in hazarding the nightmare trip across the burning downtown, Tinkham considered the charge well worth it to him and fully deserved by the driver.

On Monday afternoon Cook County judge James Bradwell hired an expressman to carry a trunk of belongings for him and his family. After he loaded the wagon with the Bradwells' trunk, the driver became too frightened to proceed. When he saw the man trying to remove the trunk, Bradwell, who was six foot two, told the driver to choose one of three options: carry the trunk and the Bradwells to safety, die with them in the attempt to do so, or have Bradwell kill him then and there. "For God's sake, come on," the cowed driver replied, lifting the trunk back on the wagon.

With the fire bearing down on them and the streets mobbed, people adjusted their original ambitions of saving their goods to the exigencies of the moment. Even more than on the West Side, the South Division's thoroughfares became obstacle courses full of items abandoned to the insatiable flames. Alexander Frear remembered how "the streets and sidewalks presented the most astonishing wreck. Valuable oil paintings, books, pet animals, musical instruments, toys, mirrors, and bedding, were trampled under foot." He was struck in the arm by a bird cage thrown from an upstairs window. Most fire refugees just took what they could carry in their arms, holding tight to young children, aged relatives, and portable possessions of significant financial or sentimental value, such as a jewelry box or a portrait of a deceased loved one.

Of the many works of art saved on a night during which many more were lost, the largest by far was John Peter Rothermel's sixteen-by-thirty-two-foot depiction of the Battle of Gettysburg, which was on temporary display in the Academy of Design (predecessor to the Art Institute of Chicago) on Adams near State Street. Rothermel's painting was in Chicago on a national tour before it was to be hung in the Pennsylvania capitol building in Harrisburg. Commissioned by the state for $25,000, the work had taken Rothermel three years to complete. With smoke rising over thousands of soldiers locked in a death struggle, the epic scene on Rothermel's canvas made a fitting companion piece to the battle being fought in the streets of Chicago.

Too valuable to be torn roughly out of its frame, the painting was instead carefully cut away and rolled up by two artists who shared a studio in the building. One of them, F. L. Rockwell, wrapped it in drapery and lugged it clumsily to the lakeshore, where he guarded the painting all night and through Monday. Rockwell repeatedly soaked his face and hands with wet cloths to protect them from the heat.

Others tried to save possessions by burying them. Before he hired a driver to transport his trunk, Judge Bradwell had first dug a hole for it in Dearborn Park. In a preview of Bradwell's confrontation with the wagon driver, a policeman who did not fully grasp the larger situation tried to stop the judge from "defacing" the park with his digging. Bradwell raised his shovel and responded, "You go on or I'll make you see more stars than you ever saw in your life." The policeman decided to go on.

Size was no object to a determined digger. A day after the fire, Mary Fales, wife of attorney David Fales, wrote to her mother that before they piled a few things in their small buggy, David had entombed their books, china, and, most remarkably, their piano. William Gallagher said he "saw many a cook-stove in the process of burial, stuffed with all sorts of cooking utensils and useful articles."

Many could not bear to leave beloved pets behind. At the last minute Horace White seized the cage containing "a talented green parrot," which he put down next to the driver of the wagon he hired. As they proceeded, the parrot would pipe up, "Get up, get up, get up; hurry up, hurry up; it's eight o'clock." James Bradwell's wife Myra swept up their family's bird as she made her exit.

Myra Colby Bradwell, who at forty was three years younger than her husband, was an exceptionally intelligent and ambitious woman who would be remembered far better than he. Her goal was to become the first female attorney in Illinois. She had helped draft the state's Married Women's Property Act of 1861 and the Earnings Act of 1869, which gave married women rather than their husbands control of their earnings and property. While there were no doubts about her intellectual qualifications to be a lawyer, the state of Illinois denied her application on the basis of gender. The US Supreme Court would uphold the decision in 1873 in the noted case of *Bradwell v. Illinois*. Not to be deterred from a legal career, Bradwell became founding editor of the *Chicago Legal News*, which covered the profession, as she continued to fight for certification.

Bradwell kept her sense of humor even in this fraught moment. In addition to the bird, she seized her husband's Masonic hat from a closet and stuck it on her head, announcing, "Masonry will certainly be an aid at a time like this."

The accounts of those who experienced the fire as children frequently focus on their concern for an article of clothing, a beloved toy, or other treasured object. The Bradwells' resourceful twelve-year-old daughter Bessie, who had earlier helped her father retrieve rare law books from his office, decided that the best way to rescue her favorite dresses was to put them on in layers, one on top of another. This freed her arms to carry the *Chicago Legal News* subscription book, which her mother was determined to preserve.

With the greatest regret Jennie Otis left behind the new high-button shoes that had cost six dollars, more than some Chicago workers earned in a week. Knowing she might have to walk several miles, she chose instead an old pair because of their proven comfort and durability. Jennie

*Myra Colby Bradwell. Photograph by Charles D. Mosher,
who did formal portraits of many prominent Chicagoans.
(Chicago History Museum, ICHi-009585)*

was delighted to find out later that someone else in the household had
swept up the fancy shoes in a last hurried gathering of goods.

As the flames pushed northeast, the larger buildings they had already
ignited burned on, so at any one time the wall of fire was as much as a
half mile thick. Meanwhile, there were countless pieces of flaring wreck-
age swirling in the wind. To Alexander Frear, it was completely bizarre,
"a snow-storm lit by colored fire." The intensity of the flames turned
stone to dust while bending iron and melting glass, which requires a
temperature of over 2,500 degrees Fahrenheit.

Wooden buildings did not so much burn as disappear. As Arthur
Kinzie explained, "the front would melt away, exactly as a sheet of

paper laid on a bed of burning coals will smoulder [*sic*] awhile, then suddenly flash up, and be gone." In a letter written a week after the fire, Board of Public Works president William H. Carter told his brother, "The flames were rushing most frantically, leaping from block to block— whole squares vanishing as though they were gossamer."

Eleven-year-old Fanny Boggs lived on the southeast corner of Michigan Avenue and Twenty-Third Street in the South Division, well south of the fire. On the opposite corner was a vacant lot. When Fanny and her parents awoke on Monday morning, they were surprised to see the lot filled with visitors to Chicago who had stuffed their belongings into pillowcases and sheets they had appropriated from the hotels where they had been staying. Parked in front of the Boggs house was a hearse its owner had used to move his possessions. On the seat beside the driver's, she remembered, was a marble mantle clock.

Many people in the upper portion of the downtown could not retreat southward because the fire blocked the way. Their choices were to flee to the West Division, above where the flames had reached, or to the North Division, where the fire had not yet arrived.

This required crossing the river on a bridge or by one of the two tunnels the city had recently built to facilitate carriage, wagon, and passenger traffic between the divisions. One tunnel ran under the South Branch of the Chicago River at Washington Street, the other beneath the Main Branch at LaSalle. The tunnel at Washington opened in 1869, the other only the past summer, on Independence Day.

The masses of panicky people forcing their way through the LaSalle Street Tunnel and across the bridges created dangers of their own. The tunnel became a crush of humankind, all the more terrifying since it went totally dark once the Chicago Gas Light and Coke Company works shut down. Long after the fire, George Payson, editor of *Freeman's Illinois Digest*, who retreated to the North Division carrying copies of the publication, could "still seem to hear the oft repeated cry of 'Keep to the right,' 'Keep to the right,' by which the hurrying fugitives gave each other notice of their approach in the pitch darkness."

The tunnel, being underwater and made of brick and stone, was fireproof. The bridges, out in the open and constructed largely of wood, were just so much more fuel. The bridges at Madison, Randolph, and Lake Streets would barely survive, but those at Clark, Van Buren, Rush, Polk, Adams, State, and Wells Streets caught fire and dropped piece-meal into the river. These bridges opened the way to river traffic by rotating on a central pivot. The tender of the Van Buren Street Bridge tried to turn it in order to avoid the approaching fire, but he was too late. As Alexander Frear wrote, the bridge became "a grand fantastic frame-work of flames." The wind pushed a young girl so forcefully against the girders of the State Street Bridge that her father had to extricate her.

Harper's Weekly illustrator John R. Chapin, who was in Chicago when the fire struck, took an eyewitness sketch and wrote an account of what the magazine titled "The Rush for Life over Randolph Street Bridge." Thanks to its location directly west of the Courthouse, and because it did not burn, this bridge was a major exit route from the South Division to the West Side. Chapin's drawing was one of several of this terror-filled scene.

"Vehicles of every kind and character were crossing and recrossing the bridge, bringing away goods of all kinds, and sometimes of the most ludicrous description," Chapin reported. "One party had a platform store truck with three wheels, on which they had piled desks, chairs, cushions, and office furniture to a height of six or eight feet." Soon the load slid off, "and an immense express wagon, dashing along, went over the pile and crushed it into splinters." Then a fire department steam engine, pulled by "four splendid horses," barreled through, its driver "either wild with excitement or crazy drunk."

Chicago Evening Post reporter Joseph Edgar Chamberlin witnessed the "torrent of humanity . . . pouring over the bridge." Chamberlin recalled how "drays, express wagons, trucks, and conveyances of every conceivable species and size crowded across in indiscriminate haste. Collisions happened almost every moment, and when one overloaded wagon broke down, there were enough men on hand to drag it and its contents over the bridge by main force."

A South Division undertaker whose wagon could not accommodate his entire stock of coffins hired a half dozen boys to help him carry

Chicago in Flames—The Rush for Life over Randolph Street Bridge.
From Harper's Weekly, *October 28, 1871, based on an eyewitness sketch
by John R. Chapin. (Chicago History Museum, ICHi-002901)*

away the remainder. "The sight of those coffins, upright, and bobbing along just above the heads of the crowd, without any apparent help from anybody, was something startling," Chamberlin wrote. It was as if the coffins "were escaping across the river, on their own account, to be ready for use when the debris of the conflagration should be cleared away." The effect was more amusing than macabre: "Just as men in the midst of a devastating plague carouse over each new corpse, so we laughed merrily, with grim enjoyment of the ominous spectacle."

The downtown to the east of the bridge was an "infernal gorge of horses, wagons, men, women, children, trunks, and plunder," Horace White wrote. "It was every person for himself and the fire-fiend take the hindermost," Cassius Milton Wicker recalled.

Police captain Michael Hickey summed it up well: "There was such confusion! Men, women, and children hollering and yelling and drawing out their things—the streets were just perfectly thronged with these human beings trying to get out of these patches, and they

Panic-Stricken Citizens Rushing Past the Sherman House, Carrying the
Aged, Sick and Helpless and Endeavoring to Save Family Treasures.
From Frank Leslie's Illustrated Newspaper, *October 28, 1871.*
(Chicago History Museum, ICHi-002909)

were all hollering and running in every direction. It was nothing but
excitement."

Sometime between one and two o'clock on Monday morning, October 9, Mayor Mason and his son exited the Courthouse through the
west exit on the LaSalle Street side of Courthouse Square. The city's chief
executive, Mason was now as helpless as tens of thousands of other Chicagoans. Blazing buildings blocked the way to his home on South Michigan Avenue at Twelfth Street (Roosevelt Road). When the mayor looked
down LaSalle Street, the street appeared as full of flame as a furnace. He
and his son fixed on a roundabout route. They would go north a block to
Randolph, east to Michigan Avenue, and only then southward.

The Masons discovered that the fire had also made eastbound Randolph Street impassable. So was Lake Street, a block farther north. They concluded that they needed to trace an even larger loop by taking the LaSalle Street Tunnel to the North Division, turning eastward, and finding their way back across the Rush Street Bridge, which would bring them back to Michigan Avenue.

Amid the chaos, the Masons ran into commodities dealer Julian Rumsey. Rumsey and his brother George moved to Chicago from Batavia, New York, in the 1830s as teenagers and subsequently made their fortunes in grain commissions and banking. Rumsey had served as mayor in 1861–62. He had risked coming downtown from his house in the North Division to retrieve $40,000 in grain receipts and other valuable documents from his office. Like the Masons, he planned to return through the LaSalle Street Tunnel. When the Masons and Rumsey saw how packed the tunnel was, they walked west another block and made it to the North Division via the Wells Street Bridge. Rumsey invited the Masons to accompany him to his home. In spite of the ease with which the fire had jumped the South Branch, he clung to the belief that the Main Branch would prove an effective obstacle.

Mason very possibly did not share Rumsey's optimism, or he just wanted to get to his own house in any case. Whatever the reason, he declined. He and his son followed their revised path, though this was far more harrowing than they anticipated. It took them three hours to go two miles. They finally made it back at four thirty on Monday morning, unharmed but very much the worse for wear.

Mason had plenty of time along the way to contemplate the wholesale destruction of the city of which he was mayor. All he could do now was wait, watch, and worry.

5

"I GAVE UP ALL HOPES OF BEING ABLE TO SAVE MUCH OF ANYTHING"

The North Division

About 1:30 a.m. on Monday, October 9, approximately a half hour before the Courthouse cupola imploded, the flames leaped the Main Branch of the Chicago River to the North Division as easily as they had earlier jumped the South Branch. They ignited Lill's Brewery, right below the Pumping Station of the waterworks and more than a half mile above the river.

That fire did only limited harm. The North Side's fate was sealed an hour later, however, when at about 2:30 a.m. flames seized upon a string of Chicago and North Western Railway cars full of kerosene above the river at Wolcott (State) Street. Within minutes Andrew J. Wright's large stable, a block north on Kinzie Street, was also ablaze. The stable gave way so quickly that the animals were trapped awfully in the flames. At close to the same time, the fires still burning in the West Division again jumped into the South Division, this time landing at Polk Street, a half mile south of where they had earlier crossed the river, and moved east and north from there.

The North Side blaze swept deeper into the division, ultimately razing the legion of humbler homes occupied, and often built, by German and Scandinavian skilled workers. It leveled virtually all the churches in which they worshipped, the stores in which they shopped, the saloons where they drank, and the *verein*, the multipurpose community centers where German people gathered.

The fire even threatened the North Side's most remote residence, which was not exactly in the division at all. To John Tolland and his wife, home was the modest quarters atop the Lake Michigan water

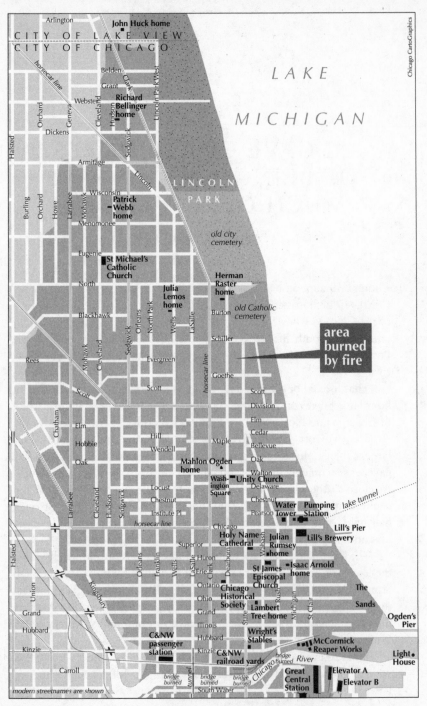

The fire in the North Division, the most extensively burned of the three divisions.

intake crib two miles from shore. As early as eleven o'clock on Sunday evening, flaming boards from the South Division, some six inches long, began to bombard the Tollands. The assault lasted most of the night, reaching peak intensity between two and three in the morning.

Tolland said that the possibility that he would be burned alive seemed so likely that he would have "sold out my chances . . . for a dollar to any man that came along." It was not, unfortunately, the kind of place where people "came along." Equipped with only a broom and buckets, Tolland labored feverishly to sweep away cinders and keep the crib wetted down.

Since the Chicago Water Tower and Pumping Station, on either side of Pine Street (Michigan Avenue) at Chicago Avenue, were clad in limestone and stood in a relatively isolated spot almost two miles north of the Main Branch, there was a reasonable chance that the flames might spare them. The fire did leave the Water Tower unharmed.

Not the Pumping Station. At approximately 3:20 a.m., with the main body of the conflagration still well to the south, an enormous brand— by some descriptions twelve feet long—sailed by the Water Tower and lodged in the northwest corner of the Pumping Station's roof. Within minutes the interior was ablaze, and the three steam engines that delivered water to Chicago, including the hydrants used by the fire department, broke down.

The burning city's predicament was similar to that of the Tollands, only writ much larger. *Chicago Tribune* editor Horace White noted the irony of it all. Once the engines broke down, "though we had at our feet a basin sixty miles wide by three hundred and sixty long, and seven hundred feet deep, all full of clear green water, we could not lift enough to quench a cooking-stove."

Chief Fire Marshal Robert A. Williams had his men soaking down the Sherman House hotel at Clark and Randolph when he received the bad news from Chicago Avenue. "I couldn't hardly believe it," he recalled. He had to see for himself. Williams sped to the waterworks in his chief's wagon. When he beheld the damage to the Pumping Station, Williams stated later, "I gave up all hopes of being able to save much of anything."

Not quite all hopes. Enlisting a few firefighters to accompany him, Williams set off to where he and his wife Harriet lived. He was taking

no chances with her safety and, so it would seem, that of their piano.
The chief did not do any of the heavy lifting, though he made the others'
work easier by unscrewing the piano's legs before they carried it down
from the second floor and into the street. On his way out, he also rolled
up a carpet, which one of the firefighters helped him remove. "That was
all I got of my things," he lamented. He especially regretted having to
leave an expensive new stove behind.

The personal errand was understandable in human terms, but it was
not the kind of action that wins service commendations. His private mission accomplished, Williams returned to public duty.

The North Division was the location of the oldest well-to-do neighborhood in the city, a narrow rectangle of blocks west of Pine Street (Michigan Avenue) between the businesses along the north bank of the Main
Branch and Division Street. This part of Chicago included Washington
Square Park, between Dearborn and Clark Streets and about four blocks
south of Division. The area was at once so near and so far from both
the bustling downtown and the much humbler dwellings—some to
the west and most to the north—of the mainly German workers who
had settled heavily in the North Division and constituted most of its
population.

A few residences here were more like country villas than urban mansions, with broad verandas, burbling fountains, flourishing gardens,
and both carriage houses and conservatories. Among the most gracious
properties was the home of attorney Isaac N. Arnold, who came from
the upstate New York village of Hartwick, about ten miles west of
Cooperstown. He had arrived in 1836, the year he turned twenty-one,
with a few hundred dollars and some law books. His current house and
grounds took up the entire block bordering the west side of Pine Street
(Michigan Avenue) between Erie and Huron Streets, amid mature oak,
ash, maple, cherry, elm, hickory, and cottonwood trees. Over the years
Arnold assembled a personal library of eight thousand volumes, one of
several distinguished collections in the city. He also owned a large collection of memorabilia relating to Abraham Lincoln, who had been a
close friend.

Isaac N. Arnold (Chicago History Museum, ICHi-037723) and Julian Rumsey. (Chicago History Museum, ICHi-027270)

The Rumsey brothers had removed trees to clear the way for Huron Street, where both lived. Behind Julian Rumsey's house was a yard where the family kept chickens. In the garden was a fountain in a pool stocked with trout. While Rumsey went downtown to retrieve his valuable grain receipts, his wife, older children, and a few neighbors huddled fretfully in their rambling home. Still in bed upstairs were the four youngest— all girls—of Julian and Martha Rumsey's ten children. Ada and Lida shared one room, Dora and Emily another.

The commotion below awakened thirteen-year-old Ada, who asked her mother if she could join the grown-ups. Martha Rumsey said yes, as long as Ada got dressed. Their conversation apparently awakened Ada's younger sisters, since soon all four girls were downstairs with the others, including two older siblings, awaiting their father. The four oldest Rumsey children were away at college or boarding school.

Ada noticed that "the sky kept getting redder and redder; the wind, already high, was increasing with the heat, and huge burning cinders were settling in every direction." The children hosed down the flower beds and fallen autumn leaves, both dried out by the lack of rain and recent hot spell. Family servant Christian Larson sprayed water on the roof.

By the time Julian Rumsey returned, it was close to three o'clock. The North Division fires had advanced so far that he knew the house was beyond salvation. The entire ménage prepared to decamp in the family's several vehicles. Larson harnessed two black ponies to the phaeton used by Ada's older sisters and loaded it with the family silverware and linen, oil portraits and other paintings, and a tin box with the grain receipts.

With the house now on fire, Julian risked entering it to save one more painting, a landscape titled *Deerfield*, the first work of art the Rumseys had purchased following their marriage twenty-three years and ten children earlier. After he emerged, Rumsey implored a man heading up Cass Street (Wabash Avenue) to carry the painting northward to who knew where, as long as it was beyond the fire. The most persuasive part of the imploring was Rumsey's offer of twenty-five dollars, half the cash on him.

At the last moment Rumsey also recalled and removed from his safe government bonds he had purchased for his children. Then he drove north with his wife and daughters in the family carriage. Ada described the trip as "a terrific struggle . . . , the hot wind almost knocking us down and the burning cinders falling about us."

Nine-year-old Philena Maxwell watched her father intently as he surveyed what to take from their two-story frame home on Erie Street between Clark and Dearborn, a half dozen blocks southwest of the Rumseys. He chose the family's Fletcher Bible, which he and his wife had purchased right after moving to Chicago from Maine fifteen years earlier. The book's name derived from its editor, nineteenth-century Scottish minister and reformer Alexander Fletcher. Philena's father removed his coat and wrapped the Bible in it. Tucking the bundle under his arm, he rushed into the family's burning barn to fetch his horse, whose fetlocks were on fire. Maxwell smothered the flames and led the horse out, calming the animal by covering its eyes with his hat. They joined the rest of the family in the crowded procession trudging north on Clark Street.

Attorney Isaac Arnold had connected hoses to two different hydrants in order to keep his house and outbuildings wet. While the Arnolds' three older children and the servants stayed to assist him, his wife Harriet left with nine-year-old Alice. In spite of their efforts, the storm of cinders ignited the barn, the lawn, the front piazza, one of the greenhouses, and the roof of the house. Any hope of success ceased when the engines in the Pumping Station broke down. Arnold understood that the fight was lost and that it was now too late to try to salvage his most precious possessions, including his library and irreplaceable collection of Lincoln memorabilia.

Some families who were members of the Chicago Historical Society carted their things to its building on the northwest corner of Dearborn and Ontario Streets. Founded at an 1856 meeting in J. Young Scammon's office that included Isaac Arnold, the society had moved into its current home in 1868. Intended to protect as well as hold the society's collections, the building was supposedly one of the city's most fire-resistant structures, which is why members were eager to stash their belongings there.

When Samuel Stone, the society's assistant librarian, arrived at the building a little after two o'clock on Monday morning, he was surprised to see librarian William Corkran busily accepting personal trunks and boxes. Knowing this put the collections at risk, Stone decided to seal the building immediately. Those who had not arrived in time to store their goods cursed Stone out. He barely closed the door to the overfilled basement by canting a trunk against it.

Sophie Raster, wife of *Illinois Staats-Zeitung* editor Herman Raster, was too ill to walk to safety from their home on North Dearborn Street below North Avenue, but a man the paper described as "an American" offered her a ride in his buggy. The *Staats-Zeitung*, which would criticize others ("Germans too") for demanding up to fifty dollars "for such a favor," praised Sophie's savior, "who would not even give his name, much less accept any payment." A German milkman named Miller, who had stacked all his furniture in his wagon, gallantly unloaded it in order to make room for a pregnant woman. "He saved her, and permitted all his goods to burn," the *Staats-Zeitung* reported approvingly.

Patrick Webb, a day laborer for the Chicago and North Western Railway, lived in a North Division frame house on Church (Hudson) Street. Webb had built the home with his own hands in 1869. Unable to hire a wagon for his goods and his family, he joined other men digging a pit in which to bury their furniture, bedding, and kitchen goods. They stopped when they hit water under the area's shallow soil. As their wives filled this hole with the items they hoped to save, the men started on another. The sparks and burning brands landing all about spurred them to work more quickly. Overheated from exertion, Webb took off some of his outer garments. Just before the family fled, Webb asked his wife for the clothes he had doffed. They had been buried with everything else.

Sixteen-year-old Mary Kehoe and her younger sister Kate led their three-year-old twin stepsisters to crowded Washington Square Park, from which they could see the destruction of Holy Name Cathedral, about three blocks to the southeast. Separated from the rest of the family, the Kehoe sisters were unnerved to come upon the corpse of a cow that had caught its head in a sewer, evidently in an attempt to escape the smoke and fire. Dreading that the flames might overwhelm Washington Square, they walked westward toward the North Branch of the river.

The Kehoes ended up finding shelter under an abutment of the Division Street Bridge. Teamster James Roche, his wife, and their six children spent a similarly grim Monday night wedged under a raised sidewalk a half mile farther north, near the North Avenue Bridge. They had stuffed the family's $300 in greenbacks into a mattress atop a wagon, but a piece of burning wood landed on the vehicle and set the mattress—and the money—on fire.

While some refugees from the burning North Division crossed the North Branch of the Chicago River to the West Side, most made their escape either east or north. Those who went east were mainly people who lived below Chicago Avenue. They huddled along a ragged eastern edge of the city above the Main Branch. Through much of the late nineteenth century, the Sands, as this area was called, was a socially as well as geographically marginal neighborhood. By the early 1850s it had become notorious as a locus of gambling and prostitution. In April 1857, Mayor "Long John" Wentworth led a posse of policemen in pulling down the shacks that hosted these illicit activities. The raid scattered the occupants, who did not disappear but resumed their callings elsewhere in the city. The Sands' unsavory reputation persisted.

In a letter he sent to his friend Philip Prescott (whom he addressed as "Dear Chum") about a week after the fire, twelve-year-old Justin Butterfield, the youngest of his family's three children, described their ordeal in trying to reach the Sands. Awakened at about 1:30 a.m. on Monday, October 9, by loud knocking by an unknown person, the family "saw a perfect shower of sparks" flying over their home. Justin and his brother Charlie spent about two hours trying to drench the house before they gave up. The Butterfields could not get a wagon, so they put two trunks on a wheelbarrow and carried what else they could by hand.

Justin held up the rear, leading his pet goat. He included a drawing of the procession in his letter. He made sure to show his father William Butterfield's glasses and beard, and he put a smile on his mother Sarah Butterfield's face.

The journey was no smiling matter, however. The smoke from a burning lumberyard made it difficult to breathe, and then Sarah Butterfield's broad skirt caught fire. After they stifled the flames, the Butterfields continued on until they came to a shanty on the shore, which they decided

Justin Butterfield (identified as "me") trailing his family and leading his goat. (Chicago History Museum, ICHi-063792)

to use as a shelter. William Butterfield and Justin's older brother Charlie went back for the trunks they had set down along the way, but the blowing sand, which cut into their faces, reduced visibility so much that they could only recover one of the trunks.

Attorney Lambert Tree had moved to Chicago from his native Washington, DC, in 1855. Voters selected him as a Cook County Circuit Court judge in the election of 1870. With the help of servants, Tree wetted down the roof of his house east of Wolcott (State) on Ohio Street, but by about three o'clock Monday morning he decided it was time to find "a safer place." After his wife Anna, their eight-year-old son Arthur, Lambert's father and sister, and a French female servant left, he dragged out a trunk with the family silver and then made a last-minute decision to save a portrait of Arthur. He pulled the trunk across the street with one hand while holding the portrait in the other. Once he was a short distance away, it occurred to Tree that he had forgotten to turn off the gas, not that it mattered anymore.

The Trees intended to stop at the nearby house of Anna's elderly parents, H. H. Magie and his wife, and take them along. He set down the portrait in the Magies' large garden, thinking it would be safe there. He never saw it again. He had the Magies' gardener, whom he referred to as "old Matthew," bury the silver.

The group, now including the Magies, had great difficulty finding their way through all the smoke. Anna Tree nearly fainted, but the French maid helped her move along. At one point they feared they were trapped by a burning fence, but it fell away just in time to let them through. The Trees then realized to their horror that they had been separated from the Magies. The smoke was so dense and the fire so near that they knew it would be useless, possibly even fatal, to try to find Anna's parents.

They could only hope that the Magies were escaping on their own. When the hem of Anna Tree's dress took fire, her husband ripped away the burning section of cloth. She abandoned as too ponderous a burden the jewelry and other valuables she had hoped to take with her.

The Trees went a block north to Ontario Street and walked east toward the lake. Between the smoke and the flying cinders, which set aflame mattresses carried by other refugees, they had great difficulty. Once at the shore, they saw "thousands of men, women, and children, and hundreds of horses and dogs who had already fled there for refuge. The grounds were dotted all over at short intervals with piles of trunks, chairs, tables, beds, and household furniture of every description."

Tree saw families huddled around the few pieces of furniture that were now all that was left of their property. "Here and there a mother sat upon the ground clinging to her infant, with one or more little ones, who, exhausted by the prolonged interruptions to their slumbers, were now sleeping, with their heads reclining on her lap, as peacefully as if nothing unusual was transpiring."

Elsewhere "several invalids lay helplessly stretched upon mattresses, but still surrounded by relatives and friends, who were endeavoring to soothe their fears." Sitting near Tree was a young girl trying to shield her pet canary. She covered the cage with a shawl, which she raised periodically to check on its well-being. Tree later saw the bird tumble from its perch. "It was dead; and the poor child, who doubtless had met her first sorrow, burst into tears."

While sparks and cinders fell "as fast and thick as hailstones," Tree wrote, "man and beast alike rushed to the water's edge, and into the water, to avoid suffocation." Many walked out until the water reached

as high as their waists, turning their backs to the city to avoid the waves
of heat.

By midday on Monday, October 9, the fire reached North Avenue,
a mile above the waterworks and about twice that far from the Main
Branch. The easternmost stretch of North Avenue, which ended at the
lake, was a half mile below what was then the southern edge of Lincoln
Park, the largest public space in the North Division.

The park was established in 1864 and then named for Abraham Lincoln shortly after his assassination the following year. At the outset it
was only eighty acres. It was soon to be extended south to North Avenue, which involved annexing what was then the city cemetery. Public
health advocate Dr. John H. Rauch had convinced the city that it was
necessary to Chicago's well-being to remove the bodies of the deceased
in the city cemetery and reinter them in private burial grounds in adjoining towns. Given the local topography and the cemetery's proximity
to the lake, Rauch explained, the conditions were "peculiarly favorable"
to carrying the "noxious compounds" of decaying bodies into the public water supply.

In the southeast corner of the cemetery were both the pest house,
where victims of cholera and smallpox were kept in isolation, and the
potter's field, the burial ground for indigent Chicagoans. In another section were the remains of about four thousand Confederate prisoners of
war. Most had died of illnesses attributable to the horrible conditions
of their confinement at the southern edge of the city in Camp Douglas, once part of the estate of the late senator Stephen Douglas. There
was also a small Jewish section. The Catholic cemetery was on the
south side of North Avenue at the top of what became the Gold Coast
neighborhood.

As Chicago burned, this habitation of the dead provided asylum for
the living who were escaping north. It teemed with terrified and fatigued
evacuees in search of safety and respite. *Harper's Weekly* staff artist
Theodore Davis, who seven years earlier had depicted the merciless march
of Union general William Tecumseh Sherman's army through Georgia,
prepared a haunting sketch of the "rush of fugitives through the Potter's Field toward Lincoln Park." In the center, a tattered parade of disconsolate Chicagoans files toward the viewer. The light from the flaming
city, far in the background, silhouettes the trees, reflects off the lake,
and illuminates the cemetery. The refugees pass desks, chairs, paintings,

Rush of Fugitives through the Potter's Field toward Lincoln Park,
based on a sketch by Theo R. Davis. From Harper's Weekly,
November 4, 1871. (Chicago History Museum, ICHi-002881)

and other goods carted all this way only to be discarded amid the simple
crosses marking the graves of the impoverished and forgotten.

Even more desolate were scattered encampments in the expanses of prairie a mile farther north, near the Chicago–Lake View border. These
outer reaches of the city, about three miles from the Courthouse, were
very thinly settled. The center of the early suburb of Lake View was
another two miles away, at Halsted and Addison, near the site of what
would later be Wrigley Field. A farming area that had become popular as a summer resort, Lake View was readily accessible by train,
whose tracks crossed these undeveloped spots where fire refugees
camped out.

A. S. Chapman remembered the "flood of stricken humanity"
that flowed up Lincoln Avenue. "Without thinking," he wrote, "it

was possessed by one thought—on, onward—away from the burning city to the green country beyond. Nobody might stop to rest; he was pressed on by others as tired as himself. Men pulled buggies loaded with all they had on earth; women carried burdens larger than themselves; children pushed baby carriages containing the little saved from their homes. On they went to Fullerton Avenue to scatter over the prairie—to drop in their tracks and wait for they knew not what."

Railroad laborer Patrick Webb, who had inadvertently buried his clothes, led his wife and four children to the prairie because it was a place where there would be "no houses to burn." Amid hosts of others, all without shelter, blankets, or food, the Webbs tried to settle down for the night. Among other refugees in this area was the family of Julia Lemos. Her father was Eustace Wyszynski, a Polish nobleman who had been exiled after his country's failed 1831 uprising against Russian rule. Her mother, Johanna, was a cousin of former president Martin Van Buren. Julia had married Nicolas Lemos when she was sixteen, but he had passed away.

When the fire struck, Julia was a twenty-nine-year-old widow struggling to support five children and her aged parents on her income as an artist at a downtown lithography company. The family rented its home on Wells Street, a block below North Avenue. In addition to writing a long narrative of her fire experience decades later, Lemos painted a vivid bird's-eye view of her neighborhood during the fire. In the painting, families cluster together in terror in the foreground, as behind them their world collapses in flames. Especially striking are the great clouds of red-tinged smoke.

Johanna Wyszynski had been ill of late, so Julia, as was not unusual for hard-pressed parents, temporarily placed four of the children in an orphan asylum. When Lemos saw the fire approaching, she hurried to the orphanage to retrieve them. Lemos had the presence of mind to ask her landlord for a refund on the rent she had just paid since it was clear that within a very short time the fire would evict them. The landlord refused but offered instead to haul the family and its possessions, including her father's hunting dog, to a spot beyond the fire.

After the landlord dropped them off, Lemos put her children to bed on the mattresses that were part of the load. They were asleep only an hour when their watchful mother saw that the fire was approaching.

Julia Lemos, Memories of the Chicago Fire, *1912.*
(Chicago History Museum, ICHi-062293)

They had to move farther out, this time on foot and without their goods. Once Lemos was satisfied that the family had reached a safe place, her father tore down a board fence so the children could lie on something other than the bare ground. Lemos now worried that they had survived the fire only to contract a serious illness from exposure.

Baron Wyszynski stumbled through the dark in search of any kind of shelter for the group. He discovered a shed and returned to get the others. It was pitch-black inside. Lemos and her mother held the two youngest children in their arms as everyone tried to go back to sleep. They were awakened around midnight when others joined them. Not until daylight did Lemos see that the newcomers were a woman and her little boy.

It was "an awful night for the people on the prairies," William Gallagher wrote to his family. "No one would ever know of the suffering or of the number that died that night from hunger, exhaustion and the cold." Rumors attributed both untimely deaths and premature births to the stress. A semiliterate woman named Amelia (there is no record of

her last name) told her sister in a pencil-written letter of rumors that
there had been five hundred deliveries on the prairie on Monday.

The necessities of hurried flight, with limited options for where to go
and how to get there, pushed some of the city's wealthiest residents and
those far less advantaged into unaccustomed intimacy. Lambert Tree
was struck by their common demoralization, which reminded him of a
shipwrecked crew. He noted how indifferent people were when an extremely ill poor woman who had been carried to the lakefront "died in
the midst of a mixed crowd of men, women, and children."

Horace White, in contrast, stated that the common plight created a
kind of mutual aid society that ignored class divisions. White claimed to
witness "a great many kindly acts done as we moved along. The poor
helped the rich, and the rich helped the poor (if anybody could be called
rich at such a time), to get on with their loads." Emma Hambleton, wife of
lawyer Chalkey J. Hambleton, reflected to her mother on October 11,
"The fire was a wonderful leveler, if I may use that expression. Life was
the only question then."

If leveling there was, it moved exclusively in one direction. For the
moment, at least, the fire reduced everyone to misery. "Women who had
never before lacked comfort, spent Monday night in the open air,"
James W. Milner wrote to a friend four days after the fire. According to
nineteenth-century Chicago historian A. T. Andreas, writing of refugees
on the prairie, "The millionaire, the pauper, the innocent, the prostitute,
the young, the old, the strong, the sick and dying—all gathered on the
level of corporal deprivation, and shivered under the same chill wind;
were parched by the same thirst, gnawed by the same pangs of hunger,
felt the same suspense concerning absent relatives and friends, the same
grim hoping against hope."

Although White suggested that this created a kind of community of
suffering that brought people together in positive ways, in some instances it heightened simmering resentments. Alexander Frear said he
saw an angry and drunken worker standing defiantly atop an abandoned
piano in the midst of piles of other goods left on the street by exclusive
downtown stores and moneyed Chicagoans. The man declared trium-

phantly that "the fire was the friend of the poor man," if only by hurting the rich, who might now learn what it meant to live in poverty. "He wanted everybody to help himself to the best liquor he could get; and continued to yell from the piano until some one, as drunk as himself, flung a bottle at him and knocked him off it." To Frear, "The brutality and horror of the scene made it sickening."

Here and there a reporter noted that working people were particularly hard hit. "Hundreds of poor families were being rendered homeless, presenting pictures of squalid misery most pitiable," the *Chicago Times* observed. A writer on the scene for the *Chicago Tribune* pointed out that the O'Leary's West Division laboring community "were nearly all poor people, the savings of whose lifetime were represented in the little mass of furniture" they dragged out into the streets. He added that "every now and then a woman, wild with grief, would run in and out among the alleys, and cry aloud her grief," presumably over a missing child.

For the most part, however, the sympathies of reporters for the leading dailies and authors of contemporary published accounts of the fire—two groups that overlapped—were heavily on the side of the well-to-do. After observing that as a result of the fire the "inequalities of societies were now leveled off as smooth as the beach itself," Elias Colbert and Everett Chamberlin, local journalists and co-authors of *Chicago and the Great Conflagration*, considered the wealthy the greatest victims of the fire. A rich and cultured person was obviously worse off than "the boor who now jostles him." After all, "he is allowed to lose more and to suffer more, and is required to lament less."

Colbert and Chamberlin were wrong. As is the case in most disasters, the prosperous were in fact far better off, even if they apparently had more to lose and farther to fall. While many of the city's leading citizens endured a harrowing trial, their social position and financial reserves eased their plight in ways unavailable to most Chicagoans. Like the Arnolds, the Rumseys, and the Trees, they had servants to help them defend their homes and then carry their things away. They either owned a carriage (sometimes more than one) or had the means to hire a wagon, even if the price was exorbitant. They also benefited from a network of relatives and friends to take them in afterward and help them find each other after being separated.

Isaac Arnold's resources finally brought him and his three older children to safety after a remarkable odyssey. They went straight east from their home on Erie Street to the Sands, then proceeded as far south as they could, just beyond the reach of the fire, to a pier on the north bank of the Main Branch at the river's mouth. From the pier they took a small rowboat to the lighthouse a short distance out in the lake. Here they remained for several hours, hoping for some kind of deliverance. They looked on anxiously as a boat moored in the river burst into flame and threatened to float with the current directly toward their lighthouse refuge. It sank before reaching them.

They spent much of Monday in the lighthouse, with little to do but agonize about what happened to Arnold's wife Harriet and daughter Alice, who had departed their home before the others. Then, between three and four in the afternoon, the tugboat *Clifford*, itself fleeing the burning city, chugged down the river and moored at the lighthouse. Arnold talked the *Clifford*'s pilot into trying to escape the fire by going right through it, back up the narrow river and past the collapsed bridges and the burning warehouses, docks, grain elevators, offices, and factories on its banks.

When the wind blew the hat off the head of thirteen-year-old Arthur Arnold, his father dipped his handkerchief in the river and draped it over Arthur's face. As they passed Wells Street, Arnold asked the pilot hopefully, "Is not the wors[t] over?" The man answered, "We are through, sir." Arnold spent the next twenty-four hours combing the city for Harriet and Alice. He finally discovered that they had reached the suburban home of a friend. By Tuesday evening, October 10, the family was reunited.

Terrible as the experience was, Arnold's money and position assisted him and his family in ways available to a very limited number of their fellow Chicagoans. Not coincidentally, the lighthouse was occupied by wealthy friends and neighbors who, even in these terrible circumstances, found a way to cleave to each other, apart from the common mass. A. T. Andreas notes that when the Arnolds arrived at the lighthouse, they "were hospitably received" by others in their circle.

It took bravery and nerve to risk running the fiery gauntlet along the Chicago River, but it doubtless also required a substantial financial exchange to convince the pilot of the *Clifford* to chance it. Arnold's social network came through for him by taking in his wife and daughter and then the rest of the family.

Lambert Tree's experience was similar. His family headed north along the Sands. After much wandering, they spied a one-horse grocery wagon moving east on Superior Street toward the lake. Judge Tree quickly made a deal with the driver to carry them across the ruins of the North Division to the West Side. At the Kinzie Street Bridge, the driver asked where to drop them off. They had no idea. It was by now seven o'clock Monday evening, more than twenty-four hours since their last meal.

The driver came to their aid. He took them to a West Division boarding house he knew on Washington Street. Its usual clientele were people with incomes well below the Trees', but this was no time to be choosy. As the family was getting out of the wagon, they were spotted by an acquaintance, who offered to host them. In his account of the fire, Tree noted that his friends the Butterfields ended up staying in the boarding house, though he did not indicate where Justin's goat spent the night.

The Trees were thus able to sleep without charge in cozy quarters among congenial company, while most refugees would not have been able to afford the boarding house. After three days of heartache, the Trees reconnected with the Magies, Lambert's elderly in-laws. The couple had lingered behind their daughter's family in order to gather some keepsakes. They escaped, though not without suffering burns on their ears, noses, legs, arms, and hands. The Magies fled north toward the prairie until, like the Trees, they by chance met an old friend, a physician, who housed them and treated their injuries.

When Thomas Hoyne's family needed to move their goods, "friends were constantly coming in, pressing our hands, in tears, and soliciting us to take shelter with them." Two brought wagons to help carry things away. The voluminous family of Julian and Martha Rumsey was even more fortunate. Julian had to make do with a horse blanket for an overcoat, but they made their escape by an overground railroad of sorts, from one friend's house to another, until they caught a Chicago and North Western train to the southern Wisconsin resort town of Lake Geneva, where they had vacationed the previous summer. They discovered that they still had a few hundred dollars in the local bank. This would conveniently cover their expenses for the time being. According to Ada, "the townspeople helped to make articles to replenish our wardrobe."

Neither Julia Lemos's nor Patrick Webb's family, forced to spend the night out on the damp prairie, had much chance of running into acquaintances with a wagon or a warm bed. In one of the infrequent mentions of the sufferings of the poor in contemporary published accounts of the fire, Colbert and Chamberlin speak of those "who had no twenty dollars to give to an exceptionally liberal cartman" and "no sympathizing friends down the avenue to give them shelter and other comforts, and generally no hour's or even a half hour's time in which to calculate upon the means of escape from the devouring element."

The personal accounts of wealthy refugees take as a given the sacrifices of their faithful servants. Christian Larson did not join the Rumseys in their escape but slept on the prairie, where an outbreak of smallpox put him in quarantine. As soon as he was released, he found Julian Rumsey and restored to him the belongings that had been entrusted to Larson's possession and which he had somehow kept secure throughout his ordeal. He had also happened to come upon the man to whom Julian had given twenty-five dollars to carry the painting *Deerfield* beyond the fire and retrieved that as well.

When the Arnolds rowed to the lighthouse, they left behind the servant who had rescued their horse, pony, and cow. After the fire, Tree wrote of how he recovered the silver that his in-laws' gardener, "old Matthew," buried, but he did not say what became of old Matthew. He also did not mention the name of the French maid who stood so steadily by his wife's side throughout their long escape.

There was at least one group of down-at-heels Chicagoans for whom the fire did a fortunate turn. In the course of police captain Michael Hickey's transfer of fifty dangerous prisoners from the jail of the burning Courthouse to the North Division, twenty slipped away. He incarcerated the others in the North Avenue station. When the advancing fire threatened this building, the police moved them once again, to the West Side station on Madison Street. More than half the remaining thirty took advantage of this second opportunity to escape custody, so by the time the officers reached this destination, they had only fourteen inmates in tow. The rest disappeared into the city's far larger population of desperate fugitives.

- 6 -
ENDGAME

Besides the Courthouse, the most important government building in the prefire city was the three-story Romanesque Post Office and Custom House three blocks to the southeast, on the northwest corner of Monroe and Dearborn Streets. Through the early hours of Monday, October 9, the eastern edge of the fire had been moving in its direction, and by dawn the flames were at hand.

The post office occupied the entire basement, where mail was received, and the main floor, where it was distributed. At the time of the fire, Chicago was handling more mail than any other US city besides New York. On the second floor were the offices of the collector of customs, the collector of internal revenue, the steamboat inspector, the US marshal, the US commissioner, and the administrators of the post office. On the top floor were the federal court and district attorney's office.

"It may be interesting to know how this Government building took fire," Francis William Test, who worked there, wrote to his mother four days later. As Test noted, the Post Office and Custom House was another of a handful of Chicago buildings meant to be as impervious to fire as possible. The exterior was solid stone. Iron window shutters and internal doors provided additional protection. When Test and several of his colleagues realized that the building was in the fire's path, they remained hopeful it could withstand the assault.

It could not. A falling wall blew in the shutters at the north end of the basement, "and in less than five minutes the first floor (the Post Office proper) was in flames." Test still thought the upper stories might survive. In the course of a renovation, however, workmen had unintentionally created a passage through which the fire quickly spread upward and "bounded through the hall" to the customs offices.

Even had the post office renovation been flawless, a fire of this magnitude and intensity would almost certainly have destroyed it. Evidence for this lies in the fate of another "fireproof" building, the *Chicago Tribune's* home on the southeast corner of Madison and Dearborn Streets, a block above the Post Office and Custom House. In 1869 the paper had moved into this four-story limestone, marble, and brick edifice, designed in the ornate Second Empire style of midcentury France. Its ceilings were made of arched corrugated iron held in place with wrought iron I-beams embedded in cement.

Tribune part-owner Joseph Medill, who had watched the flames jump the South Branch, crossed to the South Division on the Randolph Street Bridge in time to see the Courthouse catch fire. Since the blaze was between him and his building, Medill had to take an indirect route to get to the *Tribune*. When he arrived, he found the staff maniacally at work on the Monday morning paper, which they knew would be full of the biggest story in the city's history.

The storm of flying embers in the air filled Medill with "lively fears" for the building's fate. He summoned employees to join him on the roof, where there were large water tanks specifically intended for fighting fire. Medill ordered the others to direct the water wherever it was needed. "The air was like that of a furnace—fearfully hot," Medill remembered. "With the hot air, the stifling smoke, and a perfect storm of sparks and blazing fragments falling on the *Tribune*'s 'fireproof' roof, we had a trying time in our efforts to extinguish the incipient fires all about us." Lacking protective clothing, the men took brief breaks behind the east side of the building's chimneys, which shielded them from direct exposure to the heat.

When he peered down to see what was happening on the street, four floors below, Medill observed masses of panicked Chicagoans rushing every which way. "Over all this terrible scene was a sullen roar," he recalled, "much like one hears when close to Niagara Falls, but mixed with crackling sounds and constant reverberations, loud as thunder, from falling walls and explosions, and I could see the great brick buildings tumbling and masses of flame thrown high in the air." It reminded Medill of descriptions of the Battle of Waterloo.

War metaphors appeared in many other firsthand descriptions of the fire. According to the *Chicago Evening Post*, firemen "charged up to the blazing foe only to be driven back to another position by its increasing fierceness" and uncanny ability to "outflank" them. Horace White observed, "Nobody could see it all—no more than one man could see the whole of the Battle of Gettysburg." It was all "too vast, too swift, too full of smoke, too full of danger" to take in, let alone process.

Allusions to natural catastrophes, especially watery ones, are likewise everywhere in accounts of the fire. "The flames, propelled by variable gusts of wind, seemed to pour down Randolph Street in a liquid torrent," recalled Joseph Edgar Chamberlin. In a letter to friends less than two weeks after the fire, Aurelia King, wife of Lake Street clothing wholesaler Henry W. King, described how she fled with her four young children "literally in a shower of fire." King was one of the many who saw Chicago's great conflagration as an apocalyptic struggle. As she held fast to her brood, fearful that the wind would lift them from her, she "thought the day of judgment had come." When Julia Lemos tried to comfort her son Willie, he asked her if this was "the Last Day."

"What a sight," Jonas Hutchinson told his mother, "a sea of fire, the heavens all ablaze, the air filled with burning embers, the wind blowing & fiercely tossing fire brands in all directions, thousands upon thousands of people rushing frantically about, burned out of shelter, without food, the rich of yesterday poor today, destruction everywhere—is it not awful?" He said that one could only exclaim, "My God, when will it end."

Many personified the raging conflagration as the "fire fiend," implying that the devil himself was behind it. White, who threw all the figurative language he could muster at the conflagration, said it was as if "the dogs of hell were upon the housetops of LaSalle and Wells Street, just south of Adams, bounding from one to another."

In his 1889 novel, *Daniel Trentworthy: A Tale of the Great Fire of Chicago*, John McGovern, who was twenty-one in 1871 and had been at the *Tribune* before moving to the *Chicago Herald*, has an editor shouting at his reporters, "All sit here and write whatever comes into your heads!" Few matched the bravura of a reporter for the *Chicago Evening Post*, who ingeniously conveyed its terrors by describing the instinctive reactions of animals in the city:

> The horses, maddened by heat and noise, and irritated by
> falling sparks, neighed and screamed with affright and
> anger, and reared and kicked, and bit each other, or stood
> with drooping tails and rigid legs, ears laid back and eyes

wild with amazement, shivering as if with cold. The dogs
ran wildly hither and thither, snuffing eagerly at every one,
and occasionally sitting down on their haunches to howl
dismally. When there was a lull in the fire, far-away dogs
could be heard baying and cocks crowing at the unwonted
light. Cats ran along ridge-poles in the bright glare, and
came pattering into the street with dropsical tails. Great
brown rats with beadlike eyes were ferreted out from
under the sidewalks by the flames, and scurried along
the streets, kicked at, trampled upon, hunted down.
Flocks of beautiful pigeons, so plentiful in the city,
wheeled up aimlessly, circled blindly once or twice,
and were drawn into the maw of the fiery hell raging
underneath.

The reporters and the pressmen in the *Tribune* building labored
bravely on by the light of the flames until the fire whose story they were
trying to tell made that telling impossible. It became so hot that windows
snapped and the rollers on the presses began to melt. Suffocating smoke
was everywhere.

At about seven o'clock on Monday morning, October 9, Medill and
his staff fled. They attempted to save rare early issues of the paper, only
to realize that this meant carrying a heavy load of highly combustible
material through a roaring fire. They dropped the papers. Looking back
on the burning structure, Medill now thought it resembled a volcano.

Earlier the night before, the flames that had destroyed the Courthouse blew along Randolph and Washington Streets east of Clark and
took down the many theaters and other attractions in this area. The most
curious of Chicago's "amusements," as the papers called even serious
playhouses, was the five-story, banner-bedecked Col. Wood's Museum,
on the north side of Randolph Street between Clark and Dearborn. For
twenty-five cents, visitors entered Wood's grab bag of natural history
specimens and random oddities. Alongside displays of reptiles, insects,
and birds were what Wood presented as Daniel Boone's rifle, mummies
owned by Mormon Church founder Joseph Smith, and a ninety-six-foot-
long whale skeleton he called the Great Zeuglodon. With his eye for the
sensational, Wood had also acquired the silver-plated revolver onetime
chambermaid Mollie Trussell had used to murder her unfaithful lover,

CHICAGO IN FLAMES—BURNING OF THE CHAMBER OF COMMERCE.—[SEE PAGE 1010.]

CHICAGO IN FLAMES—BURNING OF THE CROSBY OPERA-HOUSE.—[SEE PAGE 1010.]

Chicago in Flames. *Top, the Chamber of Commerce;
bottom, Crosby's Opera House. From Harper's Weekly,
October 25, 1871. (Chicago History Museum, ICHi-063127)*

sportsman and gambler George Trussell, by shooting him through the heart in a Randolph Street saloon in September 1866.

On the north side of Washington Street between Dearborn and State was the most magnificent of Chicago's theaters, Crosby's Opera House. Its Italianate exterior was adorned with allegorical figures representing painting, sculpture, music, and commerce. This was one of several hybrid buildings with both performance and retail space. The first floor along Washington Street was rented out as retail stores, the second and third as offices. The fourth housed an art gallery and studios.

On the immense ceiling of the three-thousand-seat auditorium were portraits of Daniel François Esprit Auber, Ludwig von Beethoven, Gaetano Donizetti, Christoph Willibald Gluck, Charles François Gounod, Wolfgang Amadeus Mozart, Gioacchino Antonio Rossini, Guiseppe Verdi, Richard Wagner, and Carl Maria von Weber. On the wall above the stage, flanked by the masks of the characters Comedy and Tragedy, was a forty-foot reproduction of seventeenth-century baroque master Guido Reni's *Aurora*, the original of which is in Rome.

Crosby had encountered a series of misfortunes since the completion of his building in the spring of 1865, when Abraham Lincoln's assassination forced him to delay the theater's debut. After that he had lost and then regained ownership of it. In the summer of 1871 Crosby closed the theater for a complete renovation. He scheduled the reopening, to be celebrated with an orchestral performance conducted by German maestro Theodore Thomas, for Monday evening, October 9.

The fire next ravaged State Street, laying waste to the two jewels in Potter Palmer's real estate empire. Palmer, who grew up on a farm thirty miles southwest of Albany, New York, was one of the many easterners who settled in Chicago after living for shorter or longer periods in other towns along the way. The forty-five-year-old Palmer made a fortune in the dry goods business before switching to real estate development and turning State Street into one of the finest commercial addresses in the city. On Monday morning the flames destroyed both his luxurious Palmer House hotel, under construction at State and Monroe, and the six-story Field, Leiter & Company department store, the biggest retail establishment of its kind outside New York. Palmer had previously sold his dry goods business on Lake Street to Marshall Field and Levi Leiter and then persuaded them to rent this palatial emporium.

The dramatic closing act of Crosby's Opera House became one of the few sources of humor in accounts of the fire. In his long and otherwise sobering letter to his sister, William Gallagher posed her a riddle that referred to Theodore Thomas's scheduled performance at Crosby's grand reopening on Monday evening: What was the difference between Thomas and Emperor Nero? "One fiddled away while his Rome was burning, and the other roamed away while his fiddles were burning."

As if bored, the fire began to play new tricks. In spite of the prevailing southwest wind, a portion of it barreled southward down Michigan and Wabash Avenues, the two north-south streets closest to the lakefront. By three o'clock Monday afternoon this south-moving fire intersected with an east-heading spur of flames at Terrace Row, on Michigan Avenue north of Van Buren Street, where only a few hours earlier J. Young Scammon and Robert Todd Lincoln had breakfasted with a feeling that they were secure from harm.

One of Scammon's Terrace Row neighbors was William Bross. Bross was born in New Jersey in 1813 and came to Chicago in 1848, where he prospered in a range of investments and became one of the city's most bombastic boosters. In 1859 he drove the first spike of the Chicago City Railway Company's streetcar tracks at the corner of State and Randolph. Like Joseph Medill, ten years Bross's junior, he entered journalism and Republican Party politics, investing in the *Tribune* and serving a term as Illinois lieutenant governor in the late 1860s.

Bross evidently was not aware of the fire until he was awakened by a houseguest about 2:00 a.m. Monday. After making a personal inspection of the progress of the flames, he was sure that Terrace Row was far enough south and east to escape their wrath. When he returned home, he was surprised to find his wife Mary Jane, their seventeen-year-old daughter Jessie, and the family's servants readying for flight. He instructed them to stop packing and instead to prepare to assist the many who would be burned out. "The result of this night's work will be awful," Bross told them. "At least ten thousand people will want breakfast in the morning; you prepare breakfast for one hundred," he ordered. At

William Bross. (Chicago History Museum, ICHi-168958)

about 2:30 a.m. he rode off to check on the *Tribune*, where he saw "no cause for apprehension" and left not long after he arrived. The others in the household meanwhile did as he had directed, but, unconvinced by his assurances, soon returned to packing.

They made the right decision. By late Monday morning Bross and other occupants of Terrace Row acknowledged that the townhouses were lost. They transported what possessions they could across Michigan Avenue to the lakeshore.

Many, but not all, of the belongings made it safely. After Bross's coachman had loaded a buggy, an opportunistic thief took the reins and drove it away. Bross said that he encountered a different stranger at his door who looked "decidedly corpulent." He claimed that he said to the man, "My friend, you have on a considerable invoice of my clothes, with the hunting suit outside." Instead of stopping or even reprimanding this robber, Bross waxed philosophical, "Well, go along," he continued, "you might as well have them as to let them burn."

Aurelia King told her friends that there was a story going around that described Bross's exit from Terrace Row in a very different way than he did: "It was said that when the fire was raging, one citizen left his house and family, and fled on horseback down Michigan Avenue with his portrait under one arm and his lecture, 'Across the Continent,' under the other." Her friends would know the "one citizen" was Bross because of their familiarity with his much-repeated talk on "The Resources of the Far West" (which King called "Across the Continent"), based on a trip Bross made after the Civil War.

According to Bross, his family and the other tony occupants of Terrace Row perched by the lakefront on their relocated furniture, which provided them a front row seat to the spectacle of their burning homes. "There I sat with a few others by our household goods," Bross wrote, "calmly awaiting the destruction of our property—one of the most splendid blocks in Chicago."

They had plenty of company. Just to the east of Michigan Avenue was a thin and scraggly forty-four-acre stretch of land known as Lake (or Lake Shore) Park. In 1871 the Chicago White Stockings—ancestors of the Cubs, not, as their name would seem to imply, the White Sox—built a baseball diamond in the park. The team sported white flannel shirts with a blue C on the pocket, blue pants, and, of course, white stockings. The day before the Great Fire, the White Stockings easily defeated an amateur squad in spite of having only eight players, two of whom covered the entire outfield. Now many other Chicagoans joined the residents of Terrace Row in Lake Park.

In a spot where a wooden fence blocked the way into the park, "a benevolent laborer" pulled up a loose post and used it to knock out the boards, enabling Horace White and his family to pass through. F. L. Rockwell and the rolled-up canvas of Rothermel's painting of Gettysburg were marooned a few blocks farther north, as were James and Myra Bradwell and their son Thomas. The Bradwells were deeply worried about their daughter Bessie, from whom they had been separated.

Bross's description notwithstanding, the South Division shoreline was by no means a comfortable refuge. Cassius Milton Wicker said that the wind was "strong enough to blow a chair left alone clear across the park." The gales raised so much dust and sand that the fire was almost invisible, close though it was. People certainly felt it. Like Rockwell and plenty of others, the Bradwells dipped their faces in the lake "to keep from burning up."

As on the North Side, the fire in the South Division created a community of exhausted exiles out of otherwise very different individuals. By the lake, where "the air was so full of dust and sand that it was impossible to see the fire," Wicker wrote, "lay the lowly and the proud."

As in the North Division, the proud fared better than the lowly. Servants helped William Bross carry his family's belongings across Michigan Avenue. He was subsequently able to hire wagons to deliver these possessions to the homes of friends who lived in large houses south of the fire. The Brosses soon found safe and comfortable refuge at the South Wabash Avenue home of his brother-in-law.

Late Monday afternoon, James H. Hildreth and gunpowder made a second appearance in the South Division. According to Hildreth, Mayor Roswell B. Mason's son provided him with a fresh supply the mayor had ordered from a factory a few miles south of the city. After considerable confusion and delay—Hildreth still did not seem to understand why he had difficulty convincing others to assist him in moving gunpowder through a burning city—he decided to make a stand at Wabash and Harrison, about a block south and west of Terrace Row.

While the claim has skeptics as well as believers, Hildreth later contended that it was "self-evident of itself" that this time his blasting was effective. Whether thanks to Hildreth or not, it was here that the South Division fires finally ended late Monday afternoon.

Hildreth had a run-in with a far more celebrated resident of the city, lieutenant general and Civil War hero Philip H. Sheridan. Born in Albany, New York, of Irish Catholic immigrant parents in 1831 and raised in Ohio, Sheridan attended the US Military Academy at West Point and then rose quickly through the ranks during the Civil War, when he was still in his early thirties. His height, or lack of it—Sheridan was at most five foot five—earned him the nickname "Little Phil." His strong nose, dashing vandyke mustache and beard, high cheekbones, and, most of all, his uncompromising spirit made him nonetheless a daunting presence.

General Philip H. Sheridan, ca. 1876. Photograph by
Charles D. Mosher. (Chicago History Museum, ICHi-063957)

Sheridan had a well-earned reputation as a relentless warrior. Away from his troops for a strategy meeting during the 1864 Shenandoah Valley campaign, he galloped back in time to rally them to victory. "Sheridan's Ride," Thomas Buchanan's poem about this exploit, turned him into a figure of legend, as Henry Wadsworth Longfellow's poem had done for Paul Revere. The following year Sheridan played a critical role in trapping Robert E. Lee's forces and ending the conflict. In 1869 Sheridan was appointed head of the Army's sprawling Department of the Missouri, which stretched from the Mississippi River to the Rocky Mountains and from Canada to Mexico. He shifted division headquarters from St. Louis to Chicago, renting offices in the Merchants Building, across LaSalle Street from the Courthouse.

Sheridan's first response to the fire was the same as that of others with offices in the downtown. He attempted to retrieve Army records from the Merchants Building, including his own Civil War correspondence, but he was too late. Although he was a federal military officer with no civilian authority, he assisted in this extraordinary crisis with the special resources at his disposal. Sheridan telegraphed US Army headquarters in St. Louis for rations and military installations in Jeffersonville, Indiana, and Omaha, Nebraska, for tents and troops.

Sheridan helped even more directly. At the time Hildreth embarked on his second foray with gunpowder, Sheridan and some of his men were trying to create a firebreak in the South Division by knocking down small wooden buildings with axes. Wishing to speed up the process, Sheridan sent a messenger to Hildreth requesting some gunpowder. Hildreth contemptuously refused him, claiming that there was no need for Sheridan's men do anything since he, Hildreth, had already stopped the fire.

Whether this was true or not, the fire ceased just before it reached the Michigan Avenue Hotel, at Congress and Michigan, a block south of Terrace Row. One of the oft-repeated anecdotes of the disaster involves John B. Drake, a part owner of the Tremont House hotel at Lake and Dearborn. Having lost the Tremont to the flames much earlier on Monday (it was the third iteration of the hotel to burn down), Drake reached a hurried agreement with the owner to purchase the Michigan Avenue Hotel even as the flames licked at other properties nearby. Drake was betting that the Michigan Avenue Hotel would survive, its owner that it would not. Drake won the bet.

By early Monday evening the fire in the North Division was entering its final phase. The flames reached the city's Fullerton Avenue northern border and encroached a little into Lake View late Monday night. The last house the fire claimed was that of a man named John A. Huck, who lived near the shore just beyond the Chicago city line. In the early hours of Tuesday, October 10, the fire finally burned itself out. Mother Nature provided some relief—too little, too late—as rain began to fall. Early Tuesday morning, about thirty hours after the shouts of Daniel Sullivan that their barn was burning awakened Patrick and Catherine O'Leary, the Great Chicago Fire ended.

Its full story had only just begun.

7

"PRAY FOR ME"

The Great Chicago Fire earned its name. The so-called Burnt District was, by the conservative estimate of the city's Board of Public Works, four miles from end to end and an average of just under two-thirds of a mile wide. It comprised 2.64 square miles of the most built-up and densely populated part of the city.

The board stated that the conflagration claimed some 122 miles of sidewalks and 2,162 street lamps. Of the $2,680,856.90 in losses sustained by the municipality of Chicago, $470,000 were due to the burning of the Courthouse, almost $250,000 to damage to the waterworks (including some $100,000 in water that escaped through melted pipes), and a similar amount to the destruction of schools. The private property loss of just under $200 million in 1871 dollars represented about one-third of the total valuation at the time. Close to eighteen thousand buildings were gone.

The North Division was hurt far more extensively than the others, losing 13,300 of its 13,800 buildings, many of them homes of immigrant workers. The toll in the South Division was "only" 3,650 buildings, but a significant number of these, like the Courthouse, were among the city's largest and most valuable structures.

The flames reduced to rubble almost all of Chicago's principal banks; 3 of its 4 downtown railroad depots; the offices of its daily and weekly newspapers, brokerage houses, insurance companies, and law firms; and some 1,600 stores, 28 hotels, and 60 factories. Within the Burnt District were 10 school buildings, including 7 of the 9 in the North Division, and 39 of Chicago's 165 churches. "Our losses are enormous," Catholic bishop Thomas Foley wrote to an associate, adding, "Pray for me."

The fire burned up the records held in the Courthouse and millions of critical documents in the possession of attorneys, brokers, and surveyors. It turned to ashes the collections of the Chicago Historical Society,

Map Showing the Burnt District in Chicago, *3rd edition, 1871. West is at the top. The O'Leary cottage was located near the upper left, the South Division downtown in the center left, and the North Division, which was almost completely destroyed, to the right. The concentric rings are mile markers. As indicated, this map, one of many like it that appeared at the time, was published to help raise money to assist Chicagoans after the fire. (Chicago History Museum, ICHi-002870)*

including its most precious possession, Abraham Lincoln's original draft of the Emancipation Proclamation. It destroyed the Chicago Academy of Sciences' eighteen thousand specimens, the Audubon Club's four hundred mounted game birds and mammals, and countless trees, shrubs, and flowers along streets and in parks, yards, gardens, and conservatories. All that was saved from the "immense collection of curiosities" in Col. Wood's Museum was Mollie Trussell's silver-plated pistol.

Warehouses and stores lost their inventories, hotels their furnishings, skilled craftsmen the tools of their trade. Two days after the fire officially ended, dry goods were still smoking in the basement of the Field, Leiter & Company store, emitting a terrible stench.

The human displacement was staggering. Over ninety thousand people—equivalent to the population of Cleveland, then the fifteenth biggest city in the country—were homeless, most with neither a fixed place to sleep nor access to food and basic hygiene. A larger number no longer had a place of work.

Judge Lambert Tree was shocked to come upon not just dead animals but also a human body, "burned beyond recognition," on Dearborn Street between Ohio and Ontario Streets. After spending the night outdoors under the Division Street Bridge abutment, the Kehoe sisters saw that they had slept a stone's throw from blackened corpses now being retrieved from the river below the bridge.

Considering the scale of destruction, the death toll was miraculously low, probably in the low to mid-hundreds, even if one takes into account incinerated bodies that were never accounted for. As terrible as the fire was, most Chicagoans had the opportunity to flee.

In a terrible coincidence that speaks to the extreme dryness of the Upper Midwest, many more individuals lost their lives in another enormous blaze the same night. A flash firestorm trapped people residing in and around the small northern Wisconsin lumber town of Peshtigo, fifty miles north of Green Bay and almost 250 miles from Chicago. A third fire occurred at virtually the same time across the lake in Manistee, Michigan. The human cost of the Peshtigo fire was appalling. About 1,500 people burned to death, to this day the worst loss of life to fire in American history.

While Peshtigo's death toll was far greater than Chicago's, it does not lessen the colossal property damage the city endured or the pain and suffering its hundreds of thousands of residents were forced to bear. Many spent anxious hours and even days seeking out missing loved ones. The *Chicago Republican* told of haggard refugees looking for their lost children, commenting, "In many the extent of their calamity completely obliterated ambition, affection, sensibility."

The losses of material things frequently involved much more than these objects in themselves. "The Homestead built by my own hands out of my own hard earnings, is gone—a total wreck," Board of Public Works head William H. Carter told his brother. "The spot had become endeared to me by many fond associations. It was the first home I could call my own, where my children were born, where I had hoped to live to educate them, where I had welcomed kind brothers and sisters and friends in the past and where I had hoped to do it often in the future. It was the spot above all others where a half century of toil had centered and where at some time I had hoped to live more at ease. No other spot will seem like it to me."

As the sun rose on Tuesday, October 10, there was little movement in the Burnt District besides the belated collapse of heat-weakened walls. Chicago's downtown, normally one of the most hectic places on the planet, was more still and silent than it would ever be again. "There was no running of the street-railroad cars, or other of the signs of life which usually are visible, even on Sabbaths and holidays," Elias Colbert and Everett Chamberlin wrote. "In short, the day seemed a *dies non*—a day burnt out of the history of the city." The only comparable hush was the twenty-four somber hours in early May 1865 when Abraham Lincoln's body lay in state in the Courthouse. Chicago was his funeral train's last stop on the slow, sad dirge of a journey from Washington, DC, to his burial in Springfield, Illinois.

The devastated areas possessed an otherworldly quality, especially at night. "The clouds are very dark and on these the light from the burning coal heaps reflects a living red that is surely visible for miles," Francis William Test told his mother. The burned-out cityscape was profoundly disorienting. "One is unable to form any idea of where he is—lost among the streets that contain not a house for miles," Cassius Milton Wicker remarked.

On Tuesday morning Anna Higginson's husband George reconnoitered their North Side neighborhood. He found "all landmarks . . . obliterated, all street signs destroyed." Higginson struggled to locate their home on Dearborn Street. He finally identified it by the iron frame and wire strings of the family piano and, partially buried in fallen bricks, the stone jars in which Anna had put up preserves a few days earlier. In the extreme heat the jars had become crucibles. They remained intact; the preserves were "burnt to a crisp."

"Even the distances seem to have been burned up with all things else, and any of the few landmarks left would suddenly come up and confront one, like an apparition, when he thought it far away," Colbert and Chamberlin wrote. The intense heat twisted lamp posts completely out of shape. It turned iron street car rails red and yellow and curled them into what struck A. S. Chapman as "great bows."

Besides the Water Tower, two North Division homes in the path of the fire escaped destruction. The first was the mansion of wealthy attorney Mahlon Ogden, directly to the north of Washington Square Park. Ogden was out of town when disaster struck. His servants spread carpets over the wooden mansard roof of the house and repeatedly wetted them down. Police officer Richard Bellinger lived about a mile and a half north of Ogden in an area full of the frame homes of working people like himself. Bellinger enlisted the help of his brother-in-law in clearing away dry leaves and tearing out the wooden fence and sidewalk along the border of his lot. Lacking Ogden's supply of carpets, they soaked the house directly.

The only finished building in the downtown left unharmed was the five-story Lind Block, tucked into the northwest corner of the South Division at Randolph and Market (North Wacker Drive) Streets. The flames had barely bypassed it. More surprising was the survival of the nearly completed six-story Nixon Block, since it was directly in the fire's path, two blocks south of the Courthouse on the northeast corner of Monroe and LaSalle Streets. The Nixon Block was a formidable combination of iron joists, concrete-covered beams, brick arches, marble floors, and plaster of Paris ceilings. Still, its escape, like that of the Water Tower, the Mahlon Ogden mansion, and the Richard Bellinger house, was more a fluke than a tribute to either stout construction or staunch defense.

"You can scarcely imagine the desolation," James W. Milner wrote in a letter to a friend four days after the fire. "If a man wants his mind impressed with what the end of the world will be, let him come here."

While the stricken portion of Chicago looked nothing like it had just a few days earlier, it conjured powerful associations with other places. One association was very fresh. The Burnt District recalled to mind proud Confederate cities after they had been assaulted by Union forces. George N. Barnard, who during the Civil War had photographed the ruins of Atlanta, now performed the same service for burned-out Chicago.

George N. Barnard, The Van Buren Street Bridge after the Fire.
From a Lovejoy & Foster stereograph.
(Chicago History Museum, ICHi-019792)

He had moved to the city in the spring of 1871, in time to be both a witness to and victim of the fire.

Barnard lost the studio he opened on Washington Street two blocks east of the Courthouse but rescued or borrowed enough gear to photograph Chicago right after the fire. There are no known photographs of Chicago during the conflagration by Barnard or anyone else, whether because of the logistical and technical limitations of photography at the time, the destruction of equipment, or the photographers' decision that surviving the disaster was a higher priority than recording it.

To the more fanciful, the ruins evoked the grandeur of ancient far-away places, as if in the act of destroying Chicago the fire had in an historical instant invested the young city with the past it lacked. In *The Great Conflagration,* James W. Sheahan and George P. Upton described

George N. Barnard, Among the Ruins in Chicago: Court House Seen through Ruins of East Side of Clark Street. *From a Lovejoy & Foster stereograph. (Chicago History Museum, ICHi-021546)*

ruined downtown Chicago, so recently alive with all the energy of the present day, as a place "where there is no feeling of newness." It seemed like "a page taken from middle age[s] history." The wreck of the dynamic metropolis was "full of the charm of mystery and darkness," a fitting spot for "creatures who lurk among the ruined tombs and devour the belated wanderers there." Like Colbert and Chamberlin, Sheahan and Upton were a pair of seasoned Chicago newspapermen who hastily put together a book-length history of the fire.

The Reverend E. J. Goodspeed, minister of Chicago's Second Baptist Church, quickly turned out a series of fire histories, starting with his 78-page *Earth's Holocaust*, followed by the 144-page *The Great Fires in Chicago and the West*. Before the end of 1871, he published a

Jex Bardwell, View of Trinity Church after Fire of 1871. *The British-born Bardwell, based in Detroit at the time of the fire, was one of the many out-of-town writers, photographers, and artists, as well as tourists, who rushed to the city following the disaster. Trinity Episcopal Church was erected in 1860 on the south side of Jackson Street between Michigan and Wabash Avenues. (Chicago History Museum, ICHi-063815)*

Jex Bardwell, Ruins of the Court House after the
Fire of 1871. *(Chicago History Museum, ICHi-038923)*

third version, *History of the Great Fires in Chicago and the West,* that
ran 667 pages. He, too, envisaged more ancient places in devastated Chicago. "Arabia Petra looks upon us from the stone walls of the Post-
Office," he wrote of that building's ruins, "and the Catacombs of Egypt
stare at us from the embrasure-like windows of the Court-House wings."

Goodspeed extended the comparisons: "Cleopatra's Needle and the
Tower of Babel find duplicates in the water-tower and the smoke-stacks
of ruined factories, . . . and the pillared ruins of Cairo in the roofless
front of the Honoré Block, . . . while the Parthenon, the Acropolis,
and the gladiatorial arena of ancient Greece and Rome find their counterpart in the fire-built ruins of last week's palaces."

Jex Bardwell, Farwell Building after the Fire.
(Chicago History Museum, ICHi-039415)

Chicago's attraction for disaster tourists verged on the ghoulish. The
city "is beginning to fill up with aesthetic sight-seers," read a story in
the *New-York Tribune* on October 14. They were drawn by the novelty
of this juggernaut of American urban vitality turned overnight into a
ghost town by the greatest fire of the time. The proud inland metropolis, a triumph of human aspiration and capability, had proved no equal

Jex Bardwell, View of the Union Depot after the
Fire of 1871. *(Chicago History Museum, ICHi-059804)*

to the elemental forces of nature. Many of the visitors were reporters,
photographers, and illustrators dispatched to Chicago by newspaper
and magazine editors competing with each other to capture its desolation for the millions of others who could not see it firsthand. "The artists of the illustrated papers are seated at every coign of vantage, sketching
for dear life" against their deadlines, the *Tribune* observed.

Accuracy sometimes took second place to speed. The October 28
Harper's Weekly bird's-eye view of Chicago's disaster depicts the flames
tilted in the wrong direction, to the south rather than the north, an

Depiction of the fire with the flames heading south. From Harper's
Weekly, *October 28, 1871. This was likely a reworked version
of an illustration of Chicago from before the fire.
(Chicago History Museum, ICHi-002935)*

error repeated in a lithograph of the scene produced by Currier &
Ives, which was perhaps based on the *Harper's Weekly* illustration.

Unlike the sightseers and journalists, Chicagoans could not indulge in
an appreciation of the ruins. Having just passed through terrors that left
them physically and mentally shattered, and with few resources at hand
besides the clothes on their backs, they now faced the terrible circumstances of the present and the uncertain prospects of the future.

The homeless and hungry struggled to secure a decent place to sleep
and something to eat. After their night under the bridge, the Kehoe sisters
thought they had found a shanty in which they could stay, but it was
already so crowded with other refugees that there was not enough space
to lie down. The woman named Amelia who told of all the births said

in her penciled letter that there were still hundreds of people out on the prairie, since "there is [sic] no houses for them to live in their suffering is terrible as they have no stoves to keep them warm and are obliged to lie on the ground."

Forlorn families without friends or relatives to take them in shuffled into impromptu shelters. After spending a "long cold night" on a patch of prairie on the edge of the city with many other unfortunates, Patrick Webb, his wife, and children joined a "shivering crowd" that filled a Lutheran church. Webb obtained a little bread and meat for himself and the others, who had not had any food in almost twenty-four hours. Union Park, on the West Side, well outside the Burnt District, became an outdoor dormitory whose occupants washed themselves in its small pond.

Twelve-year-old Bessie Bradwell, separated from her family in the confusion, never let go of the ponderous *Chicago Legal News* subscription book she had rescued for her mother. Following the separation from her relatives, she had run into a couple who knew her parents, and she fled with them to the North Division and then the West Side. On the State Street Bridge, she overheard a man crying, "This is the end of Chicago." Bessie answered, "No, no, she will rise again." When her coat caught fire, others in the crowd tamped out the flames with their bare hands.

The next evening her father attended a refugees' meeting at which he spoke of his missing child. He was overjoyed when a man with whom Bessie had breakfasted that morning rose up to announce, "Don't worry, Judge Bradwell, your daughter is safe on the west side and she carted that great heavy *Legal News* subscription book for nine hours."

George Payson, who had similarly lugged his annotated copies of the *Freeman's Illinois Digest* through the LaSalle Street Tunnel, searched all day Tuesday across the North Division for his daughter and her nurse. He was relieved to find them, but he feared that the nightmare was not over. He thought the smoking coal piles might set the city aflame again. In order to be prepared to flee at a moment's notice, Payson remained dressed in the same clothes and barely slept the entire week following the fire.

Payson's fears reveal the brittle mental condition of the survivors. Historian A. T. Andreas wrote that the fire bestowed upon Chicagoans a legacy of "shattered nerves, premature age, disordered minds." It proved a "baleful influence over lives that, up to then, were vigorous, healthful and sound."

Francis William Test confided that it made him "heart sick to go through the ruins." *Illinois Staats-Zeitung* editor Herman Raster lost virtually all his worldly goods except for a few articles of laundry and a single chair. His furnishings, books, paintings, and "a carefully kept correspondence of thirty years with friends, writers, and statesmen" were burned away.

Aurelia King could not help mourning "the dear things that can never be replaced—my books, the gifts of dear friends, the treasured locks of hair, my Mother's Bible, relics of my little daughter Fanny, my wedding dress, and a thousand things I had saved for my children." These children meanwhile grieved over "their little treasures and their books," she wrote, "and I cry with them." She would fall asleep only to slip into nightmares in which she was "forever running from fires."

When Patrick Webb returned to the site of his family's cottage, now burned away, he discovered the shovel he had used to bury their possessions and, mistakenly, some of the clothes he had been wearing. When he started to unearth his belongings, he recalled, the contents were still so hot they burst into flame on contact with the air. His home and the rest of his possessions, which he had earned "by hard labor, honesty and sobriety," were no more. Now fifty-eight years old, he believed he was reduced to a beggar, with no way to recover from this setback.

Thirty-one-year-old lawyer Jonas Hutchinson also thought that his prospects had disappeared. "I am stripped and you may conclude I am about vanquished," he confessed to his mother. He had come to Chicago because it had seemed so much more promising than the New Hampshire he left. He wondered if he should give up and return home.

Faith in the future, previously Chicago's most ample commodity, seemed suddenly in short supply.

Even as the city mourned, help was on the way. A lot of help.

Mayor Roswell B. Mason had not been able to do anything to stop the fire, but the telegrams he sent to other cities asking for assistance produced remarkable results. Milwaukee put fire engines on a train that arrived about ten o'clock on Monday morning, October 9, and went right to work, if in a lost cause. Chicago also received engines and other equipment from Allegheny City, Pennsylvania; Cincinnati; Detroit; Louisville, Kentucky; New York City; Pittsburgh; and the Illinois towns of Aurora, Bloomington, Freeport, Quincy, and Springfield.

Communities convened emergency meetings and relief rallies to aid Chicago at which they passed resolutions of sympathy, pledged cash contributions, and solicited goods for the benefit of "sufferers by the fire." Cleveland mayor F. W. Pelton summoned residents of his city to a meeting at 3:00 p.m. on October 9, while much of Chicago was still aflame, to provide aid. The poster for the gathering exhorted, "HELP, HELP, HELP."

Bostonians streamed into historic Faneuil Hall, where Senate Radical Republican champion Charles Sumner and clergyman and author Edward Everett Hale beseeched them to donate to the cause. On Tuesday, October 10, Boston mayor William Gaston wired Mason the very welcome message, "You are authorized to draw on Kidder, Peabody & Co. of this city, for the sum of one hundred thousand dollars for the relief of the sufferers by the late fire." Three prominent Bostonians meanwhile telegraphed that they would arrive by Saturday "to offer their services in cooperation with you for the relief of your suffering people."

On Monday evening, when the fire was alive in the upper reaches of the North Division, food and supplies by the box and barrelful—hams, roasts of beef and pork, turkeys and chickens, clothing, and bedding—began appearing from more nearby locations. At 3:00 a.m. Tuesday, a Louisville, New Albany, and Salem Railroad train reached the city bearing Indianapolis police chief Eli Thompson, a pair of his city's fire engines, and two carloads of cooked provisions from his fellow citizens. By Tuesday afternoon every train to the city was bringing relief supplies; some had little room for anything else.

Shipments arrived from Fort Wayne, Indiana; Louisville; Pittsburgh; and St. Louis, as well as the downstate Illinois towns of Cairo and Springfield. The suburb of Evanston, on the lake about a dozen miles north of downtown Chicago, delivered food and supplies to those still camped out in Lincoln Park. Within twenty-four hours of the end of the fire, Chicago received more than $1,500,000 in pledges, as well as 650 wagonloads of provisions. In numerous instances a delegation of

Poster calling people to the relief rally in Cleveland.
(Chicago History Museum, ICHi-020590)

leading citizens from the donor city accompanied the contributions and stayed to help distribute them.

The outpouring was extraordinarily wide and deep. The legislature of Illinois voted to pay Chicago ahead of schedule the state's pledged contribution for the Deep Cut, the project to reverse the flow of the river. This sum was earmarked for reconstructing bridges and public buildings, maintaining the police and fire departments, and making payments on the city's bonded debt. In addition to Boston, other large American cities—Baltimore, Brooklyn, Philadelphia, and Pittsburgh—each sent $100,000.

The donations of many smaller places, such as Fall River, Massachusetts; Hartford, Connecticut; Jersey City, New Jersey; Sacramento, California; San Francisco; St. Paul, Minnesota; and Syracuse, New York, were in the $20,000 to $30,000 range. Salt Lake City; Albany, New York; Bridgeport, Connecticut; Lawrence, Massachusetts; Oakland, California; and Portland, Maine, donated about half that. James Roosevelt, father of future president Franklin Delano Roosevelt, sent $1,000 raised in the family's hometown of Hyde Park, New York. Even Richmond, Virginia, and other southern cities joined in, as did remote Santa Fe and even remoter Honolulu.

Pledges and contributions arrived from a roll call of foreign cities and nations near and far. Halifax, Nova Scotia; Montreal; and Toronto sent aid, as did Basel; Belfast; Berlin; Birmingham, London, and Manchester, England; Dundee, Scotland; Frankfurt; and Paris. The emperor and crown prince of Prussia promised assistance, thanking Chicago citizens for their support during the recent war with France. Japanese ambassador Iwakura Tomomi, on a two-year around-the-world diplomatic mission for his rapidly modernizing nation, promised $5,000.

Individuals, organizations, and businesses shipped large donations to the crippled city. New York department store owner A. T. Stewart contributed $50,000. Financier Junius Spencer Morgan, father of John Pierpont (better known as J. P.) Morgan, sent $5,000. President Ulysses S. Grant, who was scheduled to travel to Boston, asked that city to forgo a public reception and instead give the budgeted funds to Chicago. The New York Produce, Cotton, and Gold Exchanges joined in, as did dozens of brokerages, banks, and insurance companies. The Peekskill, New York, Mutual Stove Works shipped twenty-five stoves.

Theaters in Albany, Baltimore, Boston, Brooklyn, Buffalo, Cleveland, Fort Wayne, New York City, Philadelphia, Pittsburgh, Rochester, St. Louis, and Syracuse donated the receipts from a designated regular or special performance. Eugenie Johanna Wilhelmina de Roode Rice, the Dutch-born "pianiste" who had recently moved to Chicago from Cincinnati, returned to Cincinnati briefly to perform a "monster concert" for the benefit of her new home.

Prize fighters in St. Louis offered to stage a money-raising exhibition. Fire companies raised contributions specifically intended for the families of their burned-out Chicago brethren. New York and European artists organized sales of their works to assist Chicago painters and sculptors.

Those in other callings also sent aid to their Chicago counterparts, as did religious denominations, ethnic groups, and fraternal lodges.

Some contributions were very modest. The coal miners of St. Mary's, Pennsylvania, raised $65, and the Methodist Episcopal Church of Rural Grove, New York, $34.50. Young Arthur Hardy of Boston Highlands, Massachusetts, donated ten dollars for "the little suffering boys and girls." He included an apology: "If I was a man, I would give you more, but this is all I could raise from my schoolmates at this time."

Buccaneering speculators Jim Fisk and Jay Gould organized an especially high-profile errand of mercy. Two years earlier, Fisk and Gould had precipitated a financial panic when they attempted to corner the gold market. The manipulations behind their recent takeover of the Erie Railroad and Fisk's notorious womanizing (which led to his fatal shooting by a jealous rival early the following year) set the unsavory ethical and moral tone of the early years of the Gilded Age. Chicago's plight provided them a chance for favorable publicity. Fisk and Gould arranged for a seven-car "lightning train," reputed to have reached speeds up to a mile a minute, to carry $250,000 in food and clothing from New York to Chicago.

Illustrations in the national newsweeklies depicted the mustachioed Fisk, shiny silk hat atop his head, with a whip in one hand and reins in the other, commanding the driver's seat of a six-horse wagon loaded with supplies to be transferred to the freight cars. The train reached Chicago on Wednesday, October 11, barely a day after the fire ended. As it careered along the tracks, people tossed on additional bundles of food and goods.

A *Harper's Weekly* engraving titled *The National Hand of Fellowship* depicted an outstretched palm set against a background of smoke billowing up from burning Chicago. The sleeve is secured by a cufflink bearing the initials *US*. In the upturned palm is a thick stack of thousand-dollar bills bound in a wrapper labeled "FOR THE BENEFIT SUFFERERS CHICAGO."

Disasters on such a scale, especially ones that leave so many people in need, almost always stir interest and spur charitable giving. Still, the response to the Great Chicago Fire was extraordinarily spontaneous,

Aid for the Suffering Thousands—Col. Jim Fisk Drives a Team of
Six-in-Hand through the Streets of New York City, *1871.*
(Chicago History Museum, ICHi-002873)

broad, and generous. Two related factors explain this exceptional outpouring: the particular city that suffered the destruction, and the way
the world learned of it.

Chicago's prodigious growth and its emergence as a major mercantile and manufacturing center had already captured the world's attention.
The city's distress resonated because people felt its presence in their lives.
"As the greatest primary market for produce on the face of the globe,"
Colbert and Chamberlin explained, "Chicago had long been regarded
as the cornucopia of modern civilization, while the energy and enterprise of her citizens had made her an object of envy to many other cities, and the wonder of the world."

This is why Chicago's destruction attracted so much more attention
than did the fire in Peshtigo, Wisconsin, even though the latter conflagration covered a much larger area and took the lives of many more people.
To be sure, all the papers covered it, including those in Chicago. In its first
postfire issue, the *Chicago Evening Mail* admitted that by some measures

The National Hand of Fellowship. *From Harper's Weekly, November 4, 1871. The artist was Frank Bellew, a popular illustrator at the time. (Chicago History Museum, ICHi-063817)*

Peshtigo's disaster was worse. "Chicago Outdone by Wisconsin Terrors," read a headline. But the destruction of a remote lumber town could not come close to the interest Chicago's destruction generated.

The city's visibility and national importance turned the act of coming to its aid into a patriotic obligation. With memories of the Civil War still fresh, this latest catastrophe recalled earlier sacrifices to preserve the nation. After reminding Bostonians how much they relied on Chicago for the beef and pork on their dinner plates, Edward Everett Hale compared assisting the city to supporting the recent struggle for liberty and union. "There has fallen by this calamity one of our noblest fortresses," he declared to his listeners in Faneuil Hall. "Its garrison is without munitions." He called on Bostonians to "reconstruct that fortress" and resupply the garrison.

The second factor that made the rescue of Chicago a national and international sensation was the telegraph network that linked every

American city and thousands of smaller places. Following the success-ful completion of the transatlantic cable in 1866, that network included the cities of Europe. As a result, the Great Chicago Fire was the first in-stantaneously reported international news event, details of which reached an audience in the tens of millions while it was happening. As people read and discussed the latest news reported in the local papers, their shared spectatorship brought these far-flung individuals psychically to-gether in a community of interest that transcended their physical distance from Chicago and each other.

During the fire, Western Associated Press agent William Henry Smith, who directed the agency from rented space in the *Chicago Tribune* head-quarters, shared with the world his four reporters' running account of Chicago under siege. Although its offices in the downtown were burned out, telegraph company Western Union enabled Smith's team and other journalists in the city to disseminate the story by keeping open a facility outside the Burnt District.

Recipients of the *Kansas State Record*, the *Sacramento Bee*, and the *London Times* could pore over details of the disaster within hours after the O'Leary barn went up in flames. For the better part of two days, people across the nation and even the Atlantic Ocean knew far more about what was happening in Chicago than a person who was right there but had no access to a newspaper.

Papers far afield gathered and then printed in a single day's edition successive telegraphed updates from Chicago, one after another, so readers could proceed through them with a sense of following the pro-gress of the fire. If they wanted even fresher information, they could join the crowd outside the nearest newspaper office, where the latest word was posted on a public bulletin board. Wherever they went in the course of the day, they could expect to see other people who knew about the fire and were eager to discuss it. The disaster that threatened to de-stroy Chicago secured its position on everyone's mental map.

Other recent technological advances besides the telegraph sped the circulation of information. Major newspapers and the national news-weeklies employed Hoe rotary steam presses, named after inventor Rich-ard Henry Hoe, that in the middle decades of the century began replacing much slower flatbed presses. The *Chicago Tribune* had recently invested sixty thousand dollars in two state-of-the-art eight-cylinder machines that could turn out ten thousand pages an hour. Other leading Chicago papers owned four-cylinder models. These presses imparted the news on plentiful and cheap wood pulp paper that became available at about the same time. While lithography was invented around 1800, the ability to reproduce images quickly and in large runs was another midcentury breakthrough. Faster locomotives streaking across the nation's ever broader and denser railroad system carried all this printed matter to disparate audiences in record time.

Harper's Weekly, which normally printed 175,000 copies of each issue, stated that because of the fire it was filling orders for 300,000. Over 120,000 were requested by three of the nation's new mass distributors, the American News Company in New York, the New England News Company in Boston, and the Western News Company in Chicago.

The rapid—the word today would be *viral*—spread of the shocking news from Chicago became part of the story. The *New York Herald* of

The Reading Room of the Fifth Avenue Hotel—Discussion the News from Chicago. *From* Every Saturday, *October 28, 1871.*
(Chicago History Museum, ICHi-002916)

October 10 spoke of the mixed crowd of urban types—"from the kid-gloved exquisite, laying aside for once his nonchalant air, to the hard fisted mechanic or apple woman"—who pushed against the bulletin boards, hungry for information. Businessmen gathered in hotels and club reading rooms to learn the latest news from Chicago and discuss it with their friends and associates.

Professional writers capitalized on the fascination with Chicago and its fire. By November, a scant month after the disaster, booksellers advertised the earliest of a dozen or more illustrated instant histories of the kind written by Colbert and Chamberlin, Sheahan and Upton, and the Reverend Goodspeed. Some appeared in German translation. These were forerunners of contemporary books on subjects like 9/11 that are rushed into print immediately following a major event. The fire histories, which mixed original material with written and visual content lifted from newspapers and magazines, devoted up to half of their pages to a prefire history of Chicago worthy of any booster. While all were rich in stirring narratives aimed at capturing the reader's attention, they varied considerably in tone and fidelity to fact, from measured and carefully detailed to wild and woolly.

After reading of Chicago's distress, venerable Massachusetts poet John Greenleaf Whittier, champion of proper literary form and even more proper moral sentiments, immediately composed a ten-quatrain poem, simply titled "Chicago." It opens with a two-line summary of Chicago's sudden demise:

> Men said at vespers: "All is well!"
> In one wild night the city fell.

It then speaks of the postfire pessimism:

> Men clasped each other's hands, and said
> "The City of the West is dead."

Yet spontaneous assistance arrives from everywhere:

> From East, from West, from South and North,
> The messages of hope shot forth,
> And, underneath the severing wave,
> The world, full-handed, reached to save.

Whittier made special mention of the technology that inspired and facilitated this largesse:

> A sudden impulse thrilled each wire
> That signaled round that sea of fire;
> Swift words of cheer, warm heart-throbs came;
> In tears of pity died the flame!

The fire provided a rare point of coincidence between Whittier's writings and those of Bret Harte, who at thirty-five was almost three decades younger and made his name chronicling the rough-and-tumble mining camps of California. Harte also quickly penned a poem on Chicago's tragedy. Both poems were snapped up and reprinted multiple times by publishers and editors who wanted a known luminary's reflections on an event already in the public mind.

By early November a producer mounted a traveling exhibition featuring a five-hundred-foot panoramic canvas. When it was unrolled before them, audiences could marvel at scenes of Chicago before and during the fire. The artist was H. H. Cross, who would become better known for his portraits of Native Americans. Popular humorist Charles Henry Harris, who wrote under the pen name Carl Pretzel, enhanced the visual experience with lively patter. One-fifth of the proceeds were to go to the sufferers.

The fire was immediately the subject of popular song. One of the street-level retail businesses in the Crosby's Opera House building was the Root & Cady store, which sold sheet music to be played on the inevitable piano in every middle-class parlor in this age before sound recording and radio. The firm itself published the output of co-owner George F. Root. During the war Root composed songs both maudlin and martial, from "Just before the Battle, Mother" to "The Battle Cry of Freedom," of which over a half million copies were printed.

Root made the best of the firm's setback by finding a press outside the Burnt District to print his several solemn and emotionally touching compositions on the tragedy, among them "Lost and Saved" and "From the Ruins Our City Shall Rise." For another, titled "Passing Through the Fire," Root rejected a standard tempo like *largo* or *andante* and instead prescribed *con fuoco*—that is, "with fire."

Picturesquely fallen Chicago attracted a hoard of stereograph photographers with their double-lens cameras. Stereographs, another midcentury innovation, consist of two approximately three-by-three-inch images mounted next to each other on a piece of stiff cardboard. When placed in a special viewer, they appear to be a single three-dimensional image. Stereograph companies marketed thousands of stereographs of the ruined city following the fire. A specialty was paired "before-and-after" stereographs of the same structure, such as the Field, Leiter & Company store.

The fire also inspired much fiction. The most popular by far was the Reverend E. P. Roe's *Barriers Burned Away*. Roe was minister of the First Presbyterian Church of Highland Falls, New York, located on the west bank of the Hudson River within walking distance of the US Military Academy at West Point. In his spare time, Roe pursued his favorite hobby, the cultivation of berries.

The Sunday of the fire found Roe tending neither his flock nor his garden. The thirty-three-year-old clergyman was fifty miles to the south, where he was considering a possible move to a vacant pulpit in New York City. He had been invited by the congregation to guest preach, a tryout that could lead to a job offer. According to Roe, his guest sermon was a success. The leaders of the church invited him to remain to meet with other members. The offer seemed a sure thing.

Roe did not wait to find out. Soon after he arose on Monday morning, October 9, he joined the multitude of New Yorkers who, in his words, "held their breath as they read the startling head-lines in the morning papers." An impulse to rush to the stricken city so overpowered him that he was soon on a train to Chicago. As he put it, he had "no clear purpose, no definite plan, beyond that of seeing humanity at a time when it appealed so powerfully to one's sympathy and interest." Wandering the city one moonlit night, Roe was struck with a new inspiration. Although he had never done anything like it before, he would write a novel about Chicago's tragedy.

Top: *Field, Leiter & Company department store before the fire;
stereograph, P. B. Greene, circa 1871 (Chicago History Museum,
ICHi-064398). Bottom: Ruins of Field, Leiter & Company;
stereograph, Lovejoy & Foster, 1871. (Chicago History Museum,
ICHi-021537)*

Once back in Highland Falls, Roe stole time to put eight chapters on paper. He placed them in the *New York Evangelist*, a periodical issued under the auspices of the Presbyterian Church, which had published some sketches he had written as a Union Army chaplain during the Civil War. The chapters began appearing in the magazine in February 1872, under the title *Barriers Burnt Away*. Thanks to the positive response to the serialized version, Roe landed a book contract with Dodd, Mead and Company. Frank Howard Dodd and Edward S. Mead had formed their partnership only the year before, during the postwar expansion of publishing driven by the same new printing and distribution technologies and mass reading audiences on which national periodicals like *Harper's Weekly* and major dailies like the *Chicago Tribune* depended.

Dodd, Mead released the book under the slightly revised title *Barriers Burned Away* in early December 1872. Sales took off. By March 1873 the public had purchased thirteen thousand copies. A cheap edition costing fifty cents soon sold another 100,000. By 1900 total sales reached a million, making *Barriers Burned Away* one of the top bestsellers of the late nineteenth century. Roe quit the ministry and wrote sixteen more novels in as many years, with another unfinished when he passed away in 1888 while reading aloud to his family from Nathaniel Hawthorne, his favorite author. A few of the novels similarly hinged on a contemporary disaster of one kind or another, though no other book sold as well as his tale of Chicago's fire. Roe's royalties enabled him to move to a larger house with a bigger garden. In addition to all of those novels, he published three books on horticulture, including *Success with Small Fruits*.

The fire does not figure at all in the convoluted twists and turns of *Barriers Burned Away* until near the end of the narrative, when Roe employs it to provide a thrilling climax that resolves the central love story. Like many actual Chicagoans, protagonist Dennis Fleet emigrates from New England to Chicago as a young man, arriving not long before the fire. His devout but ineffectual father has just passed away, and Dennis, the oldest child, hopes to make enough money in the city to support the impoverished family.

Dennis is as fine a Christian as his father, but he is far more ambitious and capable, a good match for Chicago's opportunities. He nonetheless has trouble landing a job until he secures a place as a humble man-of-all-work in the gallery of a wealthy German immigrant art dealer. Baron Ludolph plans to accumulate a large fortune and return to Europe, where he will use the money to reestablish the luster of the family name for himself and his beautiful daughter Christine.

The Ludolphs are arrogantly contemptuous of Dennis's faith in Christianity and democratic ideals. Dennis nonetheless falls hopelessly in love with Christine. His work ethic, intelligence, and taste win him promotions from Baron Ludolph, but he gets nowhere with his employer's haughty daughter, who toys with his affections. Or so it seems. She senses an attraction to Dennis in spite of herself. Roe's figurative language is more than a little heavy-handed: "She had not realized that in kindling and fanning this [i.e., Dennis's] flame of honest love to sevenfold power and heat, she might be kindled herself."

At long last the actual fire intervenes, killing Baron Ludolph and wiping out the gallery, which forecloses Christine's prospects of returning to Germany as Baroness Ludolph. The disaster also provides Dennis with multiple opportunities to display to her his selfless heroism and devotion. This wins Christine over to Dennis, Christ, and Chicago, more or less in that order. When he sees her praying for the first time in her life, he remarks, "Well, now I can almost say, Praise God for the fire."

For an emerging culture of mass-produced and mass-marketed print content, the Great Chicago Fire—a tale of epic destruction and high human drama—was a perfect subject. The most riveting component of this new culture was Chicago itself, the emblem of American urban modernity, now in such awful and affecting straits. In attending aid rallies, poring over news dispatches, reciting poetry, absorbing instant histories and novels, viewing stereographs, singing *con fuoco*, and, most of all, talking endlessly about the disaster, people experienced a riveting moment of national unity and reaffirmation.

8

"CHICAGO SHALL RISE AGAIN"

On Monday morning, October 9, with the fire still raging through the South and North Divisions, Charles C. P. Holden, alderman from the West Division's Tenth Ward and president of the Common Council, decided the city government needed to act.

Holden's life reflects the restless aspirations of so many individuals in the developing nation during this period. His first ancestors in North America sailed from England to the Massachusetts Bay Colony in 1634, four years after the Puritans landed on the flagship *Arbella*. His maternal grandfather served as an officer in the Continental Army from Bunker Hill to Yorktown. In 1836, nine years after Holden's birth, his parents decided to move themselves and their ten children from Vermont to Illinois. The family became pioneer farmers in Skunk's Grove, on the Sauk Trail thirty miles south of Chicago. As a boy, Holden helped guide a five-oxen plow that broke the fertile prairie soil. School was a three-mile trek.

When Charles turned fifteen, his father found him a job with a grocer in Chicago. Six years later, Holden volunteered to fight in the Mexican-American War. In 1850, two years after the conflict ended, he joined the California Gold Rush, journeying overland from Illinois to the Middle Fork of the American River. (Several other successful Chicagoans, including George Pullman, meatpacker Philip Armour, and architect Daniel Burnham, also ventured as young men to the mining areas of the West before settling permanently in Chicago.) By 1851 he was farming and raising stock in the Napa Valley, north of San Francisco. Two years later Holden concluded it was time to return to Chicago.

For the first leg of the trip, he booked passage to Panama on the *Winfield Scott*, named after the general who led troops against the British,

Native Americans, Confederates, and Mexicans, with a break in 1852 to run an unsuccessful presidential campaign against Democrat Franklin Pierce. Lost in fog, the *Scott* struck a reef near Anacapa Island, about sixty miles west of Los Angeles (the population of all of Los Angeles County was then under eight thousand) and sank. Holden and the other survivors were rescued by the *California*, also en route to Panama. After crossing the isthmus and sailing to New York, he finally made it back to Chicago. He had been gone four years.

Now twenty-seven, Holden quickly made up for lost time. Within a year he was married and working for the Illinois Central Railroad, where he was more of a real estate dealer than a railroad man. His job was to sell off chunks of the Illinois Central's massive 2.6-million-acre land grant from the federal government, one of many gigantic parcels given to railroads in the nineteenth century to finance construction and encourage western expansion.

Holden became active in politics. He was a delegate to the 1858 Republican state convention that nominated Abraham Lincoln for the US Senate. First elected to the Chicago Common Council in 1861, Alderman Holden zealously recruited Union Army volunteers from his ward. He also pushed hard for major infrastructure projects, including the new waterworks. In December 1870 his colleagues on the council elected him their leader. He also became a West Side parks commissioner. (At the time the parks in the three divisions were administered separately.)

Holden had thick dark hair, prominent eyebrows, and a full, trimmed beard. According to the 1870 census, he owned $100,000 in real estate and $5,000 in personal property, not a fortune by the standards of Chicago's wealthiest businessmen but more than enough to support his wife Sarah and their adopted seven-year-old daughter in comfort, as well as to hire the two young Norwegian women who kept house for them.

Holden's West Division home was more than a mile from the Courthouse and safely to the northwest of the fire. On Monday morning, accompanied by his neighbor Orren E. Moore, an insurance executive, he ventured eastward in Moore's carriage to see how badly Chicago had been hurt so far. At Jefferson Street they turned south and into the section of the West Side that had burned the previous two nights. Near the corner of Harrison Street, they had a gruesome view of eight bodies discovered in the ashes.

Charles C. P. Holden. (Chicago History Museum, ICHi-024446)

As they continued on, Holden later wrote, "the sights were too terrible to behold!—men, women and children in endless confusion, gathered in vacant lots, in the alleys, in the streets, indeed, everywhere." Since the Adams, Van Buren, and Polk Street Bridges had been destroyed, Holden and Moore's nearest access to the South Division was via Twelfth Street (Roosevelt Road), two blocks south of DeKoven, where the fire began. The Twelfth Street Bridge was crowded with people fleeing westward, however, so they drove six blocks farther south to the Eighteenth Street Bridge and crossed to the South Division there.

The two men felt their way east and north to Wabash Avenue and Eldridge Court (Ninth Street), just below where the fire would end late Monday afternoon. "Every nook and corner in that vicinity appeared covered with goods and human beings," Holden recalled. Reluctant to get closer to the flames, the two men opted to return to the West Division.

Holden hoped that along the way they would encounter other Chicago officials with whom he could confer about what to do. The only person in authority they came across was Chief Fire Marshal Robert A. Williams, who told them what they could plainly see with their own eyes: the city had "gone up."

The "great masses of living people" they passed were "appealing most piteously for help." Foremost in his mind, Holden contended later, was the question, "Who was to care for these sufferers then everywhere to be seen?" Holden decided that "it was for the city, in its corporate capacity, to step to the front" lest "suffering humanity die for the want of help."

While Holden and Moore did not find other members of the city government, they ran into several people they knew, whom they told to pass word to any aldermen these people might see of an emergency Common Council meeting. It would begin at 1:00 p.m. in the First Congregational Church, located on the corner of Washington and Ann (Racine) Streets in Holden's West Division ward. Everyone was "to come prepared for active work." Holden and Moore drove to a nearby police station, where he ordered the captain to dispatch officers to notify Mayor Roswell B. Mason, City Clerk C. T. Hotchkiss, other aldermen, and leading citizens of the meeting.

Holden spoke with First Congregational's pastor, who granted permission to use the building as a temporary Common Council chamber and all-purpose relief center. With only a handful of people in attendance, including City Clerk Hotchkiss and Thomas B. Brown, head of the Board of Police and Fire Commissioners, the rump government started making plans. They determined that the top priorities were to ensure public safety and establish temporary shelters and distribution centers for food and clothing.

Mayor Mason arrived at the church at about 2:40 p.m., by which time some half dozen of the city's forty aldermen were also present. Within a half hour Mason, Common Council president Holden, Police and Fire Board president Brown, and city comptroller George Taylor issued a proclamation. "Whereas, in the Providence of God, to whose will we humbly submit," it began, "a terrible calamity has befallen our city, which demands of us our best efforts for the preservation of order and relief of suffering."

The proclamation pledged the faith and credit of the City of Chicago in facing its financial obligations, a step vital to the city's future as

The rebuilding city. A number of the sites indicated here are discussed in later chapters.

Map labels:

LAKE MICHIGAN

Patrick Webb home
barracks
St Michael's Catholic Church
Julia Lemos home
Herman Raster home
North
Sedgwick
LaSalle
horsecar line
Clybourn
Halsted
Elston
Division
Oak
Washington Square
Mahlon Ogden home
barracks
Chicago
Sedgwick
LaSalle
State
Grand
Cook County Court House
Milwaukee
horsecar line
Racine
Morgan
1st temporary City Hall (First Congregational Church)
barracks
Second Precinct Police Station
Union Depot
South Water
Lind Block
Lake
Iroquois Theatre
Court-house Square
Kerfoot "Block"
Michigan
Fire Cyclorama
Inter-State Exposition Bldg
Madison
Nixon Block
3rd temporary City Hall
Van Buren
horsecar line
site of May 1872 labor rally
barracks
Harrison
temporary Post Office
Harrison
2nd temporary City Hall
area burned by 1874 fire
Taylor
O'Leary house
Roosevelt
site of Dec. 1873 labor rally
Standard Hall
horsecar line
18th
Wirt Dexter home
George Pullman home
Field, Leiter & Co. temporary store
Marshall Field home
railroad depot temporarily used by Illinois Central RR & Michigan Central RR
Archer
State
Michigan
Cermak
Chicago CartoGraphics

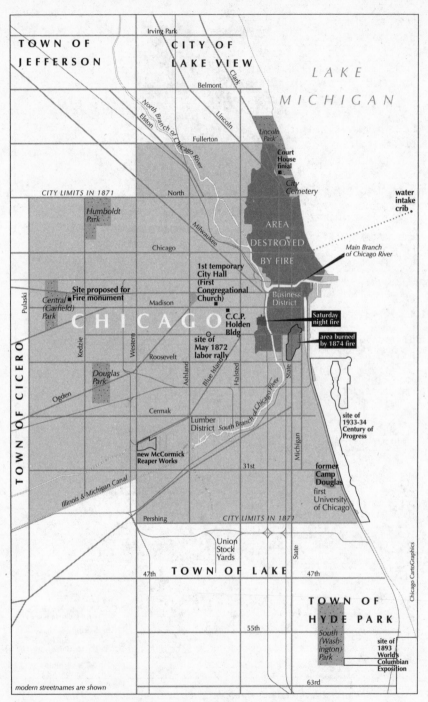

TOWN OF
JEFFERSON

CITY OF
LAKE VIEW

Irving Park

Belmont

Clark

North Branch of Chicago River

Elston

Fullerton

Lincoln

Lincoln Park

LAKE
MICHIGAN

CITY LIMITS IN 1871

North

Milwaukee

Court House finial

City Cemetery

Humboldt Park

Chicago

AREA
DESTROYED
BY FIRE

water intake crib

Main Branch of Chicago River

Pulaski

Central (Garfield) Park

Madison

1st temporary City Hall (First Congregational Church)

Site proposed for Fire monument

C.C.P. Holden Bldg

Business District

Saturday night fire

area burned by 1874 fire

Kedzie

Western

Roosevelt

site of May 1872 labor rally

CHICAGO

TOWN OF CICERO

Douglas Park

Ogden

Ashland

Blue Island

Halsted

State

Cermak

Lumber District

South Branch of Chicago River

new McCormick Reaper Works

Michigan

site of 1933-34 Century of Progress

Illinois & Michigan Canal

31st

former Camp Douglas first University of Chicago

Pershing

CITY LIMITS IN 1871

Union Stock Yards

State

47th

TOWN OF LAKE

47th

Chicago CartoGraphics

TOWN OF
HYDE PARK

55th

South (Washington) Park

site of 1893 World's Columbian Exposition

63rd

modern streetnames are shown

Chicago and surrounding areas following the fire.

a commercial center. It both issued a warning and offered reassurance to Chicago residents: individuals caught committing crimes would be prosecuted, and everything soon would be well. By five o'clock Monday evening, as the fire was ceasing in the South Division and winding down in the North, runners posted the proclamation throughout the city, and other messengers alerted refugees on the outskirts of the Burnt District that they would receive help. For the moment, there was no other way to communicate with the population at large.

The next day Mason put his name to another proclamation. It instructed citizens to be extremely careful with fire generally and specifically forbade the use of kerosene. With no gas and so many street lamps destroyed, Chicago was a very dark place at night. Eleven-year-old Fanny Boggs Lester's family relied on candles, which her mother, just to be extra sure, set in glass containers so she could surround the candles with water.

More proclamations followed. Mason designated several unburned railroad facilities around the city, in addition to the First Congregational Church, as places where the hungry could obtain the food arriving from elsewhere. He warned Chicagoans to avoid the Burnt District, where fire-weakened buildings were collapsing. He allowed saloons, which he had previously ordered closed, to reopen, but for the next week they were required to stop doing business by 9:00 p.m. or risk heavy fines and loss of their licenses. While citizens outside the Burnt District were instructed not to light their ovens, large bakeries were exempted so they could furnish emergency food supplies. Smoking was prohibited until the restoration of regular water service. Concerned about profiteering, the city set price controls on basic goods and services. For the next ten days, bakers could charge no more than eight cents for a twelve-ounce loaf of bread. Hackmen, expressmen, draymen, and teamsters had to abide by regular prefire rates.

Over its owners' objections, the self-constituted committee of aldermen and citizens appropriated another West Side building, a former church, as a dining hall for refugees. The makeshift government directed that surviving public schools would serve as shelters. It also declared the city's right to take possession of any unoccupied building as needed and approved a volunteer corps of lookouts, both male and female, to be on constant watch for new fires. Three West Division churches and Mercy Hospital, near Chicago's southern border, agreed to serve as provisional infirmaries for the sick and injured.

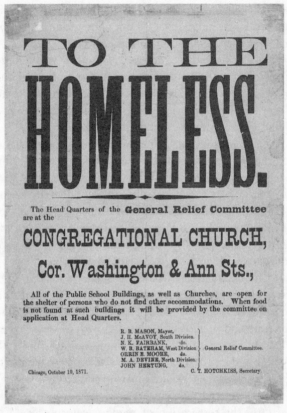

Poster distributed by the General Relief Committee,
October 10, 1871. (Chicago History Museum, ICHi-006194)

For those trying to locate missing relatives and friends, an intelligence office was opened at Twelfth (Roosevelt Road) and State Streets. A temporary "dead-house," or morgue, was set up in a livery stable in the West Division. Some of the bodies showed signs of terrible death agonies, while others were burned beyond recognition. By midweek, forlorn Chicagoans searching for family and friends were filing through at a rate of three hundred an hour, torn between a need for closure and a desire to keep hoping.

The Board of Public Works put men to work immediately repairing the Pumping Station. In the meantime, the fire department turned engines into miniature waterworks by laying hose in the river and pumping its contents to thirsty and dirty residents. *Chicago Tribune* editor Horace White, boasting of the success of the Deep Cut in cleansing the Chicago River, claimed that "twenty-four hours had not passed before tens of thousands of people were drinking the water" of the formerly "horrible, black, stinking river"—which he claimed the deepening of the canal had cleared—"with no unpleasant taste or effects."

Nonetheless, a week later the *Chicago Republican* was advising readers to boil or filter water from this source. Physician E. M. Hale agreed, warning against diarrhea, dysentery, and "gastric irritation." Wagons and teams pressed into duty under threat of confiscation delivered healthier lake and well water throughout the city. An illustration in *Harper's Weekly* shows others fetching water from artesian wells.

Convinced that the fire-caused chaos and confusion left the city vulnerable to looting, some Chicagoans armed themselves with gas pipes, laths, and baseball bats. Amid rumors that "thieves were already plying their trade," the Commercial National Bank, where one of Jennie Otis's older brothers worked as a bookkeeper, issued revolvers to him and other young employees and put them on duty watching over the vault. Famed detective Allan Pinkerton, now the Chicago-based owner of a private security company, posted a warning to "Thieves & Burglars" that he had authorized his men to kill suspected offenders. "No Mercy Shall be shown them," Pinkerton promised in bold type, "but Death shall be their fate."

Even before Mayor Mason arrived, the group Holden convened realized that it needed to devise a coordinated approach to public safety. It requested that Police and Fire Commissioner Brown swear in citizen volunteers as members of a special patrol that would protect residents and their property from "incendiaries and all other malicious persons." Sixteen-year-old Allan Culver prepared badges for the volunteers, which were nothing more than rectangular pieces of cheap white cloth on which he printed the words "Police" or "Special Police" with his hobby press.

In subsequent statements Mayor Mason specified that the citizen volunteers would be arranged into three groups of five hundred, one for each of the three divisions, all under the direction of the police department. According to Horace White, it seemed as if "the whole male population of the city was organized by spontaneous impulse into a night patrol, with applied determination to put every incendiary to instant death." This was an obvious overstatement, but many citizens did sacrifice their sleep to stand guard.

Divinity student William Gallagher volunteered for one of the special police units. Its members chose a captain and marched to the temporary city hall in the First Congregational Church, where they removed their hats, raised their right hands, and swore before God to do their duty and obey the police commissioners. After receiving their badges, they followed orders to appropriate every cart they found and to arrest drivers who resisted. They used the carts to fetch families camped on the prairie and convey them to emergency quarters in churches and schools, where the fire victims would also get clothing and food.

Eben Matthews, a bookkeeper who worked for the grain brokerage firm of Jones & Raymond, remembered how citizen sentries marched up and down the streets after dark, demanding every passerby to state his or her destination. Once approved, the person could proceed to the next patrol. With the city so on edge, the special police were given extraordinary authority. They were told to use deadly force if a person refused to identify himself after a second request to do so. As Holden observed, "This city was, and probably never will be again, so thoroughly guarded and watched with so many anxious eyes, as it was on that fearful Monday and the few succeeding days."

Mason, Holden, and the others knew they needed to develop a systematic way to receive and distribute all the clothing and provisions that were arriving. To accomplish this, they appointed a General Relief Committee consisting of five aldermen and a similar number of private citizens. One of the aldermen was William Bateham, whose West Side buildings had been one of the early casualties of the fire.

The committee chose Orren Moore as president, City Clerk C. T. Hotchkiss as secretary, and Charles Holden as treasurer. Board of Trade president John W. Preston was to oversee the receipt of relief supplies and, to that end, could hire or requisition the horses and wagons he needed to transport them. Physician and sanitary expert John H. Rauch was in charge of health. Banker and commodities trader Joseph Reynolds chaired a Lost and Found subcommittee, whose primary purpose was to reunite families the fire had separated.

The General Relief Committee set to work with energy and alacrity. Under its direction, hundreds of men and women volunteers—among them the spouses of Holden and Moore, Joseph Medill's wife Katherine, and the Medills' daughters Kate and Elinor—worked around the clock assisting victims. Numerous others pitched in. By one count, one-third of Chicagoans outside the Burnt District hosted fire fugitives.

Many fire victims were eager to leave town, at least until after it recovered. Railroads empowered the Relief Committee to grant free passage from Chicago to residents who wanted to get to friends' or relatives' houses outside the city or to make a fresh start in a new place. The distribution of train passes quickly evolved into a regular procedure. Printed forms, to be signed and countersigned by specified individuals, replaced earlier informal notes of authorization. In the days following the fire, some thirty thousand people boarded outbound trains. The trains were so crowded that some men and boys rode atop the cars.

Relief administrators and city officials soon started to curtail free passes when it dawned on them that Chicago's rebuilding would require the labor of many of those whose departure they were now facilitating. In any event, many who left Chicago returned later, although not immediately. Twenty-two-year-old Maria Charlotte Lindsten and her sister came to the city from Sweden the year before the fire to live with their brother, a tailor in the North Division. She requested a train ticket to her aunt's home in Paxton, Illinois, a hundred miles downstate. Lindsten lingered a month before returning to Chicago in November to rejoin her siblings and help her brother get his business back on its feet. "We had to sleep on the floor on piles of rags," she wrote. "It was a very hard winter but we came through it all right." Mary Kehoe and her sisters secured railroad passes to Des Moines, Iowa, where there was employment waiting, but they never got on the train. "We were too scared to go there," Kehoe admitted.

To widow Julia Lemos, the sole support of her five young children and her parents, it made sense to request tickets to New York, where her mother's sister lived. From the West Division church where the family was staying, Lemos sent her father to obtain passes for all eight of them. He succeeded, but they still had to get to the train, and the terminal for lines to and from the East, now at Michigan Avenue and

Twenty-Second Street, was diagonally all the way across the Burnt District. Lemos agreed with the janitor of the church to swap her father's hunting dog for transportation to the train in the janitor's wagon. Along the way they had to maneuver around streetcar tracks bent into curlicues by the intense heat, as well as menacing "rowdies," the common term for toughs and ne'er-do-wells. Once they were on the train, things improved. Other passengers treated the children to cake and candy; Lemos herself did not have even a dime to purchase them anything.

On arrival in New York, she waited in the station with the children while her parents sought out the aunt, whom they had been unable to notify in advance. Lemos claimed that a well-dressed stranger approached her and inquired if she was one of the Chicago outcasts. When she said yes, he pressed a bill into her hand. Lemos objected, but he insisted. As he walked away, she looked at the bill and saw that it was ten dollars, two-thirds of her weekly salary. Convinced that the man had given her more than he intended, Lemos pursued him, but he assured her that he knew what he was doing. An onlooker told her father, who had just returned from a successful search for his sister-in-law, that the Good Samaritan was "the richest man in New York." He was making a personal project of helping Chicago refugees, not by giving to charities but directly to individual fire victims, and only after he investigated the cases himself. Lemos said she could not remember his name.

As the terrible and fascinating news of Chicago's distress circulated far and wide, the only one of the city's several dozen English- and foreign-language newspapers and periodicals that somehow managed to publish an edition on Monday, October 9, was the *Evening Journal*. It was a limited edition extra, reprinted the next day. Copies of both editions and of subsequent postfire papers were in high demand. This was true even of dailies in some other towns, which people wanted as collector's items.

After surrendering the supposedly fireproof *Chicago Tribune* building to its fate, Joseph Medill wearily returned to his home on the West Side, where he drank a cup of coffee, yanked off his boots, and collapsed into bed. Besieged by frightful dreams, he did not sleep long. Besides, he was determined to resume publication of the *Tribune* right away.

Within hours he had rented a three-story job printing office at 217 Canal Street in the West Division that he agreed to share with the *Chicago Journal*. Since the *Tribune* was a morning paper and the *Journal* appeared in the afternoon, the plan was to take turns using the printing press. This machine could not approach the output of the *Tribune's* Hoe models, and the available type was short on lowercase letters, but Medill was happy to have it. The first postfire edition of the *Tribune* appeared the next morning, Wednesday, October 11.

Soon a shipment of used fonts arrived from Cincinnati. The source was Murat Halstead, owner of the *Cincinnati Commercial*, coming to the assistance of fellow journalists. "That well-worn type looked new and beautiful" to Medill, whose staff gratefully used Halstead's gift until the *Tribune* could acquire more type of its own. When Medill heard there was a four-cylinder Hoe press available in Baltimore, he telegraphed an offer to buy it at the asking price, specifying express delivery, and then procured a boiler big enough to power the machine.

The city's most popular paper was the *Chicago Times*, which boasted a daily circulation of about thirty-five thousand. The *Tribune's* was about thirty thousand, and four other dailies had ten thousand or more. Wilbur Storey, owner of the *Times*, was everything leaders like Joseph Medill and Horace White believed they were not. They thought of themselves as individuals of learning, culture, refinement, and probity who represented the moral and intellectual backbone of the city. While Storey's paper's slogan was "Temperance in All Things," Storey himself was unapologetically intemperate in every way, including in his relationship with alcohol and women. Born in Vermont in 1819, he moved westward and through a succession of newspapers in other towns before purchasing the *Times* in 1861. A tall man with a long white beard, Storey was despised by virtually everyone in Chicago who had the displeasure of knowing him—even those who admired his nerve and business sense.

Storey was a bitter racist who questioned the Northern cause during the Civil War and greeted the Emancipation Proclamation as "the most wicked, atrocious and revolting deed in the annals of civilization." Union Army general Ambrose Burnside briefly shut the *Times* down, only to be overruled by Abraham Lincoln, partly on advice from Isaac N. Arnold. Arnold believed in freedom of the press, and, as a practical matter, he feared that suppression of the *Times* would only make the newspaper more popular. If Storey was grateful to the president, he did not show it. Five weeks before Lincoln's assassination, the *Times* called him "a noisome stench thrust under the nostrils of the community." To be fair to a man who never was fair himself, pro-Union newspapers could be just as vituperative toward Lincoln. And while Storey constantly attacked the *Tribune*, as it did his paper, he had no disagreements with its contempt for ethnic politicians and the foreign-born Chicagoans they represented.

According to longtime *Times* editor and contributor Franc Willkie, the headstrong Storey was so uncharacteristically discouraged by the fire that he at first wished to shut the paper for good. In the next few days Storey changed his mind, and the *Times* returned on October 18, a week after the *Tribune* and most other dailies. To help the *Times* get back on its feet, the staff agreed to work at half salary for five weeks. Instead of showing appreciation, Storey insisted that the arrangement last another week even though he could afford to pay them. Between the demand for newspapers and advertising space, business at the resurrected *Times* was booming. As Willkie explained, Storey treated employees "as mere machines—to be operated but in no sense to be human beings."

The *Illinois Staats-Zeitung*, with a daily circulation of twelve thousand copies, was the most widely read foreign-language newspaper in the city. It bemoaned the fact that "no other paper has found it so difficult . . . to give even a sign of life after the horrible catastrophe . . . because the personnel of none has been burned out so completely." Editor Herman Raster turned for help to the German-language *Milwaukee Herald*, which enabled him to issue the first postfire issue on October 11, the same day as the *Tribune* and several other leading dailies.

Papers priced at three cents or a nickel now had a street value of a quarter or more, but any newsboy who wanted to get a stack to peddle on the street had to wait on a long line outside the temporary newspaper offices and hope the supply did not run out.

Besides detailed accounts of the disaster, the earliest postfire issues of Chicago papers included stories of the world's reaction to the disaster, notices of meetings of different groups within the city to discuss emergency measures, bits of news from elsewhere, a smattering of ads from surviving businesses, and lists of the deceased who had been identified. They also included columns headed "The Sufferers" and "The Missing,"

Joseph Medill (Chicago History Museum, ICHi-016828) and
Wilbur Storey. (Chicago History Museum, ICHi-021288)

one a tally of individual property losses and the other names of individuals, many of them children, whose whereabouts were unknown.

There were also longer personal inquiries. One sought information anyone might have about "Hartwig Staats, a gentleman 26 years old, just arrived from Germany, on Friday, the 6th." Another hinted at a poignant backstory: "MISS MACK (FORMERLY of Montreal), will much relieve the anxiety of her friends if she will communicate at once with the undersigned, or accept for herself and relatives the hospitality of his house, which he will glad afford her and them." It was signed, "HENRY W. DARLING (formerly of Montreal), Hamilton, Ontario."

Joseph Medill and William Bross agreed that Bross should travel to New York as soon as possible. He was to purchase additional equipment the *Tribune* needed, but the much more pressing need was to convince

Chicago's current creditors and prospective investors that the city was far from through. Bross was on his way Wednesday morning, October 11. When he arrived in Buffalo late in the day, members of the Board of Trade of that city, hungry for an eyewitness account of the devastation and tumult, asked Bross to speak. He offered a positive spin on the disaster, promising that Chicago would "rise from its ashes in all its pristine rigor."

Impressing Buffalo, the eleventh largest city in the United States, was all well and good, but Bross made certain that he caught the evening train that would take him east across the state and then down the Hudson River valley to the nation's financial capital, New York City. Once there, he immediately set to work putting out the story that Chicago was very much alive. *New-York Tribune* editor Whitelaw Reid sent two reporters to interview Bross in his room in the posh St. Nicholas Hotel on lower Broadway. Reid integrated the upbeat story they filed with his paper's on-the-scene reporting from Chicago.

Bross was delighted to receive an invitation from the Chicago Relief Committee of the New York Chamber of Commerce to address the chamber's membership. It consisted of exactly the sort of movers and shakers he had to persuade of Chicago's financial soundness and continuing promise for investment capital. Bross began his speech by reminding the New York money men that when he had addressed them five years earlier, he had predicted that the transcontinental railroad, then three years from completion, would be a tremendous boon to the national economy. They had thought he was taking a brighter view than the facts supported, he said. Now everyone would agree that his prediction had been fulfilled.

So they should believe him when he insisted that Chicago's future was bright as ever. But that future relied on the same kind of external financing that had created the city in the first place. Putting cash behind Chicago's recovery would be the shrewdest investment they could ever make. Far from foreclosing past opportunities, Bross insisted, the fire opened new ones. It might take a little time to realize a large return, but the certain reward far exceeded any apparent risk. After all, "braver and truer, nobler and better men do not live, than the leading business men of Chicago."

Bross advised his listeners to send more than their money to the city. There was no better place than Chicago for their sons to begin their careers, since there they would be under the tutelage of the city's exceptionally capable entrepreneurs at the most exciting of moments. Working in Chicago would also save these privileged young men from the pitfalls of inherited wealth: "Better a thousand fold encourage the sons of the rich to honorable exertion than to allow them to waste their energies in ease and luxury."

Shrewd investors could not afford to withhold the means to rebuild Chicago. "What she has been in the past she must become in the future, and a hundred fold," Bross declared. If his listeners failed to seize the moment, they would miss a spectacular opportunity to profit from the fulfillment of Chicago's "manifest destiny."

Back in Chicago, the local business community was taking its own first postdisaster steps. On Tuesday afternoon, October 10, about twelve hours after the fire ended, downtown merchants, bankers, brokers, and manufacturers met to discuss how to deal with the current crisis. They convened in Standard Hall, a two-story Romanesque building at Thirteenth Street and Michigan Avenue, less than a mile south of the Burnt District. Standard Hall was almost brand new, having been erected in 1870 to house the Standard Club, the social, charitable, and civic organization founded the year before by the city's successful Jewish leaders, mainly midcentury immigrants from Germany like banker Henry Greenebaum. North Division businessmen met for similar purposes that Wednesday morning. With almost every building above the Main Branch destroyed, they gathered outdoors, at the corner of Kinzie and Clark Streets.

Bankers convened in the Wabash Avenue home of C. T. Wheeler, vice president of the Union National Bank and former president of the Board of Trade. Union National Bank president W. F. Coolbaugh chaired the meeting. Coolbaugh and a handful of others, among them J. Young Scammon of the Marine Bank and Julian Rumsey of the Corn Exchange Bank, formed a leadership committee. Just as Mayor Mason had guaranteed the faith and credit of the city, so these bankers stated that they would meet all their obligations.

Members of individual professions also conferred with each other—retailers and wholesalers with other retailers and wholesalers, attorneys with attorneys, ministers with ministers. The same was true for organized labor. John M. Farquhar, president of the Typographical Union, called members to its headquarters on the West Side to consider how to find jobs in a city that had just lost its major printing facilities.

The editorial that appeared in the initial postfire edition of the *Chicago Tribune* on October 11, titled "CHEER UP," was an inspiring exercise in positive thinking. The *Tribune* commended Chicagoans for how magnificently they were faring under the circumstances. It predicted in no uncertain terms (and capital letters) that "CHICAGO SHALL RISE AGAIN." The enormity of the damage, rather than a crippling blow, was merely another sign of Chicago's greatness. An article in the column adjoining the editorial claimed that there had never been—not in London, Moscow, or anywhere else—a calamity of such magnitude as far as property loss was concerned. Chicago would respond to the world's greatest disaster with the world's greatest recovery.

The *Tribune* was not a lone voice crying in the wilderness but part of a chorus. The *Chicago Republican* printed its own version of "CHEER UP" the following day, proclaiming, "Thursday dawns with a bright sun in the east and a brighter hope and faith in the breasts of the citizens of Chicago. No night so black was ever followed by a day so full of promise." Six days after that the *Times* issued a similar message in its first postfire issue. "Chicago can be beaten, but it cannot be conquered," the *Times* asserted. In a short time, "the world shall see us marching on as cheeredly and determinedly as if naught save victory had ever perched on our banners."

In private letters, some Chicagoans shared this optimism. "It is my painful duty to write to you and inform you of the sad misfortune that has befallen Chicago," Joel Bigelow wrote to his brothers immediately following the fire. After recounting at length all the losses and "the precariousness of the situation," Bigelow added a postscript: "Don't you think it would be well to take advantage of the present to invest a little money out here?"

- 9 -

CONTROVERSY AND CONTROL

In the first twenty-two months of his two-year term, Chicago mayor Roswell B. Mason had been a low-key administrator who did not try to stretch the limited powers of his office. Following the fire, in his two most important actions as mayor, he made exceptionally powerful use of what authority he could exercise, though in a paradoxical manner—by giving it away.

On Wednesday, October 11, Mason bypassed the police department, the elected board that ran it, and the Common Council when he announced that he had entrusted the "preservation of the good order and peace of the city" to Lieutenant General Philip H. Sheridan.

Two days later, on Friday, October 13, Mason designated a private organization, the Chicago Relief and Aid Society, as the recipient and dispenser of "all contributions for the suffering people of this city." He directed the existing General Relief Committee, formed on the Monday of the fire, to surrender its responsibilities and resources to the Relief and Aid Society and then immediately disband.

Both actions made some practical sense. Both were legally questionable. And both were made possible by the unprecedented nature of the situation and the current disarray of the Common Council. Taken together, the appointments of Sheridan and the Relief and Aid Society constituted a coup by the city's native-born economic and social elite, who were certain that they knew best how order should be maintained and the world's contributions distributed, as opposed to the voters and the incompetent and corrupt people these voters elected. The advocates of these two measures refused to admit, and perhaps were even unable to see, that what they claimed were the city's best interests were indistinguishable from their own.

Sheridan maintained at the time and after that he did not want the job. To his surprise, he told Secretary of War William W. Belknap, prominent citizens implored him to take military control over incapacitated Chicago. He said the public mind was panic-stricken, believing "the wildest and most improbable rumors of arson and robbery" and indulging in "the greatest apprehensions . . . of another conflagration, together with riotous demonstrations" by the general population.

Thinking that the visible presence of soldiers would be helpful in quieting such apprehensions, Sheridan had already requisitioned more troops and supplies in addition to the ones he had originally requested. He revealed that he was most concerned about people of means when he said that this force would "aid in the protection of treasure and property until public confidence could again be restored."

By the time these additional federal troops arrived on Wednesday, October 11, a considerable public safety force had been assembled. Augmenting the seven hundred regular soldiers in Chicago were the volunteers sworn in as special police officers, as well as private guards hired by some larger companies. On top of that, on Tuesday evening Illinois governor John M. Palmer had sent to Chicago a contingent of five hundred state militia members, among them the Champaign Cadets, the Rock Falls Zouaves, the Springfield Volunteers, and the Sterling City Guards. They were commanded by Colonel Hubert Dilger and armed with a thousand muskets.

The total number of individuals charged with maintaining order approached three thousand men; there were also the neighborhood volunteer watches. Chicagoans still remained skittish and suggestible, prone to generating, spreading, and crediting rumors based in free-floating fears and traumatic stress.

Newspaper coverage of the fire fanned anxieties. The *Chicago Evening Journal* worried that the wind might shift and ignite the city all over again. "Then, alas, this is not the only source of danger," it warned. "The city is infested with a horde of thieves, burglars and cut-throats, bent on plunder, and who will not hesitate to burn, pillage and even murder, as opportunity may seem to offer to them to do so with safety." This infestation consisted of more than local thieves. There were stories that the same trains bringing relief supplies, reporters, and aesthetic sightseers to Chicago also conveyed professional crooks based elsewhere. The *New-York Tribune* stated that some of its city's most notorious crimi-

Orgies in the Doomed City—Men and Boys Drinking from the Casks of a Burning Liquor Store, *1871. (Chicago History Museum, ICHi-002897)*

nals had descended on Chicago, "trusting to reap a rich harvest, amid the confusion consequent on the appalling catastrophe."

Newspapers and periodicals also published tales of drunkenness, robbery, looting, arson, and sexual assault having taken place during the fire, when saloons, stores, and homes were abandoned and the police were distracted by the universal pandemonium. An illustration depicted men and boys breaking open casks of liquor with hatchets, apparently so possessed by their beastly thirst that they disregarded the fact that the store they were looting was ablaze. The terrors and excitement of the fire allegedly caused even refined and respectable people, including women, to deaden their senses with alcohol. More than a decade after the fact, A. T. Andreas was still perpetuating these tales. The Sands, which he characterized as a "stretch of sandy purgatory" was the scene of the worst transgressions, as "the spirit of infernal revelry prevailed" and "purest girlhood was forced to endure the leering of the vile."

Letters written right after the fire show that Chicagoans believed such stories and spun out more of their own. Lawyer Jonas Hutchinson told his mother in New Hampshire that "the city is thronged with desperadoes who are plundering & trying to set new fires." Bookkeeper

Eben Matthews recalled that anyone who was not there at the time "can hardly imagine the fear of incendiarism, looting, etc. which prevailed. Stories of all kinds were afloat concerning thefts murders and the like."

The anecdotes of robbery and arson often ended in lurid retributive violence, as outraged citizens treated malefactors to rough justice. Readers of the *Chicago Evening Journal* could feast on a list of reports under the headline, "Death to Incendiaries." One of these stories informed them that a boy arsonist caught in the act by firemen now "sleeps in the valley." News sources outside the city amplified the grisly details. The *St. Louis Dispatch* of October 11 stated, "It is learned at police headquarters that forty-one persons were shot in making arrests last night. The station houses are filled with prisoners."

People credited the descriptions of vigilante executions. Writing to friends and family two days after the fire, Phillip C. Morgan, who worked for National Life Insurance, told his parents, "There has [*sic*] been a good many roughs shot dead and quite a number *hung. Immediately* upon their hellish deeds such as setting new fires and stealing." "Many fires have been started," Cassius Milton Wicker explained to his relatives, "but in most cases the party caught in the act has been shot on the spot." He repeated a preposterous tale of righteous vigilante action in which Catholic priests shot seven men who were trying to torch a church.

Even newspapers that took pride in their reasoned restraint approved of this supposed summary treatment. According to the *Chicago Tribune*, "instant death is the just and equitable punishment in every case where the guilt of the party is perfectly assured." The paper talked out of both sides of its mouth, admitting that shooting or stringing up someone on the spot would not be a sign of good judgment while also asserting that the city would be much safer if every would-be arsonist knew he would not live five minutes beyond the moment he was spotted setting a fire.

Asked later if there had in fact been an influx of thieves and assassins, police captain Michael Hickey avoided a direct answer. He praised Chicagoans' aggressive watchfulness more for preventing rather than punishing crime since it scared criminals away. He admitted, however, that agitated and angry citizens had set upon blameless suspected perpetrators, one a member of the fire department prudently moving gunpowder to a safer location. Two nights after the fire, he stated, the police had rescued a "peaceable man" and "good citizen" in the nick

Fearful Retribution. Thieves and Incendiaries Are Hanged
by the Heels and Brained. *From George L. Barclay,* The Great
Fires of Chicago, *1871. (Chicago History Museum, ICHi-064421)*

of time from an overexcited mob of five hundred people who would have lynched him had police officers not spirited him off to the safety of a station house, thus preventing an actual crime.

Reporters and editors in Chicago who knew that reports of violence, whether substantiated or not, sold papers, eagerly passed them along as if true. They rarely identified the supposed sources of these stories by name, nor did reporters claim to have witnessed the events they described. Private citizens did the same thing, creating an echo chamber for a cacophony of invented horrors. In Joel Bigelow's October 10 letter to his brothers, he told them, "I am informed 30 are missing on the North Side," and that "there are some who assert that it is a preconcerted plan by a lot of villains to meet here and burn the city—for plunder." He added that he met someone "who says that two parties were caught in the act of setting fire to side walks in the West Division—and that they were both hung to lamp posts—the party asserted that he saw the bodies hanging—an acquaintance of mine says that he is reliably informed that in the South Division two men have been hung and one shot." Even as he spread such tales, Bigelow admitted he was not sure he believed them, though under the circumstances he was "inclined to accept these statements with some degree of allowance."

Some of Chicago's fears may have been inspired by the Paris Commune uprising at the close of the Franco-Prussian War in the spring. Newspapers in cities throughout the United States, including Chicago, closely followed the Paris Commune and its bloody collapse under military attack, during which the Communards set buildings ablaze, including the famed Tuileries Palace. The *Chicago Evening Post* compared the use of explosives to try to prevent the fire's spread to "the booming of heavy siege guns," so that it seemed as if "the commune and the reign of terror were being realized in the very heart of the Garden City of the West."

It was all too easy for someone already antagonistic to immigrants and workers in Chicago to portray them as terrorists. Four months before the fire, alongside an account of the Commune by a *London Times* correspondent, the *Tribune* included an angry letter to the editor who insisted "there was a striking similarity" between the German residents of Chicago who attended a "large and enthusiastic" antitemperance rally "to the reports of the proceedings of the late Paris Commune." Right after the fire, the *New York Evening Post* published a poem, titled "Paris and Chicago," that posed the question,

> Did out of her ashes arise
> This bird with a flaming crest,
> That over the ocean unhindered flies,
> With a scourge for the Queen of the West?

On October 23 the *Chicago Times*, which five days earlier had dismissed rumors of incendiaries, published on its front page the purported "confession" of an unidentified American Communard in which he stated that he and several accomplices started the fire by setting off bombs. He said that he had recently come to Chicago from Paris as part of a worldwide plot to visit chaos on other great cities. The damage would have been a lot worse had he not experienced last-minute remorse and decided not to ignite another explosive that would certainly have killed many Chicagoans as they fled the fire. The *Times* evaded the issue of the authenticity of the document, which did not keep the paper from wondering out loud if the terrorist's tale of multiple bombs explained why the great conflagration was several simultaneous fires, not just one.

In the November 4 issue of the Boston-based newsweekly *Every Saturday*, artist Alfred Fredericks depicted the city besieged by merciless enemies. In this intense allegorical scene, brave and noble young women in classical gowns assist their dazed sister, Chicago, to her feet. As they raise her up, other maidens of mercy fend off savage hounds closing in for the kill. Fredericks set this life-and-death struggle against the postapocalyptic backdrop of the burning city, with vultures circling the smoky sky.

The message was clear: the forces of good could rescue Chicago only if they were prepared to battle the minions of evil. In case any reader missed this meaning, the *Every Saturday* editors made it explicit. The dogs embodied famine and pestilence, they explained, while the vultures "represent those human birds of prey which swooped down upon Chicago in the midst of her calamity."

Whether or not there was any truth to the stories of rampant criminality and terrorism in Chicago, people believed such appalling things were possible—people influential enough to convince Mayor Mason to appoint Sheridan and persuade the general to agree. As Sheridan told

Chicago, October 10, 1871, *based on a drawing by*
Alfred Fredericks. From Every Saturday, *November 4, 1871.*
(Chicago History Museum, ICHi-063771)

Belknap, during the afternoon of Tuesday, October 10, several leading
citizens approached him a second time, insisting that "nothing but
prompt action on my part could save the balance of the city, restore confidence and maintain order." One of these citizens, he specified, was
Thomas W. Grosvenor, a prosecuting city attorney. Colonel Grosvenor,

as he was still called, was a Civil War hero who had lost the use of an arm to a battle wound.

When Sheridan dismissed as nonsense the tales of incendiaries, robbers, murderers, and lynch mobs, he found to his astonishment that even some of Chicago's "best citizens" believed the baseless rumors, though he was "utterly unable to find a single individual who had seen in person any of the alleged outrages." Sheridan said he remained reluctant to assume control. In his view, Mayor Mason was doing everything possible, albeit with the "worn out force at his disposal." Although the general felt that as a resident of Chicago it was his duty to assist as he could, it was Sheridan's "earnest desire" that civilian authorities should bring the city through its troubles.

Sheridan said that when, after more pressure, he agreed to serve, he did so only after stipulating that the mayor's proclamation putting him in charge must include a paragraph stating that his powers were in no way to interfere with those of the city government. Police and Fire Board president Thomas Brown, who was involved in the discussions, later said that Sheridan actually rejected the idea that he share leadership with Superintendent of Police W. W. Kennedy. Brown said that General Sheridan insisted that "there can be but one hand in this," that he "was not willing to have anything to do with it in any other way"—he would withdraw his troops if he were not in charge. "I am not anxious for the job," he reminded Mason, thus challenging the mayor to give him sole command or lose him entirely.

For Mason and the influential citizens who could not wait for Sheridan to take over, the decision was easy.

On Thursday, October 12, Sheridan met with Illinois governor John M. Palmer, who was in the city to inspect conditions in person. Since Palmer planned to address the legislature in Springfield on the situation the next day, he stayed less than twelve hours. Before leaving, the governor approved the arrangement Mason and Sheridan had made, which included assembling a local regiment of volunteers consisting of existing militias and new recruits. He requested that Sheridan send home as soon as possible members of Illinois militia companies whose members lived some distance from Chicago. In a related action, the Board of Police revoked the powers of the citizen special police, who were glad to get back to their personal lives.

Authorized to serve for twenty days, the First Regiment of Chicago Volunteers consisted of nineteen companies of sixty men each, around 1,100 in all. Some of the new recruits among them had no military experience or training. The latter included the University Cadets, drawn from students at the original University of Chicago, also known as Chicago or Douglas University, located next to Camp Douglas at the southern edge of the city, also on land formerly owned by the late senator Stephen Douglas. As Palmer had requested, Sheridan sent Dilger and the downstate militia members home.

For the next week and a half the general was the supreme policing authority in the city. The headquarters of order-keeping in Chicago was an office building on South Wabash Avenue, where Sheridan sat at a pine table and issued directives. Sheridan used the temporary military force to supplement the regular soldiers and the city's policemen. He and his second in command, Assistant Adjutant General James B. Fry, assigned their men to posts and watches. Some of these military guardians of the peace bivouacked on the lakefront, where the White Stockings had so recently played baseball and local residents had fled from the fire.

In the letter he wrote to his mother on October 13, Francis William Test said of Sheridan, "He is a little God here." The de facto martial law reminded Test of the war: "Soldiers march our streets; the citizens are patrolling the squares; every alley is guarded and woe be to him that lights a match or smokes a cigar in the street after nightfall." Mayor Mason sent handwritten orders to Sheridan rather than to the police department when he made decisions requiring someone to back them up.

Sheridan concentrated his regular infantry troops in the ruins of the downtown. He provided less protection to the burned-out North Division. Members of the First Regiment of Chicago Volunteers mainly served night duty in areas that were untouched by the fire, making sure that saloons observed the curfew, that no one was smoking, and that merchants and hotel keepers were not overcharging. Sentries restricted the movement of civilians, including in their own neighborhoods. They demanded that people moving about the city state their business and provide a password. Even Chicagoans doing essential cleanup work needed written permission after dark. "Of course such procedure was illegal," Eben Matthews reflected, "but it had the force of public opinion back of it, and so was most effective in giving us the much needed security."

Alfred Waud was one of the magazine illustrators who had rushed to Chicago from wherever they were—in his case, St. Louis—at first reports of the fire. In one of Waud's several on-the-scene sketches, titled *Halt! Who Goes There*, a lone infantryman with a bayonet affixed to his rifle confronts two well-dressed men, one carrying an umbrella and briefcase, on the perimeter of the Burnt District. They are obviously not criminals but citizens going about their business.

Most contemporary commentary strongly approved of Sheridan's appointment and exercise of his authority, which they saw as of great and timely benefit, halting disaster profiteering as well as more serious crimes. Test repeated to his mother a story making the rounds. Supposedly the general had entered a hotel and asked the price of a room, to which the proprietor responded, "I am charging $10.00, sir." This was far above the normal rate. He then asked Sheridan, "Will you register your name?" The general reportedly replied: "No, sir, but I will inform you that if you cannot give room and board at $3.00 per day I can find someone that can."

The veracity of the anecdote is uncertain, but Sheridan's forces did take steps to discourage profiteering. Businessmen were conscious of the prevailing wariness about gouging customers. In their ads in the newspapers, they included promises of "Regular Prices" or "No Change in Prices!" Test said that people sometimes took matters into their own hands. When a farmer set up a wagon from which he offered beans "at an exorbitant price" and asked fifty dollars for a calf, "a crowd gathered around him and drove him from the city."

The soldiers made their rounds in a Chicago that was generally peaceful, if always on edge. On October 12, Sheridan informed the mayor that there had been no cases of "outbreak or disorder" and no authenticated instances of incendiarism. Nevertheless, he counseled, citizens should not "relax in their watchfulness." Five days later he told Mason that newspaper stories of disorder were "without the slightest foundation" and added that the agitated public mood was settling down. Francis William Test agreed: "Sheridan has control here now and this has done much to stay the confidence of the people," he informed his mother. James W. Milner commented, "The presence of soldiers is, undoubtedly, a good thing as so many men thrown idle, with the unsettled condition that such ruin induced in their minds, makes every precaution advisable."

Alfred R. Waud, Halt! Who Goes There?
(Chicago History Museum, ICHi-002990)

The soldiers seemed at times as likely to create disorder as stifle it. Captain Jerry Crowley of the Montgomery Light Guards militia company reported that the barroom of a German social hall at Twelfth and Halsted Streets in the West Division had been "open and at full blast" at ten thirty the previous evening, which was well after the curfew. A few days earlier, however, police captain Hickey sent a complaint to Sheridan about the members of another company who brandished bayonets and cocked rifles not only at citizens but also at Chicago policemen. "These men claimed to be acting under your orders," Hickey wrote, "but they were evidently intoxicated."

Sheridan received especially favorable reviews from those who importuned him to take over in the first place. They attributed the city's calm and the good behavior of residents to the presence of troops, not the law-abiding character of Chicagoans. William Bross was thrilled to see "Sheridan's boys, with knapsack and musket," marching smartly into the city. "Never did deeper emotions of joy overcome me," he recalled. "Had it not been for General Sheridan's prompt, bold, and patriotic action," Bross contended, "I verily believe that what was left of the city would have been nearly, if not quite entirely, destroyed by the cutthroats and vagabonds who flocked here like vultures from every point of the compass."

While Sheridan's men were trying to ease fears, the General Relief Committee was providing for the city's tens of thousands of displaced and despondent people. By Wednesday, October 11, two days after it was formed, the committee was far better organized and had adopted bylaws. Donations of supplies and cash were inundating the city. To Charles C. P. Holden, "it appeared as though there was to be no end to the world's charity."

On that Wednesday, a delegation from the Chicago Relief and Aid Society called on the General Relief Committee at the First Congregational Church. The delegation stated that the Relief and Aid Society, not the General Relief Committee, should administer the resources being sent to Chicago. Its members asserted that the contributions from around the nation and the world "of right, ought to be turned over to them."

The society had been incorporated in 1850 as a private philanthropic organization of a type established in several American cities around the same time. Its founders were men who had been critical to the city's early development while they made fortunes of their own, but the current board members represented the city's younger business leaders who had arrived more recently. They included department store proprietor Marshall Field, railroad car manufacturer George Pullman, soap and lard magnate Nathaniel K. Fairbank, and clothing wholesaler Henry W. King, who had come to Chicago from upstate New York in 1854 and made his fortune in the new industry of ready-to-wear apparel. Throughout the society's history, virtually all of its leaders and members were white, male, native-born Protestants. In 1871 attorney Julius Rosenthal, who was Jewish and born in Germany, was the only exception on the Executive Committee, which governed the organization.

The group's driving force was Executive Committee chair Wirt Dexter. Though still in his thirties, Dexter had already become one of the most highly regarded and well-connected attorneys in Chicago. Dexter's grandfather and father, both named Samuel, were Boston-born Harvard University graduates. The elder Samuel Dexter represented Massachusetts in the US House and Senate before joining President John Adams's cabinet, first as the nation's fourth secretary of war and next as its third secretary of the Treasury. The younger Samuel Dexter moved to New York and then Michigan Territory, which did not become a state until 1837. He built a lumber mill and founded the village of Dexter, northwest of Ann Arbor. His son Wirt attended the University of Michigan before entering the lumber business. Dexter also studied law, which was his profession by the time he moved to Chicago in 1865, the year he turned thirty-two. A mere four years later he was one of the small group of influential men, along with Pullman, Anson Stager of Western Union, and dry goods merchant Charles Farwell, who started the exclusive Chicago Club.

Dexter kept a distinguished wine cellar but supposedly never took more than an occasional glass. He was a physically fit man who walked to and from work and in the evenings rode horseback an hour or more. By one flattering description, he was said to have a "high broad forehead," a more positive way of indicating that he was prematurely bald.

The society prided itself on its businesslike and "scientific" approach to philanthropy, which it said was based on objective and measured evaluation of need rather than sentiment and impulse. A great believer in the developing field of statistics, it directed its staff to maintain detailed records of all of the organization's work. While the first generation of leaders took a more hands-on approach to managing the organization, current board members, several of whom ran much larger and complex companies than their predecessors, hired a professional full-time general superintendent, O. C. Gibbs, who in turn engaged salaried "visitors," forerunners of professional social workers, to screen applicants, often in their homes.

The society's mission was based on its belief in individual responsibility for one's status in life. It aided a small subset of the impoverished, normally independent and solvent people who for reasons beyond their control required assistance to weather a temporary difficulty. In

Wirt Dexter. Photograph by Charles D. Mosher.
(Chicago History Museum, ICHi-176532)

all cities, the society explained, "there is a class of worthy and industrious poor who in their prosperity have a hard struggle to obtain what are deemed the necessaries of life." For such people, who had limited savings and credit, an illness or accident, or the loss of a job, could be disastrous. The timely and judicious administration of charity until their lives stabilized would keep them and their families from slipping into "permanent pauperism." The society also assisted previously self-reliant people who were unable to get by on their own for reasons they could not amend, such as widows with dependent children, the aged, and the infirm.

The society distinguished these "deserving" poor from those who by implication were "undeserving"—that is, people who dwelt in poverty because of their low habits and lack of resolve. Like all but the most progressive Americans at this time, the Relief and Aid Society's members believed that the miserable conditions in which they saw many Chicagoans living, especially the immigrant underclass, were these people's own fault, not some systemic problem. Life might be tough, they argued, but it was fair, especially in the United States, the land of opportunity. Character determined environment, not the other way around.

The society assumed that applicants for assistance were undeserving until they proved otherwise. The board instructed its visitors to sniff out "imposition," by which it meant any attempt to receive help through chicanery. Visitors screened potential clients in their homes so that they could see for themselves how applicants lived, lest the society squander its funds on those who in its judgment were capable of supporting themselves but too lazy to do so. Not trusting those it aided to spend money wisely, the organization assisted successful applicants by furnishing them with food and essential supplies rather than cash, lest they spend it on something of which its donors did not approve, especially alcohol.

The organization credited itself with bolstering the moral fiber of recipients while also protecting Chicago's overall well-being. In 1868 it established a work department that required physically able clients to split wood, stack lumber, and shovel coal in the supply yards the society maintained, or to take positions the society found for them. It denied provisions and goods to those who refused to do so, even if that job required a person to move to some distant town or village. The society candidly admitted that one purpose of this policy was to limit dependency in the local population.

Like those who urged the appointment of Sheridan, the Relief and Aid Society had a plausible argument that it should take control. After all, theirs was a state-chartered charitable body that "possessed all the paraphernalia and facilities" now needed. Still, the society had never dealt with anything approaching the size and complexity of the fire relief. The society's clients currently numbered a little more than 1,200 poor but generally not homeless families. In addition, its resources were the contributions of the same small group of wealthy individuals who decided how the money was spent. Now it proposed to distribute funds and goods donated by thousands of outsiders in a devastated metropolis of well over 300,000 people, at least one-third of whom were in serious distress.

The General Relief Committee members who were present when Dexter's delegation paid its call heard him out but neither accepted nor rejected the idea that the society should take over the committee's work. Dexter and other Relief and Aid Society leaders were determined to get their way. They returned to the First Congregational Church the next day to state again that they should assume control of the relief. According to Holden's account, Nathaniel K. Fairbank—who was a member of both the Relief and Aid Society and the General Relief Committee—presented a formal resolution that the society "be adopted as the means of distributing the food and supplies received for the sufferers." The resolution stated that the present General Relief Committee, along with the mayor, comptroller, city treasurer, and two aldermen from each division would also "be added to the directory of said Society." Holden's account gives no details of the discussion of Fairbank's motion and does not indicate the Common Council president's position on the matter, but it states that the resolution passed.

Chicago had never faced as disruptive a crisis as the Great Fire, and there was no precedent or set procedure for handing over such a large responsibility and amount of resources. When he endorsed the transfer on Friday, October 13, Mason offered reasons but no legal justification. Though the society had been founded only twenty-one years earlier, he said it was an "old" and "established" organization that enjoyed the trust of the community. It was familiar with the kind of work to be done. Although its staff was not at the moment sufficient to deal with the far larger duties the society now faced, it would expand as required.

Mason was probably eager to turn the administration of aid to the Relief and Aid Society. Its leaders were the kind of individuals he had worked with throughout his long career as a high-level corporate employee. Another likely factor in the mayor's willingness to cede authority was an implicit threat from a group called the Committees of the Nations, which was made up of representatives of the out-of-town delegations currently in Chicago to assist in the relief. In most instances these philanthropic emissaries were men very much like the leaders of the Relief and Aid Society, whom they knew personally through commercial dealings and a network of friendships.

On the evening of the day Mason appointed the society, the Committees of the Nations issued a statement to "The Citizens of Chicago." While acknowledging "most heartily" the "unselfish and arduous service" of the General Relief Committee, the statement asserted that it was "absolutely essential that the work be systematically and economically extended" and that the reception and distribution of supplies be handled "by an organization which will satisfy yourselves and encourage your friends to continued action." This implied that "your friends"—that is, benefactors like themselves—might withdraw aid if the Relief and Aid Society were not appointed. Lest anyone be in doubt of just why the society deserved such an endorsement, the address referred to its leaders as "your best men."

Mason's decision to defer Chicago's distribution of aid to the Relief and Aid Society was even more questionable than his appointment of Sheridan to assume what were normally the duties of the city's police department. First of all, he could not justify the decision by pointing to widespread fear and panic. Second, while everyone understood that Sheridan's authority would be brief, directing the relief would be a sustained major undertaking that involved tens of thousands of people and affected the city's economy for many months, perhaps even a few years.

Nor was there an overwhelming need for the handover other than that the Relief and Aid Society and its supporters desired it. The General Relief Committee, a semipublic body formed in response to the crisis, appeared to be doing a creditable job under the most trying conditions. It was improving its operations steadily during the very short time it was in control. In the three days following the fire, it had assisted about seventy thousand Chicagoans. Its leadership was an impressive mix of elected officials and private citizens. As it added members, it selected people with sterling business credentials for key positions, like Board of Trade president J. W. Preston, who was in charge of receiving supplies. It had already appointed the Relief and Aid Society's superintendent O.C. Gibbs to be head of the subcommittee on distribution of relief.

It also made provisions for financial oversight. The day before the Relief and Aid Society's takeover, the General Relief Committee announced through Mayor Mason that all funds sent to the city would be entrusted to city treasurer David Gage, who, like Mason, had been elected on the Citizens Party ticket in 1869. Gage would deposit relief funds in a special account on which only the mayor could draw, overseen by an auditing committee of trusted citizens.

The Chicago Relief and Aid Society was aware of the shaky legal grounds for its request. Attorney Dexter, a master at such things, constructed a strained technical argument to justify the society's position. He told the newspapers that Chicago's thousands of benefactors had in fact contributed not "to the city as a corporation, but to the citizens at large." Having just posited this distinction as if it were irrefutable, he then parsed it to suit his purposes. "It must be plain," he claimed, that "no official bond or liability given or assumed by the officers of the city" covered anything like the distribution of this money, while the Chicago Relief and Aid Society had been specifically formed as a philanthropic organization and accepted legal liability for its actions in this capacity.

In other words, the city government was not qualified legally or in any other respect to do the job at hand, while the Relief and Aid Society was. It was somehow a far more proper steward for the people of Chicago than the officials they elected. He neglected to say that the society was far from the only charitable and philanthropic organization in the city, any of which could make the identical argument that he presented.

The same kind of people who praised Mason for the appointment of Sheridan affirmed his selection of the Chicago Relief and Aid Society. The *New York Times* was one of several voices of respectable thought across the nation that expressed approval. In so doing it revealed the deeper rationale behind the desire of "the best men" to put the society in charge, the fear that otherwise crooked and incompetent members of the Common Council would seize control. The society's leaders and backers insisted that all principled donors would have stipulated in advance that contributions should be kept from the aldermen had they thought this was a possibility.

The *Times* said that the continuing tension between an honest mayor and crooked council members had broken out anew, this time over the aid funds. Fortunately, the *Times* noted, after the gathering of the Committees of the Nations "there has been considerable plain talk." The mayor had wisely removed the world's contributions from the greedy and grasping aldermen and entrusted them to private citizens well known nationally for their integrity.

Not content with just commending the Relief and Aid Society, the *Chicago Tribune* condemned what it said were the haphazard and sloppy operations of the General Relief Committee. The paper ignored the fact that the committee started from scratch amid unprecedented destruction and desperation, and that its members (which included some leaders of the Relief and Aid Society) had to build a large volunteer organization and devise working procedures immediately.

The real challenge ahead, the *Tribune* contended, was not to assist the tens of thousands of people whose lives the fire had shattered. It was to guard the relief resources against those greedy impostors who were salivating at the chance of bellying up to the aid trough. It described these fakers in sexualized terms, as "lusty men and women" who assumed they would now be fed and clothed by others.

The paper pointed out that the stricken city most of all needed people to get to work. A thousand men were wanted, "at good wages," to rebuild the Burnt District. But no laborer would lift a finger if he received relief assistance regardless of whether or not he found a job. There were another thousand domestic positions "in respectable families," also at good pay, but Chicago women were turning them down in the expectation they could obtain aid even if they remained idle.

Like Sheridan, the Relief and Aid Society would be bravely riding to rescue Chicagoans from themselves.

- 10 -

"MORE STRENGTH AND GREATER HOPE"

Getting Going

Slowly at first, and then with increasing momentum, Chicago began to revive. On Thursday, October 12, Mayor Roswell B. Mason moved his office from the First Congregational Church in the West Division to a building at Wabash Avenue and Hubbard Court (Balbo Street), thus reestablishing the city's executive headquarters closer to Courthouse Square and more or less in the center of the city, or what was left of it. Mason predicted that local government would soon resettle in temporary quarters in the square, which would be an important step in resurrecting the downtown.

The Common Council now met in the courtroom of the Second Precinct police station at Union and Madison in the West Division, where the central administration of the police department also relocated. Local courts took over Chicago's lone public high school (in this era most students ended their education at the eighth grade, if not sooner), also on the West Side, until early in 1872.

On Monday evening, October 17, a week after the fire ended, repair crews that had been working around the clock had the 1867 engine in the waterworks Pumping Station running again. By Wednesday it generated enough pressure to raise water to the second floor of buildings. The two older engines in the Pumping Station would not be functional until the end of November, and some fifteen thousand melted and leaking service pipes needed repair or replacement.

The disaster inevitably precipitated a major budget crunch because the city faced the mammoth expenses of rebuilding at the same time all the destruction lowered projected tax revenues. Mayor Mason dismissed municipal employees deemed nonessential while reducing the salaries of those still on the payroll. The city's remaining public schools

*The corner of State and Madison Streets shortly after
the fire. The bricks in the rectangular receptacles were likely
intended for reuse. (Chicago History Museum, ICHi-002811)*

partially reopened October 18, but students whose schools had burned down had to cram into those that had been spared. The city fired music, art, and foreign language instructors. The *Illinois Staats-Zeitung* attacked the dismissal of German teachers as "impudent nationalism," another sign of "the bigoted nativism of the fossils on the school board." It predicted revenge in future elections.

The commercial heart of the city started to beat again. Within a week downtown streetcars returned with limited service, charging riders half fare. The intense heat had weakened some of the thousands of safes and vaults in businesses and professional offices so badly that they crumbled like mortar at the tap of a hammer. Most had held up, however, though many had been buried beneath bricks and stones.

Robert Todd Lincoln confided to a friend that the fire had left his family "in a very bad condition as you can imagine but so far as I can learn I am in better shape than most of my confreres as my vault stood the fire." When Cassius Milton Wicker heard that the Tremont House hotel safe had not withstood the flames, he assumed that the watch and bonds he had stored in it were gone. He was surprised and relieved to learn that proprietor John B. Drake had presciently emptied the safe and taken its contents, including Wicker's property, to a spot beyond the fire.

Since the locking mechanisms of some safes were damaged, they had to be opened by brute force. According to A. S. Chapman, "safe-breaking was a popular industry for a few days, conducted with the full approval and in the presence of safe-owners by skilled men who sprung into sudden demand." And even if a safe itself seemed to emerge from the fire intact, the high temperatures might still have destroyed the vital papers inside. This reportedly could also happen if one opened a safe too soon. In scenes similar to Patrick Webb's unearthing of his belongings, relief would turn to horror as owners saw their cash and securities ignite on exposure to fresh oxygen.

Chapman remembered watching safes dragged into Randolph Street, where "men grimed with soot and ashes work[ed] like fiends with sledge hammers and steel wedges" to break them open before the eyes of nervous owners. Chapman heightened the drama with his use of the present tense: "The air rushes in and I see their hopes turned to ashes as rolls of bills crumble at its touch." In a postfire stereograph, a lone man stands amid broken columns and rubble, pouring water from a bucket on an overturned safe to cool it.

According to his twelve-year-old daughter Bertia, jeweler John Ashleman's papers caught fire when his safe was opened, though not his precious inventory. Ashleman unceremoniously dumped the smoke-stained jewelry into a wheelbarrow and set Bertia to work picking out the diamond rings. "I found them," she recalled proudly years after the fact.

Eben Matthews was greatly relieved that the notebook in which he kept a pencil-written record of the insurance held by his employer, grain broker Jones & Raymond, survived. The pages were "black as a hat," but "the lead pencil marks glistened when held to the light so that they could be deciphered and the insurance proved up." A local company hawked an "ink developer" that promised to reveal what had been written on burnt paper. "Writing Perfectly Restored," it promised. Manufacturers of fireproof safes filled the local papers with advertisements,

Pouring water on a safe to cool it before opening. From a Lovejoy &
Foster stereograph. (Chicago History Museum, ICHi-021520)

some bragging of how well their models had withstood the fire. There were also plenty of ads for fire extinguishers, though none of them would have done much good against a conflagration of this scale and intensity.

Prominent businessmen displayed the kind of public bravado that they hoped would reassure creditors and the general public. Away from the city when disaster hit, Potter Palmer announced by telegraph that he was "perfectly reconciled" to his losses and had "an abundance left." He stated that he would immediately complete the new Palmer House hotel under construction at State and Monroe. Less wealthy and well-known Chicagoans expressed similar resolve. Jared Bassett, a fifty-seven-year-old physician, wrote to a friend on October 21, "I must help myself. I don't see any other way, for me." He said that in a day or two

"I shall commence picking up my bricks, preparatory to building." Like many others, he was already looking even further ahead. "Now, if you know any one who wants to lend me $4000, for 5 years at 8 pr. Ct. pr. Annum," he continued, "I will pile it up on a piece of ground worth $100,000 and Mortgage to secure it."

William H. Carter, head of the Board of Works, reflected privately to his brother, "Chicago is burned down but not despairing—she has the energy and push and will rise phoenix like from the ashes." This was far from the first application of this metaphor to a city that had experienced a major fire, but it was probably the most repeated. Over the next several decades, the phrase "phoenix-like, from the ashes," appeared countless times in characterizations of Chicago's recovery.

When the fire struck, sixty-six-year-old William B. Ogden was living in semiretirement at Villa Boscobel, his estate in the Bronx, which was still largely a rural suburb of Manhattan. Ogden was from the town of Walton in New York's Delaware County, near the northeast corner of Pennsylvania. In 1835, when he turned thirty, he traveled to Chicago to arrange for a title change on 182 acres in the North Division that his brother-in-law Charles Butler had purchased, partly with Ogden's money. On inspecting the property, he advised Butler, "You have been guilty of the grossest folly."

Ogden quickly changed his opinion when he saw the insatiable demand among investors for Chicago real estate. He moved to the city, bringing his lawyer brother Mahlon with him. In 1837 he was elected Chicago's first mayor. There was hardly an area of commercial enterprise in which Ogden was not central, starting with real estate, in which he became the city's largest player. He was a prime mover in Chicago's rise as a transportation center. In 1848 he and J. Young Scammon started the Galena and Chicago Union Railroad, Chicago's first, which was pulled by a secondhand locomotive appropriately named the *Pioneer*. It ran west, first to the Des Plaines River, then to Elgin by 1850, and onward to the lead mines and wheat fields near the Mississippi River.

Fire not only wiped out Ogden's buildings in Chicago, including his North Side home, but also severely damaged his lumber interests in Peshtigo, Wisconsin, where he owned 200,000 acres of pine forest. He had visited the town just the month before. Many of those who had been burned to death in the Peshtigo fire were employees he knew.

William B. Ogden. (Chicago History Museum, ICHi-011943)

This double disaster slashed Ogden's estimated $12 million fortune by one-third. He caught a train to Chicago shortly after he received the bad news by wire. After attending to matters there for a few days, he boarded a lake steamer to Peshtigo. He stayed five weeks.

Courage and determination could only carry even a William Ogden so far. All the fatalities in Peshtigo shook him deeply, as did the physical destruction in Chicago, where he had put so much of himself for so long. He wrote to his niece Julia Wheeler that he had no choice but to accept the fire "without speculation or complaint as an event we can only deal with by trying to repair as far as we may its injury." He told her he was doing his best to maintain his good cheer, though "hardly in the expectation of ever seeing the past literally restored."

The personal situation of Ogden and many other individuals notwithstanding, there was good reason to have confidence in Chicago's future. The Great Fire had amazed the world with its ferocity and scope, but in fact it left much of Chicago in place as a basis for its recovery. While the downtown was gone, the flames had not touched many of the city's most valuable assets. Over two-thirds of developed commercial property was still standing, as were the same portion of homes. The fire disabled the railroad depots, transportation infrastructure, and communications facilities in the downtown, but the tracks, docks, and telegraph lines outside the Burnt District were fine.

Eleven of Chicago's seventeen grain elevators, which held 75 percent of the grain on hand when the fire began, escaped harm. The largest reserves of coal and lumber were still stacked in storage yards along the South Branch of the Chicago River near most of the city's newer heavy manufacturing facilities. The mammoth Union Stock Yards, meat provisioner to the world, was well beyond the southern city limits. Most of the West Division's factories were also unscathed. And the fire did nothing to alter Chicago's location, which had enabled it to become an essential linchpin in the national economy.

Chicago's tragedy caused a downturn in stock exchanges in New York and abroad, but by the end of the month prices stabilized in the expectation that the city would recover. Locally, the *Weekly Post* objected to a prediction by the *St. Louis Republican* that Chicago had now lost its preeminence. "Chicago is a national city," the *Post* responded, "the only one in America except New York"—much as St. Louis might wish it otherwise. "Her prosperity, credit, and stability are in the jealous keeping of all America, and hence she is safe from the financial catastrophe which might otherwise follow this severe trial."

John Stephen Wright, the most enthusiastic and unflagging of Chicago's army of boosters, had long argued that there was nothing about Chicago that did not guarantee its greatness. Born in the Berkshire Hills town of Sheffield, Massachusetts, in 1815, Wright came to Chicago in 1832 with his father and began investing in real estate immediately. Shortly before the fire, he published the Chicago booster book par excellence, *Chicago: Past, Present, Future*, in which Wright declared that God and nature had decreed that Chicago would become the "Hub" of "our National Wheel of Commerce." Faced with the destruction of much of the city in 1871, he was unperturbed, predicting, "Chicago will

have more men, more money, more business, within five years than she
would have had without the fire."

The first rebuilding in the Burnt District was necessarily quick and cheap.
The Board of Public Works announced less than three full days after the
fire that it would approve permits to owners of land within the Burnt District to erect temporary one-story wooden buildings on their property.

The city also decided to lease twenty-five-by-two-hundred-foot lots of
Lake Park public land on the east side of Michigan Avenue between

Jex Bardwell, Temporary Frame Commercial Buildings on
Michigan Avenue, *1871. (Chicago History Museum, ICHi-064149)*

Randolph and Twelfth (Roosevelt Road) Streets. The charge was $500 a year, $750 for a corner lot; after the year was up, tenants were legally obligated to tear down what they had built and move out. The row of wooden storefronts that soon rose along Michigan Avenue could have been mistaken for the main street of a frontier town, except for the fact that they stood next to scorched trees and in front of a body of water that seemed as vast as an ocean. The tenants were substantial if not large wholesalers like grocer F. D. Cossitt and milliner Mayhon, Daly & Company.

One of the scores of out-of-town journalists covering the fire was John Hay, currently a correspondent for the *New-York Tribune*. Hay, who in his early twenties had been a private secretary to President Abraham Lincoln and would later serve as secretary of state under presidents William McKinley and Theodore Roosevelt, turned thirty-three on the Sunday the Great Fire began. Three days later he was on a train to Chicago.

Hay had nothing but praise for Chicagoans' spirit. He encountered attorney, banker, and real estate man J. Young Scammon by the ruins of his Terrace Row home. Scammon was deeply absorbed in the construction of three temporary business structures on the site. Hay was amazed by the purposeful optimism of the man, who was nearing sixty. "The indefatigable owner is everywhere present," Hay wrote, "ordering and directing everything, and shedding about him a fresh and breezy atmosphere of hope and energy."

The first store in the Burnt District bore the impressive name of Schock, Bigford & Company, but it was merely a battered chest turned into an open-air stand that peddled cigars, grapes, apples, and cider at "Old Prices." The pioneer of the return to the business center proper was, not surprisingly, a real estate dealer. William D. Kerfoot had been in the business since he came to Chicago in 1854 at the age of seventeen. Eight years later he opened his own real estate company at 89 Washington Street, a half block east of Courthouse Square.

When Kerfoot saw that the fire would claim his North Division home, he bundled his wife and children into his horse-drawn carriage. With no room left for himself in the vehicle, he mounted the horse and led them away. When they passed another man pulling his wife in their buggy, Kerfoot generously hitched it to the rear of his rig. Kerfoot quickly found homes for both his family and his business in the West Division. Three days after the fire, he also knocked together a wooden shanty at

J. Young Scammon.
(Chicago History Museum, ICHi-176511)

89 Washington. The shanty stood in the middle of the street for a week, by which time his lot was finally cool enough for him to move it within the property line. He raised the shanty off the ground, much like the O'Leary cottage, to keep it above the rubble, with access by a wooden ramp.

Kerfoot nailed a tongue-in-cheek sign on the building that christened the shanty the "Kerfoot Block" and declared it "First in the Burnt District." The rest of it conveyed a message very similar to the content of the ads he was running in the papers, which read:

W D. KERFOOT
Is at 59 Union Park Row
All gone but WIFE
CHILDREN and ENERGY

Schock, Bigford & Co. doing business in the ruins.
(Chicago History Museum, ICHi-068193)

Kerfoot's modest structure assumed a vital role in the reviving city. The exterior of its pine board walls served as a bulletin board for notices stating where fire-evicted businesses had relocated. General Philip H. Sheridan employed it as a headquarters of sorts for troops guarding this crucial area. It provided a reference point for giving directions, as the Courthouse had been before the fire.

By the middle of the week following the disaster, the *New-York Tribune* reported that photographers, "alarmed by the prospect of speedy reconstruction, are training their cameras upon every unprotected point of picturesque ruin." An anecdote published in several places told of a

Hand-painted wooden sign from the "Kerfoot Block"; 59 Union
Park Row was Kerfoot's temporary West Division address.
(Chicago History Museum, ICHi-064473)

The "Kerfoot Block" before being moved onto the lot at 89 Washington
Street. The hand-painted "All gone but wife children and energy" sign is
next to the window on the left. (Chicago History Museum, ICHi-026898)

man from East St. Louis, Illinois, who, upon hearing news of the fire, rushed to the railroad station. "I have to get to Chicago to-morrow on this train," he breathlessly explained, "or those people up there will have built up the whole d—d town again, and I won't see them ruins—!"

In late October the *Chicago Republican* estimated that there were ten thousand men working amid the South Division ruins. Shortly before that, the market in downtown real estate resumed. The first significant property exchange took place on October 19, ten days after the fire, when H. W. Hinsdale sold Thomas B. Bryan a forty-one-by-eighty-two-foot lot at the corner of Dearborn and Randolph, a block east of Courthouse Square, for $50,000. The land had been valued at $60,000 right before the city burned, but the seller had purchased it only a year earlier for $40,000, so he still made a 25 percent profit, in spite of the fire.

Bryan was owner of the Fidelity Safe Depository Company, which had protected the money and valuables of many Chicagoans during the inferno. He had built Bryan Hall on Clark Street, opposite the Courthouse, which was the city's premier entertainment venue until it was surpassed by Crosby's Opera House, and he founded Graceland Cemetery in Lake View, which became the fashionable final resting place for the city's most prominent families, including the Arnolds, the Dexters, the Fairbanks, the Fields, the Medills, the Palmers, the Pullmans, the Rumseys, and the Trees.

The same day Bryan made his purchase, architect John M. Van Osdel moved into an office in the lightly damaged Nixon Block at LaSalle and Monroe, where he worked on several commissions, including a new Tremont House hotel.

These were encouraging developments, but it would take time before business on any scale could resume in the former commercial center, where rebuilding could not begin until the ruins and rubble were removed. Knocking down walls and then lifting all the dead weight by hand into wagons and wheelbarrows to be carted away and unloaded elsewhere was a tedious and backbreaking job. Unlike stone, bricks could be reused.

There were other delaying factors. The loss of property records complicated negotiations between landowners; the price of materials and labor threatened to rise in response to the heightened demand; and a long, cold Chicago winter, during which major construction usually ceased, awaited. About half of the approximately $200 million in property loss

was insured (a higher percentage in the downtown), but payouts came
slowly and irregularly, if at all. Sixty-eight of the 201 companies insuring
Chicago property failed as a result of the fire. As a general rule, the farther
away one's insurer was located the more likely it was to be solvent enough
to honor a claim, and the richer one was the more likely one had insurance with a sound eastern US or British company. By 1872 less than
40 percent of the amount claimed had been disbursed.

The initial resumption of significant economic activity took place
outside the prefire downtown. Many businesses, among them most
newspapers and the Board of Trade, temporarily resettled in buildings
unhurt by the fire, just across the South Branch of the Chicago River in
the West Division. North Division German businessmen also relocated
in the West Division, but usually west of the North Branch rather than
the South. The *Staats-Zeitung* reported that grocer Henry Schollcroft
and musical instrument store Bauer and Company were among those
setting up shop on Milwaukee Avenue. "Germans don't take second
place after the Americans as to energy," the *Staats-Zeitung* boasted.
The West Division became a center of new construction, with 103 new
buildings by mid-December. The Lull & Holmes Planing mill, a casualty of the Saturday Night Fire, was running again.

Many small and large businesses, and a large number of professional
practices that had been burned out, resettled in the neighborhood below
the Burnt District in the South Division, where the mayor's office was
now located. The Chicago Relief and Aid Society moved into Standard
Hall at Michigan and Thirteenth. The post office reopened two weeks
after the fire in Burlington Hall, at State and Sixteenth Streets, before
moving on Christmas Day into the Wabash Avenue Methodist Church
on the northwest corner of Harrison and Wabash, very close to where
the fire ended in the South Division. The post office registry, cashier, and
distributing department took over the classrooms of the Sunday school.

In what John Hay labeled the "sudden confusion of quarters," homeowners in this heretofore largely residential district leased their houses
to commercial tenants. "The finest parlors on Wabash-ave. are for rent
to banker [*sic*] and Real Estate brokers, and the most exclusive families
find themselves living over shops," Hay reported. Surveyor Samuel Greeley rented the kitchen and laundry of a fashionable brick mansion.
Other churches besides Wabash Avenue Methodist became commercial
landlords, conducting their religious services elsewhere.

With a mix of mock and genuine disapproval, journalist W. A. Croffut, who in his career worked for papers in Minneapolis; New Haven, Connecticut; New York City; Rochester, New York; and Washington, DC, as well as the *Evening Post* in Chicago, derided this development as "the terrible descent of the barbarians upon our aristocratic thoroughfares." Among the barbarians were the aristocratic property owners themselves. "Many a man who has done a business of half a million a year," Croffut noted, "has invaded his own front parlor on the Avenue, has whisked the piano, the gorgeous sofas, the medallion carpet and the clock of *ormulu* into the capacious upper stories, and has sent his family to keep them company; while show-cases have been arrayed through drawing and dining rooms, and clerks now serve customers with hats, furs, shoes, or jewelry, where they formerly spooned water ices at an evening party."

There might be three or four businesses within one house—a shoe store in the basement, a button factory upstairs, lawyers and doctors seeing clients and patients in the bedrooms. All this moving around was a boon for one profession in particular. "Ever since the fire, Chicago has been the Mecca of sign-painters," Croffut observed, "and every man commanding a brush and paint-pot was sure of constant employment at high wages, whether he could spell or not."

The Burnt District was dotted with the wooden signs to which Croffut referred, which told where the firms previously located on this or that spot had gone. As soon as the newspapers reappeared, customers, clients, salesmen, and suppliers could find the latest information on new addresses in the classified listings or display advertisements. Henry King, president of the Relief and Aid Society, placed one of the biggest ads on the front page of the October 20 *Chicago Tribune*. "Notice!" it read; "Henry W. King & Co., Wholesale Clothing will resume business at Nos 28 and 30 Market-st. [Wacker Drive], next door to the drug house of Fuller & Fuller, within the next ten days, with as full a stock as before the fire." Hotels handed out cheap pocket directories with current addresses of local businesses. These booklets often contained a brief account of the disaster.

Jeweler John G. Ashleman prepared a form letter alerting customers to his new store on 10 Peck Court (Eighth Street). Despite his losses, he told them, he still had $10,000 worth of gold and silver chains, watch movements, and cases. He was leaving for New York very soon to restock, so they could look forward to excellent Christmas shopping. He politely requested that his clients "reserve their orders for me until my return."

During the fire, Field, Leiter & Company employees had removed an estimated $200,000 worth of the store's finest merchandise from the store. This was less than 10 percent of the value of its inventory. The company shipped the salvaged goods to a railroad roundhouse and paint shop in LaPorte, Indiana, about seventy miles southeast of Chicago. On November 6, less than a month after the fire and a brief three weeks after it signed a lease, Field, Leiter & Company reopened in a former streetcar and horse barn of the South Side Railroad. This was a two-story brick building with 130 feet of frontage on State Street and 150 feet on Twentieth, situated a little more than two miles south of the store's former and far more sumptuous home at State and Washington. Silks and laces were by the Twentieth Street entrance, gloves near the State Street door.

W. A. Croffut was astonished by the quick and nimble relocation, especially the total makeover of the building, in record time. "Here, where ready-made dresses hang," he wrote, "then hung sets of double-harness; yonder, where a richly-robed body leans languidly across the counter and fingers point-laces, a manger stood and offered hospitality to a disconsolate horse."

When members of the Board of Trade argued about where they might find a temporary home equal to the board's status as a major commodities exchange, William B. Ogden advised them to be humble and practical. There was no use in waiting for some palatial mansion to become available. For the time being, they "could work just as well in a shanty as in a marble house." He also told the doomsayers among the traders that they needed to put the current situation in historical perspective. Ogden recalled the grim conditions following the Panic of 1837, when it had been impossible to borrow money and real estate prices collapsed. By contrast, at present there was plenty of accessible investment cash in other financial centers and Chicago land would hold its value.

Ogden also warned his fellow traders against shortsighted selfishness and greed. "If we can only keep from being plundered by the jackals around us," he predicted à la John Stephen Wright, "five years hence will see scarcely a trace of the present desolation; ten years from now the place will be better off than a month ago, and fifteen years in the future our city will have a population of half a million." As it turned out, Ogden underestimated that number by 325,000.

With Holy Name Cathedral destroyed, Bishop Thomas Foley moved his pulpit to Holy Family, the church Father Arnold Damen had built on Twelfth Street (Roosevelt Road). Congregation Sinai, the first Reform synagogue in the city, founded in 1861, lost its building at Van Buren Street and Plymouth Court, near the current site of the Harold Washington Central Library. After the fire, the congregation rented a Presbyterian church and shared Zion Congregation's choir.

As activity picked up and the public mood became more buoyant, many Chicagoans were arguably participating in what has been called a disaster utopia, which sometimes follows cataclysmic events, especially those attributed to natural forces rather than clearly human-instigated violence like wars and riots. The first shock gives way to feelings of confidence and fellowship. "Our people began the week yesterday with more strength and greater hope," the *Republican* proclaimed on Tuesday, October 17. The next day the *Tribune* chimed in, "A week is enough time for Chicago to plume herself for a new flight."

The *Staats-Zeitung* maintained that the fire would solidify the city's German community. "Whatever existed before the ninth of October in the way of small frictions, cavils, and animosities among the Germans should be buried with so many other things under the giant heap of debris," it counseled.

Private citizens concurred. Aurelia King, spouse of Henry W. King, wrote near the end of her long postfire letter to friends, "We are all cheerful and hopeful. I have seen only one complainer and that was a millionaire." Anna Higginson observed, "Men are full of excitement now & hope." James Milner called the generally positive outlook "an honor to humanity." He was pleased that Chicagoans stood cool and cheerful without whining, demonstrating "a grand manliness of feeling that shows American character of the highest type." Like the recent war, the fire experience was an example of "individual character made deep and earnest by the experience of real trouble." This calamity, which had cut away "the froth and foam of vanity and ostentation," would make residents all the stronger.

Such positive feelings alternated with bouts of exhaustion and pessimism. Chicagoans would ride an emotional roller coaster for a long time. Landscape architect and cultural observer Frederick Law Olmsted visited the city a few weeks after the fire to report on it for the *Nation*. Olmsted noted that by the time he arrived, the period when people were "unreasonably cheerful and hopeful" had passed. "In its place there is sternness; but so narrow is the division between this and another mood, that in the midst of a sentence a change of quality in the voice occurs, and you see that eyes have moistened."

On Sunday, October 15, a week after the fire began, the Chicago Relief and Aid Society assumed control of contributions sent to help fire victims. Continuing the General Relief Committee's reliance on volunteer workers, it took over the task of assisting tens of thousands of people a day. John J. Healy's family received bread and meat on a street corner in the burned-out North Division from a wagon that Field, Leiter & Company had loaned to the relief effort. Fanny Boggs Lester's mother handed out food and clothing for many weeks in the Baptist church two doors away from the Lester home.

The Relief and Aid Society later explained that it first gave out food "indiscriminately, and in uncertain quantities, for want of conveniences in measuring and weighing." As soon as it could, however, the society switched to a system of standardized allotments, first what it calculated as enough for two or three days, then for a week, and moved from an emphasis on prepared foods such as bread to cheaper raw ingredients like flour. Its staff calculated precisely what they believed recipients needed and what it cost to provide it to them. They determined that a week's rations for a family of two adults and three children consisted of

    3 pounds pork, at 5 ½ cents
    6 pounds [preserved] beef, at 5 cents
    14 pounds flour, at 3 cents
    1 ¼ peck potatoes, at 20 cents
    ¼ pound tea, at 80 cents
    1 ½ pounds sugar, at 11 cents
    1 ¼ pounds rice, at 8 cents; or 3 ½ pounds beans at 3 ¾ cents

1 ¼ pounds soap, at 7 cents
1 ½ pounds dried apples, at 8 cents
3 pounds fresh beef, at 5 cents
Total $1.98

Substituting bread for flour added forty-two cents, while giving out coffee instead of tea cost an extra seventeen cents.

The relief received as much attention near and far as the disaster that prompted it. Illustrations in the national newsweeklies showed well-dressed upper-class women like Fanny Boggs Lester's mother fitting grateful women and children with clothing.

For all the good work it undoubtedly did, however, the Relief and Aid Society continued to base its policies and procedures more on suspicion of the needy than on either timeless sympathy or the modern "scientific" approach it claimed to be following. The society viewed assisting the bereft not as an end in itself but as a means of reconstructing Chicago, which it insisted must be accomplished according to the vision of its elite leadership. Society Executive Committee chair Wirt Dexter said that his organization would "help men and women to help themselves," but it would "check any attempt at roguery on the part of applicants for aid." The administration of relief was "a matter of business, and not [of] maudlin, wishy-washy sentiment, and rascals have no mercy shown them."

To enforce this policy, the society applied its prefire screening methods to an immensely larger and far more varied clientele. Applicants needed to fill out forms detailing their property, losses, and present financial condition. They were required to provide written references from the kind of people the society considered trustworthy, such as pastors of churches and officers of other benevolent associations in Chicago. Finally, they had to pass inspection by a Relief and Aid Society visitor. Only then might they receive help.

The class and ethnic assumptions of the Relief and Aid Society's leaders undermined its claims of objectivity. For homeless Chicagoans with the lowest income, property, and skills, the society provided housing in one of four clusters of barracks erected immediately after the fire, two in the North Division and two in the West. Together these housed about a thousand families. Each family received two rooms furnished with a stove, utensils, chairs, table, crockery, beds, and bedding. The

The Chicago Fire—Ladies Distributing Clothing to Sufferers of Both
Sexes. *From* Frank Leslie's Illustrated Newspaper, *November 4, 1871.*
(Chicago History Museum, ICHi-002894)

organization claimed that this housing was at least as good as what the
occupants had known before the fire.

Insulting as such assertions were, these buildings were the best
alternative available to those who would otherwise be homeless. A
large family might find the quarters very tight, but some enjoyed living there, at least in good weather. Mary Kehoe wrote favorably to a
friend of her new kitchen stove and the daily food delivery. "Good
times," she said of life in the barracks, "so we were [not] the worse
for our awful experience."

The barracks had significant shortcomings, even in the opinion of
the society. The buildings were a potential breeding ground for commu-
nicable illnesses. For this reason, the society explained, "The barracks
were subject to a careful daily inspection by sanitary officers, and regulations best calculated to maintain health were rigidly enforced." Given
its low opinion of most of the city's poor, the society also worried that

the barracks might encourage the spread of maladies of character that were harder to root out—notably, "idleness, disorder, and vice."

The barracks constructed in Washington Square Park raised a different set of class concerns because they put a very small group of rich people in an "involuntary association" of sorts with the much less fortunate. This group of several cheap and quickly made long one-story buildings could not contrast more with the only residence within sight to have survived the fire, the handsome Mahlon Ogden mansion directly across the street.

In the Ogdens' defense, they shared their good luck by accommodating a few dozen burned-out friends. But these were other well-to-do people whose temporary quarters with the Ogdens, while far more crowded than what they had known, were worlds more comfortable and congenial than the barracks. The Ogden guests also expected that they would soon find good quarters to rent or purchase, while the barracks dwellers had little idea what the future held.

To those in the city's upper social circles, the Ogdens and their boarders were the ones to be pitied. "I think Mrs. O. feels worse, living in her elegant, untouched house, than we do who are altogether homeless," Anna Higginson confided to her friend Elizabeth Skinner. "I do not wonder at it, as they live in fear of their lives, with their house watched day & night by policemen."

Illinois Staats-Zeitung editor Hermann Raster complained in print to General Sheridan that the current use of the Ogden mansion was a waste of a precious resource. Raster demanded that Sheridan "should now in Heaven's name take possession of Ogden's house in which 300 shelterless could be put up." This step would correct "the partiality of providence," as he put the building's escape from the flames. Otherwise, "the conviction will become general that the rich Yankeedom wants to reconstruct Chicago as a Yankee city, at the cost of the poor Germans and Scandinavians."

Raster hinted that "Mrs. O," as he acerbically referred to Ogden's wife, had good reason to worry, and in so doing he dangled the fears of the Yankee elite in their faces: "How if one of these unfortunates, with the idea of compensating an injustice of fate, were to put the burning torch to the millionaire Ogden's house?" If Sheridan seized the house and opened it to working people, this would demonstrate the compassion of the rich for the poor far more than all the lip service about sympathy.

When it came to distributing food, the society's Executive Committee again put its preconceptions about recipients ahead of their actual needs. Idleness struck its leaders as a greater danger than hunger since they believed it encouraged bad and even criminal behavior among the poor while depriving Chicago employers of cheap labor in a time when there was so much that needed to be done. As before the fire, the society linked its food distribution policies to a strict work program, though no donor had specified this condition.

The society set up a labor exchange near the ruins of the Courthouse through which it matched jobless individuals with openings on offer. If someone currently receiving aid from the society did not accept an available position, its staff could decide to suspend food delivery. On October 24, barely two weeks after the fire, Relief and Aid Society general superintendent O. C. Gibbs issued a memo to the organization's superintendents, assistants, and visitors. In it he made the questionable assertion that any able-bodied man, boy, or single woman who was still unemployed "is so from choice and not from necessity" and so should be denied assistance. People with jobs, however, could receive essential food, fuel, clothing, bedding, and furniture that their new salary could not cover, so that the society would in effect be subsidizing those who paid low wages and thus keeping those wages down.

The Relief and Aid Society treated trade craftsmen, who were indispensable to the city's rebuilding, more generously than it did the unskilled. It expressed concern about placing "the better class of laboring people," who were "thrifty, domestic, and respectable," in debilitating proximity to the barracks residents. If these people were able to move back into a home of their own on their own land, the society reasoned, this would raise their spirits and their property's value, providing "all the incentives to industry" on which Chicago's future depended.

The society devised a plan for the many members of this "better class" who owned lots but could not currently afford to rebuild the houses they lost in the fire. The Shelter Committee, chaired by lumber tycoons T. M. Avery and Turlington Harvey, supported the construction of two sizes of temporary shelter homes. This initiative began a week after the fire. The smaller model, intended for three or fewer people, was twelve by sixteen feet. The larger, for four or more inhabitants, was commonly sixteen by twenty feet. Lot owners received plans, framing lumber, boards, felt paper, windows, doors, and an iron chimney pipe.

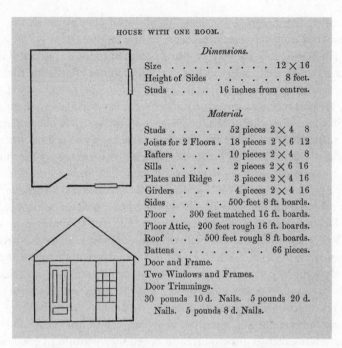

HOUSE WITH ONE ROOM.

Dimensions.

Size . . . . 12 × 16
Height of Sides . . . . . . 8 feet.
Studs . . . . 16 inches from centres.

Material.

Studs . . . . . 52 pieces 2 × 4 8
Joists for 2 Floors . 18 pieces 2 × 6 12
Rafters . . . . 10 pieces 2 × 4 8
Sills . . . . . 2 pieces 2 × 6 16
Plates and Ridge . 3 pieces 2 × 4 16
Girders . . . . 4 pieces 2 × 4 16
Sides . . . . . 500 feet 8 ft. boards.
Floor . 300 feet matched 16 ft. boards.
Floor Attic, 200 feet rough 16 ft. boards.
Roof . . . 500 feet rough 8 ft. boards.
Battens . . . . 66 pieces.
Door and Frame.
Two Windows and Frames.
Door Trimmings.
30 pounds 10 d. Nails. 5 pounds 20 d.
Nails. 5 pounds 8 d. Nails.

House with One Room. *From Chicago Relief and Aid Society,* Report of the Chicago Relief and Aid Society, 1874. *(Chicago History Museum, ICHi-063835)*

The estimated cost, including the same minimal furnishings as in the barracks, was around $125. The society evidently did not press recipients on covering this expense. The Shelter Committee assumed skilled workers could erect these structures themselves or easily find someone to do so. It arranged to have them built for widowed, aged, or infirm people who had a spot on which to put them.

The family of young John A. Healy lived in one of these shelter homes. His father built it in the rear of his North Division lot, planning to put up a sturdier house in front as soon as he could afford to do so. Healy remembered that the stove was set in a box with sand on its bottom to keep the very flammable building from catching fire. Another beneficiary was Patrick Webb, whose tiny patch of real estate was the only thing his family owned that had not burned. He had purchased fire insurance, but it proved worthless. Webb called his family's shelter cottage a "hut," which conveys his sense of how minimal it was.

The Relief and Aid Society also designated funds to replace skilled workers' tools that had been lost in the fire, in the knowledge that the expertise of carpenters, masons, tinners, bookbinders, locksmiths, tailors, shoemakers, and mechanics was otherwise worthless to them and to Chicago. The society similarly assisted professionals like engineers and surgeons in obtaining the instruments necessary to resume work. It provided women, especially seamstresses, with Singer sewing machines, which the manufacturer offered at a discount. Sometimes the workers paid a portion of the price, but always the purpose was "to relieve him [or her] from the necessity of any further application for assistance."

This program was administered by the society's Committee on Special Relief. In another area of its work, this committee extended help in inverse proportion to need. It singled out for preferential treatment previously wealthy people who were now "suddenly reduced to conditions of the greatest privation and distress." The rationale was that since they had fallen so much further than the burned-out poor, they were "the keenest sufferers of all." Far from being suspicious, the Relief and Aid Society was eager to dispense what it called the "warmth of good-will" to such victims, certain that they were not the kind of people to resort to imposition.

A sister organization, the Ladies' Relief Society, went an additional step. Founded on October 19 at a gathering in the home of Wirt Dexter and his wife Josephine, the Ladies' Relief Society proactively sought out those "who shrink from making their wants publicly known even to the Bureau of Special Relief," so that they could be helped as quickly and "delicately" as possible.

Prosperous Chicagoans were not above criticizing acquaintances who accepted alms. Just short of two weeks after the fire, city engineer Ellis Chesbrough, who had planned Chicago's current waterworks (and, a few years earlier, its first sewer system), wrote to his son at Harvard University to request that the young man cut down on his expenses, though there was no need for him to move to cheaper housing in Cambridge, Massachusetts. Chesbrough mentioned family acquaintances who had asked the Relief and Aid Society for clothing, expressing regret that in some cases "respectable people have gone for aid, who ought to have waited a little while for their friends to come forward."

Wealthy people taking public assistance invited gossip. "You may imagine how I felt on meeting Mrs. Arnold coming from the Relief Society with a bundle of clothing for Mr. [Isaac N.] Arnold," Anna Higginson confided to Elizabeth Skinner. Higginson added that she thought Harriet Arnold seemed to feel uplifted by the necessity, "appearing somewhat in the character of a martyr." Higginson said that when a minister at St. James Episcopal Church spotted Arnold with her bundle of charity clothing, he seized her hands and exclaimed, "You noble woman." Arnold seemed anything but embarrassed. "I am sure she felt abundantly repaid for all she had undergone," Higginson commented sharply.

The Chicago Relief and Aid Society allotted cash to designated charitable institutions, particularly orphan asylums and homes for those unable to care for themselves. It also managed the $50,000 fund endowed by New York department store magnate A. T. Stewart for the specific benefit of working women—domestics, seamstresses, saleswomen, bookbinders, milliners, and office workers—who normally supported themselves, as well as poor widows and children. Before the fire, Field, Leiter & Company employed about 230 women who sewed ready-to-wear clothing, mainly in their own homes. The company rehired most of them afterward, but many Chicago women had difficulty getting any work at all, let alone at prefire wages.

Though the Relief and Aid Society was the designated distributor of the contributions given to the city generally, there was nothing to prevent dozens of other organizations from assisting fire victims with resources they raised or that had been donated to them. Members of religious, trade, and ethnic groups, such as the United Hebrew Relief Association, the National Typographical Union, and numerous German groups targeted their own people among the fire victims. They dispensed assistance without the hurdles, forms, and suspicion that characterized the society's procedures. A few organizations, however, were as interested as the Relief and Aid Society in maintaining the current social order as in helping others, if by a different route. Presbyterian minister Robert Patterson said of the Ladies' Christian Union, "If they were to succeed in keeping down the revolutionary spirit in this city, it could be done only by kindness."

The society's imperious exercise of its authority in the distribution of resources drew multiple criticisms. Common Council members demanded that the city have more control of relief funds, as the society originally stated it would, charging that Dexter and his Executive Committee ignored the informed advice of aldermen. At the Common Council meeting on October 26, North Division alderman John Buehler protested that there were too few distribution points. Others cited instances in which "incompetency was exhibited to a marked degree." Deserving people frequently did not get relief; some of those who did receive provisions found it "of a character unfit for food."

The *Illinois Staats-Zeitung* complained repeatedly about the "small consideration" the Relief and Aid Society granted to Chicago's Germans, who made up both the city's largest ethnic group and, since so many of them lived in the devastated North Division, the portion of the population that the fire injured most. It charged that the society stuck to its narrow prejudices even in the face of broad need. The *Staats-Zeitung* noted that the requirement of references from clergy was discriminatory because many Germans did not belong to any religious congregation, and that the society provided no translators for non-English speakers.

Perhaps most telling were criticisms of the Chicago Relief and Aid Society from members of the same elite as its Executive Committee—notably, a few well-to-do native-born women. They objected to the policies of the male-run organization, which included ignoring the wants and opinions of female Chicagoans. These women spoke from personal experience ministering to fire sufferers.

A handful who had the means to do so started their own female-led assistance initiatives. Annie McClure Hitchcock, who lived south of Chicago in Hyde Park, joined with none other than Joseph Medill's wife, Katherine, in distributing goods from the Medills' West Division home. Hitchcock told a friend in Boston that the Relief and Aid Society's rules were "so hard to follow." She asked the friend to send donations directly to Hitchcock and Medill's group. "It would be such a comfort if some Boston ladies felt like sending some boxes of clothing to be distributed in violation of all general rules."

Even Aurelia King, whose husband Henry was president of the Relief and Aid Society, was more than ready to circumvent the society's policies. She advised Elizabeth Skinner that wealthy women would do better "to send their supplies where they would reach some of the sufferers directly." King explained that in so large an undertaking as the Relief

and Aid Society's current work, "there must of course be some donations misapplied." She divulged that even her husband agreed with her.

The attempt to preserve safety by imposing extralegal martial law
brought its own deadly violence. General Sheridan's authority over postfire Chicago was always expected to be much briefer than that of the
Relief and Aid Society, but no one anticipated that it would end in a
tragedy of errors and a morass of recriminations.

On the evening of Friday, October 20, prosecuting attorney and dec-
orated Civil War officer Thomas Grosvenor—whom Sheridan later
singled out as one of the Chicagoans who wanted him to lead the protection of the postfire city—enjoyed dinner with a friend. It seems likely
that there was plenty to drink. Afterward Grosvenor boarded a streetcar toward his home at the southern edge of the city, near the University
of Chicago. He stepped off at Cottage Grove Avenue, which was de-
serted under a bright midnight moon. As he passed the university cam-
pus, about two blocks from his residence, Grosvenor was confronted
by twenty-year-old undergraduate Theodore Treat of Janesville, Wisconsin, who had joined the University Cadets, one of the militias under
Sheridan's command. Treat, armed with a musket, had never loaded or
fired a gun before he volunteered for the Guards.

When Treat demanded that Grosvenor halt, Grosvenor testily refused. When he ignored a second order to stop, Treat shot him. The
bullet passed through Grosvenor's left arm, shattered his tenth rib, and
penetrated his diaphragm, stomach, and liver. Crying out, "O! God, O
God! My wife my wife!" Grosvenor crumbled to the sidewalk, his blood
pooling around him.

He struggled to his feet and lunged a few steps toward home before
collapsing. He got up, only to drop again. Grosvenor rose and managed
a few more steps before crumpling a final time. Firemen in a nearby station who heard his cries carried him first to the station and then home,
where he lay in agony for several hours. Grosvenor died just before
dawn.

The police arrested Treat, who told reporters that Grosvenor had
barely paused even when Treat cocked his rifle. "He told me to go to h—l,

and to bang away," Treat contended. "I let him go some distance, and, remembering that I was under orders, and liable to be court-martialed and punished for disobedience of orders, I thought I was bound to fire." Treat said he had no idea that Grosvenor was an important person. "I did not know but he was a rough," he explained. "It was dark, and I could not exactly see what sort of a looking man he was in the face."

Fearing that Grosvenor was armed (which he was, though he did not draw his revolver) and "playing possum," Treat did not attend to Grosvenor but left to report the incident to his sergeant. "I did not realize that I had shot him," he claimed, "because I did not think I could, knowing nothing at all about firearms."

Grosvenor's killing became the flashpoint for a verbal brawl in which principles and politics were indistinguishable. Outraged by the killing, Illinois governor John Palmer claimed that he assumed the general would exercise limited powers and only for a few days. At stake, to his mind, were states' rights and civilian authority. If the city of Chicago needed extra protection, as governor of Illinois he was the only one empowered to provide it.

Palmer contended he did not hear of the mayor's proclamation entrusting the city to a mixed military police force under a US Army officer until October 17, almost a week after he was briefly in Chicago. He would never have agreed to this since it would have been a violation of both his duty and self-respect. He thought Sheridan would briefly help out, not take over. As for the militiamen Sheridan assembled, he thought they would be experienced local veterans willing to serve for a few days, "old soldiers" rather than college students.

Palmer did not explain why he waited two more days after he learned all this to wire his objections to Mayor Mason, or why his one-line message at that time did not speak to constitutional principles but only asked what additional help Mason needed once the federal troops were gone. Mason responded immediately but evaded the issues Palmer raised, saying only that within ten to fifteen days no supplemental force, federal or otherwise, would be necessary. During the day of October 20, a few hours before Treat shot Grosvenor, Palmer wrote a long letter to Mason criticizing him for abandoning his mayoral duty and demanding he dismiss Sheridan. The presence of the US Army was "in violation of law."

Mason defended his actions, stating that "the emergency required me to take the step that I did." He did not try to rationalize the appointment of Sheridan on legal grounds, insisting that as mayor his primary goal was to protect Chicago when the lives and property of so many people were in such peril. This worthy end justified the otherwise questionable means. Palmer admitted that the circumstances under which Mason acted were exceptionally difficult, and that Sheridan deserved thanks. Still, he argued in the October 20 letter, it was very regrettable that Mason did not call on the legitimate power of the governor and the state rather than submit Chicago to unlawful military control. In any event, there was no longer any reason, "either real or imaginary," to continue "this anomalous state of things."

Mason afterward stated that even before receiving Palmer's letter he was preparing to dismiss the troops. Not until October 22, however, the day after Grosvenor died, did he ask Sheridan's opinion on when a military presence would no longer be needed. Sheridan replied on October 23 that it was time to discharge the volunteers and end his command. The next day the First Regiment was mustered out of service and the federal troops sent back to the bases where they had been stationed.

Governor Palmer may have had mixed motives in criticizing Sheridan's temporary assumption of power. On one hand, he sincerely believed in states' rights. In his inaugural address in 1869, he said that with the Civil War concluded public welfare demanded "recurrence to the true principles that underlie our system of government," of which one of the most firmly established was that "the federal government is one of enumerated and limited powers."

On the other, he harbored a dislike of Sheridan dating back to the war, in which he, too, had been a general. Unlike Sheridan, Palmer neither attended West Point nor intended to become a soldier until hostilities began. Like many Union officers who left civilian life to fight, Palmer was wary of career military men holding public office, as he knew they were of nonprofessional soldiers like him in command of troops. Taken as a class, Palmer wrote in his memoirs, "they are profligate and reckless and profoundly ignorant of everything outside their own profession."

Sheridan continued to serve the bidding of the city's top businessmen even after his brief command was over and in spite of Palmer's objections. On October 29 he told army adjutant general E. D. Townsend that as soon as the troops were gone "the turbulent spirit commenced to manifest itself, and seems to be increasing." His use of "seems to be" suggests that this increase was open to doubt, if not in the minds of the unnamed "prominent citizens" who wanted him to bring four companies of infantry back for the winter. Sheridan was now more willing to do the bidding of these people than he had been right after the fire. "I am satisfied of the necessity of their [i.e., regular army soldiers'] presence here," he told Townsend. The request was approved by Sheridan's fellow war hero, General William Tecumseh Sherman, now the commander of the US Army.

Sherman sent to Chicago soldiers from the Eighth Infantry, currently based in Philadelphia. Sheridan had them make camp just south of the city, near the Union Stock Yards, so they would be right at hand if needed. They never were.

In his final report to Secretary of War W. W. Belknap on the matter, in which he specified that Colonel Grosvenor had been among those who, right after the fire, entreated him to take charge of keeping order in Chicago, Sheridan maintained that he "never for one moment thought of infringing or abrogating any of the civil laws," only of helping out after "an unparalleled calamity." Sheridan's contempt for his critics is hard to miss. If Palmer, whom he called "His Excellency Governor Palmer," had offered some better ideas at the time, the general would have followed these "wise suggestions."

As for himself, Sheridan stated, "I was as pure in my motives as are those of the whole world who are now sending their charities here to relieve the distressed."

11

THE TRIUMPH OF THE FIRE-PROOF TICKET

The ability of Chicago's business and professional elite to convince Mayor Roswell B. Mason to place the safety of the city in Philip H. Sheridan's hands and the world's charity in the care of the Chicago Relief and Aid Society was impressive. Neither of these steps gave these men control of local government, however. In the 1869 election they had successfully backed Mason for mayor on the Citizens Party ticket, though in their opinion the Common Council remained thoroughly corrupt.

Several past and current aldermen were willing to sell their votes and help arrange questionable deals—notably property transactions and contracts involving the city. But sometimes the most serious flaw of this or that alderman in the eyes of a Joseph Medill or a Wirt Dexter, who were anything but above politics, was not that he was for sale but that he did not vote their way.

The same elite thought it especially opportune that the next municipal election was coming up on Tuesday, November 7, a month after the fire. This was soon enough to invoke the catastrophe in demanding reform while affording sufficient time to strategize how best to be rid of the "professional thieves and jobbers" on the Common Council. In selecting candidates for mayor and aldermen, they knew they would need the support of a substantial number of the immigrants and workers who constituted a majority of the electorate.

Mason himself gave no public indication that he wanted to run again, nor did he enjoy wide and enthusiastic support to do so. Those who had backed his candidacy two years earlier said little to encourage him. He faced daily criticism and ridicule from Wilbur Storey's *Chicago Times* for his handling of the fire and especially for the appointment of Sheridan. The presence of federal troops in Chicago under the command of a Union hero reawakened Storey's opposition to the war. Although his paper stirred up fears of lethally armed radical conspirators on the loose in Chicago by publishing the alleged Communard's "confession," it excoriated Mason for taking measures commensurate with such a threat when he appointed Sheridan. The mayor, whom the *Chicago Times* called "Granny Mason," was "an old idiot" who abdicated his office by elevating the general to the level of "an imperial satrap."

As for the University Cadets to which Theodore Treat belonged, the *Times* said that a more fitting name for them was "University Assassins." The paper, which condemned the army's enforcement of Reconstruction in the former Confederacy as a "reign of terror" and sympathized with Southerners who resisted it, now compared the "military usurpation in Chicago" to that "in the Ku Klux districts of the south."

On October 20—coincidentally the same day that Treat killed attorney Thomas Grosvenor—the *Times* proposed William B. Ogden to succeed Mason. The idea possessed a powerful nostalgic appeal. Since Ogden could claim to be the most dynamic figure in the building of the city, he could be seen as the best person to rebuild it.

There is no evidence that Ogden wanted the job. He was sixty-six years old and living in New York, though he still kept his home in Chicago (which had been burned in the fire) and voted there. He needed to husband his energies to face the major blows he had suffered to his holdings in Chicago and Peshtigo, Wisconsin, at a time of life when he thought he would be taking his ease.

The *Chicago Tribune* countered by recommending banker Henry Greenebaum, who had been born in 1833 in the town of Eppelsheim, Germany, and come to the United States with his family in the 1848 cohort of refugees. A small man with a widow's peak and a full dark mustache, Greenebaum was highly respected by both the city's predominantly native-born bankers and its German immigrants. His civic credentials were impeccable. He had been elected the city's first Jewish alderman, and he devoted himself to many cultural and philanthropic organizations within the Reform Jewish community and beyond, from the United Hebrew Relief Association to the Chicago Historical Society. A resident of the West Side, Greenebaum served with Charles C. P. Holden on the division's park commission. His "well developed form, though *petite*," gushed the editors of *Sketches of the Leading Men of Chicago* in 1868, "incloses [*sic*] as big a heart and soul as we often find in a mortal frame."

Henry Greenebaum.
(Chicago History Museum, ICHi-176510)

The *Tribune*'s forwarding of Greenebaum's name seemed compelling for several reasons. He had always put principle above party. Once a Democrat supporting Stephen Douglas, he had become a Republican backing Abraham Lincoln upon the outbreak of the Civil War. Greenebaum had energetically recruited and generously equipped Union troops, notably the Eighty-Second Illinois Infantry regiment, in whose ranks were a large number of immigrants, and Jews in particular. He had already thrown himself into the postfire recovery, using his position as the Chicago banker with the best connections in Europe to encourage financiers on the Continent to put their money behind Chicago's future. As a German immigrant, he could expect the support of that substantial bloc, including editor Herman Raster of the *Illinois Staats-Zeitung*. As for whether Greenebaum might be too foreign, the *Tribune* pointed out that he had resided in Chicago longer than 95 percent of its native-born population, who had either come to the city or were born there after he arrived.

This idea went nowhere. Medill and the *Tribune*, either knowing that Greenebaum would not run or that he would not gain wide and enthusiastic support—the *Times* opposed his possible candidacy—may have used him as a decoy.

At a meeting of Republicans on October 23, Medill made another proposal, this one about the ticket as a whole. He recommended that Chicagoans who wanted honest and capable government should, as in 1869, nominate a list of candidates to a slate consisting of men of unquestionable ability and integrity without regard to their party affiliation. In all senses of the word, he argued, this was just the ticket to steer Chicago to full recovery. The spotless reputations of these paragons would not only attract votes but also encourage investors elsewhere to fund Chicago's recovery.

Not surprisingly, Medill's paper enthusiastically endorsed the idea. By the next day, other Republicans expressed their agreement. For the moment, Chicago's Democrats held back, suspecting they would not be offered a satisfactory share of power. A few days of additional discussion among members of both parties produced a consensus on a combined slate, with none other than Joseph Medill as its mayoral candidate. They cleverly named themselves the Fire-Proof Party. Even the *Times* assented. The once and future virulent foe of the *Tribune* and its leadership now proclaimed that Medill was "a citizen of sterling character, excellent good sense, and unquestionable integrity."

Besides Medill, the Fire-Proofers nominated former mayor Julian Rumsey for Cook County treasurer, Lambert Tree (a Democrat) for circuit court judge, Jacob Rehm for police superintendent, and David A. Gage for city treasurer. Rehm, who was twelve when he arrived from Alsace-Lorraine, had divided his career between the police department and the brewery business. New Hampshire native Gage, with his brother George and John B. Drake, had run the Tremont House hotel. The party slated William B. Ogden's brother Mahlon for alderman from the North Division's Nineteenth Ward, of which he was the lone legal resident currently able to live in his own home.

While its ostensible purpose was to rise above existing divisions, the creation of the Fire-Proof Party instead highlighted them. This may have been its organizers' unstated intention. The supposed unity gambit split political Chicago all the more clearly into an "us" against "them," the men of supposed capability and character versus the conniving hacks whose only skill was lining their pockets. It could not help but rankle those excluded from the righteous chosen—not just Nineteenth Ward alderman James McCauley and his allies, known as McCauley's Nine-teen, but also politically active Chicago businessmen of as sound reputation as those on the Fire-Proof ticket.

The Republicans and Democrats on the outs responded by forming their own coalition. Their mayoral candidate of what they called the People's Union slate was alderman and Common Council president Charles C. P. Holden, whose qualifications were as good as or better than anyone's on the Fire-Proof ticket.

As was true of most elections in this period, the two-week campaign consisted of heavy helpings of name-calling, mudslinging, and unsubstantiated accusations, with the daily newspapers full-throated partisans, savaging each other as caustically as they did opposition candidates. Led by the *Tribune* and the *Times*, supporters of Medill and his slate accused Holden—now suddenly "Boss" Holden—and his "sorehead" adherents of plotting a Chicago Tammany. It escaped no one's attention that New York's William M. "Boss" Tweed was arrested for corruption on October 27, less than two weeks before election day in Chicago. While conceding that Holden was not exactly a crooked "bummer" politician himself, these newspapers condemned him for the sordid company they said he was now keeping. The *Tribune* jumped on his profusion of initials to brand him "Chief Caucus Packer" Holden.

Three days before the election, backed by a statement from Wirt Dexter, Medill's paper falsely accused Holden of withholding cash during the transfer of contributions from the General Relief Committee to the Chicago Relief and Aid Society. He had supposedly pocketed $15,000 in relief contributions after Dexter and other Relief and Aid Society leaders rejected his demand that some members of the society's board resign their roles in the administration of the relief in favor of aldermen. The society had in fact pledged to give aldermen a significant say when it took over the relief funds, but it had never followed through. It now accused Holden of compounding his sins by asking reimbursement for bloated carriage bills incurred during the brief life of the Relief Committee, when, it charged, he rode about the stricken city in luxury as widows and orphans went cold and hungry.

Some of the wealthiest and most influential Chicagoans thus portrayed themselves as indignant, honest citizens who took it as their duty to wrest control of the city from the selfish and corrupt. This was in spite of the fact that they were the ultimate insiders everywhere that mattered except the Common Council. To fail to elect the Fire-Proof candidates, the *Tribune* warned six days before the election, "would be to advertise that Chicago is not worthy of the charity or the confidence that has been bestowed upon her, and to stop both the supplies contributed for the relief of the destitute, and the influx of capital to rebuild the city"—that is, the projects in which affluent Chicago businessmen were heavily invested.

Holden's strongest advocate among local newspapers was the *Chicago Republican*, which had less than half the readership of the *Times* or *Tribune* and was struggling to survive. The *Republican*'s opposition to the Fire-Proof ticket was based less on enthusiasm for Holden than the long-standing antipathy of its leadership toward Medill and to the *Tribune*'s opposition to some national Republican Party policies. It now spoke as if it were the true champion of democracy and of the mass of working people in the city, whom it did not particularly like and who did not read it. Holden, it contended, was the choice of an openly constituted group of "wide awake" men, as opposed to the "Star Chamber" Fire-Proofers who nominated candidates that represented wealth and privilege. Medill and his running mates, not Holden and his slate, were the actual corrupt bummer politicians since they were bent on a wholesale hijacking of the public good for their own selfish interests.

"Let every laboring man remember that Mr. Joseph Medill has always been, and still is, in favor of reducing the rate of wages to every man employed by the city," the *Republican* warned. The Fire-Proofers were "an unscrupulous clique of designing men." The Executive Committee of the Relief and Aid Society, Medill supporters to a man, had their hands "deep into the relief fund," which they had ripped away from honest public servants like Holden. In response to the accusations of malfeasance aimed at Holden published in the *Tribune*, the *Republican* leveled the equally spurious charge that the Relief and Aid Society had diverted $20,000 that donors intended for fire victims to the election of "Joe Medill and his gang." The supposedly "eminent and respectable" Wirt Dexter was guilty of "the venal sin of heavy lying."

Three weeks before the election, the *Times* warned that the greatest danger to the city was that in the upcoming election "the good citizens"— that is, well-to-do members of the native-born population—would be so preoccupied with getting their personal affairs back in order that they would not take time to vote for candidates who would oust the crooks from office. On the morning of election day, the *Tribune* reminded its readers of how less than two months earlier, with Chicago in ruins, stalwart citizens like themselves had joined special police patrols to defend their city against "villains and cutthroats."

This very moment, the *Tribune* advised, a far worse threat was at hand in the form of the Holden ticket. Chicagoans no longer needed to stand a post with musket in hand but instead faced a no less critical duty, "a day's faithful service at the polls." The demagogues and scalawags had no chance of winning "*if business men will only turn out and get their friends out.*" And once businessmen did cast their votes, they needed to stick around the polling places to make sure the bummers did not pull any dirty tricks.

The *Tribune* instructed wives to get their menfolk in line. On the morning of election day, it told them to remind their husbands to vote on their way to their offices. When the man of the house came home for his midday meal, his wife should "put the question direct, 'Sir have you voted?'" If he said no, she must make him promise to do so on his way back to work. "Deal with him kindly but firmly," the paper counseled. And if her spouse ran a business that employed others, "use your influence to have them vote, and vote the right ticket."

Conducting an election in a city that had just suffered a major fire and in which virtually all government buildings and records had been lost was a challenging exercise. Chicagoans normally voted near where they lived, but in one-third of the city both the residences and polling places were gone. With registration records now in ashes, election judges could not readily certify any voter even if he lived outside the Burnt District.

Chicago Corporation counsel Murray F. Tuley ruled that fire-evicted citizens should vote in the same precincts where they had lived, even if little was currently standing. To make this possible, the city erected sheds like the "Kerfoot Block" to serve as polling places. In the absence of records, Tuley told voters to be able to produce trusted acquaintances who could vouch for them, much as if they were applying for aid from the Chicago Relief and Aid Society. Both sides posted loyalists to certify supporters and to monitor fraud by the other side. Mason called for a suspension of business on election day so that people could focus on voting. He also told them to obey the law stating that no liquor could be sold or given away during the voting. Chicagoans apparently heeded neither recommendation.

Arguably the biggest difference between the election that took place on Tuesday, November 7, and a normal one was how dull it was, especially in light of the intensity of the campaign. "Every man deposited his vote quietly and then walked away, about his business," observed the *Times*. "There was none of that thronging together and lingering about the polls, which has been common." The fire suppressed the overall turnout. The total of 22,113 votes cast was more than ten thousand fewer than in the mayoral contest of two years earlier.

Be that as it may, the outcome was decisive. Medill crushed Holden, 16,125 votes to 5,988, a majority of almost 73 percent. Six of the twenty aldermanic candidates on Holden's ticket were victorious, but otherwise it was a rout for the Fire-Proof Party. James McCauley was one of the victims. "CHICAGO HAS INDEED RISEN FROM HER ASHES," the *Tribune* shouted in triumph. The *Republican* called the election "Chicago's Darkest Day," grousing about crooked judges, roughs, and shysters intimidating Holden supporters, and it suggested that foremen in the factories and railroad machine shops accepted bribes to prevent workers from getting to the polls. In a phrase that would be familiar to observers of Chicago elections in the next century, the *Republican* spoke of repeat voters hired by Medill backers to head to the polls "early and often."

Medill and his allies had played their cards well, especially in getting Storey's support and floating Greenebaum's name, which helped win over the *Illinois Staats-Zeitung* and a large portion of the German vote. Anton Hesing, the paper's owner, returned to Chicago on the eve of election day following a year-and-a-half trip to Europe. Hesing, born in the Grand Duchy of Oldenburg forty-eight years earlier, was also a powerful political figure—he was sometimes referred to as "Boss" Hesing—insofar as German-born voters were concerned. After taking in the ruins, he visited Fire-Proof Party headquarters in the West Division, where he was greeted warmly and urged to speak at a preelection rally. In his remarks Hesing said that when he passed through New York on his way back, his creditors urged him to throw his weight behind the Fire-Proof candidates. Medill enjoyed "an enviable national reputation" that would bring the city the continuing financial support it needed.

Anton Hesing.
(Chicago History Museum, ICHi-059606)

Even Andrew Cameron, editor of the *Workingman's Advocate*, the national labor weekly newspaper based in Chicago, jumped on the Fire-Proof bandwagon, rejecting Holden's contention that he would be a better defender of working people and their interests than Medill. Cameron's paper said that the choice of Medill was "an eminently proper one" that would "redound to the best interests of the city." Cameron hardly spoke for all of Chicago's workers, who did not have an effective voice at the time, but his backing of Medill reveals how weak the opposition was.

On election night, with the outcome sure, Mayor-Elect Medill addressed his supporters. The path ahead would be hard, he warned them. Changes would be needed. Under current law the mayor's powers were too limited. This might be acceptable in smooth and prosperous times, but postfire Chicago required the kind of efficiency, retrenchment, and reorganization that only a strong and sure executive hand could accomplish. He favored a bill under consideration in the Illinois Legislature to strengthen the authority of the state's mayors. Medill evoked shouts of agreement when he declared that aldermen and the mayor must work together "to do all in their power to strengthen the public credit, economically apply the public resources, and aid in the resurrection of our beloved city now rising from its ruins."

Governor John M. Palmer meanwhile failed to muster widespread support for his denunciation of Mayor Mason and General Sheridan for the institution of martial law and the homicide of Thomas Grosvenor. Besides the *Chicago Times*, an exception was Chicago police and fire commissioner Thomas Brown, who maintained that the US Army had never been needed and in fact turned out to be "more detriment than service." Brown derided as a class the wealthy Chicagoans who were so eager to put Sheridan in control of the city. "Capitalists don't generally fight except in defense of their property," he remarked, implying that the reason the rich wanted Sheridan and troops on duty was to defend them and their interests, not the city and citizenry as a whole. Brown spoke up for working Chicagoans, who he said were very unlikely to riot or destroy property, as their supposed betters insultingly feared. Since so many workers owned their own houses, they were as in favor of law and order as the rich. Any person afraid of them had to be "very timid or very wicked."

The *Tribune* and others who called for and praised Mason's appointment of Sheridan continued to exalt the general as a hero, attacking Palmer as a self-aggrandizing complainer. Grosvenor's death, while deeply regrettable, was partly the result of his own behavior, since he did not halt when Treat ordered him to do so. The Illinois General Assembly was split on the matter. The seven-member select committee that investigated the military occupation of Chicago backed Palmer's position, but only by a bare majority of four to three. The minority agreed that Sheridan's appointment was unlawful but nonetheless supported Mason's action. The mayor's decision was understandable under the circumstances, his motives beyond question.

In Chicago a grand jury refused to indict Treat for murder, let alone Mason and Sheridan. It instead took the unusual step of issuing a kind of anti-indictment that commended both the mayor and the general. It praised the "wise discretion" of Mason "in thrusting aside the petty vanity of place and position, and summoning to his side the wisest counsels in our midst"—that is, people like the members of the grand jury—"in the appalling emergencies of the late conflagration."

In short, the grand jury applauded Mason for appointing Sheridan and then getting out of the way. As for Sheridan himself, in the grand jury's opinion he usurped no authority and fulfilled his responsibilities effectively. It did not quite blame Grosvenor for his own very regrettable demise, but it came close when it observed that he "unfortunately was found [away] from home at a very unreasonable hour."

By the time of the November 7 election, Chicago's downtown ruins were rapidly disappearing. Attracted by the prospect of earning six dollars a day, area farmers with heavy-duty wagons and sturdy horses to pull them joined local teamsters in the hauling. The city turned the rubble into a resource by using it to continue the filling of the basin between the Illinois Central Railroad tracks and the lakeshore.

Everyone seemed to benefit. For debris haulers, this spot was conveniently close. To the city, the ruins were free landfill. An estimated five thousand wagonloads of prefire Chicago were deposited in the basin between the lakeshore and the Illinois Central tracks. By the end of November, the basin was virtually gone.

Harper's Weekly for October 28 was full of images of Chicago aflame; the following issue's cover featured two illustrations of the city on the mend. In one, the Reverend Robert Collyer of Unity Church stands on a piece of rubble, his arms outstretched and a Bible in his left hand, as he preaches to congregants gathered in the open air outside what is left of his sanctuary. Unity stood on Dearborn Street, opposite the northeast corner of Washington Square Park.

Collyer, who was born in Yorkshire in 1823 and apprenticed to a blacksmith, emigrated to the United States in 1850. He lived in Pennsylvania prior to settling in Chicago. While still a blacksmith, he also became a Methodist preacher. His considerable appeal lay in his principled directness. Collyer was a fervent abolitionist whose theologically liberal ideas led to his expulsion from the Methodist Church for heresy and his transition to Unitarianism. He attracted many followers in Chicago, which enabled him to found Unity Church. Proud of his origins, he had his old anvil mounted in the church.

On the Sunday following the fire, Collyer led the ecumenical gathering of members of several congregations that was pictured on the *Harper's Weekly* cover. Elias Colbert and Everett Chamberlin likened it to "a convention of early Christians in the catacombs." *Harper's Weekly* reported that Collyer told listeners "he had once preached for seventy-five cents a year, and was ready for their sakes to do it again; and that, if the worst came, he could still make as good a horseshoe as any blacksmith in Chicago."

The other illustration on the cover of *Harper's Weekly* for November 4 depicts the bustle of activity in the burned-out downtown the day after Collyer's service. Workers pull wheelbarrows along temporary planks set over the ruins as the employees of contractors Mortimer & Tapper lay the cornerstone of what the magazine called the first postfire building in the center of the city, Kendall's Bank at Washington and Dearborn. Dozens of Chicagoans bear witness. Behind them is the Courthouse, which looks to be in better shape than it was. While its walls remained, the fire gutted the Courthouse's interior. Soon it, too, would be knocked down and carted away.

Before the fire, the downtown slum buildings along Market, Franklin, and Wells Streets, including Conley's Patch, had persisted because of the profits they returned to landlords. With the overnight disappearance of these hazardous eyesores, the area was ripe for redevelopment. The firm of John V. Farwell & Company, the biggest wholesale dry goods company in the West, purchased a large piece of property for its new building. Field, Leiter & Company soon joined Farwell, acquiring an enormous plot on Madison Street for its future wholesale operations.

Workers in the building trades had reason to expect a boost in work and wages, since there seemed to be plenty of demand for their skills. Higher pay did not materialize with any consistency or without considerable pushback. Contractors attacked union leaders as traitors to the good of the community for wanting improved wages, which would raise the cost of new buildings. Businessmen criticized skilled workers of trying to discourage men in the trades living elsewhere from moving to the city.

HARPER'S WEEKLY.
A JOURNAL OF CIVILIZATION

Vol. XV.—No. 775.]   NEW YORK, SATURDAY, NOVEMBER 4, 1871.   [WITH A SUPPLEMENT. PRICE TEN CENTS.

Entered according to Act of Congress, in the Year 1871, by Harper & Brothers, in the Office of the Librarian of Congress, at Washington.

CHICAGO IN RUINS—THE REV. MR. COLLYER PREACHING ON THE SITE OF HIS CHURCH.—[SEE PAGE 1028.]

CHICAGO IN RUINS—LAYING THE CORNER-STONE OF THE FIRST BUILDING AFTER THE FIRE.—PHOT. BY THOMAS S. SWEENEY.—[SEE PAGE 1028.]

Cover of Harper's Weekly, *November 4, 1871.*
(Chicago History Museum, ICHi-063128)

Employers attacked workers as unpatriotic if they asked for more money, an argument that did not deter landlords from using the housing shortage to justify hiking rents. Only two weeks after the fire, there were rumors of an impending bricklayers' strike. The union charged that this was a false report generated by contractors trying to squeeze both property owners and workers by asking more from the former while paying less to the latter.

Too much had been destroyed for Chicagoans to return to the old normal, but people did their best to put the pieces of their lives back together and proceed with personal plans made before the fire. Rebecca Moore had looked forward to marrying Sam Collyer, the son of the Reverend Robert Collyer, in a formal wedding at the residence of family friends. The fire had taken both the fancy gown she ordered and the friends' home. Moore managed to rescue a trunk containing some of the rest of her wardrobe, including the far plainer calico dress she wore when she married Collyer at the West Division house of a different friend on October 11, the day after the fire ended. The Collyers postponed their honeymoon to save money. One of Mayor Mason's sons, recently married, sold his and his wife's wedding presents to the luxury retailer Tiffany & Co. in New York and used the proceeds to purchase inventory for his postfire business.

On the lookout for such human interest features, reporters and illustrators made much of other nuptials in reduced circumstances. The *New-York Tribune* published an account of the wedding of the daughter of a fashionable North Division family planned for October 12. The burning of Field, Leiter & Company had destroyed her wedding dress and veil just before they were to be delivered. She made do with a white cambric morning dress and the same veil her married sister had worn at her nuptials. The rest of her outfit, as well as that of the groom, was also borrowed from what friends and relatives had at hand. Instead of vases filled with fresh flowers, there was a slop-jar containing green and crimson autumn leaves. All but one of the forty guests had lost their homes. "But never have I seen, among rich or poor, a sweeter and more holy-seeming wedding," the reporter commented. The ceremony included prayers of thanksgiving for everyone's preservation. Instead of cake and wine, the celebrants afterward shared warm biscuits and cold water.

In an illustration from Frank Luzerne's *The Lost City! Drama of the Fire Fiend!*, one of the instant fire histories, a bride and groom clasp

The Wedding Amid the Ruins—A Romantic Incident Following the Destruction of Chicago, *1871. (Chicago History Museum, ICHi-002931)*

hands as the guests stand outside amid the rubble of the church where they are being wed. The minister rests his prayer book atop the remnants of a brick chimney or wall as he raises his hands, perhaps in benediction.

The White Stockings finished the season strong, battling the Philadelphia Athletics for the championship of the National Association of Professional Base Ball Players. The decisive game took place on October 30 in front of six hundred spectators at the Union Grounds in Brooklyn, with bettors favoring the Athletics. The fire had cost the Chicago squad its uniforms, as well as practice time. Teams from other cities loaned the White Stockings what they had to spare, so that no two players on the squad were dressed alike.

However generous, this gesture came with certain liabilities. "Where so much depends on the freedom of limb," an account of the game read, "it is very necessary that the uniforms of the players should fit them well and easily." The players' performance "with tight shirts, short pants, and hose in many cases a world too wide, was indeed as creditable as it was surprising." Alas, the White Stockings could not quite complete the Cinderella story. In the bottom of the ninth inning, third baseman Ed Pinkham drove in the team's lone run on a fielder's choice in a 4–1 loss.

The city's cultural life slowly resumed. Colonel J. H. Wood launched a new venture, renting the Globe Theater in the West Division from the German Workers Association a week after the fire. By the end of October, Blanche De Bar, niece of actor and Lincoln assassin John Wilkes Booth, was starring at the Globe in the comedy *The Soldier's Daughter*.

The audience was small. Perhaps patrons of the arts were short on disposable income or not quite ready to step out for an evening on the town. They also may have stayed away because the Globe was, in the description of one reviewer, "dirty, dingy, and forbidding," and the voices of the actors "barely audible." Another play, with the intriguing title *Divorce*, did better for Wood, as did *Bertha, the Sewing Machine Girl* for DeBar.

Throughout the fall, even as they struggled with the fire's destruction, Chicagoans with the means to do so attended numerous lectures by nationally known figures, usually as parts of "courses," or series, to which they could subscribe. There was no other way to see or hear such luminaries except in person. Edward Everett Hale, who had raised money for stricken Chicago in the rally at Boston's Faneuil Hall, read his new story, titled "His Level Best," at Union Park Congregational Church on the West Side. Women's rights champion Elizabeth Cady Stanton delivered "The Coming Girl" as part of the Star Lecture course.

When Victoria Woodhull came to Chicago to lecture, the *Times* expressed disapproval of her free-love views of marriage, sex, and family, attacking her as "the woman who glories in her dirty ideas." Displaying its typical fondness for contemptuous alliteration, it called former slave and current author and activist Frederick Douglass "the darkey Demosthenes." According to the *Times* reviewer, "His wavy ringlets fell in thick profusion at the rear of his cranium, and his jet black eye glistened with pleasure as he surveyed the goodly assemblage of respectable white folks that had come together to hear him have his say."

A pair of titans of American letters visited the city that fall. In late November, Ralph Waldo Emerson addressed a rapt house on "Nature and Art." "Taste is the love of beauty," he told Chicagoans, while "art is the description of beauty." While a reviewer considered Emerson's manner "stiff and awkward," he praised the Sage of Concord for "flashing some great truths into the mind of the auditor, by a happy word or a well-turned phrase." The reviewer questioned the reputed superior intellectual life of eastern cities when he pointed out that while there had been a sea of empty rows when Emerson visited Philadelphia earlier in his tour, Chicagoans filled the 2,500 seats in the auditorium.

Emerson, now almost seventy (or "three score and ten," as the paper put it), represented a passing generation of American literary greats. Mark Twain, who came to Chicago to recall his experiences in the West by reading what would become part of *Roughing It*, was half Emerson's age, and his books about Tom Sawyer and Huckleberry Finn were still ahead. A reporter described him as "a youngish man of perhaps thirty-five, not handsome, but having a bright intelligent look, and an eye with a humorous twinkle that put him at once *en rapport* with an audience." Twain was an even bigger draw than Emerson; extra seats were needed in the same hall.

Some of the picking up of the pieces entailed actual pieces of the prefire city. A reporter told of "old men and women, begrimed with smoke and white with dust, . . . groping for multifarious treasures, flat-irons, sofa springs, boilers, currycombs, all sorts of odds and ends, discolored and out of shape." Heat-twisted bottles and dishes, as well as melded clusters of screws, washers, and nails, were reminders of how unearthly hot was the conflagration.

The fire endowed objects that survived it with a special aura, and especially those things that bore signs of what they had been through. When the Rumseys sifted through the ashes of their house on Huron Street, they discovered the watch that Julian had placed under his pillow on October 8. The watch would never again function, but they treasured it as a reminder of their prefire world, gone with the flames. Jeweler John Ashleman's daughter Bertia was pleased that the ceramic

The fire's handiwork: fused screws (Chicago History Museum,
ICHi-064558) and a bent bottle. (Chicago History Museum, ICHi-064471)

head of a favorite doll survived without a crack, even if it had been
blackened and its cloth body burned away.

Charles R. Lott, fifteen at the time, took advantage of the local hunger for news and the shortage of local papers immediately after the fire
by peddling Milwaukee dailies in Chicago at the premium price of fifteen cents apiece. After that he started a new business on Madison Street,
where he sold fragments of the burned city that he had collected. In a
postfire illustration titled *Enterprising Young Merchant Disposing of
Relics Opposite the Ruins of the Sherman House*, the "merchant" sits
inside an overturned safe on which he has placed a board displaying several fire-touched objects, like the doll he is selling to a well-dressed
couple and their daughter. Wedged in the rubble next to the safe is a
business relocation sign.

A stereograph from the time shows the crowd around a stand cluttered with pieces of Chicago touched by the fire. A resourceful Chicagoan built an oddity known as the Relic House, a one-story building

Enterprising young merchant disposing of relics opposite the ruins of the Sherman House, 1871. (Chicago History Museum, ICHi-063818)

Left, View of the Courthouse bell after the fire. Shaw Photographer, stereograph, 1871. (Chicago History Museum, ICHi-064280) Right, Souvenir of the Courthouse bell, fashioned in metal taken from it. (Chicago History Museum, ICHi-063853)

made out of salvaged stones, pipes, bottles, plates, sewing machines, doll's heads, and iron toys.

The single most actively marketed fire relic was the fallen bell from the Courthouse cupola. Another stereograph depicts a boy sitting in a large fragment of it, his hand resting on his chin. Two men squat on the rubble next to the bell, and a uniformed policeman stands by, perhaps guarding it from those who picked through the debris at night for anything that might be valuable. The city placed the bell in storage before auctioning it off in mid-December. The successful bidder was Thomas B. Bryan of the Fidelity Safe Depository Company, who had been the first to buy land in the postfire downtown.

Bryan resold the bell two days later to H. S. Everhart & Company, retaining a small portion to be remade into an alarm for his office. Everhart melted down the rest and molded it into souvenirs. Most were either commemorative medals or small replicas of the original bell in a range of sizes, available in sets that were tastefully arranged on purple velvet in a polished wooden box and accompanied by a certificate of authenticity signed by members of the city's Board of Public Works.

A reporter derided the souvenir hunting, gathering, and peddling, calling many of the relics of Chicago "extremely apocryphal." He missed the point, which was that Chicago and the rest of the world treasured these souvenirs, authentic or not, for what they represented—talismans of a titanic and world-altering catastrophe beyond the grasp of imagination.

12

WHO STARTED THE GREAT CHICAGO FIRE?

The *Chicago Evening Journal*, the only local newspaper to publish on Monday, October 9, reported that the fire began with "a cow kicking over a lamp in a stable in which a woman was milking." Since then this story and the fire have been inseparable. People who know nothing else about the Great Chicago Fire have heard of Mrs. O'Leary and her cow.

Several factors made Catherine O'Leary a convenient person on whom to pin the blame. Eyewitnesses located the first flames as flaring from the barn where she attended her cows. There was considerable comfort in tracing the origin to a specific cause, as opposed to not knowing how and why the fire began. Attributing it to an accident was much less disturbing than believing that a person or persons, with or without a specific motive, purposely set Chicago afire. Tying the enormous destruction to a humble source also offered a certain ironic satisfaction, and a suggestive precedent lay in one of the few comparably large urban conflagrations. The London Fire that began on Sunday, September 2, 1666, originated in baker Thomas Farriner's kitchen on Pudding Lane.

Catherine O'Leary already had at least five strikes against her: she was a poor immigrant Irish Catholic woman. In this very unsettling moment, she provided a place for settled opinions—xenophobic, anti-Irish, anti-Catholic, and sexist prejudices—to find confirmation. She was also defenseless and illiterate, with no effective means to counter her accusers.

Other theories about the fire's origins surfaced at the time in the newspapers, most of them placing a similar person in or near the barn when the blaze broke loose. Some suggested that the McLaughlins, the tenants in the O'Learys' front cottage, or one of their guests that evening had ventured into the dark barn to draw fresh milk for a celebratory punch. Others speculated that the fateful spark came from the pipe of Daniel Sullivan, the one-legged neighbor who awakened Patrick and Catherine O'Leary, or that boys shooting dice or playing cards in the barn ignited the hay. Perhaps it was a wayward cinder from someone's chimney. Maybe spontaneous combustion. Or an arsonist who just liked to see things burn. Or those Communards or other sinister enemies of the established order.

None of these alternatives could budge Catherine O'Leary from her unenviable position as prime suspect. Reduced to a caricature whom unsympathetic and even hostile journalists could shape any way they pleased, especially since there were no photographs or accurate like-nesses of her, she remained guilty in the court of public opinion. The fact that the fire spared the O'Leary home while destroying others all around it reinforced the idea that she was blameworthy.

While most accounts depicted her as too ignorant and inept to have committed the act intentionally, some reporters suggested other-wise. In its first postfire issue, the *Chicago Times* vilified the hardwork-ing O'Leary, who was not on any dole, as a welfare fraud who, when cut from the rolls, swore that "she would be revenged on charity that would deny her a bit of wood or a pound of bacon." The paper likened her to "any one of the vermin which haunt our streets." While she was actually around forty, the *Times* described her as a bent-over crone of seventy.

For a few days after the fire the O'Leary neighborhood was a cir-cus. A photographer led a cow (some say a bull) next to their home and snapped a picture. Illustrators, none of whom ever laid eyes on Cathe-rine O'Leary, joined the *Times* in aging her by decades. They depicted her looking on with shock and dismay, or as comically falling backward head over heels and skirts in the air, as the lamp goes flying.

To the mainstream daily English-language press, the O'Learys and their world were so alien to respectable sensibilities that reporters de-scribed the investigations of their neighborhood as a journey into the primitive unknown. In March 1871, about six months before the Great Chicago Fire, the *New York Herald* had sent Henry Morton Stanley to deepest Africa in search of long-lost British explorer Dr. David Living-stone. When he found the object of his quest by the shores of Lake Tanganyika in early November, Stanley famously asked, "Dr. Living-stone, I presume?"

W. O. Mull, Origin of the Chicago Fire, *ca. 1871.*
(Chicago History Museum, ICHi-064420)

By that time the *New-York Tribune* had put John Hay on a train to Chicago to report on the fire. "Curious to see the first footprint of the monster who had trampled a great city out of existence in a day," Hay set forth across the Twelfth Street Bridge and into the O'Leary neighborhood, a place "wholly foreign and not quite reputable." Hay's account, which was reprinted in the Chicago papers, was a reprehensible exercise in condescension and disdain, as vicious in intent as it was elegantly written. On his way to interview Mrs. O'Leary, Hay explained, he first encountered German relief volunteers guarding supplies from hungry Czechs who communicated with each other in broken English, which made him fear for "the final doom of our language."

Hay called the block where the O'Learys lived "a mean little street of shabby wooden houses, with dirty dooryards and unpainted fences falling to decay." It did not seem to belong in this city of vitality and enterprise. As he put it, "It had no look of Chicago about it."

At last he reached the "the squalid little hovel" he dubbed "the Mecca of my pilgrimage." Hay beheld "a warped and weather-beaten shanty of two rooms, perched on thin piles, with the plates nailed half way down them like dirty pantalets. There was no shabbier hut in Chicago nor in Tipperary." Adapting the story of Chicago's tale of destruction to the framework of the nursery rhyme "The House that Jack Built," Hay wrote of the O'Leary home, "For out of that house, last Sunday night, came a woman with a lamp to the barn behind the house, to milk the cow with the crumpled temper, that kicked the lamp, that spilled the kerosene, that fired the straw, that burned Chicago." To which he added, with a flourish of personification, "And there to this hour stands that craven little house, holding on tightly to its miserable existence."

Hay claimed that he interviewed Patrick O'Leary, who greeted him with "sleepy, furtive eyes" and whom Hay belittled by using capital letters to refer to him as "the Man of the House." When O'Leary said he had nothing to do with starting the fire, Hay felt that "there was something unutterably grotesque in this ultimate atom" discussing his possible relation to "a catastrophe so stupendous." Hay aimed his most elevated sarcasm at Catherine O'Leary, with whom he did not deign to speak: "Our Lady of the Lamp—freighted with heavier disaster than which Psyche carried to the bed-side of Eros—sat at the window, knitting."

In the few apparently legitimate interviews Catherine O'Leary did grant immediately after the fire, she repeatedly said that she was asleep when it began, and Daniel Sullivan had awakened her by rapping on the door. She explained that her house was saved thanks to the many friends who threw water on its walls and roof. While the reporters did not seem to notice, she thus described her neighborhood as a community, not Hay's forlorn wasteland of pathetic outcasts.

A fellow Irish Catholic immigrant named Michael McDermott tried to assist the O'Learys in presenting their side of the story. Unlike them, he was an educated professional, a civil engineer and surveyor. On October 15 McDermott took sworn affidavits from the couple and Sullivan that soon appeared in the *Chicago Tribune*. In her statement Catherine O'Leary said that she milked her cows daily at 5:00 a.m. and 4:30 p.m. On the evening of the fire, she made her last trip to the barn at about seven o'clock, when she fed the horse and put him in for the night. She carried no lamp. Patrick O'Leary attested that he had nothing to do with the animals, which his wife and oldest child, fifteen-year-old Mary, fed and milked. The family was in bed when the fire started.

The couple pointed out that they, too, were its victims. It had cost them their barn and livestock, on which they had no insurance. In his affidavit, Daniel Sullivan stated that he had called on the family between eight thirty and nine o'clock but left as soon as he discovered they had gone to sleep. He spotted the fire from across DeKoven Street a short time later. He had tried to save the animals but the only one he could rescue was the calf. All three signed their statements with an *X*.

McDermott sent a note to the *Tribune* along with the affidavits. "A great deal has been published respecting the origin of the great fire," he wrote, "which all reports have settled down on the head of a woman, or as the *Times* has it, an 'Irish hag' of 70 years of age." Even if the O'Learys had in fact been blameworthy, "there was a great want of charity in the epithets used by the *Times*." But in fact they were innocent. "The following facts [i.e., the accounts in the affidavits] are stubborn things, and will cause the public to look for the cause in other sources, and perhaps attribute it to the love of plunder, Divine wrath, etc."

We cannot be sure just what McDermott meant by his reference to "Divine wrath," but many Americans understood experience generally and cataclysmic events in particular through a conceptual framework of sin and punishment. Shortly after the fire, a few clergymen interpreted Chicago's suffering as a straightforward example of Old Testament–style justice. The Reverend Edgar J. Goodspeed of the Second Baptist Church, author of those successively longer fire histories, read the disaster as God's response to the city's violations of the Sabbath, its drinking and materialism, and its profusion of theaters, brothels, and "gambling-hells."

Granville Moody, a Methodist minister in Cincinnati, concurred. Moody was an unusually militant parson. He joined the Union Army not as a chaplain but as commander of the Seventy-Fourth Ohio Volunteer Infantry, attaining the rank of brevet brigadier general. Afterward he returned to the pulpit with the imprint of the battlefield still on him. He viewed urban life as a constant clash between the armies of righteousness and evil. The fire was "a retributive judgment on a city which has shown such a devotion in its worship to the Golden Calf."

Even Mayor Roswell B. Mason nodded to this view in a proclamation that set aside Sunday, October 29, as "a special day of humiliation and prayer" in acknowledgment of "those past offenses against Almighty God, to which these severe afflictions were intended to lead our minds."

Other believers preferred to envision the fire as the work of a loving God who, in spite of all the destruction, cared deeply for humankind. The most prominent spokesman for this outlook was the best known clergyman in the country, Congregationalist minister Henry Ward Beecher. Based in the Plymouth Church in Brooklyn, the fifty-eight-year-old Beecher spread his ideas nationally on the lecture circuit and in newspapers, magazines, and books.

Beecher was the younger brother of Harriet Beecher Stowe, author of *Uncle Tom's Cabin*, the extraordinarily popular 1852 novel credited with widening opposition to slavery and hastening the Civil War. Their late father Lyman Beecher had been another noted man of the cloth. Henry agreed with some of Lyman's views, such as his father's championing of temperance, but he saw God as far more compassionate.

Like many other ministers across the country, Beecher devoted his sermon the Sunday after the fire to the inferno that was the talk of the nation. Beecher took as his text "Thy judgments are a great deep" from Psalm 36. He began by acknowledging that events like the fire raise the question of why God causes terrible things to happen that inflict as much pain on the upright as on the wicked. Beecher advised against expecting an answer to theological conundrums like this. "If you pursue them," he warned, "that way lies atheism."

Beecher did not concern himself with the story of the O'Learys, the cow, the broken lamp, or any other proximate cause of the fire. To him the most interesting aspect of the entire experience was what it revealed about one of the great issues of the day, urbanization, bundling under this heading the modern forms of communication on which the nation increasingly relied.

"This great national disaster is a revelation of *the structure and function of cities in the organization of society*," he asserted. One could see this most clearly in the gloriously generous reaction to Chicago's misfortune, a sign that so many people felt it personally. The wholehearted way humankind at large reacted to Chicago's blow indicated that "a city is, for the time being, the point where God enthrones himself in wisdom and power." No person could be a good citizen, patriot, or Christian who did not care about what happened in places like Chicago, on which every business's prosperity and each family's well-being depended.

Beecher urged his listeners and readers to embrace all the affirmative aspects of the fire. He admitted that there was nothing as hideous as the reports of crime, looting, and debauchery, but he noted how few such stories were in comparison to those of bravery and selflessness. Most wonderful of all was the current rush of support from around the country to the fallen city, overflowing as it was with "moral riches" as well as material ones.

Far from a visitation by an angry God, the fire was "a great national blessing" that demonstrated the triumph of selfless Christian love. The tragedy that leveled Chicago broke down existing divisions—from doctrinal differences between religious denominations to lingering bad feeling between Britain and the United States attributable to the former mother country's support of the Confederacy—by reminding us of the sympathy all feel for suffering humanity. "We are richer to-day with Chicago burned, than we were last month with Chicago unburned," Beecher declared, leading into a resounding double negative: "We could not have afforded not to have had her burned."

In closing, Beecher looked his congregants in the eye and asked them directly for donations. A note to a published version of the sermon states they responded with $5,000 in pledges.

Several visual representations of the world's response to Chicago's ordeal echoed Beecher's message. These provide a counterpoint to Alfred Fredericks' drawing of the young women protecting fallen Chicago from being torn apart by wild dogs. In an 1872 painting by Jules-Émile Saintin, a French artist who spent time in the United States, dark birds circle over the burned-out city much as they do in the Fredericks drawing. Saintin does not emphasize Chicago's vulnerability, however, but

Jules-Émile Saintin, Relief for the Sufferers of Chicago, *1872.*
(Chicago History Museum, ICHi-062440)

the world's sympathy and charity. In the foreground stands a dignified
young woman dressed in mourning, a somber expression on her face.
She slips a gold coin into a crudely made lockbox on which is inscribed,
"Relief for the Sufferers of Chicago."

Even more closely related to the Frederick drawing was a very large
1873 painting by Englishman Edward Armitage, a member of the pres-

tigious Royal Academy of Arts. *In Memory of the Great Fire at Chicago* was commissioned as a gift to the city from the staff of the British illustrated weekly, the *Graphic*. A beautiful nude female lies prostrate in a pose reminiscent of paintings of Christ's deposition from the Cross, her head supported by the leg of a seated woman in a classical gown. The afflicted figure looks up into the eyes of a second similarly attired woman, who joins the first in succoring her.

Flanking the trio are a lion and an eagle, signifying that the two women represent Britain and the United States watching over Chicago in the spirit of Christian benevolence. At the bottom of the painting is the inscription, "I was thirsty and ye gave me drink . . . naked and ye clothed me," from Matthew 25:35. The scene was reproduced in multiple variations, including the version that serves as the frontispiece to the second volume of A. T. Andreas's *History of Chicago*, in which

In Memory of the Great Fire at Chicago. *Lithograph based on the painting by Edward Armitage. (Chicago History Museum, ICHi-063132)*

Britain and the United States have changed into Renaissance costume
and Chicago's lap is discreetly draped.

Practical-minded Chicagoans considered themselves good Christians,
but they had had little use for the cow anecdote, the sermonizing, or
the high-minded paintings. As gratified as they were by all the aid sent
to the city, they probably did not agree with Beecher that the nation in
general and Chicago in particular could not have afforded not to have
had the fire. They definitely knew that they could not afford to have their
city burn a second time, and so they focused on how they could stop
that from happening.

One way was to improve the fire department. First hailed as valiant
and selfless heroes, firefighters were soon denounced for their poor performance. Charges against the men fell mainly into two categories. The
first was that some of them were drunk during the fire. New Yorker
Alexander Frear said that he spotted several members of Little Giant
Engine Company No. 6 in a South Division saloon even as the city
burned. "One of the men was bathing his head with whisky from a
flask. They declared that the Fire Department had given up, over-
worked, and that they could do nothing more," Frear wrote. The second accusation was that some firemen accepted bribes from building
owners to prioritize the rescue of their properties.

By mid-November the criticisms gathered into a drumbeat of demands for a thorough official inquiry into the causes of the fire and the
quality of the firefighters' efforts. The commissioners on the board
that supervised the police and fire departments promised that they would
conduct one soon. The *Chicago Tribune* intensified the pressure for an
inquiry with a multiarticle investigation of its own titled "Boring for
Facts." It based these stories on interviews with the chief fire marshal
and his assistants, who contradicted and criticized each other in ways
that made the department's leadership look bad.

When Chief Fire Marshal Robert A. Williams stated for attribu-
tion that he did not see First Assistant Marshal John Schank at any
point throughout the entire struggle, the *Tribune* hunted down Schank,

who angrily shot back, "It's a d—d lie." Schank said that the two of them had met and conferred on DeKoven Street, as Williams would later confirm. Schank went on the offensive, condemning Williams for ignoring his advice to get more men in front of the flames in order to halt their progress. "If the engines had been brought to lead the fire fifteen or twenty minutes earlier we could have stopped it easily," he maintained.

Williams prepared a long statement defending himself against both Schank and irate citizens who had been attacking him in published letters to Chicago papers. He pointed out that some of these critics lacked the courage to sign their names. The firefighters, he insisted, lost the battle because they were so poorly equipped.

The investigation finally began on Thursday, November 23. It lasted twelve days, during nine of which the fifty witnesses presented testimony, with Courthouse telegraph operator William Brown and watchman Mathias Schaefer submitting theirs in the form of affidavits. False rumors of Williams's resignation—perhaps wishful thinking— were in circulation as it began. The panel consisted of the four elected police and fire commissioners who oversaw both departments, though apparently not all were present for every witness.

The inquiry took place in the captain's office of the Second Precinct police station in the West Division. Since this was a relatively small room furnished with a desk, a table, a stove, ten chairs, and a cot, there was barely enough room for the questioners, the press, and the current witness, who got to sit on the only chair in the room with a cushion. Twenty-seven witnesses—slightly more than half—were members of the fire department. The questioners also heard from police captain Michael Hickey. On the list of civilians were both Catherine and Patrick O'Leary and a few of their neighbors, such as their tenant Catharine McLaughlin, Dennis Regan, and Daniel Sullivan, as well as former alderman James Hildreth, who described his use of gunpowder.

After the first day, when someone took notes in longhand, a stenographer recorded what was said. The full transcript totals about 1,170 foolscap pages. The hearings started with the submission of the statements from William Brown and Mathias Schaefer. This was followed by the testimony of the first firemen to arrive on DeKoven and then that of the O'Learys and their neighbors. Catherine O'Leary appeared the second day with her infant in her arms. The merciless *Times* now described her as "a tall, stout, Irish woman with no intelligence." While she was on the stand, it reported, "the infant kicked its bare legs around and drew nourishment from immense reservoirs."

O'Leary said that she was so frightened at the time of the fire that it was hard for her to remember details clearly, but she recalled that, because of the wind, the flames grew to dangerous proportions in no more time than it took to "clap your two hands together." Of the roar of the flames that evening, she stated, "You never heard such a thing." Her testimony closed with her bemoaning the loss of the barn and the livestock. Snapping her fingers for emphasis, O'Leary stated, "I couldn't save that much out of it, and upon my word I worked hard for them."

The next day Patrick O'Leary corroborated his wife's account. The *Times* was no easier on him. It called O'Leary "a stupid-looking sort of man, who acknowledged himself he could neither read nor write," and it made fun of the stenographer's inability to keep up with his runaway brogue. In his responses to the commissioners, O'Leary said that once the firefighters arrived, they made small effort to put out his fire. "My little shanty wasn't worth much. They didn't care much about it," he charged. Asked if he had any idea of how the fire started, O'Leary answered, "No sir. If I was to be hanged for it, I don't know who done it."

The *Times* showed a rare soft spot for Daniel Sullivan, characterizing him as "a rough, honest-looking, hard working man" who dutifully handed over his pay to his mother. As in the case of other witnesses, the paper included give-and-take not in the official transcript. It said that Sullivan's testimony was rich "with original bits of Irish eloquence and frequent jokes," and that he sneered at the marshals and winked at the visitors. Sullivan evidently went off on such tangents that Commissioner Thomas B. Brown at one point instructed him to stick to the fire. The procession of witnesses ended with the three assistant fire marshals and finally Chief Marshal Williams.

The method of interrogation was more open-ended than tightly directed. Commissioners asked each individual to offer his or her recollections of what happened rather than pursue a clear line of questioning themselves. No one followed up on Williams's account of how he took a break to rescue his piano. The appearance of some witnesses, like waterworks crib keeper John Tolland, seemed irrelevant to the causes of the fire and how it was fought, while a few individuals who might have had something important to say, like drugstore owner Bruno Goll, did not testify.

The panel specifically asked fire company foremen whether charges of drunkenness and bribery were true. Foreman William Mullin of Illinois Steamer Company No. 15 recalled that although grateful bystanders tried to reward his men with whiskey and brandy, the firefighters did not accept. They were not averse to a little fortification on the job, but on this occasion it was too risky to drink because their stomachs were empty. He said that the strongest liquids the firemen consumed amid the inhumanly dehydrating conditions were cider and wine, which was nothing unusual at the time.

On the issue of bribery, Leo Myers, foreman of Tempest Hose Company No. 1, remarked, "I do not hardly think there is a fireman in the department that would take the responsibility of moving his engine at the request of any individual for personal gain for himself." Michael Sullivan, foreman of Waubansia Company No. 2, admitted that he had received offers of a hundred dollars from building owners and one as high as a thousand from the proprietor of a furniture factory to pay special attention to their property, but he turned them down. "I could not do it," he said. "I referred them to the marshals. I was working under orders." The most that anyone would admit to accepting was a small amount of cash or a few cigars, which they said some individuals proffered in gratitude for what the firemen were doing, not as inducements to get them to do it a certain way.

Chief Fire Marshal Williams, who testified last and longest, earnestly defended his men and his decisions. He said he had refused to place or keep firefighters in situations where the likelihood of their perishing was far greater than of doing any good. He admitted that he had heard that some of his men were intoxicated, but he insisted that while it was possible a few had taken a drink, no firefighter was drunk. If any man seemed to be staggering, it was due to exhaustion, not alcohol.

He reminded the panel that the department had battled a major fire on Saturday and then an epic one on Sunday and Monday, with virtually no time in between to recover. Singed by flame, blinded by smoke, drenched under their heavy gear, they were completely wrung out in body and spirit. Williams asserted that no city had been better at fighting fires than Chicago. But this conflagration was unstoppable, "and if we had had all the fire departments in the world here, I don't think it could have been prevented."

The commissioners submitted their findings at their December 11 semiweekly meeting. About two thousand words long, it was a small report on a big fire. They said there was no proof any person had been in the O'Leary barn when the drama began. Whether it "originated from a spark blown from a chimney on that windy night, or was set on fire by human agency," the commissioners stated, "we are unable to determine."

Their chronology of the event omitted the failures of the alarm system and its operators. The report said only that the watchman in the America Hose Cart No. 2 firehouse eleven blocks away had spotted the flames, and that firemen "repaired to the fire . . . with the usual celerity" after hearing the alarm that subsequently sounded. By then, it noted, the blaze had a fifteen-minute head start (though it was very likely twice that). When the department arrived, the fire was already "fiercely burning" and the southwest wind was driving it "from building to building in a neighborhood composed wholly of dry wooden buildings, with wood shavings piled in every barn and under every house." What small chance the men had to halt it disappeared once the conflagration took hold of the steeple of St. Paul's Catholic Church.

The commissioners found that the firefighters had been sober and did all they could, working selflessly to save others when their own homes were burning. The board underlined the fact that most of the department had been on brutally demanding duty from late Saturday night until three o'clock Sunday afternoon, only to be summoned less than seven hours later to an even bigger fight that no department had hope of winning. To their great credit, the men answered the call bravely and professionally.

The panel found no evidence that firemen took bribes to try to save particular buildings. What gifts they did receive were merely a thank you after the fact. In addition to overlooking the failure of the alarm system, the report did not mention contradictions either in the testimony or between what some witnesses stated on the stand and what they had said to reporters earlier.

In conclusion, the commissioners blamed the fire on the way the city had been constructed and the shortsightedness of its mayors and aldermen, who bent to the wishes of property owners who wanted low building costs and taxes, no matter what the risk in skimping on fire prevention and protection. If more of the West Division had been built of brick or stone, the fire would probably have been stopped before it could cross the river. Once it did reach the South Division, all the wooden cornices and signs, as well as the tar and felt roofs, accelerated the destruction of the downtown. Although the Pumping Station (which was overseen by the Board of Public Works) housed three pumps that together were large enough to serve a city of 330,000 people, it had no apparatus that could raise even a drop of water to its own roof in order to put out a fire that started there.

The report complained that past recommendations had gone nowhere because of the lack of proper restrictive legislation on building materials and necessary funding for the fire department. Chicago had paid a far higher price than implementing these recommendations would have cost. Year after year, fire marshals and boards warned about the dangerous way the city had been built up. They had advised clearing piles of combustible materials like wood and coal from where they could cause harm, requiring fireproof materials in buildings, installing more hydrants, placing cisterns at major street intersections, purchasing additional and better equipment, and increasing water pressure. These steps would have made the fire department much more effective, even without more personnel. Unfortunately, the recommendations had been ignored. If the citizens of Chicago did not follow similar advice now, "they will after the next great fire sweeps out of existence the greater portion of the wooden city which now remains."

Though limited and self-serving, the report was accurate as far as it went. Instead of easy accusations aimed at the O'Learys, its authors took the couple at their word and implicitly absolved them of blame. The commissioners skipped the talk of Christian punishment, with or without redemption, and of Communards and incendiaries. The perpetrators of the fire were the people who built Chicago so heedlessly and the officials who let them do so. The problem lay not with some Irishwoman or arsonist or whomever, but in the city's fundamental nature. It was as if Chicagoans had purposely intended to construct a city they wished to burn down and then voted for aldermen and mayors who did little to stop that from happening. If things did not change, Chicago would burn again.

In his *Nation* article on Chicago, which was published a month after the disaster and a few weeks before the official inquiry began, Frederick Law Olmsted anticipated many of the same points the commissioners would make. He did so more thoroughly and with greater eloquence, if also with more than a hint of condescension toward most Chicagoans.

Olmsted paid little attention to the O'Leary neighborhood, critiquing instead Chicago's prefire downtown. While its numerous large buildings were constructed mainly of brick, stone, and iron, he noted, they "were mostly lined, to the fourth, fifth, or sixth floor, with pine-wood shelves, on which, or in pine-wood cases, a fresh stock of—larger at the moment than ever before—dry goods or other inflammable materials, was set up, with plentiful air-space for rapid combustion." Olmsted had no patience for the stories of incendiaries and Communards. These were "delusions growing out of the common excitement." The cause of the fire was nothing more or less than "a commonplace accident" to be expected as part of the normal course of things. The real question was why this accident could lead to such wholesale destruction.

The true firebrands were property owners, elected officials, and city employees. The city was a firetrap because real estate interests had convinced the Common Council to modify a law against such density of construction and to ignore the objections of the Board of Health. Meanwhile, underwriters, merchants, and capitalists said nothing. Olmsted criticized Chicago's prideful booster mentality, its "weakness for 'big things.'" This produced architecture that was objectionable on aesthetic grounds, but far more disturbing was the insubstantiality of so much of the aspiring great metropolis. Olmsted could not say with absolute certainty that sounder building methods in the downtown would have stopped the flames once they leapt the South Branch of the river, but he was sure that "the heat thrown forward would have been less intense, the advance of the fire less rapid, the destruction of buildings less complete, the salvage of their contents greater, and the loss of life smaller."

The key site on which Olmsted based his secular sermon was the Courthouse, about which he remarked that there was "much more beauty in the walls now, where they have been chipped and crumbled by the fire, than ever before." A well-built structure set off by itself in a parklike square would never have surrendered to the flames as easily as did this defective building. When the city planned the Courthouse expansion that was completed shortly before the fire, it had done so "under such conditions that no respectable architect could have been employed." He suggested that corruption in the Common Council was to blame when he alluded to charges that "some of the legislators of the city were interested in the building contracts, and that much money was made on them."

The wise course would have been to declare the Courthouse a botch and tear it down, but that would have embarrassed those who had already wasted so much money on it. There was a lesson of sin and retribution here, but the teacher was not an angry God. It was the conflagration itself: "The fire, true to its mission of instructive punishment, made a long leap forward to seize upon this [i.e., the Courthouse]."

Olmsted had some positive things to say about the disaster as a whole. Chicagoans behaved well through the ordeal, which was a test of character that they clearly passed. He attributed the low death toll to "an active volunteer rear-guard of cool-headed Christians." Olmsted offered faint and patronizing praise of the city's great mass of working people, commenting that "their conduct seems to have been as satisfactory as could have been reasonably expected."

Olmsted believed that Chicagoans had been usefully chastened. He expected to find "a feverish, reckless spirit, and among the less disciplined classes an unusual current setting toward turbulence, lawlessness, and artificial jollity," but was glad to report that "Chicago is the soberest and most clear headed city I ever saw." Drunks were scarce, people were law-abiding, there were no beggars on the streets. Best of all, the city's business and professional men had learned their lesson. Olmsted looked forward to the impending election of Joseph Medill and the Fire-Proof ticket, which he treated as a fortunately foregone conclusion.

He explicitly approved of the takeover of contributions by the Chicago Relief and Aid Society, whom he called "men of great good sense" who "have taken time to devise and bring others into a comprehensive and sufficient organization, acting under well-guarded laws." They only did so, "it is said," after "a hard struggle with political speculators." Now, Olmsted urged, it was up to Chicagoans to create a finer and safer city than the one whose destruction had been its own fault.

Easier said than done.

13

THE LIMITS OF LIMITS

On Monday, December 4, 1871, the provisional city hall on South Wabash Avenue was filled to overflowing for the swearing in of the new mayor and Common Council. After a last roll call of the 1870–71 aldermen, council president Charles C. P. Holden introduced Mayor Roswell B. Mason for his farewell public remarks.

In his short statement, Mason offered a final oblique defense of his postfire actions. Referring to himself in the third person and resorting to labored syntax, Mason omitted specifics. "His [i.e., Mason's] sole object and aim," he said, "was to secure means that would be the most effectual, and the soonest available to meet the emergency, and it is believed this was done without lowering the dignity of his office or abrogating any of its powers." After a few words of his own, Holden declared the outgoing council adjourned. He invited those members who were retiring to conduct newly elected aldermen to their seats.

The 1871–72 council's first order of business was to choose a president from among its ranks. On the third ballot the members elected John H. McAvoy of the South Division's Third Ward by a one-vote majority. Although he was an Irish Catholic and an incumbent Democrat, McAvoy had been on the Fire-Proof Party ticket. Holden, who would not face reelection until the fall of 1872, continued on the council as one of the Tenth Ward's two aldermen.

The spotlight turned to new mayor Joseph Medill, who delivered a long and lackluster inaugural address. Medill offered a stern assessment of Chicago's financial condition and spoke of the need for further retrenchment, starting with additional reductions in the number of municipal employees and a one-year 20 percent salary cut for those staying on. He pledged that he would also save money by ending corruption. For the past several years, he said, "good men" throughout the land despaired as the "evil example" of New York "infected" local governments. Chicago had been no exception, but with the victories of Fire-Proof candidates honesty was now ascendant.

Medill endorsed the "Mayor's Bill" pending in the state legislature, which it would enact in early February. This would greatly increase the executive power of mayors in the state. Among other things, it would enable Medill to appoint the members of key city boards and of regular committees of the Common Council.

He then discussed his central priority, the extension of fire limits to the borders of the Chicago. Fire limits were an early form of zoning that banned the use of certain combustible materials, in this case wood, from use in the exposed exterior of new buildings constructed in specified parts of the city. Any change would require a new ordinance approved by the Common Council. And, unlike the existing fire limits, which covered the downtown and close-in sections of the West and North Divisions but was spottily observed even there, Medill insisted that the much broader ban needed to be strictly enforced.

The new mayor said that the fire had not been an act of God or fate before whom humans were helpless. The city had burned catastrophically because of its "blind, unreasoning infatuation in favor of pine" as a building material for external walls. Any economies wood seemed to offer were false. Buildings covered in brick and stone lasted longer, were cheaper to heat and maintain, and incurred lower insurance premiums precisely because they were resistant to fire. On top of that, they were handsomer than wood structures.

If Chicagoans now replicated the city that had burned, he warned, they faced the "moral certainty, at no distant day, of a recurrence of the late catastrophe." Medill said he agreed with those who wanted the Board of Public Works to increase the water supply and do a better job of protecting the Pumping Station against fire. But these measures in themselves would be of limited value unless the city took meaningful steps to make itself far less susceptible to another conflagration. Only a total ban on wood buildings, he contended, would guarantee security for everyone. There could be no exceptions, not only because these would jeopardize public safety but also because special privileges "are odious in a republican country."

The previous council had already extended limits slightly since the fire, but this meant little because it had not improved enforcement. The aldermen had also discussed but did not pass a more comprehensive proposal drafted by a special committee on fire safety regulations. Along with a prohibition of wooden buildings virtually everywhere in Chicago, the proposal included more stringent specifications in the use of brick, requiring twelve-inch walls for buildings of one story and thicker ones for taller structures. It required that roofs must be made of metal, slate, terra cotta, or a similarly nonflammable material, and it prohibited the use of wood trim in cornices, coping, bay windows, and other projections.

Few disputed that Chicago should rebuild more wisely, but between the scarcity of shelter and commercial space, the lack of ready cash, and the approach of winter, those whose homes and businesses had been burned out wanted to erect something quickly and cheaply, no matter how flimsy or flammable. As the mayor and the council talked about fire limits, wooden buildings were sprouting up everywhere along Chicago's scorched streets, like mushrooms after a forest fire.

Some of these structures had the blessing of the same authorities who wanted the new Chicago to be less combustible than the old. The Board of Public Works sanctioned the wooden storefronts along the lakefront on Michigan Avenue, while the Chicago Relief and Aid Society encouraged burned-out workers to erect shelter cottages on their lots. Remarkably, 7,983 of these spare pine homes were built between October 18, 1871, and May 1, 1872, furnishing provisional housing for close to forty thousand people. Wood buildings were also rising rapidly in areas outside the Burnt District.

In ways Medill and his core constituency of native-born businessmen and professionals neither acknowledged nor appreciated, many residents, including a large number who had voted for him, believed that a ban on wood everywhere in Chicago discriminated against them. Workers who either had lost their homes and wanted to rebuild or who aspired to own a house one day strongly opposed the stricter proposal. These workers and the aldermen who represented them argued that Medill's assertion about the false economies of wooden buildings was unrealistic. A working family could not afford anything else. And unless burned-out workers could erect new homes on their land, the property was virtually worthless to them. This did not mean they wanted a neighborhood filled with the Relief and Aid Society's fire cottages, which they thought gave the impression of "poverty-stricken shabbiness," but solid homes of their own choosing.

Some real estate investors also chafed at extending fire limits. If allowing special privileges to some and not to others went against the nation's principles, they argued, so did the government telling citizens what they could and could not do with their property. Opponents of Medill's plan gained support from a few prominent Chicagoans, notably William B. Ogden, who said he did not believe it was necessary for safety's sake to outlaw wood buildings in uncrowded parts of the city.

Medill faced the fact that while the city's elite might have the clout to get Philip H. Sheridan appointed, to hand over the world's donations to suffering Chicago to the private Relief and Aid Society, and to fashion the coalition that elected him, these wealthy Yankee businessmen were unable to convince a democratically elected Common Council representing all Chicagoans to adopt his fire limits plan. He was puzzled and angry when the extension proposal provoked objections from working people that blocked its passage and implementation.

Medill and his supporters raged and fumed. They took what consolation they could from the news that on December 29 a grand jury indicted four current and two former aldermen for accepting bribes to have a portion of Randolph Street cleared for certain private businesses at public expense and to back the city's purchase of a particular piece of property for a schoolhouse. Soon seven more were indicted, among them former aldermen James McCauley and none other than James H. Hildreth, he of the gunpowder. Whether justice was served remained an open question. Only four were convicted, while the rest, including McCauley and Hildreth, were either acquitted or the charges against them were eventually dropped.

Construction in Chicago, especially of brick and stone buildings, normally slacked off during winter because the days were shorter and the freezing weather prevented mortar from setting. Even if it was not abnormally cold, the winter of 1871–72 was a miserable one. Heavy rains in early November created a "a horrible condition of mud and nastiness" throughout the city. Just before Christmas a major snowstorm was followed by sleet and rain. Despite the weather and against the backdrop of the argument over expanded fire limits, within six weeks of the fire 212 stone and brick buildings were under construction in the South Division.

The Board of Public Works agreed that the interim city hall on Wabash Avenue and Hubbard Court (Balbo Street) was inadequate but decided that Mayor Mason's plan for erecting a bigger if still temporary building on the site of the Courthouse was impractical for the time being. It instead erected one on a plot of city-owned land three blocks south of Courthouse Square, on the southeast corner of LaSalle and Adams Streets. The site was called the Reservoir Lot since it was partly occupied by a large circular elevated water tank no longer in use, a relic of the previous waterworks distribution system. It was also known as the Old Rookery because of all the birds that flocked around the tank.

Work began right away, on October 17. Since speed and economy were the current priorities, the temporary city hall was a nondescript brick building that, viewed from the outside, resembled a factory or warehouse. It was L-shaped to accommodate the water tank, with legs that stretched almost 180 feet along the LaSalle and Adams Street borders of the property. The mayor's and other executive offices were

CITY HALL BUILDING.

The temporary Chicago city hall at LaSalle and Adams Streets. The water tank, flying the flag, is in the rear. (Chicago History Museum, ICHi-000446)

downstairs, the Common Council on the second floor. Soon the Cook County Circuit and Superior Courts also moved there.

Contractors for new buildings in the downtown made innovative use of derricks, forerunners to construction cranes, to facilitate the erection of taller structures. Masons lit bonfires by mortar beds to keep them workable. Crews would soon employ limelight—incandescent calcium illumination commonly used by theaters—so that they could stay on the job after dark.

The high winds that accompanied the pre-Christmas snow, sleet, and rain toppled freshly constructed brick walls held together with incompletely cured mortar. The *Chicago Tribune* complained that these walls were built "on the approved Chicago principle, with all possible speed and the smallest possible regard for stability."

The *Tribune*'s own reconstruction project contributed to the mounting toll of laborers seriously injured or killed on the job. In early November, twenty-year-old Xavier Martin, one of the workers disassembling the wreck of the paper's prefire building, fell on a spike that fatally punctured his femoral artery. Just before the New Year, bricklayer Michael McMullen plunged to his death from the third floor of the new five-story Field, Leiter & Company wholesale building on the northwest corner of Market (Wacker Drive) and Madison Streets, which the company bragged it completed in one hundred days.

While no one could deny that the Relief and Aid Society had impressively expanded its scope to serve far more people than it had before, complaints about its coldheartedness, prejudices, and onerous regulations continued. Critics, especially the *Chicago Republican*, the *Illinois Staats-Zeitung*, and some members of the Common Council, accused the society of inefficiency, maladministration of aid, favoritism, nepotism, thievery, and fraud. These were the same things the society and its supporters said would have occurred had the aid been left in the hands of the General Relief Committee and the Board of Aldermen.

In response, Society Superintendent O. C. Gibbs placed notices in the papers requesting that "all persons who feel that they have been treated with incivility, rudeness, or neglect by any visitor, clerk, or other person connected with any District Office of the Chicago Relief and Aid Society, will at once report the facts to the Superintendent of the District." Unless clients officially registered their grievances, the notices stated, "it will be impossible to correct evils and abuses, which the officers of the society are as anxious to correct as anyone in the community can be."

Register grievances they did, though not in the manner Gibbs prescribed. At a December 21 meeting that drew a thousand people, Chicago Germans again protested the irregularities and abuses in the Relief and Aid Society's distribution of aid to working people on the North Side. They demanded that the superintendent select his subordinates from the residents of the area, "it being a notorious fact" that the current functionaries had little knowledge of human nature in general and of the German language in particular. As a result, society employees "were unable to discriminate between the worthy and the unworthy or to establish a bond of sympathy between themselves and those who receive aid, or to gain the confidence of the residents of the district."

Even the *Tribune*, the mayor's newspaper and the Chicago Relief and Aid Society's strongest defender, found faults in the treatment of fire victims who had lost their homes. With the onset of freezing weather in late November, a *Tribune* reporter inspected all four of the sets of barracks. He judged the facilities at Clybourn Avenue and Halsted Street in the West Division, home to 158 families, the best; they promoted health and cleanliness by providing good drainage, sidewalks over the mud, and well-placed outhouses.

The barracks at Centre Avenue (Racine) and Harrison Streets in the West Division, however, were "simply beastly." Here as many as nine people lived in a single accommodation barely large enough to fit a stove and a single bed. These barracks lacked privacy, separation of the sexes, and appropriate spaces for children, who ran about "dirty, squalid, [and] half-clad." The floors were low quality boards with gaps between them "through which the wind sucks up from beneath." The draft "chills to the bone the wretched occupants, and brings in its train a perfect epidemic of colds, rheumatism, and pulmonary affections."

Residents who spent their own money to purchase lumber and rags to block the spaces in the floor told the *Tribune* reporter that they feared the Shelter Committee would remove these unauthorized fixes. Decent food was expensive since the Relief and Aid Society denied a family rations if any member could work, which forced barracks families whose breadwinners were employed to pay a premium price to whatever grocers they could find. "The general condition is one of poverty, degradation, and distress," the reporter concluded.

The Reverend Robert Collyer, who had become the embodiment of postfire faith and resilience when he led nondenominational worship in the ruins of his Unity Church, answered the *Tribune* exposé by conducting an assessment of his own. The paper published his findings. Collyer's defense did more to reveal the insensitivities and biases of the city's elite than to make a convincing case that the barracks provided decent housing.

The contortions in Collyer's language and reasoning would have been ludicrous had not the situation he was describing been so distressing. The best he could say about the construction of the barracks was that they were "rough and ready," the kind of shelter "as I should be glad to creep into with my family out of a barn." While Collyer admitted that he saw little of what he could call "real comfort" and witnessed much "discomfort," he claimed that no barracks resident was "hopelessly uncomfortable."

Like John Hay in his visit to the O'Leary neighborhood, Collyer blamed the squalor he saw on the inhabitants themselves. Collyer wrote that every living space he visited was "in some measure, the expression of the nature and life of those that are in it." His assessment of "the nature and life" of Chicagoans of different backgrounds adhered to stereotypes. An Irish couple lived in "one of the most cheerless places," while the rooms of a Scottish-Bohemian family that had added slats, curtains, insulation, and shelves were cheerful. It did not seem to bother Collyer that the shelves were where the children in the Scottish-Bohemian family slept. He could not resist adding that "if you should put a Yankee family" into the barracks and "give them a few pennies' worth of newspapers and a little pot of paste," they would make an appealing and decent home for themselves.

The close of 1871 brought a memorable event that distracted Chicagoans from their recent troubles and pumped up local pride, at least among civic leaders. The whole country was excited by the national goodwill tour of Grand Duke Alexis of Russia, the dashing twenty-one-year-old son of Czar Alexander II. A distant fourth in line to the throne, Alexis was beginning a career as a naval officer.

Chicago was overjoyed to be selected as one of his major stops, even if he was scheduled to visit in the dead of winter. Alexis was to arrive on Saturday, December 30, and remain a whole week, during which he would make a side trip to Milwaukee. In anticipation of Alexis's visit, Mayor Medill wrote to the grand duke to apologize for "the inadequate reception" he would receive because of the city's travails. "We have little to exhibit," the mayor explained, "except the ruins and *debris* of a great and beautiful city, and an undaunted people struggling with adversity to retrieve their overwhelming misfortunes."

A reception committee including General Philip H. Sheridan, Isaac N. Arnold, J. Young Scammon, and several aldermen joined Mayor Medill on a special train to meet Alexis at the Indiana-Illinois border southeast of the city and accompany him from there. George Pullman provided five luxury railroad cars so the party could make its entrance in grand style. When the train reached Chicago, former mayors Julian Rumsey, John Blake Rice, and Roswell Mason, as well as William Bross, Wirt Dexter, Anton Hesing, Herman Raster, and Wilbur Storey, were in the line-up of greeters.

In his speech of welcome, Medill stated that while Chicago had been "severely singed and scorched," the city's vitality was as irrepressible as ever. He went heavy on the figurative language. "She [Chicago]," the mayor assured Alexis, "still wields her business scepter as the queen of the lakes—the metropolis of the Northwest—the focus of railroads—the nation's store-house for bread and meat, and the prairies' depot for lumber, iron, and merchandise."

As they did with all visitors, Chicago's leaders planned to impress the royal visitor with how the city accomplished everything—even burning down—in a big way. His hosts arranged a New Year's Day tour of the Union Stock Yards and the areas the fire had devastated. The weather was predictably terrible: a dispiriting and chilling rain fell, and a clinging fog obscured the lake. The swampy streets made for a difficult slog.

The grand duke was game. At six foot two, with curly blond hair and bright blue eyes, he cut a striking figure, all the more so when he stood next to "Little Phil" Sheridan, one of his main tour guides. During

Alexis's stop at the Union Stock Yards, a reporter noted, he "seemed greatly interested, watching carefully the progress of the porcine slaughter, from the last squeal to the final concealment of the meat in barrels ready for shipment." The next day the royal visitor took in the North Division, including an inspection of the repaired waterworks and a drive by Mahlon Ogden's mansion, during which Alexis likely saw the barracks in Washington Square Park. Sheridan also arranged an excursion a few weeks later on the Nebraska plains during which the grand duke shot bison with William Frederick "Buffalo Bill" Cody and, less than five years before the Battle of the Little Big Horn, witnessed a Sioux war dance and met both Brulé Lakota chief Spotted Tail and General George Armstrong Custer.

During his stay in Chicago, Alexis addressed the members of the Board of Trade. "I hope that before many years have passed Chicago will be as rich, as great, as prosperous, as she was at the time the great conflagration occurred," the grand duke told them. When he announced that he would host the public at a reception, Chicagoans responded enthusiastically. By the end of the evening, Alexis had shaken hands with two thousand well-wishers in the dining room of his hotel, John B. Drake's New Tremont House.

Before he departed, the grand duke donated $5,000 to the city's recovery, which Medill distributed among several of the city's orphan asylums and foundling homes. And then the royal visitor was gone, leaving the city pleased with itself and guardedly optimistic about what lay ahead.

The Common Council began 1872 by trying to settle the contested question of extending fire limits to the entire city. After months of studies and debate, it appeared that the aldermen would finally resolve the fire limits issue at their regularly scheduled biweekly council meeting on Monday evening, January 15. What happened dramatized the divisions and resentments that made it so difficult to reach consensus on any major matter.

The Eighteenth Ward, located along the North and Main Branches of the Chicago River in the southwest corner of the North Division, led the resistance to the proposed fire limit extension. Inhabited largely by German and Irish workers, it was the sole ward that had not gone for Medill in the recent election. Two Irish Chicagoans, Thomas Carney and John McCaffrey, represented it on the Common Council.

On the Saturday night preceding the council meeting, ward residents opposed to the expansion of fire limits met at Carney's grocery store at Illinois and Market (Orleans) Streets. The crowd was angry, impatient to do more than just pass resolutions stating their objections to the extension of fire limits to where they lived. "Some hot heads even swore they would lynch the first policeman who should dare to arrest a father of a family who builds a wooden hut on his plot," the *Illinois Staats-Zeitung* reported.

Calmer attendees pointed out that they were not against all fire limits. They said that restrictions were fine in the center of the city, on both sides of the Main Branch, and in the southeastern section of the North Division between Wells Street and the lake. Many also were ready to accept limits on the height of wooden buildings. For several weeks Anton Hesing and others had been advancing such a compromise.

Hesing, who had backed Medill's candidacy, saw the fire limits fight as an occasion not only to express his sense of betrayal but also strengthen his standing in the urban immigrant community. He accused the mayor and prolimits interests of waging a thinly disguised war against foreign-born working people. He cited Wilbur Storey's paper deriding him as "Kaiser Hesing" and stating that Germans were "aliens, not Americans." Hesing's *Staats-Zeitung* called Storey "the grey old scoundrel." The protesters who attended this Saturday night gathering agreed to rally again early Monday evening and then march to the council meeting at the interim city hall at LaSalle and Adams, where Hesing would present their case.

Several of the many who assembled for the procession on Monday carried banners and illuminated signs with hortatory slogans, such as "Leave a Home for the Laborer" and "Don't Vote Any More for the Poor Man's Oppressor." At least one sign was edgier, displaying an image of a man in a noose, with the caption, "The Future of Those Who Vote for the Fire Ordinance." In addition to burned-out working-class homeowners, the demonstration attracted young male troublemakers drawn by the possibility of violent conflict, even if they had to start it.

With a band blaring away, the marchers strode southward and into the LaSalle Street Tunnel, then down LaSalle to the new temporary city hall at Adams Street.

Hearing the clamor, the aldermen in the second floor council chamber left their seats to peer out the windows. They viewed what was by then a mob, which became all the more stirred up at the sight of the alarmed aldermen. As the demonstrators pushed into the building, council president John McAvoy abandoned normal parliamentary procedure and unilaterally declared immediate adjournment.

Some in the crowd threw stones and bricks—perhaps a weaponized commentary on these as approved building materials—through the windows. One of these missiles hit police sergeant Louis J. Lull full in the face, injuring him very badly. Hesing would later express "the strongest reprobation" and regret that "boy gangsters"—certainly not honest working people—had committed this act. Soon other police officers, including Captain Michael Hickey, were on the scene to break up the riot.

Fire limits supporters stated that the protesters wished nothing less than the violent overthrow of the current order. Under the headline "COMMUNISM" the *Tribune* attacked the "howling" participants in the "torch-light procession." It distinguished between this thrill-seeking rabble and the "respectable" Germans and Irish who owned lots, but it did not scruple to emphasize Hesing's foreignness. The mob, the *Tribune* said, recalled the excesses of the *canaille* during the French Revolution and the antipopery riots (not that the *Tribune* was in favor of popery) in the same period in England.

This was mild compared to the coverage in the *Chicago Times*, which was replete with the kind of pungent detail that won the paper its large readership. The *Times* account described how the stove in Carney's store—called his "gin-shop"—was "struggling vainly with a huge hunk of anthracite" as the protesters in "Hesing's mob" assembled. It characterized them as a "horde of ruffians" and "mongrel fire-bugs." Among their number, the *Times* charged, was "a smattering" of the Communist Internationale. As they pushed through the LaSalle Street Tunnel, the paper stated, they broke into a deafening version of "Watch on the Rhine," the anthem of Prussian troops.

"The Dutch [a common term for Germans] had captured the city hall," the paper said of the marchers who forced their way into the building. The *Times* claimed that these "animals loose in the council chamber" trampled "ruthlessly" on the American flag, broke open aldermen's desks, and shredded official documents with "their dirty greasy" fingers. The mob was the fiery catastrophe of October personified. It struck "almost as much terror to the souls of the right thinking and law-abiding members of the community as did the terrible fire of which they were the sequel." After the protesters sacked the council chamber, the *Times* reported, they returned to Carney's for a "grand orgie," where "flowing bowls of lager were drained in quick succession."

Hesing answered that this kind of defamatory coverage revealed the prevailing hostility in the English-language press toward immigrants, especially ones who stood up for their rights. "All the infernal hullabaloo of [the] *Tribune* and *Times*, all the capon-like crowing of the *Evening Journal*, all the deep moral indignation of the *Evening Post* about the 'horror' of Monday night have been in vain," he declared. "The infamous nativistic maliciousness has in vain been appealed to by the aristocratic money-bags against the just demands of the workers and small-plot owners."

While there was little doubt that the meeting, one of the most embattled in the city's long history of no-holds-barred politics, disintegrated into a melee, the source of the violence was likely the troublemakers who tagged along rather than the North Division workers and property owners. Virtually all of the *Times'* details were fiction. More reliable reports have the angry demonstrators flourishing flags but trampling none. The only patriotic tune their band played was "The Star-Spangled Banner."

Though there was no recurrence of such scenes, the charges and countercharges over the next few weeks kept the cauldron of bad feeling boiling. Critics of the demonstrators demanded a hearing by a criminal grand jury. Hesing retorted that he welcomed one. "When Chicagoans heretofore proudly boasted of the rapidity with which the population of the city increased," he asked, "did they never reflect that the thousands of small frame cottages springing up in a wide circle around the business centre had a great deal to do with such increasement of the city's population?" In this city, "our thrifty laboring classes are not dependent upon the good grace of, but the *makers of* capital." The fire limits debate thus became one over who were better and truer Americans and Chicagoans, the rich native-born businessmen or the hardworking immigrants.

The issue of Americanness soon was the topic of an exchange of public letters, published in several newspapers, between Hesing and the Reverend Robert Collyer, who had recently defended the barracks and seemed to be staking out a position as an immigrant defender of Yankee leadership and of the idea that the United States was a completely open and equitable society.

Collyer initiated the exchange, perhaps unaware that he was picking a fight with someone at least as articulate as he was. The clergyman's point was how much immigrants owed the United States for the hospitality it afforded them. As a result, the proper patriotic response in the current moment was to support the expansion of fire limits. It might be acceptable to plead poverty in some other land, where the poor man had no chance to get ahead, but not in a democratic country where all enjoyed equality of opportunity. Collyer said he felt the Chicago workingmen's current pain, but if they lived frugally they would recover in time. They must not think of themselves, but of the good of the city, during Chicago's rebuilding.

Hesing begged to differ. In his icy reply to what he called Collyer's "very unctuous treatise on the duties of adopted citizens," Hesing remarked that Collyer evidently was unaware of the vast difference between being an immigrant from England and one from Germany. The good reverend obviously had no idea of the discrimination and mockery people with a German accent and name encountered in their daily lives. In spite of this, Chicago's Germans adored their adopted country and city. He was agreeable to fire limits, but they should not forbid North Division workers from rebuilding their homes with wood. Hesing directly rejected Collyer's claim that "the people" demanded what Medill was proposing. In point of fact, he countered, "Neither Mr. Medill nor the editors of two or three papers are the people of Chicago."

Previously a grand jury had decided not to charge Theodore Treat with the murder of Thomas Grosvenor. Now another one refused to indict those who disrupted the January 15 Common Council meeting.

The angry fire limits debate continued in the Common Council for the next several weeks. On February 12 the aldermen passed a revised ordinance. It extended the current limits farther to the west, south, and north, but not into the heavily immigrant worker neighborhoods west of Wells Street and north of Chicago Avenue. It placed restrictions on especially fire-prone businesses and permitted a majority of landowners on a particular block to vote to outlaw buildings with flammable materials. The new measure said little about improved enforcement.

The law was not what Medill wanted, but it was the best he was going to get. The "foreigners" had beaten the "Americans" at the game of urban politics.

14

NEW CHICAGO

Chicago's rebuilding, already robust, picked up considerably in the spring of 1872 with the advent of warmer temperatures and longer hours of daylight. The state of Illinois passed the Destroyed Public Records Act, which stated that the privately held land records of the kind that John G. Shortall carted to safety would "have the same force and effect as certified copies of the original record" that had been lost when the Courthouse burned. The documents collectively held by Shortall's firm and by two other companies were consolidated in a store on Lake Street in the West Division. Claims based on these copies were published in Myra Bradwell's *Chicago Legal News*.

Attorney and banker J. Young Scammon was a particularly active participant in the recovery. He purchased the *Chicago Republican* in late January, changing its name to the *Chicago Inter-Ocean* in March. It took as its motto "Republican in everything, Independent in nothing," to differentiate itself from the *Chicago Tribune*, which sometimes swayed from party orthodoxy. Scammon rebuilt his Marine Building, on the northeast corner of LaSalle and Lake Streets, according to the bigger-is-better trend of the postfire city. The stone structure he lost was four stories, the replacement six.

The new Palmer House hotel, not completed until 1873, came with one of the highest price tags of any building in the new Chicago—more than $2 million, plus another $600,000 for furnishings. Guests could stroll among the palms and other exotic potted plants in the rooftop tropical garden. African American men attired in white tie and tails waited upon them in the dining room. Thirty-two chairs stood in two long rows in the resplendently mirrored barbershop, where the floor was inlaid with silver dollars. Suspended from the ceiling of the lobby was a magnificent crystal chandelier. Advertisements declared that the Palmer House was the "only thoroughly fireproof hotel in the United States."

The federal government decided to move the Post Office and Custom House slightly south from its prefire location on the northwest corner of Dearborn and Monroe Streets to the block bordered by Adams, Dearborn, Jackson, and Clark Streets, though it did not complete the new home until the end of the decade. After he acquired the site of the old building, J. H. Haverly salvaged remnants of the burned Post Office and Custom House when erecting the largest theater in Chicago. Cook County constructed a three-story criminal court a few blocks north of the Main Branch of the Chicago River, between Dearborn and Clark.

The Chamber of Commerce, which housed the Board of Trade, took a starring role in the return to the reviving downtown. It scheduled a formal celebration on October 9, 1872, the first anniversary of the fire, for the opening of its new building on its old site across from Courthouse Square. At midday, members and their guests—including mayors Joseph Medill and John Blake Rice, though not Roswell B. Mason—proceeded eastward along Washington Street from the Chamber of Commerce's temporary quarters in the West Division to the new structure. A band played "Home Again," followed by a glee club's rendition of "Auld Lang Syne."

The commissioners of the West Division parks asked William LeBaron Jenney to design a monument to the Great Fire. No one seems to have proposed placing it in the downtown, or anywhere else in the Burnt District, perhaps because there was too much demand for real estate there. Jenney was a native of Massachusetts who studied architecture in Paris, where one of his fellow students was Gustave Eiffel, best known for his eponymous 1889 tower. Jenney moved to Chicago after serving as a military engineer for the Union Army, in which he rose to the rank of major. He initially proposed constructing the monument out of safes and rubble taken from the ruins, remnants of the Chicago that was. When critics rejected this as undignified, he created a plan for a Gothic tower of salvaged stones supporting a female figure holding a torch.

On the cold, gray, and windy day of October 30, 1872, dignitaries watched as workmen laid the cornerstone of the monument near the Washington Boulevard entrance of what is now Garfield Park. West Division park commissioners Charles C. P. Holden and Henry Greenebaum were present, and Mayor Medill spoke. A tin time capsule was placed in a vault beneath the stone. It contained, among several other things, a fragment of the Courthouse bell and a description of Chicago a year after the fire.

Harper's Weekly had praised the world's generosity toward Chicago as "the silver lining of the cloud." Now Chicago's boosters maintained that the fire was its own silver lining, a speedy bit of urban renewal. After all, it destroyed shabby and outdated buildings, making way for bigger and better construction and, along with it, increased property values.

The fire anniversary triggered much self-congratulation of this sort. The *Chicago Times* published a special section on the year's progress,

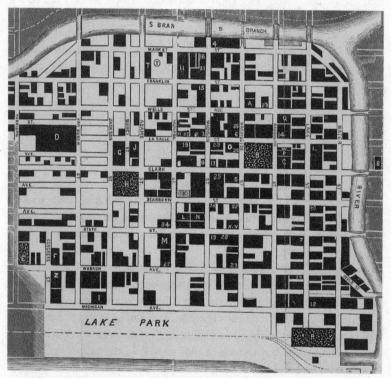

Map of the rebuilt downtown. North is to the right. The area at the bottom (east), labeled "Lake Park," which includes the former lagoon by now filled with fire rubble, is part of the current site of Grant and Millennium Parks. From New Chicago, 1872. *(Chicago History Museum, ICHi-064137)*

which it subsequently reprinted as a booklet titled *New Chicago*. The special section and the booklet chronicled the Great Fire itself, the resolve to rebuild, the work of the relief, and reconstruction to date. The most informative feature of the booklet was a fold-out map of the downtown, with new "permanent" (i.e., brick and stone) buildings marked in black. It showed plenty of blank space, especially at the western, southern, and eastern edges, but the progress was unmistakable.

J. M. Wing, publisher of the local real estate periodical *The Land Owner*, issued a similar anniversary volume, *Chicago Illustrated: One Year from the Fire*. The book was packed with large drawings of new buildings culled from the magazine's regular issues. During the previous year, *Chicago Illustrated* cheerfully noted, the air was full of "the noise of hammer and trowel," a sound "that heralds the coming of great multitudes to dwell among us." The next sentence was a Whitmanesque exhortation: "Arise, glorious and unconquered city, to be the metropolis of America!"

The *Lakeside Memorial of the Burning of Chicago*, another commemorative publication, offered essays on various aspects of the fire and its aftermath. In discussing the city's current prospects, it was mostly positive, but it included two entries that mourned the devastating effect of the fire on the higher pursuits in Chicago, notably education and the arts.

Erastus O. Haven, a Methodist minister who was president of Northwestern University in suburban Evanston, was as confident as boosters William Bross and John S. Wright that Chicago would fully recover economically because of its vital importance to the region and the nation. Summoning language that joined theology and boosterism, he stated, "It is a predestination that so long as that section of the country called the Northwest has life, here must be its heart."

Haven was far less sanguine about the city's "intellectual and moral vitality." He believed that this had been slighted during Chicago's formative years because of the emphasis on commercial growth, and he now worried that the focus on rebuilding ignored the city's hard-earned educational, spiritual, and cultural progress. The fire claimed many schools, whose space had already been inadequate for a city so populous. As a clergyman, he particularly mourned the damage to churches, which he considered "the mother of democracy and self government." Museums, galleries, and libraries would have to start again from scratch. "Magnificent wholesale palaces" were all well and good, but they were not "extraordinary monuments of the sagacity or courage of their builders, any more than the tall corn of our prairies is an indication of extraordinary science and skill in our farmers."

The author of the other essay of this kind, David Hilton Wheeler, was, at fifty-two, a decade older than Haven. As Wheeler aged and his dark hair thinned and turned snowy white, he traded the full beard of his youth for a goatee and a handlebar mustache whose tips were as far apart as his ears. He, too, was a Methodist minister, but he had also served as US consul in Genoa and as correspondent for two different *Tribune*s, first in New York and then in Chicago, before becoming a professor of English, university trustee, and, for a brief period, interim president at Northwestern.

In an article titled "The Political Economy of the Fire," Wheeler observed that the destruction of unique scientific specimens, books, art works, and heirlooms was a more severe blow than the loss of buildings, since the latter could be far more readily replaced. Like Haven, he was especially distressed by the adverse effects of the fire on cultural life. "If young men are demanded to produce grain and build houses, they cannot frequent colleges, libraries, or art studios," he observed.

Like Haven, Wheeler believed that the physical city would revive speedily, but the tone of public life would suffer for a long time. This setback "torments the thoughtful spirit with painful apprehensions," Wheeler wrote. "The vast army of counter-jumpers, bartenders, and political bummers, is recruited from among the imperfectly educated young men," who "want all forms of discipline and culture." Wheeler's attitude was narrow and snobbish—it expressed the view of people who did not worry about how to pay the rent or put bread on the table—but his thoughts about Chicago as a place to live and not just work were well worth considering.

At least a small portion of the contributions that poured into Chicago was intended to bolster cultural life. Even before the disaster, citizens complained that the city lacked a free municipal library. Public libraries were a mid- to late nineteenth-century development. One of the pioneering examples, the Boston Public Library, was not founded until 1852. Smaller libraries endowed by industrialist Andrew Carnegie would not start appearing until the 1880s. The most widely accessible private subscription library in prefire Chicago, the Chicago Library Association, lost both its home and its books when the city burned. Following the fire, the idea of finally establishing a truly public library received wide support, including from an unexpected crucial source.

On November 16, 1871, an Englishman named A. H. Burgess sent a letter to the editor of the *London Daily News* outlining a proposal that "England should present a new Free Library to Chicago, to remain there as a mark of sympathy now, and a keepsake and token of true brotherly kindness forever." The *Chicago Tribune* reprinted the letter three weeks later. The idea caught the attention of Thomas Hughes, member of Parliament and author of the popular 1857 novel *Tom Brown's School Days*. Chicago had impressed Hughes when he visited it the year before the fire. Working with an organization called the Anglo-American Association, Hughes began the campaign in Britain to help found a public library in Chicago as Burgess suggested.

Contributions arrived from publishers and learned societies, as well as from such political, philosophical, and literary luminaries as Benjamin Disraeli, John Stuart Mill, and Alfred, Lord Tennyson. A copy of *The Early Years of the Prince Consort*, a biography of the late Prince Albert, arrived with a very special inscription: "Presented to the City of Chicago towards the formation of a public library, after the fire of 1871, as a mark of English sympathy, by Her Majesty, Queen Victoria." Pending shipment of the books to Chicago, they were stored in London's Crystal Palace, the iron and glass marvel in Hyde Park that had housed the 1851 Great Exhibition, the first modern world's fair. With the cooperation of a publisher in Germany, the library also acquired books from that country, which were further supplemented by gifts from dozens of Americans.

Mayor Medill pledged fifty dollars to the campaign and appointed a special committee of twenty-two citizens to direct the project, which they approved in late January. Leading the committee was lawyer Thomas Hoyne, who five years later wrote a history of the library. "What can be made a prouder circumstance in the history of what has hitherto been the most unexampled rise and progress of any city which has ever existed," read the committee's report, "than the period of its greatest calamity was also the period from which it dated its greatest literary and moral advancement, and that side by side with its *indomitable* commercial spirit, went thenceforward also the genius of our highest modern civilization?"

On March 7, 1872, the state legislature incorporated Chicago's first public library, but the question remained of where to put it. Some suggested Dearborn Park, on the west side of Michigan Avenue between Randolph and Washington Streets. That would have required new construction at a time when public resources were thin and, as Wheeler noted, culture was taking a back seat to commerce. Instead, the library and its collection of thirteen thousand books opened on January 1, 1873, in a very unconventional space: the decommissioned and now empty water tank—sixty feet in diameter, thirty feet high, and elevated one hundred feet above the ground—behind the temporary city hall at Adams and LaSalle.

It was no Crystal Palace. A drawing of the interior shows well-dressed male and female patrons in the new "book room." Some sit at desks in the center, while others pull volumes from shelves set along the circular wall. Hot in the summer, cold in the winter, the tank was at all times a serious climb for anyone who wished to browse the collection.

By the second anniversary of the fire in October 1873, stores, offices, hotels, restaurants, and entertainment venues spread out over an area of about forty-five blocks, slightly more than double the size of the downtown before the fire. Many of these structures were four or five stories tall, some a few stories higher, and equipped with elevators, another recent advance.

While businesses were not strictly segregated by type, retail continued to shift east, toward State Street and Wabash and Michigan Avenues. Wholesale concerns, led by Farwell & Company and Field, Leiter & Company, clustered along and below Madison and Monroe Streets near Wells Street. West of the still empty Courthouse Square were lawyers, brokers, and bankers.

The public library in the converted water tank.
(Chicago History Museum, ICHi-013217)

The McCormick Reaper Works, previously on the north bank of the Main Branch of the Chicago River, joined other large industrial companies in migrating well south and west of the downtown to previously undeveloped real estate along the South Branch, between the city's center and the heretofore remote Union Stock Yards. A new manufacturing district arose farther west, between Ashland and Western Avenues, Twenty-Second Street, and the West Fork of the South Branch. In a continuation of the trend that also began before the fire, people of all income levels moved farther from the downtown. Several of the richest Chicagoans—Wirt Dexter, Marshall Field, and George Pullman, among others—built mansions on Prairie Avenue, most of them at or just below Eighteenth Street.

Wealthy native-born North Side residents knew that even if they rebuilt on their large lots, their prefire enclave was a thing of the past. The mature trees and gracious landscaping had been wiped away, and the commercial city was pushing north. For some, the elegant reaches of the South Division and the suburbs offered more attractive alternatives. Several elite North Siders did move back, however, and in a big way. Cyrus McCormick built a three-story urban chateau on Superior Street. Julian Rumsey's family tried the far western suburb of Geneva, but the Rumseys soon returned to the city, where they rented a house near the Prairie Avenue nabobs. By 1874 they were back in a big house on Huron Street. "There was a room for dancing on the third floor," Ada Rumsey remembered, "and in every way it was noted for its hospitality." They were very happy to be again so close to St. James Episcopal Church, whose prefire bell tower, now smoke-stained, was integrated into the new building.

Isaac N. Arnold, another North Division St. James congregant, was profoundly grateful to be in his rebuilt house on Erie Street by the first anniversary of the fire. He recalled how a year earlier he had wandered the Sands while escaping from the flames. "It has been a year of work and effort, not without comfort and gratification," he confided in his journal. "I desire to express gratitude and thanks to God for preservation, for health, for health of my family, and for restoration to home."

Chicagoans of comfortable if not lavish means joined the general outward migration, whether to the suburbs or to desirable neighborhoods either within or just outside Chicago near the semicircular array of major city parks: Lincoln Park on the North Side; Central (later Garfield), Douglas, and Humboldt Parks in the West; and Jackson and Washington Parks in what was then the southern suburb of Hyde Park, which Chicago would annex in 1889 along with several other neighboring communities as it expanded to close to its present size.

As they stated so emphatically during the fire limits controversy, North Division workers wished to rebuild on their old lots, and the compromise reached by the Common Council enabled most of them to do so. A large number of other laboring people who had lived elsewhere decided to move farther out in the city or beyond, whether to the south, west, or north, where they might fulfill the enduring goal of home ownership.

In 1860 only 8,000 people lived in the ring of land between three and five miles from the center of the city; by 1870 some 55,000 did so, and by 1873 nearly 100,000. Train lines to suburban towns passed through open areas, since much of the land near the city's northern and western limits was still the undeveloped prairie where Chicagoans had found refuge from the fire.

Months after the disaster, donors from far away continued to extend the hand of fellowship to Chicago. In late December 1871, William Wright, the American consul in Santos, Brazil, transmitted to Mayor Medill about seven hundred dollars donated locally "for the benefit of the unfortunate sufferers by the late terrible conflagration." The following month the Manchester (England) Relief Committee sent 249 cases and bales of blankets, quilts, rugs, scarves, shawls, skirts, velveteen, and flannel to help see Chicagoans through the winter.

In addition to the Chicago Relief and Aid Society, many different organizations within the city kept up their relief work. Women were vital to almost all of them, volunteering at the distribution centers and starting initiatives of their own. As ever, commentary on the recipients of aid was deeply condescending. The *Tribune* applauded "the ladies of our city" for "a most commendable interest in the wants of the poorer classes." The *Tribune* thanked the Ladies' Christian Union for expecting people to work if they wished for assistance, which kept away "the lazy and worthless" and gave encouragement to the "willing and industrious."

The Relief and Aid Society, however, remained by far the major distributor of relief. Its detailed records—which listed every contribution of cash and goods, from A. T. Stewart's $50,000 to a single box of clothing from the Young Ladies' Mission Circle of the First Congregational Church of Muscatine, Iowa—reveal the colossal scale and breadth of its work. In its 1874 report, the society stated that it had received $4,820,146.16 in cash donations, $3,846,032.71 of that from the United States. The cost of food and goods it administered cannot be calculated nearly as precisely, but it was almost certainly in the low millions of dollars. The value of cash, provisions, and goods contributed directly to other organizations raised the total of aid donated to Chicago by a few million more.

Between October 1871 and May 1873, the society's staff and volunteers assisted almost 160,000 people in close to 40,000 families. The society's breakdown of recipients by national origin and race (e.g., American, German, Irish, Negro, Scandinavian, etc.) demonstrated that its administrators saw them as members of separate groups and not collectively as Chicagoans needing assistance. The Employment Bureau found jobs for 20,232 people, of whom 11,811 were laborers. The society spent $281,489.03 on special relief, not counting $138,855.26 on sewing machines and $10,742.00 on other tools to help Chicagoans get back to work. The cost of the barracks and shelter houses and their furnishings was $919,680.89, the second largest expenditure behind that for supplies, which was $1,171,564.42.

The society's Health Department, under Dr. Hosmer Johnson, treated 89,724 patients and filled 76,660 prescriptions. The department vaccinated some 64,000 Chicagoans against smallpox. As a result, the society claimed, the deadly disease was a less serious problem in Chicago than other cities during the 1871–72 epidemic, and the overall mortality rate was the same as in nonexceptional times.

These numbers and all the planning, coordination, and effort they reflect were absolutely remarkable, worthy of the highest praise. Henry Ward Beecher's comments notwithstanding, the city could have done very well without the fire, but, given that the conflagration occurred, it could not have revived nearly as quickly without the efforts of the Relief and Aid Society. There was nonetheless much to criticize about the way in which the unquestionably hardworking members of the Executive Committee under Wirt Dexter understood what they were doing and formulated policy.

In the 1874 report—prepared by journalist Sydney Howard Gay, who had written favorable articles about the organization in the *Tribune* and in the *Lakeside Memorial of the Burning of Chicago*—the Relief and Aid Society stuck to its narrative that it heroically and selflessly intervened to rescue the relief contributions and thus the people of Chicago from the bummer politicians. Perhaps the society was right in contending that if aldermen had administered the aid, they would have done a worse job. But the actual story is more complicated and less flattering than the one the society told.

In late March 1872, Charles C. P. Holden and other members of the Common Council met with Mayor Medill and Wirt Dexter to pressure the Relief and Aid Society to deposit its funds in the city treasury, or at least to allow the mayor to distribute a portion of this money under the direction of the Common Council. Predictably, the society said no. Speaking in Dexter's legalese, it maintained disingenuously that its decision had nothing to do with its own preferences. The terms under which it had received the money—which it said was entrusted to the society, not the city government—made fulfilling the request impossible. It did not acknowledge that the society itself, and not the donors, had defined the terms in this self-serving way.

The businessmen who led the Relief and Aid Society had always argued that, if given the opportunity, members of the Common Council would use relief contributions to line their own pockets. They may have been right, but the society's leaders were themselves liable to conflicts of financial interest. A prominent example was the organization's position on the federal protective tariffs that were much favored by Republican administrations. Existing levies on building materials inevitably elevated the cost of construction. The 25 percent tariff on lumber, which was intended primarily to protect domestic companies from Canadian imports, was now especially burdensome, since wood was the single item most essential to the reconstruction of the city. Even buildings covered in brick and stone used large quantities of lumber. The price of lumber had risen by one-third since the fire.

Early in 1872 the US Congress considered a bill that would temporarily exempt Chicago contractors from paying duties on materials employed in the rebuilding. This was not unprecedented. Most recently it had enacted a similar measure for the benefit of Portland, Maine, after that city's conflagration of July 4, 1866. When Senator Thomas Ferry of Michigan retracted his prior support for the bill, this raised suspicions that he had changed his mind at the behest of Wirt Dexter and Chicagoans in the lumber industry, who put their own profits ahead of Chicago's needs.

On February 16, 1872, five hundred Chicago businessmen met to decide what they wanted Congress to do about the tariff. Attendees included Isaac N. Arnold, Marshall Field, Anton Hesing, Thomas Hoyne, George Pullman, J. Young Scammon, and Horace White. *Tribune* editor White was the city's most outspoken opponent of tariffs, which Scammon's *Inter-Ocean* supported.

When a speaker singled out Dexter (who had sent word that he was too ill to attend) as one of the Relief and Aid Society members who "had allowed their avarice to swallow up their own charity," others applauded. T. W. Harvey, who served on the Executive Committee of the society, countered that he and other lumber barons had been misunderstood: their industry supported temporarily lifting the tariff on wood specifically used to rebuild the Burnt District. It was only opposed to a total elimination of the duty no matter where in Chicago the lumber was employed. Other businessmen who were protariff in general supported a resolution in favor of this kind of limited and temporary suspension of tariff duties.

Dexter sent a letter to the papers claiming that he had no lumber investments himself and had only spoken up in opposition to lifting the tariff at the request of Harvey. He repeated that neither he nor Harvey had any problem with the bill as long as the tariff relief applied solely to new buildings in the Burnt District. While it was not relevant to the tariff discussion, Dexter went on to describe all he had done for the city of Chicago, implying that he deserved gratitude, not such accusations. He said he had personally lost more than $20,000 in the fire and, as chair of the Relief and Aid Society's Executive Committee, had ignored his own losses and labored "often far into the morning,—over scenes well calculated to rebuke selfishness."

The Board of Trade of St. Louis objected to the bill on the grounds that it unjustly favored Chicago. The legislatures of Michigan and Wisconsin complained that it would hurt their states' lumber industries. When Congress passed the tariff bill in late March it exempted lumber after all, but the measure proved of little actual economic benefit.

The most revealing criticism of the Relief and Aid Society did not involve mismanagement or self-interest but the Executive Committee's insistence, without authority to do so, that other organizations dispensing assistance follow its priorities and procedures. With a portion of the $100,000 Cincinnatians donated to fire victims, the Cincinnati Relief Committee bypassed intermediaries in establishing what were called soup-houses, first in the West Division and then the North, which ladled out free soup to anyone who wanted it. The street kitchens served four thousand gallons of soup daily. Chicagoans welcomed the free nourishment and almost universally praised the generosity of their sister city.

The Relief and Aid Society strongly disapproved of the soup-houses and wanted to shut them down. In late January, Dexter issued a public letter requesting their immediate closing and listing his reasons. Cincinnati, he pointed out, had never consulted with the Relief and Aid Society about the project or received its approval. Chicagoans needed solid food, not soup, which they were getting in their biweekly allotments from the society. The soup-houses did not keep records, so there was no way to evaluate their work. Standing in a line for such a meager handout was degrading; it made Chicagoans look like paupers. In sum, this form of charity was "utterly unsuited to the needs of a large population of a better class suddenly deprived of their means of support by an unparalleled public calamity."

The real reason for the society's objections was that the soup-houses distributed aid without screening takers to determine if they were needy. By Relief and Aid Society logic, this might turn potentially productive people into actual paupers who might then become permanently dependent on charity. Without careful assessments of the worthiness of recipients, "the dangers attending general, miscellaneous distribution are easily seen," Dexter wrote, the worst being "an evil influence upon character and habits." Chicago's well-being at this precarious time depended on a "resolute hand" to make certain "that no man or woman capable of work be allowed to eat the bread of idleness." Dexter's citing of Proverbs 31 (the virtuous woman "eateth not the bread of idleness") implied that his organization was following sacred Christian duty in opposing the soup-houses.

Speaking for its city's outraged citizens, the *Cincinnati Gazette* accused the Chicago Relief and Aid Society of wanting to seize what remained of the $100,000 gift. The paper noted that in the past Dexter had repeatedly asked to draw directly on the Cincinnati funds and had been rebuffed. The *Gazette* reported that because of warnings from "the best people of Chicago," it had "no confidence in [Dexter's] management." This was an especially sharp insult, since the members of the Executive Committee surely believed "the best people of Chicago" included themselves.

Cincinnati officials charged that Dexter spoke "from interested motives," that he and the society's other leaders "wanted the handling of the money donated by Cincinnati, and nothing short of that would satisfy them." For the record, the *Gazette* made clear, the Cincinnati Relief Committee did not trust Chicago's aldermen either. In the future it would work directly with the mayor and Chicago charities other than the Relief and Aid Society in deciding what to do with its remaining resources.

Even the society's usual defenders in Chicago were unhappy with its stance on the soup-houses. From the start, the *Tribune* had endorsed Mayor Mason's appointment of the society because its leaders were so trustworthy, sensible, and wise. Now it could say nothing better of Dexter's stance than that he presented it "with modesty and good temper."

In a detailed letter sent to the newspapers, thirteen prominent Chicago women, all active in fire relief work, delivered the sharpest rebuke. They responded to an article in the *Tribune* that the soup was of low quality and even unsanitary. One signer was Elisabeth Pullman, wife of Albert Benton Pullman, an executive in the railroad car company headed by his brother George, who was treasurer of the Relief and Aid Society. The women praised the nutritional value of the soup. Anyone who said the project was harmful was just plain wrong. "The very fact that thousands come daily," the letter read, "many of them from long distances, for this soup, and thankfully receive it, is, in itself, in our opinion, a sufficient refutation of the disgraceful charges alluded to above."

Medill tried to mediate the "misunderstanding" over the soup-houses. He thanked Cincinnati for its aid without directly undercutting Dexter, except to say that there was no way to tell whether or not the free distribution of aid created idleness. Time would soon resolve the controversy, he noted. With the coming of spring in a matter of weeks, when the soup-houses were already scheduled to close, there would be more work to be had and far less need for them.

As their criticism of Dexter and the Relief and Aid Society demonstrated, the many Chicago women who participated so extensively in relief efforts as both receivers and givers of aid could offer a discerning inside perspective on the way things were being done. In April 1872 they organized a mass protest meeting of widows, who now charged that the organization failed to perform its duties "in an honorable and impartial manner."

The author of the play *Relief: A Humorous Drama*, listed only as "A Chicago Lady," was almost certainly a woman of social standing in the city, and possibly a young woman, since the play is dedicated to the Philocalian Society of Dearborn Seminary, an exclusive private school for girls in the South Division that enrolled daughters of the city's economic elite. That it was published at all, and by the same company that printed the *Lakeside Fire Memorial*, also suggests that its author was well connected.

Relief is a social satire in five very brief acts that spoofs both the members of the Ladies' Relief Society and their Irish immigrant clients. The members are one-dimensional caricatures who embody their allegorical names: Miss Bombast, Miss Compromise, Miss Pry, Mrs. Pursestring, Mrs. Redtape, and Mrs. Warmheart. They are so absorbed in their virtue that they are easily bamboozled. Their canny clients, with their thick brogues, fondness for liquor and cards, and aversion to honest work, are also cardboard characters.

The clients' ringleader is Maggie O'Brien, the wife of a winning cad named Teddy. The two of them are relatively well off, thanks to Maggie's skills in manipulating the charity women. Maggie passes off the children of a hardworking Scotswoman as her own when she appears before the Ladies' Relief Society to ask for assistance. During her interview, in which she claims to be the impoverished widow of a soldier killed in the Civil War, Maggie furtively pinches the youngest to make the child cry pitiably so that her presentation will be all the more affecting. Asked about her religion, Maggie claims to be Protestant, "a loyil descindint uv the Prince of Orange." When at one point she reflexively crosses herself like the Catholic she is, arousing the suspicion of her interviewers, the quick-thinking Maggie says she is just wiping away tears.

The Ladies' Relief Society members are fussy and foolish but also generous and kind. The Irish impostors are likewise fundamentally good people, if more than a little conniving. By the conclusion of the play, Maggie and the rest are ready to wean themselves from the relief and proceed with their lives. In its own way, *Relief* is as condescending toward and ignorant of the real circumstances of the city's working poor as were Mayor Medill and the Relief and Aid Society's Executive Committee, but it exudes two qualities these men decidedly lacked: self-knowledge and a sense of humor.

With the increase in construction activity in the spring of 1872, about fifty thousand men were employed in rebuilding the city. Skilled laborers asserted their power and dramatized their resolve with a "Grand Demonstration of Trades Unions" on May 15. Several thousand tradesmen walked off their jobs to participate, braving rain and sacrificing a day's wages to join in a parade, along with marching bands, that began at 9:00 a.m. on the West Side and wound through the other divisions. The parade took a judicious detour at one point because of the muddiness of the streets. Its final stop was a rally back in the West Division. Mounted police stood watch.

The workers organized themselves by trade—stonecutters, horseshoers, plasterers, carpenters and joiners, painters, lathers, and bricklayers. The stonecutters colorfully attired themselves in blue silk sashes and white silk aprons imprinted with the image of a mallet and chisel. They stepped smartly behind a large wagon drawn by four horses. Atop the wagon was a large banner, on one side of which was a depiction of men cutting stone, on the other a portrait of George Washington. Taken together, the two sides of the banner proclaimed that Chicago's workers were true patriotic Americans.

In the days leading up to the parade, the major English-language daily newspapers either ignored it or predicted that it would degenerate into violence. They characterized organized labor as the enemy of the city for threatening to strike for higher wages. They expressed no qualms about contractors similarly working together to keep those wages down.

The *Workingman's Advocate* in turn criticized the "avidity" with which most journalists distorted the actions and pleas of "the industrial classes" with falsehood, distortion, ridicule, and demagoguery. It condemned the Chicago landlords who doubled rents at the same time employers treated the request of a raise in wages by fifty cents or a dollar a day as tantamount to "a riot, bloodshed or a resort to violence." The paper also pointed out that many workers received low pay for often hazardous work. And at best they could find employment only 250 days a year. This did not produce enough income to support a family in normal circumstances, let alone during the emergencies that life inevitably presents. Workers had no desire to halt Chicago's reconstruction, but their families had to eat.

Mayor Medill reluctantly accepted an invitation to speak at the rally. He started well enough by praising wage earners as the city's "bone and sinew" and conceding that they had the right to strike for higher salaries. He then demonstrated his political ineptitude by lecturing his audience of union members on the virtues of free market capitalism. Medill warned that employers had the right to refuse their demands and that no one could compel workers to join labor organizations. He repeated the standard businessman's position that unions undercut basic freedoms because they interfered with the rights of workers to negotiate as individuals, overlooking the fact that a single worker had little bargaining leverage and that employers often put up a united front against labor.

The mayor contended that the rise in rents was not the result of landlords banding together but of scattered individuals taking advantage of the situation. He advised workers to accept current wages and erect new buildings as quickly as possible, which would benefit them by creating additional housing. Medill engaged in some magical mathematical thinking when he told them, "You could better afford to work this season for half the existing wages than postpone the rebuilding of the city."

The final speaker of the day was William Cogswell, a union leader from Ottawa, Illinois, about eighty miles southwest of Chicago on the Illinois and Michigan Canal. Cogswell bluntly refuted Medill. The mayor had cited Charles Darwin in implying that workers should acknowledge that life is a struggle for existence. Cogswell made no such specific allusion, but he obviously preferred the insights of Karl Marx. Labor created capital, he proclaimed, not the other way around. Unions "were organized to see why men who lived in brown-stone fronts, and never earned a dollar should live sumptuously, while those who did the work lived poorly." Cogswell exhorted his audience to elect more prolabor officials who would level the playing field now so heavily tilted in favor of moneyed interests.

Anyone who read accounts of the day in the *Workingman's Advocate* and the Chicago dailies would have thought they were describing two different events. Declaring the demonstration a rousing triumph for labor, the *Workingman's Advocate* counted six thousand marchers and thirty thousand spectators. The *Times* deemed it a total failure, stating that there were only half that number in the procession and that it attracted only a small number of unenthusiastic and unsympathetic onlookers. The *Times* belied this estimate when it reported that in thronging to the demonstration workers had briefly halted the rebuilding of the Burnt District.

Labor relations during the summer were tense, though there were no major work stoppages. In the fall, the carpenters and the bricklayers staged strikes. The bricklayers were successful, the carpenters were not. Both demanded the shortening of the workday from ten to eight hours, which they said was more efficient and economical as well as more humane than present practices. William O'Brien of the Bricklayers Union stated that "there isn't a contractor in Chicago who doesn't know that ten bricklayers can do more work in eight hours, than eight can do in ten; and who also doesn't know that there are skilled workmen enough in our city to finish every building in process of construction before winter sets in under the eight hour system, without putting him to a penny's extra cost."

Mayor Medill had not won any friends at the workingmen's rally, but his worst enemies turned out to be some of those who previously had been his most fervent supporters.

The late summer and fall of 1872 witnessed a rise in serious crime. Just what caused this and whether it was a brief aberration are not clear. In any event, the situation prompted Chicago's businessmen to demand immediate and harsh treatment of lawbreakers. Under the leadership of banker Henry Greenebaum, they formed the Committee of Twenty-Five, consisting of members from all three divisions, including *Staats-Zeitung* owner Anton Hesing. Their purpose was to push the authorities to do more to protect rebuilding Chicago's citizens and the city's reputation.

Citing the fact that several of the most serious offenses had taken place in saloons, the outspoken temperance faction in the Committee of Twenty-Five insisted that the solution was to restrict the sale and consumption of alcohol. As they had the previous summer, they demanded the enforcement of the Sunday closing law that had been on the books since 1845 but not seriously enforced since the Lager Beer Riot of 1855.

The revived temperance crusade amounted to blaming immigrants and alcohol for whatever troubles, real or imagined, beset the city. German and Irish Chicagoans of all classes took offense. They opposed drunken rowdiness, but they were not going to stand for self-righteous Yankees condemning a Sunday glass of beer with family and friends as an act of moral turpitude. Greenebaum and Hesing resigned from the committee in protest.

Mayor Medill was in a difficult bind. He abjured alcohol himself, but even he was politically savvy enough to understand that implementing the Sunday ordinance would do more to provoke protests than to halt crime. Besides, enforcement was nigh impossible in a city with only 450 police officers. Medill told temperance backers "that to stop liquor drinking would require the aid of one teetotaler policeman to be stationed in every saloon, billiard hall, house of ill-fame and tavern in Chicago—say 3,000 in all." He reminded them that they already objected to paying the taxes needed to field the current force.

The temperance leaders countered that the Sunday ordinance was a law, and, like it or not, it was Medill's obligation to follow it. He dutifully ordered his recently appointed police superintendent, Elmer Washburn, to do so. Washburn, who had previously overseen the state prison in Joliet, hesitated briefly before directing officers to enforce the law. This was to start on Sunday, October 20, 1872, less than two weeks after the first anniversary of the fire. Some saloon keepers did shut down, though a few demonstrated against the new policy. Many did neither, since it was easy to serve thirsty Chicagoans without attracting attention. Proprietors kept their front doors closed and the curtains down as they carried on as usual.

Through the rest of the year and into 1873, the police board and the mayor clashed over the enforcement of Sunday closing, leading to commissioner Mark Sheridan's resignation. Having lost the fire limits fight and pleased nobody on the temperance issue, Medill was fed up with being mayor. On August 18, 1873, with almost four months remaining in his term, he submitted a letter to the Board of Aldermen informing them that for unspecified health reasons he was taking an indefinite leave of absence, effective immediately.

Within the week his family departed Chicago for New York, from where they sailed to Europe on August 27 for an extended journey abroad. The Common Council chose as interim mayor West Side alderman L. L. Bond, an attorney in the city since 1854 and a Medill ally. On the third ballot Bond received twenty of the thirty-seven votes cast, barely enough to give him the majority he needed.

By then the Sunday closing controversy had created a new and powerful political movement that threatened to reverse the achievements of those who put Medill in office. The Fire-Proof Party had morphed into the Law and Order (also known as Citizens' Union) Party. It had shown its continuing appeal in the November 1872 election by pushing Charles C. P. Holden out of his alderman's seat. That turned out to be the high point of its power. In late May 1873, German and Irish residents united with native-born Chicagoans opposed to the Medill administration to form the opposition People's Party.

It did not help the Law and Order contingent that City Treasurer David A. Gage, who had been elected on a slate that boasted of its probity, was under investigation for embezzling half a million dollars in public funds. He would eventually be convicted of the crime. In the election of November 4, 1873, the candidates on the People's Party ticket, headed by mayoral nominee Harvey D. Colvin, thoroughly defeated their Law and Order opponents, led by interim mayor Bond. Colvin received about 29,000 votes to Bond's 18,500. A handful of Law and Order candidates won seats as aldermen, but in the seesaw factionalism of Chicago politics the People's Party was now in charge.

One thing did not change. Thirty-six years after its incorporation, the city was still governed by people who had come from afar. The fifty-seven-year-old Colvin was another Chicagoan from upstate New York, where he had been a manufacturer of boots and shoes before moving to Chicago in the mid-1850s and running an express company. Seventeen members of the forty-person Common Council were born in Ireland (one was a Scotch-Irish Protestant from Belfast). Sixteen were from other parts of the United States, five from Germany, and one each from Alsace, England, and Switzerland. A single Chicago alderman was born in the city.

Mark Sheridan was back as president of the board of police and fire commissioners. James Hildreth, who had battled the fire with gunpowder and then beat charges of corruption, was the new People's Party alderman from the Seventh Ward. By the following March a new ordinance permitted saloon owners to do business on Sunday if they kept their doors closed and windows covered.

The *Tribune* seemed more upset than the *Times* that the "bummers" and the "ignorant and vicious classes" were back in charge. It bitterly described Colvin's election as "a huge practical joke." The *Inter-Ocean* reported that "our rebuilt city, the pride of the United States and the wonder of the world, became the property of a bigoted, illiterate mob of Germans and Irish." By the next day it was contending that many Colvin supporters had voted illegally.

The *Times* for once offered the most even-tempered and clear-eyed analysis. Wilbur Storey had no patience for reformers who claimed that God was with them. His paper said the takeaway from the election was that most people believed government should stay out of religion and the regulation of morality. By opening their assemblies with prayers and citing specious crime statistics, the abstinence advocates proved nothing but their own narrow-mindedness and bigotry.

Such an approach might succeed in nations where church and state were inseparable, the *Times* observed, but "in this country the Lord is generally on the side which casts the most votes."

15

CITY ON FIRE

As the battle for political control of the city took its twists and turns, the new Chicago continued to emerge. By one careful count, between the first anniversary of the fire in 1872 and the second in 1873, 37,013 lineal feet of building were added, nearly two-thirds of the total for the previous year. Earlier construction had focused on commercial buildings; more recently, residential buildings dominated.

Chicago planned two events to note the city's recovery, each far bigger than the ceremonies that accompanied the opening of the new Chamber of Commerce building twelve months after the catastrophe. The first was called Jubilee Week, though a more accurate name would have been Jubilee Days, since it ran from Wednesday, June 4, to Saturday, June 7, 1873. Visitors could take excursions to multiple sites, from Lincoln Park in the North Division to the new McCormick Reaper Works in the South and, beyond that, to the Union Stock Yards and then the commercial harbor being constructed on the lakefront twelve miles south of downtown at the mouth of the Calumet River. The most important exhibit, of course, was rebuilt downtown Chicago.

Planners arranged for a series of concerts led by Ireland-born and Boston-based composer and impresario Paul Gilmore, who had rallied Union spirits during the Civil War with the anticipatory victory anthem "When Johnny Comes Marching Home." Gilmore's program was ambitious. He planned to conduct performances by different groups of musicians playing the works of composers including Beethoven and Bellini, Handel and Haydn, Mendelssohn and Mozart. The celebration was to culminate in the Jubilee Ball.

The concert series was a debacle. With little time to rehearse, Gilmore could not get his artists to play together. His flailing at the air with his baton reminded one reviewer of a frustrated drill sergeant trying to train raw recruits at the start of the Civil War. The low quality of the concerts did not diminish visitors' positive impression of Chicago, however. A Cincinnati journalist who panned the music stated that the opportunity to view the rebuilding progress "fully compensated for my trip here." He had last seen the city shortly after its destruction, a mere twenty months earlier. He was "ready to do full justice to the enterprise, industry, and pluck which have produced this wonderful transformation." It outdid the magic worked by Aladdin's lamp. As "mournfully conspicuous" as Chicago was in her "fiery overthrow," she was "magnificent in the rapidity and grandeur of her resurrection."

The business community put great thought and effort into staging the far larger and longer second celebration, scheduled to take place over several weeks during the fall, a period that included the second anniversary of the fire in early October. The idea for what would be the Inter-State Exposition dated to 1869, well before Chicago's destruction. The fire transformed what was originally conceived of as a regional trade fair for the states of the Upper Midwest into an occasion to proclaim that the city had irrefutably risen from the ashes and was a more vibrant metropolis than ever before. Like all modern trade fairs since the Great Exhibition of 1851 in London, it paid tribute to the arts, but its main purpose, besides showing off how brilliantly Chicago had recovered, was to promote local commerce and industry.

As was the case with the London fair's Crystal Palace, the structure that hosted the event was a primary attraction in itself. The exposition's board, headed by Potter Palmer, erected an 800-by-260-foot grand exhibition hall on the lakefront, now enlarged with fire debris. Centered on Adams Street, it replaced temporary frame storefronts the Board of Public Works had permitted to be erected on the east side of Michigan Avenue immediately after the disaster.

Contractors had to sink more than three hundred oak piles, each eighteen inches across and twenty feet long, to create a reliable foundation in the uncertain ground. Two million bricks and 3.5 million feet of lumber went into the construction of the building, which enclosed some quarter million square feet of floor space. Brick and stone walls supported wooden trusses that held up the immense roof. The matching smaller cupolas at either end of the building were 140 feet high, while the larger central one rose twenty-five feet higher and measured sixty feet across.

On the evening of Thursday, September 25, a volley of cannon blasts announced the opening of the exposition. The great hall's 473 windows

The Inter-State Exposition Building.
(Chicago History Museum, ICHi-002170)

were aglow with the light from thousands of gas jets. Major manufacturers based in other cities, such as Fleischmann's Yeast and the Singer
Manufacturing Company, exhibited their products, but most participants
were from Chicago. The McCormick Harvesting Machine Company
took the occasion to show off for the first time in one place the medals it
had won at previous fairs. The earliest was the prize its reaper received
twenty-two years earlier at the Crystal Palace for what the *London
Times* called "the most valuable contribution to the great exposition."

The fine arts section displayed 167 paintings and a dozen pieces of
sculpture, from *Autumn in the Sierras* by western landscape master Albert Bierstadt to an imposing marble statue of the queen of ancient Pal-
myra, *Zenobia*, by Harriet Hosmer, the country's first female
professional sculptor. It also featured drawings from the current com-
petition for a design of the new and permanent city hall.

Viewed narrowly, the Inter-State Exposition was a great success, attracting more than 600,000 visitors before it closed in mid-November.
Unfortunately there was a skeleton at the feast, the sharp and extended
downturn in the international economy known as the Panic of 1873. A

week before the Inter-State Exposition opened, the major Philadelphia investment firm of Jay Cooke and Company went bankrupt. This set off a chain reaction of financial failures that briefly forced the closing of the New York Stock Exchange. The panic's underlying cause was overly aggressive speculation, especially in railroads.

Premonitions of trouble had worried the Chicago real estate market during the summer. With so many expensive projects in progress funded with high-interest borrowing, land prices began to soften. Chicago nonetheless fared better in the panic than did many other places. Values did not evaporate, though they did drop 20 percent, with comparable declines in industrial production, wages, and employment. Chicago's miraculous two-year recovery from the fire came close to a halt.

Hardest hurt in terms of total personal financial losses were building owners who had taken out large loans in the expectation of a continuing rise in the value of their investments and in the rents they could charge to tenants. Instead, their net worth and income plummeted while the cost of their loans did not. The most notable casualty of the collapse was J. Young Scammon, who could not make the payments on his several properties, which he had mortgaged at 10 percent. The panic placed workers who lost their jobs because of the slowdown in even grimmer circumstances, since the day-to-day lives of their families depended on their wages.

On Sunday afternoon, December 21, immigrant working people packed into Vorwaerts Turner Hall, near the corner of Halsted and Twelfth Street (Roosevelt Road), a half mile southwest of the O'Leary cottage, to hear a series of speakers. They addressed the audience variously in German, English, and French. No matter what the language, the message and demands were the same: workers needed employment, and at a living wage; in the meantime, the city must provide financial aid or provisions for suffering families; workingmen, not the wealthy, should appoint the committee managing these disbursements; if Chicago was too cash-strapped to fund assistance, it must borrow money to do so.

The speakers argued that the most significant division in the city was class, not ethnicity. Under the iron heel of capitalism, they contended, workers had been reduced to slaves. Some attacked Anton Hesing for claiming that he represented them. As a member of the economic elite, they pointed out, he was by definition as big a thief as disgraced city treasurer David Gage even if the way Hesing conducted business was technically legal. The meeting reminded the hyperbolically antiunion *Chicago Times*, always ready to use screaming capitals when lowercase letters would do, "of the COMMUNISTIC UPRISINGS in Europe."

The speakers called for a march the next evening from the West Division to the Common Council meeting in the temporary city hall at Adams and LaSalle. This demonstration proved to be very different from the raucous assault that took place the night of the fire limits debate in January 1872. That protest concerned what kind of materials a worker could use to rebuild his home; this one was about starvation.

Given the depth of resentment and the number of people—estimates were as high as ten thousand—who showed up on this cold evening, the mood was subdued. No bands accompanied the file of workers, only a muted fife and drum. The marchers carried but few signs, on which were written such terse slogans as "United We Stand, Divided We Fall," "One for All and All for One," and, more succinctly, "Work or Bread." Even the *Times* was impressed by how disciplined the mostly German and Scandinavian demonstrators were. "It was not a rabble," the paper's reporter wrote, "for in its long line, where men were standing shoulder to shoulder, there was good order."

Mayor Harvey Colvin stalled by saying that he could not respond to their demands at the moment because he was still new to the office and had yet to study the situation carefully. The next day, December 23, the mayor and seventeen Common Council members conferred with a committee of nine workingmen and their spokesman, attorney F. A. Hoffman Jr. An alderman who was skeptical of the claim that people were actually starving wondered out loud whether the protests were merely political theater. Hoffman shot back, "When men were hungry they did not think of politics or religion."

Colvin expressed concern but said that there was little the city could do to provide either work or bread. Even if there were a legal way to accomplish this, which he doubted, between the size of postfire public works expenditures and the current ailing economy, Chicago had no money for jobs or food. Nor could it borrow any, he explained, since the city was already in debt up to the legislated limit. The meeting did produce one seemingly promising idea: perhaps the Chicago Relief and Aid Society could help. Rumor had it that the society held a million dollars in its coffers. The actual figure was closer to $600,000, but this was still a substantial sum.

The next morning—Wednesday, December 24—a delegation of officials, including the mayor, visited the society's administrative office to ask for aid. Colvin tried to locate Wirt Dexter, who was nowhere to be seen, but he did encounter Relief and Aid Society Executive Committee members Nathaniel Fairbank, T. W. Harvey, and Henry King. They arranged a meeting at two o'clock that afternoon. They told Colvin that Dexter could not be present at that time because he was busy on a legal case, but he would attend a second meeting two days later.

The best the committee members offered at the Wednesday afternoon discussion was that unemployed and hungry Chicagoans could apply for help according to the much-resented Relief and Aid Society procedures, which required the usual letters of reference from respectable (in the eyes of the society) people attesting to the character and neediness of the applicant. The response would not be quick, since there was already a backlog of cases.

The workers' representatives praised Mayor Colvin for his efforts while condemning the Relief and Aid Society for withholding assistance to desperate people. They released a statement expressing hope that something would come of the meeting two days later, when Dexter, who everyone knew spoke for the society, would be present. They also strongly recommended that working people behave in an orderly manner. The statement warned, in italics, "*Beware of the influence of any evil-disposed parties that may endeavor to incite to deeds of violence.*" On the same day, the *Chicago Tribune* echoed the *Times* in referring to the protesters as "Our Communists."

The discussion on Friday, December 26, was another disappointment. Dexter reiterated the society's position that applicants must apply according to the usual rules. In anticipation of this, the hungry and unemployed had lined up "respectable" Chicagoans, including clergy, to provide the references the Relief and Aid Society demanded. On December 27 a group of workers a thousand strong assembled by the society's downtown headquarters on LaSalle Street to present their qualifications for assistance.

C. G. Truesdell, who had succeeded O. C. Gibbs as Relief and Aid Society superintendent, informed them that no one would be eligible for aid without an additional document not previously mentioned in discussions that week, a certificate of inoculation against smallpox. In Truesdell's defense, this requirement had been instituted well before this, but it was probably unrealistic to expect a person who had been inoculated some time earlier to be able to furnish proof on the spot. Staff members told applicants to sign up for an appointment and return later in the day. The society also said that it was responding to the current crisis by hiring more "visitors" to review potential clients in their homes.

What workers viewed as endless "red tapeism" tried their patience. They suspected that the Relief and Aid Society's strategy was to delay action indefinitely. "That is the way the Society means to treat us," charged a German laborer. "Monday they will tell us to come Wednesday, and then to come Sunday, and so on until the winter is over, [by which time] we and our families have died of starvation." Another complained that the problem was that employers were withholding wages due to workers for labor already performed. "The Common Council and the workingmen must find ways and means to reform that abuse," he wrote, "and then the time will have passed when workingmen wander around, penniless and shelterless, and [are] compelled to accept the charity of those who cheat and swindle them."

Protesters had been well behaved so far, but some argued that it was time to replace patience with force, not excluding firearms. For their part, the English-language papers, refusing to acknowledge that the city and the country were in a depression, parroted the society's questionable contention that many who demanded assistance were "frauds" and "deadbeats" who wanted bread without work. That it was Christmas week made the standoff all the more poignant. Suggestions from citizens abounded, some more constructive than others, from reopening the soup-houses to outlawing liquor, which temperance supporters forwarded as the solution to every problem.

The city converted a vacant police station into a lodging house for homeless Chicagoans. An industrial bakery in the West Division distributed eleven thousand loaves of bread, ten thousand of them funded at cost by the Northwestern National Bank, the remaining thousand by the Fireman's Fund insurance company.

Some families applying for aid resorted to the kind of tactics practiced by Maggie O'Brien in the play *Relief: A Humorous Drama*, but they were not impostors. Male workers, suspecting that they might be judged too hale to receive aid in spite of the fact that they were unemployed and broke, sent their wives and children to the Relief and Aid

Society's offices in the hope that an appeal from them would be more successful than from a man.

The society's board of directors found itself under siege. The minutes of its meeting on Friday, January 2, 1874, begin, "Mr. [Henry W.] King, Prest., stated that he had called this meeting to consider what action could be taken to relieve the Society of the crowd thronging the building and streets demanding relief." The minutes included the comment, without evidence, that "the majority of them" were "unworthy and impostors." The board passed a resolution "earnestly" recommending that applicants make their requests "by letter through the Post-Office, thus avoiding the annoyance and delay of applying in person." Just whose annoyance the society's leaders were trying to avoid is questionable, since many applicants were illiterate (especially in English) or otherwise unaccustomed to conducting their affairs by mail.

As the official inquiry on the 1871 disaster predicted, serious fire struck again. Chicago experienced a near miss only a week before the Inter-State Exposition opened, when firefighters managed to contain a potentially major blaze that leveled cheap wood buildings in a West Division neighborhood a mile southwest of where the 1871 fire had begun.

The return of hot dry weather in the summer of 1874 elevated the danger of fire across the nation. On Friday, July 10, a bolt of lightning ignited oil tanks in the Erie Railroad yards in Weehawken, New Jersey. On the same day, flames broke out at the corner of California and Front Streets in San Francisco and burned on for hours. A few days later, a conflagration devoured the downtown of Oshkosh, Wisconsin.

Late on the afternoon of Tuesday, July 15, 1874, a large section of Chicago was ablaze. The fire apparently started in a shanty occupied by a rag peddler near the corner of Twelfth (Roosevelt Road) and Clark Streets in the South Division, a half mile below where the 1871 fire ended. It moved north and east, reaching a short distance above Harrison Street and touching Michigan Avenue before ceasing about three thirty Wednesday morning. Attorney Thomas Hoyne, who now lived on South Michigan Avenue, described this conflagration as many had the earlier one, with a water metaphor, stating that the area was "alive with fire, while the main torrent was sweeping northward."

The 1874 fire consumed forty-seven acres. The losses encompassed 812 buildings, 619 of them wooden, and destroyed property worth close to $4 million. These numbers were paltry in comparison to the Great Fire of 1871—when well over two thousand acres burned and eighteen thousand buildings and $200 million in private property value were lost—but they powerfully recalled the recent disaster.

The similarities of the 1871 and 1874 fires were manifold: a small blaze that quickly went out of control; flying cinders everywhere; desperate efforts to soak down buildings in the fire's path; deployment of gunpowder to create a firebreak; post office workers saving much of the mail before their building (the former Wabash Avenue Methodist Church) fell; the mayor telegraphing other cities for help; crowds of gawkers; goods removed from houses and placed in the streets; stories of extortionist draymen and rumors of thievery; daring escapes and brave rescues; refugees along the lakeshore; the fire department praised for its valor and then damned for incompetence; only half the property loss covered by insurance; boosters insisting that the fire would be better for the city in the not-very-long run; and the Relief and Aid Society offering help with the usual stipulations, forms, and procedures.

It seemed that the only thing missing was the presence of General Philip H. Sheridan. Some joked that he purposely lay low because he didn't want Wilbur Storey and the *Chicago Times* after him again.

The fire of 1874 recalled the 1871 disaster in other ways. Three years earlier, Catherine O'Leary had been pilloried for her alleged carelessness. Now, if for a much briefer time, the spotlight of blame fixed on the Jewish immigrant who owned the shack where the fire started. When Nathan Isaacson was brought before a grand jury, the case collapsed from lack of evidence. Soon the prevailing theory of the cause was arson by a person or persons unknown.

The worst victims this time were residents of the African American and Jewish neighborhoods south of the downtown that had barely escaped in 1871. Two African American churches, Bethel Methodist and Olivet Baptist, and two synagogues, Kehilath Anshe Marov (Congregation of the Men of the West) and Kehilath B'nai Sholom (Congregation of the Children of Peace), were lost. The flames also destroyed the Gothic stone First Baptist Church at Wabash Avenue and Hubbard Court (Balbo Street), from whose steeple the flames rose like a bright banner. The congregation was already considering a move farther south to be nearer most of its members, but in the meantime it had left its current home underinsured.

Another casualty was the city's thriving vice business, since the devastated area included several houses of prostitution. A reporter came upon noted madam Annie Stafford, who was "pale and trembling with fright," though her bordello was spared. She claimed that she had dreamed this would happen.

While jeweler John Ashleman's business was untouched, his family's postfire home burned down. A doll belonging to one of his daughters, its head blackened but otherwise unharmed by the 1871 blaze, did not survive this latest trial by fire. Neither did the Michigan Avenue Hotel, which had temporarily been John B. Drake's New Tremont House, where Russian Grand Duke Alexis had shaken all those Chicago hands. By this time Drake had rebuilt the "old" Tremont House at Lake and Dearborn Streets.

The most prominent person to suffer losses was again J. Young Scammon. The Panic of 1873 left him teetering on the edge of ruin; the fire of 1874 pushed him over. Before his creditors could do so, the flames took possession of both the *Chicago Inter-Ocean* building and his home.

The fire department was approaching twice the size of three years earlier and improving its equipment, but critics asserted that internal conflicts and political interference by the Common Council hampered its efficiency and effectiveness. They could point to former chief marshal Robert A. Williams, who had not been in charge since the previous summer. His feud with First Assistant Marshal John Schank, whom he had wrongly accused of being missing in action during the big fire, simmered on after the 1871 official inquiry.

In February 1872 Schank retaliated against Williams by charging that the chief had repeatedly been drunk on the job and verbally abusive toward the men in his command, cursing them out as sons of bitches. After a hearing on these accusations was well underway, Schank opted to submit his resignation instead of seeing the matter through, claiming that the investigation was stacked against him. The panel holding the hearing dismissed the charges, and the department promoted Third Assistant Marshal Mathias Benner up to Schank's position.

But Williams's days were numbered, because of a soap opera of a scandal rather than poor leadership. On August 1, 1873, Euphemia Hallock, wife of fireman Isaac Hallock, approached Police and Fire Board president Mark Sheridan after a meeting of the board to say that Williams had been having an affair with her. Referring to the chief marshal, she told Sheridan, "He has wronged me." Sheridan immediately confronted Williams, who called Hallock a blackmailer and a fraud.

In short order she had signed an affidavit dripping with lurid details. According to Hallock, over the previous three years, Williams had been "holding carnal intercourse with me." He had infected her with "a loathsome disease" that made her unable to work and support her children. She implied that he had contracted this disease through "visiting houses of ill-fame and holding intercourse with [other] firemen's wives" before he started sleeping with her. He had offered her money to state that Mark Sheridan had "visited" her, but Williams never came through with any payment.

Within a day Hallock had signed a second affidavit denying everything she previously swore and now attesting "that so far as she has ever known said Williams has in every respect conducted himself as a gentleman." Then she sent a letter to the press that denied the denial.

Whatever actually transpired between Hallock and Williams, his career in the department was through. Mathias Benner became the new chief, and Denis Swenie replaced him as first assistant.

The 1874 fire justified those who had long been calling for stricter building regulations. The *Tribune* fumed, "Every cool-headed observer of the conflagration must have felt that we have paid a light penalty for allowing our magnificent business-centre to be surrounded with wooden rookeries" while indulging "the genius of free institutions—meaning the freedom of every man to keep a tinder-box and an oil factory where it suits him best."

On the evening of Saturday, July 18, three days after the fire, Chicago business and civic leaders assembled in the newly erected McCormick Hall in the North Division to express their objections to the Common Council's refusal to take sensible steps to guard against fire. Their anger and impatience raised the temperature in the room on a night that was already warm. One of the first speakers was William Bross, who, after saying he did not come for the purpose of talking, made a speech. To loud applause Bross declared that he had lived long enough in Chicago to know that wooden buildings must be outlawed. Far less well received was Anton Hesing's declaration that he had no regrets about opposing the wood ban in the North Division neighborhoods where working people lived.

Hisses turned to cheers when Hesing announced that he was now in favor of extending the limits over the whole city as far as new construction was concerned. By now many North Side residents had already erected wooden homes and businesses. He said that he still resented the hypocrisy of native-born businessmen who ignored the fact that the most dangerous firetrap in the city was the Field, Leiter & Company store. In any case, he added, individual wooden buildings were not the only problem. Chicago needed to find comprehensive fire prevention solutions and reform the fire department.

The most powerful voice in the discussion of Chicago's fire safety spoke from well outside the city. Even before the 1874 fire, the National Board of Fire Underwriters, based in New York, was threatening to instruct its member companies to stop writing fire insurance policies in Chicago. Now the board put its foot down. Chicago needed to establish and enforce higher standards or member insurers, which included most major companies, would cease doing business in the city. The board demanded fire limits coextensive with Chicago's borders, iron shutters on warehouses and stores, a thorough reorganization of the fire department, more and bigger water mains and pipes, additional hydrants, and the removal of all lumber yards from built-up areas.

In some key respects the Common Council met the board's demands before they were made. At their meeting of July 20, five days after the fire and four before the National Board of Fire Underwriters issued its ultimatum, Chicago aldermen voted 32–5 to expand the fire limits to include all of Chicago. They also discussed several other proposals to improve protection, including the Board of Police and Fire Commissioners' renewed request for equipment upgrades, the hiring of experts in the use of explosives to prevent the spread of fire, and a more ample water supply.

Two months later the underwriters declared that the city, no matter what it seemed to promise, had actually done little to reduce its vulnerability. If Chicago wanted to play with fire, so be it, but in that case its residents, and not insurers, would have to assume the risks. The

New York Times reported that 90 percent of insurance companies affiliated with the National Board of Fire Underwriters said they would withdraw from Chicago. Over the tense months that followed, the board, individual insurers, and the city government engaged in a protracted showdown over what new rules and practices would be implemented and on what timetable.

Chicago's civic-minded businessmen had already stepped in. Two weeks after the July fire, they formed the Citizens' Association of Chicago, whose membership defined more than any other organization the city's self-designated "best men." Claiming that it was nonpartisan in regard to politics, religion, and ethnicity, the association pledged to work for better government and general welfare, an end to defective laws, prompt enforcement of good ones, and improved trade.

The Citizens' Association's first priority was to get the city to satisfy the underwriters. Its key step in this regard, which it negotiated with the board, was to raise $5,000 to hire Alexander Shaler to reorganize the fire department. Still referred to by his wartime military rank, General Shaler had won the Congressional Medal of Honor for his actions at the Second Battle of Fredericksburg on May 3, 1863, when he rescued fellow Union troops under fire and repelled a Confederate attack. Since the war, he had been commissioner of the New York City Fire Department from 1867 to 1873.

Shaler's arrival in Chicago considerably eased the concerns of many underwriters. It led to incremental improvements, though not without considerable resistance from property owners to his recommendations for tighter building regulations, as well as infrastructure enhancements and an upgraded fire department. Among the problems of enhancing fire protection was, as ever, the cost of doing so, as well as the suspicion—justified or not—that providing city officials with more money, even for this purpose, might fuel the twin scourges of waste and corruption without making Chicago any safer.

Cities continued to endure major fires, both shortly before Chicago's 1874 blaze and for decades after.

On the evening of November 9, 1872, a year and a month after the Great Chicago Fire, Boston suffered the worst fire in its history. While the Burnt District in Chicago was more than thirty times larger, Chicago's losses were "only" three times greater, since Boston's flames aimed their fury at its tightly packed downtown.

Chicagoans reciprocated Bostonians' recent generosity. With Mayor Joseph Medill presiding, and Wirt Dexter and William B. Ogden on the list of speakers, residents met early in the afternoon of November 11 in the new Chamber of Commerce building to discuss how they might help. When individuals were asked to contribute, the first to step up was a peanut peddler named Kennedy. He handed over five dollars, to deafening cheers. The rally raised another $50,000, led by $5,000 from Field, Leiter & Company, a matching amount from George Pullman, $2,500 from John V. Farwell, and $2,000 from Ogden.

Chicagoans were not above bragging how much greater Chicago's fire was than Boston's. They also did not forget how some clergymen viewed the Great Fire as a divine punishment brought on by the city's "manifold sins and transgressions." It was now the obligation of those same clergymen to explain how "a fiery visitation almost as terrible of ours" struck such a metropolitan moral exemplar as Boston.

The decades ahead would visit terrible fires on Bakersfield, California (1889); Seattle (1889); Jacksonville, Florida (1901); Baltimore (1904); Bangor, Maine (1911); and Salem, Massachusetts (1914). The most extensive American urban conflagration of all, surpassing even Chicago's in area destroyed and losses suffered, were the fires triggered by the similarly legendary San Francisco Earthquake of 1906, which burned some four square miles of the city and inflicted at least $350 million in damages.

In 1916, an in-house history of the National Board of Fire Underwriters, which described the organization as "a civilizing force over the past fifty years," bemoaned the fact that the nation was still far from civilized as far as controlling fire was concerned. "The United States might well have been named Terra del Fuego—'Land of Fire,'" it stated. By the board's count, the country currently averaged 1,500 fires per day—more than one a minute—costing $600,000. "A value equal to one-quarter the total for all the new buildings erected each year is thus destroyed, and in 1906 [the year of the San Francisco Earthquake and subsequent fire] this proportion rose to one-half."

The board underlined the importance of prevention, its point being that the easiest fire to stop is one that never starts. In 1911 it persuaded several states to declare the fortieth anniversary of the burning of Chicago, October 8, as Fire Prevention Day, whose purpose was to make their citizens aware of the need for fire safety. On September 11, 1925, President Calvin Coolidge issued a proclamation designating the seven days beginning Sunday, October 4, as National Fire Prevention Week, and subsequent presidents have followed suit. The week, which is observed in Chicago, always includes the anniversary of the Great Fire, though the presidential proclamations make no mention of it.

With each successive tragedy there would be calls for improvements. The steps to greater safety were hardly mysterious: stricter restrictions on flammable materials in buildings; detailed rules regarding the installation of gas, electricity, and the machines and appliances that use them; more and improved alarms; better-trained departments; emergency drills by occupants of schools and other large buildings; expanded water supplies connected to emergency hoses and sprinkler systems; more sophisticated fire extinguishers; wider streets outside buildings and broader halls and stairways within them; ample and well-marked exits that open outward; and plentiful and reliable fire escapes. Local officials also became far more serious about regular expert inspection, with serious penalties for violations. While these measures could never eliminate all building fires, they would make it less likely that a fire would spread very far.

Such reforms became increasingly common during the first half of the twentieth century. They did not arrive in time to save the lives of those who perished in the burning of Chicago's Iroquois Theater, at Randolph and Dearborn Streets, on Wednesday, December 30, 1903. The theater had been open only a week when sparks from a spotlight set a curtain afire during the opening scene of the second act of *Mr. Blue Beard*, a strained attempt to turn the tale of the infamous serial wife murderer into a musical comedy extravaganza.

The cast escaped through the door behind the stage, but over six hundred members of the panicked audience of about 1,600 failed to find, reach, or open the poorly designed and badly marked exits in time to avoid being fatally burned, smothered, or trampled. Others jumped to their deaths from unfinished fire escapes.

Fire chief William Musham testifying before the speaker's rostrum of the City Council chamber during the Iroquois Theater fire investigation. (Chicago History Museum, DN-0001640)

It was the worst single-building fire in US history. Since the audience was attending a holiday matinee, a large number of victims were mothers and children. Because of the horror of all those deaths, and the clearly avoidable oversights that caused them, for the next several decades the Iroquois Theater fire likely seared more deeply into local memory than had the Great Fire of 1871.

The chief of the fire department when the Iroquois Theater burned was William Musham. Near the outset of his forty-eight-year career, Musham had battled the 1857 downtown fire that ended the city's reliance on volunteers. On October 8, 1871, he was foreman and acting captain of Little Giant Engine Company No. 6, the first to reach the blaze on DeKoven Street. In 1894 he was blown into the Chicago River while fighting a lumber fire, and three years later he was buried under a mass of sheet iron shortly after he saved the lives of twenty men by moving a fireboat at a critical moment.

None of this service to the city counted now. While it did not indict him, a grand jury censured Chief Musham for his department's failures in fighting the Iroquois fire. He resigned the following year and passed away in 1907.

16

CELEBRATING DESTRUCTION

Neither the Panic of 1873 nor the fire of 1874 stopped ambitious people from moving to Chicago. They came for the same reason they always had, the expectation that prospects there would be more promising than where they were. The city that burned was home to an estimated 334,000 people; the number was more than 367,000 by an 1872 count, almost 400,000 by 1874, and a half million by 1880. By 1890, less than twenty years after the city's future seemed in jeopardy (and scarcely more than fifty since Chicago had been incorporated), its population was more than a million, making it the nation's second largest metropolis after New York.

The commissioners of the West Division parks did not finish the fire monument they had hired William LeBaron Jenney to design and whose cornerstone they laid in the fall of 1872. Stalled by the Panic of 1873, the project never revived. The cornerstone and its short-lived time capsule were removed in 1882.

When the city did commemorate the Great Fire, it mainly looked ahead, not back. Chicago framed the fire as the ultimate example of creative destruction, the beginning of bigger and better things, an affirmation rather than foreclosing of the city's destiny. The city repeatedly used the memory of the fire to advance some current agenda.

On the twenty-fifth anniversary, in October 1896, the issue capturing most attention was the presidential election campaign that opposed Republican William McKinley and Democrat William Jennings Bryan. During the summer, when the Democrats had held their national convention in Chicago, Bryan had seized the nomination by electrifying the delegates with his impassioned attack on the gold standard. He famously ended the speech with the stirring warning to Republicans, "You shall not crucify mankind upon a cross of gold."

Just before this, Bryan indirectly referred to the Great Chicago Fire and the city's miraculous recovery when he insisted that farms rather than cities were the basis of American prosperity and identity. "Burn down your cities and leave our farms, and your cities will spring up again as if by magic," he declared. The best proof of this was the recovered Chicago that hosted the convention. "But destroy our farms," Bryan continued, "and the grass will grow in the streets of every city in the country."

On October 9 the two parties staged contesting parades. In a political cartoon in the pro-McKinley *Chicago Tribune*, a militant young woman hoists a banner linking "Sound Money" (i.e., a currency based on the gold standard) to "National Honor." Flanking her are two small circular vignettes, a "before" image of burning Chicago and an "after" depiction of the bright and shining city of the present, which no doubt owed its prosperity to Republican fiscal policy.

Above the cartoon is the title, "CHICAGO DAY, OCT. 9, 1896." The naming of the anniversary of the fire in this way began three years earlier with the 1893 World's Columbian Exposition, which ran from May to October in Jackson Park, on the lakefront eight miles southeast of Courthouse Square. Unlike the Great Exhibition of 1851 in London, the emblem of this exposition was not a single striking structure like the Crystal Palace but a colossal ensemble of beaux arts palaces and colonnades called the Court of Honor, which surrounded the Grand Basin.

The exterior of the buildings looked like stone, but it was nothing more than white-painted plaster over wooden framing, intended to last only to the early fall. Still, the overall effect of the so-called White City was breathtaking. One of the most popular and successful of all modern world's fairs, it proclaimed for all the world to behold Chicago's full recovery from the fire and its arrival as one of the great metropolises of the world. The embodiment of Chicago at the fair was the "I Will" woman, a noble amazon with these two words of determination emblazoned on her breastplate. Nesting in her crown was a phoenix, an allusion to the fire and the recovery.

Chicago Day, which took place on the twenty-second anniversary of the fire, was one of several themed dates in the course of the fair season scheduled to attract more visitors. It was the most successful of all, with an eye-popping total of 716,880 paid admissions, plus another forty thousand admitted on passes. The featured events included a

The Grand Basin and the Court of Honor, World's Columbian Exposition, 1893. In the foreground is sculptor Daniel Chester French's statue The Republic, *which faces the Administration Building. (Chicago History Museum, ICHi-002524)*

"monster concert," billed as the "most gorgeous display of fireworks ever seen in America," and a spectacular parade with eight floats representing stages in Chicago's growth. The poster advertising the day promised that this "Grand Columbian Carnival" would be "in Its Entirety the Most Significant and Grandest Spectacle of Modern Times."

Private promoters took advantage of all the people drawn to the fair in 1893 by building attractions well outside the fairgrounds. For fifty cents, the same price as admission to the Court of Honor and the rest of the official exhibition buildings, the curious could visit Isaac N. Reed and Howard H. Gross's Fire Cyclorama on Madison Street between Michigan Avenue and Wabash. There were cycloramas in every large city. Others in Chicago at the time depicted the Crucifixion and the Battle of Gettysburg. Spectators entered a central space where they

*Stone bust of the "I Will" woman, World's Columbian
Exposition, 1893. (Chicago History Museum, ICHi-036691)*

were encircled by an enormous 360-degree realistic rendering of a historical scene. One can call it an early form of virtual reality, since the
overall effect is of being in the middle of the action.

And what action the Fire Cyclorama offered. The point of view was
the south bank of the Main Branch by the Rush Street Bridge, as terrified Chicagoans flee the flames. The size of the five canvases was suit-
ably epic. Each was fifty by eighty feet, for a total of twenty thousand
square feet of wall space. In a promotional pamphlet, Reed and Gross
said they had hired ten master artists, who applied two tons of oil paint
to the six tons of canvas, at a cost of $250,000. The artists did a re-

World's Columbian Exposition Chicago Day poster, 1893. The "I Will" woman is at the upper left. (Chicago History Museum, ICHi-025164)

markable job. It is easy to think that photographs of the paintings are of the actual fire.

Other reenactments followed from the turn of the twentieth century to the 1930s, a mock-up of a portion of the city was besieged by flames on a regular schedule at White City, the amusement park at Sixty-Third Street and South Park. In 1903, just a few months before the Iroquois Theater tragedy, the city seemed to be tempting fate when it authorized the lighting of fires on some thirty street corners in the downtown,

Chicago Fire Cyclorama, Scene the Third: Panic at Rush Street Bridge. Burning of the North Division. Looking north up Rush Street, *1893.* *(Chicago History Museum, ICHi-063838)*

"typifying the burning of the city in 1871." Low-hanging rain clouds amplified the effect by turning rose red. It was "as if the heart of the city were wrapped in fire and mantled luridly with smoke."

The Chicago Association of Commerce led the 1921 Semi-Centennial Observance of the Chicago Fire, which stretched over the first half of October. The association proclaimed that the anniversary should be viewed as "the starting point of a great civic awakening and definite program for the building of the 'Chicago of Tomorrow'—that the next fifty years—even greater in accomplishments than the past—shall round out a century of unparalleled achievement." The official slogan of the commemoration was "Undaunted—We Build."

Judging by its program of events, the association also seemed to be responding to the enormous influx of immigrants from southern and eastern Europe over the previous decades, and perhaps even to the ugly and murderous Chicago race riot of 1919. Many events on the carefully coordinated program were dedicated to the inculcation of national and local unity as defined by the association.

Poster for the Semi-Centennial Observance of the Chicago Fire, 1921.
(Chicago History Museum, ICHi-064432)

There was the Americanization Demonstration in Grant Park, at which 648 foreign-born Chicagoans became naturalized citizens in a group ceremony witnessed by more than six thousand spectators. The association reaffirmed the greatness of the city and its people in a massive festival play, with a cast of 2,500 people accompanied by a chorus of five hundred voices and a one-hundred-piece orchestra. It was performed on several nights in a temporary lakefront stadium before a total audience of fifty thousand. There was a commemorative pageant in the West Side's Humboldt Park, *The Seven Fires: A Masque of Chicago*, that re-enacted the city's history. Only one of the six scenes of the festival play touched on the fire, which was presented as a step in "the drama of the rising glory of Chicago."

Twelve years later Chicago hosted its second world's fair, the Century of Progress, commemorating the founding of the town in 1833, four years before its incorporation as a city. The fair's explicit goal was to give the local economy, now deep in the throes of the Great Depression, a badly needed boost. For the same reason, the city decided to repeat the fair again the following summer.

The Century of Progress's art deco buildings were located mainly on Northerly Island, the artificial peninsula built out into the lake east of Soldier Field and below the Adler Planetarium, the Field Museum, and the Shedd Aquarium, all constructed in the 1920s. The "I Will" woman and her phoenix returned for a cameo appearance. Making a considerably bigger splash at the fair were burlesque artist Sally Rand's performances of her faux nude peekaboo fan dance.

The Century of Progress observed Chicago Day both years, but attendance—about 130,000 in 1933, under half that in 1934—fell far short of the mark set in 1893. The 1933 anniversary featured another pageant and fireworks show, titled *The Burning of Chicago*. In 1934 Mayor Edward J. Kelly posed with five long-retired firefighters, all in their late eighties or early nineties, the last surviving members of the force that had battled the great conflagration sixty-three years earlier.

The hundredth anniversary observances, in 1971, were less elaborate than the fiftieth. Chicago's population, which had peaked twenty years earlier at about 3.6 million, was down to a little over 3.3 million (as of 2020 it is about 2.7 million), and its industrial might was into its long decline. Mayor Richard J. Daley invoked the Chicagoans who passed through the fire in 1871 mainly to address the concerns of the late twentieth-century city. Daley said that the burned-out residents of a century earlier possessed the same wishes as did his current constituents: "Their dream for the future was a better home, a better neighborhood, a better city." The Chicago Historical Society marketed a special fire medal, while Marshall Field & Company advertised a commemorative centennial plate. The fire department sold a stamp created for the occasion.

The ceremonies at prior major anniversaries had been very serious. This time they showed a sense of play and wit. A star of the parade was an 1867 fire engine that, much to their delight, sprayed water on the fifty thousand spectators lining the streets for the parade. The main course at the banquet for 1,400 people at the Conrad Hilton was roast

*Chicago Historical Society centennial fire medal, 1971. This side
of the medal features present-day skyscrapers rising over the
burning city. On the opposite side is the official city seal surrounded
by twenty-one stars, signifying that Illinois was the twenty-first state
admitted to the Union. (Chicago History Museum, ICHi-064427)*

prime rib of beef, preceded by "Fire House Double Strength Beef Bouil-
lon" and accompanied by "Mrs. O'Leary's Baked Beans with Salt Pork."
The orchestra performed excerpts from Franz Joseph Haydn's *Fire Sym-
phony* and George Frideric Handel's *Music for the Royal Fireworks.*

In 2014 the city authorized the Redmoon Theater Company to produce a floating fire commemoration. As ever, dazzling pyrotechnics
were to be central to the program. Redmoon, which specialized in imaginative happenings in neighborhoods throughout the city, constructed
models of three fire-era Chicago houses. The plan was to tow them along
the Main Branch of the river, where they would suddenly burst into
flame, in the process revealing the flag of the city, two forty-foot fire lad-
ders, and a sixty-foot model of a skyscraper.

On October 4, despite rain and chill, some thirty thousand Chicagoans lined the Main Branch in anticipation. Instead of dazzling the onlookers with light and action, the floats fizzled. Redmoon's artistic director
offered a candid review: "This is an epic failure." The theater company

soon shut down, in its own way as much a casualty of the Great Fire
as Crosby's Opera House had been in 1871.

What little remained standing in the Burnt District after the Great Fire
did not endure long, falling victim to Chicago's abiding preference for
newer, bigger, and presumably better. The six-story Nixon Block at Monroe and LaSalle, almost finished at the time of the fire and completed
and occupied soon after it, displayed an inscription that read, "This
fireproof building is the only one in the city that successfully stood
the test of the Great Fire of October 9, 1871." Not exactly, since the
same could be said of the Mahlon Ogden mansion, policeman Richard
Bellinger's house, and the Water Tower, though all were in the North
Division.

The Nixon Block lasted only another eighteen years, to 1889. The
Lind Block, which the fire just missed because of its location in the northwest corner of the South Division, survived to 1963, but it had been
unceremoniously truncated in the 1920s when Market Street was widened and became North Wacker Drive.

The Ogden mansion, opposite the north side of Washington
Square Park, was razed in the late 1880s, and the block on which it sat
became the site of the Newberry Library, one of the leading independent research libraries in the nation. Forty-two years later a brass plaque
was affixed at the Newberry's entrance that states, "This library stands
on the site formerly occupied by the Mahlon D. Ogden Residence, the
only house in the path of the great fire of 1871 which was not burned."
Like the inscription on the Nixon Block, this is not quite true, since it
overlooks the humbler home a mile and a half farther north that Richard Bellinger and his brother-in-law successfully struggled to save. Much
renovated, the Bellinger house is still there.

Viewed from the outside, the Chicago Water Tower and Pumping
Station, on opposite sides of Michigan Avenue at Chicago Avenue, look
much as they did in 1871. A portion of the Pumping Station's interior,
viewable from a catwalk, still houses four functioning pumps. Each has a
name—Old Sallis, Old Pouliot, Old DePaul, and Old Kane—that honors
a longtime employee. Once the heart of the waterworks, the building is

now a small installation in the city's mammoth water system, which filters, treats, and distributes nearly a billion gallons of water a day.

Spaces in the Pumping Station once occupied by the Department of Public Works have hosted several other kinds of organizations, including a branch of the Chicago Public Library, a kind of echo of the original library in the water tank at LaSalle and Adams Streets. In 2011 the Lookingglass Theatre Company, by then the tenant of a different part of the building, staged *The Great Fire*, an original production that offered a reimagined version of the disaster.

Thanks to improved pumps, the standpipe inside the Water Tower has not been needed for most of the tower's 150-plus years. One of the loftiest buildings in the city when it was first erected, the Water Tower is now dwarfed by the skyscrapers that surround it, including the ninety-five-story John Hancock Center, which, at just under 1,500 feet, is over eight times taller. The Water Tower represents more than any structure the city's tenacity in the face of an overwhelming blow. In 1937, as part of the events noting the hundredth anniversary of Chicago's incorporation, the tower acquired a plaque declaring it "a principal memorial of 1871's great fire."

There are other pieces of Chicago that date from the fire, but they can be hard to locate and identify unless one knows where to look and what they are. The Reverend Robert Collyer left Chicago for New York's Church of the Messiah in 1879, but his anvil remained in Chicago. It is now in the sanctuary of the Second Unitarian Church in Lakeview, whose newsletter is *The Anvil*. Hidden in the shrubbery bordering the rear plaza of the Chicago History Museum (formerly the Chicago Historical Society) is a chunk of fused metal taken from a burned-out hardware store after the fire. The museum and its research center hold thousands of fire-related objects, publications, and manuscripts, as well as a haunting diorama of the city aflame in 1871.

The History Museum's vast collection of fire artifacts includes an 1871 alarm box, Julian Rumsey's stopped pocket watch, glass and metal objects melted in the heat, a cloth special police badge, a charred book of hymns titled *Spirit of Prayer* that is the only surviving volume from the museum's prefire library, and dolls and other beloved personal possessions rescued or salvaged from the flames. The museum also has the sign on which real estate man William Kerfoot painted "All gone but WIFE CHILDREN and ENERGY" and then nailed on the side of his "block" at 89 Washington Street. Of far more questionable provenance are cowbells that donors claimed were hanging from the neck of Mrs. O'Leary's cow that October night, and wood fragments purportedly from her barn.

In the middle of LaSalle Street, just below its intersection with Kinzie, north of the Main Branch, is a mysterious downward ramp that seems to lead nowhere. This was once the North Division entrance to the LaSalle Street Tunnel, which was such a vital escape route from the downtown for South Division residents fleeing the fire. Angry protesters filed through the tunnel in the opposite direction the evening of January 15, 1872, on their way to disrupt the Common Council meeting on fire limits. Originally designed for pedestrians and horse-drawn vehicles, the tunnel was converted into a streetcar passageway after the fire, but it has been closed to all traffic since 1939.

On the east side of Clark Street, near where Armitage Street terminates, is an odd object with a rounded top that looks like a piece in a board game played by giants. It is one of the half dozen or so extant

Courthouse finial on North Clark Street, 2011. Photograph by Stefani Foster. (Northwestern University and the Chicago History Museum)

finials that once perched on the cornice of the Courthouse. There is no sign on or near it to inform the possibly curious passerby of this.

There is not much left of structures built in the decade after the fire, either.

This is especially true of the center of the city and adjoining areas. A rare downtown survivor is the five-story limestone Washington Block, next to the Loop's elevated tracks on the southwest corner of Wells and Washington Streets, now almost lost among much larger buildings. A mile into the West Division on Madison Street, not far from the United Center, is a four-story Italianate commercial building erected in 1872, shortly after the fire. This structure survived the area's deep decline through much of the twentieth century and, perhaps more remarkably, the neighborhood's twenty-first-century gentrification. Its original owner was parks commissioner, alderman, Common Council president, and mayoral candidate Charles C. P. Holden, who proudly had his name embossed in capital letters just below the cornice. Since 2011 it has been a Chicago landmark.

There is a handsome cluster of other 1870s buildings along and near Clark Street just north of the river. The Cook County Courthouse erected on Hubbard Street between Clark and Dearborn in 1874, where the 1886 Haymarket trial was held, lasted only nineteen years, after which it was replaced by a new courthouse that reused some of its stones. That 1893 building, now converted to commercial use, is where both the 1921 Black Sox conspiracy trial and the 1924 murder trial of Nathan Leopold and Richard Loeb were held.

Shortly after the fire, Potter Palmer sold the land on which the Field, Leiter & Company store had stood to the New York–based Singer Manufacturing Company, perhaps to raise cash. Singer built another splendid building, this one with a glass dome, on the assumption that Field, Leiter & Company would rent it. Field, Leiter delayed before agreeing to terms, either in the hope of negotiating a better deal or believing that the location would not be attractive to retail customers until more of the downtown was rebuilt. For a brief time the firm moved its retail operations from the former streetcar barn at State and Twentieth Streets to the wholesale store it constructed at Madison and Market (Wacker Drive) Streets. On the second anniversary of the fire, it returned to State and Washington. "So the retail trade of the city was once again securely anchored on State Street," Francis Fisher Cook wrote in his memoir of the period.

On November 14, 1877, fire struck again. Field, Leiter & Company took up temporary quarters in the Inter-State Exposition Building on the lakefront at Adams Street, offering customers free transportation from the former site, and then in a space on Wabash Avenue. Meanwhile, the Singer Company built yet another store where the previous ones had been, again expecting Field, Leiter to return. When Field, Leiter once more delayed in signing a lease, Singer rented the building to Carson, Pirie, Scott, a rival of Field, Leiter. In order to keep its competitor from taking over the building, Field, Leiter purchased it outright and compensated Carson, Pirie, Scott for the lost lease. It reopened for business on April 28, 1879. In addition to providing a temporary home for Field, Leiter, the Inter-State Exposition Building hosted many varied activities and events. In the early 1890s it was torn down for the construction of the Art Institute of Chicago.

The Chicago Public Library, which opened in 1873 in the repurposed water tank, took almost a quarter century to find a permanent spot. By the spring of 1874 it occupied more conventional if still temporary reading rooms at Wabash Avenue and Madison Street. The library wandered from one provisional location to another until October 11, 1897, three days after the twenty-sixth anniversary of the fire, when it moved into the first home of its own, a grand beaux arts building on the rectangular plot west of Michigan Avenue between Randolph and Washington Streets where Dearborn Park had been. With the opening of the Harold Washington Library Center along State Street between Congress and Van Buren on October 7, 1991—just before the 120th anniversary of the fire—the 1897 building became the Chicago Cultural Center.

The "temporary" city hall that was hastily constructed late in 1871 next to the water tank at LaSalle and Adams lasted fourteen years, until 1885, when a new permanent Chicago City Hall and Cook County Building finally opened in Courthouse Square. The combined local government headquarters filled the square from sidewalk to sidewalk, leaving no room for greenery. The French Renaissance City Hall and Cook County Building was, like the Courthouse that burned, a design and engineering botch. The interior was too dark and cramped to be an attractive and useful space. The structure started to sink, rupturing a gas pipe and setting off an explosion in 1905. Excavation for the current eleven-story neoclassical City Hall and County Building started the following year. The City Hall portion, completed last, opened in 1911.

The Chicago Relief and Aid Society intended that the 7,983 workers' shelter cottages would be replaced by more durable buildings. Most were, but a few lingered on. At least one still stands, a half mile from the salvaged Courthouse finial. Like the Bellinger house, it has been much expanded and updated, but its origins are still recognizable.

There was talk in 1900 of moving the five paintings of the Fire Cyclorama to a private historical museum, but this idea did not materialize. Instead, the titanic canvases that had cost a quarter million dollars to create were stuffed in a warehouse on South Indiana Avenue. In 1913 they were sold as scrap for two dollars.

Wrongly accused of starting the Great Chicago Fire, Catherine O'Leary has been its most enduring victim. Although she has been repeatedly cleared of blame, starting with the official inquiry in 1871, cultural memory has refused to surrender the legend.

O'Leary quickly learned that it did her no good to talk to reporters, who were out to blame and belittle her. On fire anniversaries newspaper editors would send someone to find the O'Learys, especially Catherine. It became a ritual: she refused to answer their questions, and they would ridicule her desire for privacy as they continued to write whatever they pleased, robbing her of any identity other than the caricature they perpetuated. In 1886 a reporter from the *Chicago Daily News* said that she lived in a hovel without a front door and with pieces of clothing covering the unglazed windows. As one approached the home, "the pungent odor of distillery swill and the effluvium of cows proclaim that old habits are strong with Mrs. O'Leary and that she is still in the milk business."

The book-length instant histories of the fire, several of which were in production and some already in print by the time of the fire inquiry, took Catherine O'Leary's guilt as settled fact. The best of these, Elias Colbert and Everett Chamberlin's *Chicago and the Great Conflagration*, reached a very different verdict from that of the official report. "The blame of setting the fire," Colbert and Chamberlin declared, "rests on the woman who milked, or else upon the lazy man who allowed her to milk." If she had not been late and clumsy with her milking, she would not have needed the kerosene lamp, and the cow would not have kicked the lamp over. Colbert and Chamberlin refused to identify Catherine O'Leary by name, they said, because they had "no desire to immortalize the author of the ruin of Chicago at the expense of the noble and indefatigable pioneers" who built the Chicago that she so heedlessly destroyed.

In his *History of Chicago*, published in the 1880s, A. T. Andreas stated that the precise origin "must ever remain a mystery," adding, "There is no proof that Mrs. O'Leary is responsible for the fire." He correctly predicted, however, that "for all time, the legend of Mrs. O'Leary will be accepted." And he helped keep the legend alive by citing the story of an O'Leary neighbor named Joseph Dushek, who contended that shortly after the fire he found a broken kerosene lamp in the barn. Andreas included drawings of the fateful moment when the cow kicked over the lamp and a lamp of the kind that Dushek supposedly found.

In his 1940 study of the fire, H. A. Musham offered as fact that sometime between 8:30 and 8:45 p.m. Catherine O'Leary went out to the barn to milk or nurse a cow and placed the lamp on the floor, and then the "frisky" animal kicked over the lamp with her right hind foot, the kerosene spilled over the floor, the burning wick set it aflame, and Mrs. O'Leary screamed. Musham, who was generally careful about presenting evidence, did not provide a source for this beyond citing questionable information supposedly collected by Andreas.

To complicate matters further, others have stated that they, not Catherine O'Leary, started the fire. In 1903 a woman named Mary Callahan said that she and a few of her friends were responsible. They had been guests at the party the McLaughlins hosted October 8, 1871, in the cottage they rented from the O'Learys. Callahan stated that she was one of four "lads and girls that wanted to play a joke on our old friend, Mrs. O'Leary." The "joke" consisted of sneaking into the barn to get milk for their tea. Callahan said that one of the "lads" either knocked the lamp over or caused the cow to do so. The four kept mum when their joke ended up burning the city down.

The *Tribune* presented this belated confession as if it proved Catherine O'Leary's innocence. In 1997, the same newspaper retold the tale of a man named Louis M. Cohn, who had died in 1942. Cohn had claimed that the fire began when he and some other boys, including an O'Leary son, were shooting dice in the hayloft of the barn and one of them knocked over the lamp.

In 1915 Michael Ahern, who had been a reporter for the *Chicago Republican* in 1871, offered a different kind of admission of guilt. Ahern said that he and two other journalists fabricated the O'Leary story almost immediately after the fire began. To deepen the confusion, a friend of Ahern's maintained that he had ghostwritten Ahern's revelation for him since Ahern was now so addled by alcoholism that he could not do it himself.

Not that Catherine O'Leary lacked for latter-day defenders, though their stories are as doubtful as the others. In 1894 a physician named Swayne Wickersham, who maintained that O'Leary was his patient at the time of the fire, revealed that she was "shocked at the levity" with which she had been treated and the "satirical use" of her name, which led her to refuse interviews or any attempt to reproduce her likeness. He said that he tried to assist the Fire Cyclorama owners in getting her to help advertise the attraction. They supposedly offered her a payment and Patrick O'Leary a job if she cooperated. Wickersham said that Catherine O'Leary turned the offer down, telling him that that she did not need the money and would not take it even if she did.

He added that O'Leary said her tenants the McLaughlins were the ones who had set the barn on fire. The reporter who interviewed Wickersham blamed both the O'Learys and the McLaughlins. Whether or not Wickersham actually knew Catherine O'Leary, he spoke highly of her character. "She was a strictly honest woman and afraid of debt," he asserted. "She kept her money in an old sock and paid me for every professional visit I made before I left the house."

In 1933 Catherine O'Leary's daughter and namesake Catherine O'Leary Ledwell, who herself had consistently refused to talk to the press, broke her silence. Ten years old at the time of the fire, Ledwell said she recalled the family being awakened by Daniel Sullivan, which proved her parents were sleeping when the fire started and so had nothing to do with it. Ledwell's son told the reporter who interviewed his mother that she was so sensitive about the subject that she had ordered him out of the house recently for singing the ditty about the origin of the fire, familiar to this day to scouts and summer campers, set to the

tune of "There'll Be a Hot Time in the Old Town Tonight." One varia-
tion goes:

> Late last night, when we were all in bed,
> Mrs. O'Leary left a lantern in the shed.
> Well, the cow kicked it over, and this is what they said:
> "There'll be a hot time in the old town tonight!"

Another staunch defender was Ledwell's younger brother, James Patrick O'Leary, who had passed away in 1925. He was born in the shanty
on DeKoven Street in 1869, so he was only two when Chicago went up
in flames and had no memory of it. He was reputed to have made a lot
of money running a book on horse racing, which enabled him to open
a fancy saloon. "Big Jim" O'Leary would supposedly bet on anything,
from the outcome of a presidential election to Chicago's fickle weather.

James O'Leary was widely respected as a man of his word. When he
died, politicians from the two major parties attended his funeral. Former First Ward alderman Mike "Hinky Dink" Kenna, one of the most
storied of the all the ward bosses who so confounded and outraged reformers, praised him as "a square shooter" who "never welched on a
bet." To his dying day, O'Leary testily denied that the fire's origin had
anything to do with his parents, who told him that the story of the cow
and the lamp was "a monumental fake."

A 1985 book raised the possibility that a comet ignited not only the
Great Chicago Fire but also the fires in Michigan and Wisconsin, which
supposedly explains their simultaneity. The most ingenious and tightly
reasoned search for the fire's precise origin is that of Richard F. Bales,
who published his findings in the late 1990s. Basing his case on a me-
ticulous scrutiny of the testimony at the inquiry and land records from
the period, Bales suggests that Daniel Sullivan, whom some suspected
at the time, accidentally started the fire with his pipe before rushing to
awaken the O'Learys.

As the fire retreated into the past, Catherine and Patrick O'Leary and
the cow evolved from villains into affectionately remembered heroes of

urban legend. The meanness disappeared, if not the condescension and stereotyping.

On the fortieth anniversary of the fire, a woman costumed as Catherine O'Leary, carrying a milk pail and accompanied by a Patrick O'Leary impersonator, led a cow through Chicago's streets as part of the commemorative parade. On Chicago Day in 1934, popular *Tribune* cartoonist John McCutcheon presented a courtroom scene in which Mrs. O'Leary's cow sits in a chair beside "Judge Posterity" as the jury foreman announces, "Our verdict is *not guilty* of arson, as charged sixty-three years ago."

A sure sign that Mrs. O'Leary and her cow had entered the front ranks of national folklore is noted American artist Norman Rockwell's

Norman Rockwell, Mrs. Catherine O'Leary Milking Daisy, *1935.*
(Chicago History Museum, ICHi-064474)

1935 oil painting, *Mrs. Catherine O'Leary Milking Daisy*, now owned by
the Chicago History Museum. "Daisy" is one of the several names post-
humously invented for the cow over the years. Rockwell's version of
Catherine O'Leary is a plump middle-aged woman in kerchief and apron.
She smiles contentedly as she sits on a stool milking away. We view Daisy
from the rear, as she turns her head to look back toward both the viewer
and the kerosene lamp irresistibly placed behind her left hind hoof. Rockwell recalled wryly that the painting, which was intended for a calendar,
was his "worst failure." "Not that it was a bad painting," he explained,
"but who wants to look at the rear end of a cow for 12 months?"

The painting's attitude toward Catherine O'Leary is far kinder
than the ones in the early depictions of the scene in the barn, but it is
still a patronizing projection of cultural attitudes rather than an attempt to portray her accurately. Although the work is realistic in style,
it is as much of a caricature as the cruelest of the cartoons, an expression of Rockwell's nostalgia for a simpler time that ignores the challenging circumstances of Catherine O'Leary's life and elides the trauma
of the fire.

The theme of the January 1, 1960, Tournament of Roses Parade in
Pasadena, California, whose grand marshal that year was Vice President Richard Nixon, was "Tall Tales and True." The city of Chicago
entered a smoke-puffing float starring Mrs. O'Leary's cow fashioned out
of carnations and chrysanthemums. It won the grand prize.

It was left to the O'Learys to move on as the world would let them. They
evidently remained on DeKoven Street for a few years before selling the
property to a Bohemian immigrant named Anton Kohler and moving
to the Bridgeport neighborhood, near the Union Stock Yards. Kohler
knocked down the wooden buildings and put up a solid three-story
brick and stone house. On the tenth anniversary of the fire in 1881, the
Chicago Historical Society placed a tablet on the house inscribed with
an extremely brief summary of the disaster: "The Great Fire of 1871
Originated Here and Extended to Lincoln Park."

Eighty-four years after the great conflagration, the city fire department deliberately burned down the home that Anton Kohler erected

on the O'Leary lot. The purpose was to combine a training exercise with clearing the block for urban renewal. The irony did not stop there. Six years later, on May 15, 1961, Chicago opened a $2 million brick center for training firefighters on the O'Leary's block. In 1978 Chicago named the building the Robert J. Quinn Fire Academy. Quinn had recently retired after twenty-one years as head of the fire department and, like William D. Musham, almost fifty years of service.

When it built the training center, Chicago finally—ninety years after the fire—erected a monument to the conflagration. Chicago sculptor

Egon Weiner, Pillar of Fire, *in front of the Robert J. Quinn Fire Academy, 2011. Photograph by Stefani Foster. (Northwestern University and the Chicago History Museum)*

Egon Weiner's thirty-three-foot-high *Pillar of Fire*, on the plaza in front of the academy, is an abstract representation of the disaster in three gracefully intertwined metal "flames."

Inside the building, framed and protected by a slender chain held in place by posts that resemble the nozzle end of fire hoses, is a section of flooring marked with the outline of a fireman's shield, inside which is an image of Weiner's *Pillar* and the number 1871. "This emblem," we are told with perhaps unjustified precision and certainty, "marks the exact spot where the Great Chicago Fire began."

The arc of the moral universe eventually did bend a little closer toward justice for Catherine O'Leary. On October 6, 1997, two days before the fire's 126th anniversary, the City Council Committee on Fire and Police, with plenty of reporters on hand, held a good-humored hearing in the Quinn Fire Academy during which members passed a resolution officially clearing her name. Three weeks later the full council

Emblem marking the spot where the Great Chicago Fire began,
Robert J. Quinn Fire Academy, 2011. Photograph by Stefani Foster.
(Northwestern University and the Chicago History Museum)

voted 47–0 to "forever exonerate Mrs. O'Leary and her cow from all blame in regard to the Great Chicago Fire of 1871."

By then Patrick and Catherine O'Leary had both been dead for over a century. On September 15, 1894, Patrick suffered a fatal heart attack on the threshold of their residence at 5133 South Halsted Street. Catherine died of acute pneumonia the following July 3. Both were waked at home and buried in Mount Olivet Cemetery, on the South Side of the city. The local papers ran longer obituaries for Patrick, most likely because he was male, but it was Catherine's death that received at least a squib in newspapers across the country. All of them attributed the fire to her and the cow. As many people still do.

ACKNOWLEDGMENTS

In writing this book I have accumulated a large number of intellectual and personal debts to a long list of institutions and individuals. I am glad to have the opportunity to acknowledge them here.

I have benefited greatly from access to several exceptional research centers. The most important has been the Chicago History Museum and its extraordinarily rich and varied holdings on the fire, including manuscripts, printed sources, visual materials, and artifacts of all kinds. I have also made extensive use of the Chicago Public Library, the Huntington Library, the Newberry Library, and the Northwestern University Library. In exploring their collections I have received critical financial support from the institutions themselves and also from the American Council of Learned Societies, the Mellon Foundation, the National Endowment for the Humanities, and, multiple times and in many ways, Northwestern University.

I am very grateful for the wisdom and generosity of the several people who have provided the kind of knowledge and expertise on which any researcher profoundly depends. At the Chicago History Museum's Research Center, I am especially indebted to Lesley Martin for all she has done over the years to help me find what I was looking for, as well as many things I did not know about but proved invaluable. I am deeply appreciative of the enthusiastic and sustained support I have received from the director of print and multimedia publications, Rosemary Adams; senior curator Olivia Mahoney; senior photographer John Alderson; and Chicago History Museum presidents Lonnie Bunch, Douglas Greenberg, and Gary T. Johnson. Katie Levi of the museum's Rights and Reproduction department did remarkable work in making available the large amount of visual material in this book. I owe particular thanks to the late Russell Lewis, executive vice president and chief historian, who through a variety of projects consistently provided not just every possible sort of assistance and access but also constant inspiration and warm friendship.

I discovered a new world and enjoyed myself thoroughly while working long hours side by side with several exceptionally dedicated and talented people at Northwestern University on *The Great Chicago*

Fire and the Web of Memory, the online exhibition we produced in collaboration with the Chicago History Museum. I want to single out in particular Jon Fernandez, Stefani Foster, Joseph Germuska, Paul Hertz, William Parod, Robert Taylor, Rodolfo Vieira, Harlan Wallach, and Eric Whitley.

I am very fortunate to have had exceptional help from a series of notably resourceful and intelligent Northwestern University undergraduate research assistants—namely, Peter Golkin, Christina Powers, and especially Joseph Rathke. I want to thank the wonderful Leopold Fellowship Program of the Nicholas D. Chabraja Center for Historical Studies at Northwestern, as administered by assistant director Elzbieta Foeller-Pituch and director Sara Maza, for providing me with Mr. Rathke's indispensable assistance.

I have learned a tremendous amount about the fire in conversations with Ross Miller and Karen Sawislak, as well as from their excellent books on the subject. I have relied on Dennis McClendon's deep knowledge of Chicago history, especially in the course of his preparation of the maps included in this book. In multiple instances Louis Cain and Ellen Skerrett generously shared their remarkable learning with me. I am also very appreciative of discussions with Daniel Immerwahr, Theodore Karamanski, Ann Durkin Keating, Dominic Pacyga, and Mark Tebeau. In this project, as in all of my teaching and scholarship, I have drawn on Henry Binford's masterful knowledge of Chicago and urban history, not to mention his great good will.

I am very grateful for the advice and support of Peter and Amy Bernstein of the Bernstein Literary Agency, and of the several people at Grove Atlantic who have worked on this book with me, especially George Gibson, Joan Bingham, Emily Burns, and publisher Morgan Entrekin. My thanks to my copyeditor, Brian Bendlin, and senior production editor Melody Negron.

I have long owed the greatest thanks and appreciation to Jane S. Smith, an extraordinary partner in research and writing, as she is in every way that matters.

NOTES

1. "Kate! The Barn Is Afire!"

1   *inflicting damages estimated at $750,000*   On the Saturday Night Fire and those in the weeks that preceded it, see Musham, 89–94; *CTrib*, September 30–October 8, 1871; and Andreas, 2:704–7. As noted, estimates of the cost of the damage from this and other fires frequently vary widely. Andreas and Musham include diagrams of the Saturday Night Fire. The account of Chief Fire Marshal Williams comes from his testimony at the official inquiry on the fire, included in Bales, 271–93, and *CTrib*, November 15, 1871. Address information here and elsewhere is from Chicago city directories published at the time, many of which are available online. See, for example, Newberry Library, "City Directories," https://www.newberry.org/city-directories; and Chicago Genealogy, "How to Find Chicago City Directories," http://chicago genealogy.com/find-chicago-city-directories.html. As already indicated, many street numbers in Chicago were changed early in the twentieth century.

2   *causes ranging from more worker carelessness and mischievous boys to defective chimneys and outright arson*   For a listing of these and other fires during this period, see City of Chicago, *Report of the Board of Police, in the Fire Department, to the Common Council of the City of Chicago, for the Year Ending March 31, 1872* (Chicago: Hazlitt and Reed, 1872), 106–8.

2   *winds out of the southwest put everybody on edge*   On weather conditions in Chicago at the time, see Musham, 87.

2   *"If a fire should start, Chicago will burn up."*   A. S. Chapman, "A Boy's Recollections of the Chicago Fire" (1910), 2. This is a typescript in the collections of the Chicago History Museum.

2   *he returned home and at last made it to sleep*   There is conflicting information on the location of Robert and Harriet Williams's residence. City directories for 1871 place them in a rooming house at Adams and Halsted Streets on the West Side, about a half mile northwest of the scene of the Saturday Night Fire. Williams's account of his movements during the official inquiry have him crossing the South Branch of the Chicago River to get from his home to the West Side, which would mean that his home was in the South Division.

3   *many could barely open their swollen and bloodshot eyes*   Musham gives the total number of employees in the fire department as 219. For detailed lists of its roster and equipment, see Musham, 75–87, 181–87; Bales, 207–10; and City of Chicago, *Report of the Board of Police*, 28–87, which is full of splendid illustrations of the department's equipment.

3   *"we were going to have a 'burn.'"*   Bales, 271, 283n8; *CTrib*, November 15, 1871.

4   *so the light would not disturb him*   Bales, 271, 273.

4   *some two hundred feet east of Jefferson Street*   According to the 1870 census, Patrick and Catherine O'Leary had four children when the census was taken: Mary (fourteen), Cornelius (twelve), Catherine (eleven), and James (eight). Birthdates in censuses are not always reliable, and they can differ from one census to another. An obituary

of James O'Leary states that he was born in 1869, which would have made him two years old at the time of the fire; *CTrib*, January 23, 1925. In her testimony at the official fire inquiry, Catherine O'Leary said she had five children; Bales, 217. The 1880 census indicates that a fifth sibling, named Patrick, was born in 1871, and at least one report of Catherine's testimony at the inquiry says she was nursing an infant. The 1900 and 1910 censuses state that this child was born in 1873 and was then living with the family of his married older sister Catherine O'Leary Ledwell, who as a girl was called Katie. Censuses accessed through Ancestry, https://www.ancestry.com.

4   *and everything of wood*   Joseph Edgar Chamberlin, fire narrative, in McIlvaine, 1.

4   *serve in the Union Army*   The 1870 census lists Catherine and Patrick O'Leary's ages, respectively, as forty and forty-three. The 1880 census states that Patrick somehow aged twelve years over the decade, while Catherine gained only five (i.e., it lists him as fifty-five and her as forty-five). His obituary in the *Chicago Tribune* states that he was seventy-five at the time of his death in 1894, which would mean he was born in 1819, making him about fifty-two at the time of the fire. The *O'* was often dropped on names like theirs, so in some records they are listed as Leary. *CTrib*, September 17, 1894. See also Musham, 94–95; and Andreas, 2:708.

4   *had made a significant investment*   On wages, see Pierce, 2:500. In his deeply detailed study of daily experience in the city, Perry Duis estimates there were ten thousand head of cattle in "the backyards and barns" of Chicago by the 1870s; see Duis, *Challenging Chicago: Coping with Everyday Life, 1837–1920* (Urbana: University of Illinois Press, 1998), 135, 95.

5   *speed and economy mattered more than solidity*   The dimensions of the buildings vary in different sources. Musham, 94–95, gives the depth of the cottage as thirty-six feet, but it appears a little shorter in images. It would have been difficult, though not impossible, to fit two cottages that size, plus the barn, on the lot. On the method of construction, see Joseph C. Bigott, "Balloon Frame Construction," in *EC*, http://www.encyclopedia.chicagohistory.org/pages/105.html. See also Bigott, *From Cottage to Bungalow: Houses and the Working Class in Metropolitan Chicago* (Chicago: University of Chicago Press, 2001), 21–26.

6   *spare as those homes might be*   Of the approximately sixty thousand buildings in 1871 Chicago, two-thirds were wooden houses with an average value of around $1,000. In 1870, 20 percent of skilled workers and 17 percent of unskilled workers owned real estate. See John B. Jentz and Richard Schneirov, *Chicago in the Age of Capital: Class, Politics, and Democracy during the Civil War and Reconstruction* (Urbana: University of Illinois Press, 2012), 122.

6   *buildings jammed together like this were commonplace*   Bales, 51; Musham, 94–95. It is not clear which of the two homes was built first.

6   *he hobbled about on a wooden leg*   Bales, 138, has discovered records that Sullivan occupied a separate dwelling from his mother's, also on the south side of DeKoven Street, though other evidence suggests that he lived with her. The information on the O'Learys' neighbors is from the 1870 census.

6   *"the barn is afire!"*   Bales, 217–24, 234–36; *CTimes*, December 3, 1871.

2. "To Depress Her Rising Consequence Would Be Like an Attempt to Quench the Stars"

7   *which emptied into the lake*   John C. Hudson, *Chicago: A Geography of the City and Its Region* (Chicago: University of Chicago Press, 2006), 44–52; Libby Hill, *The Chi-*

cago River: A Natural and Unnatural History (Chicago: Lake Claremont, 2000), 32–33. See also David M. Solzman, *The Chicago River: An Illustrated History and Guide to the River and Its Waterways* (Chicago: Wild Onion Books, 1998).

7   *about thirty thousand Illinois, Kickapoo, Miami, Ojibwa, Odawa, and Sauk*   Ann Durkin Keating, *Rising Up from Indian Country: The Battle of Fort Dearborn and the Birth of Chicago* (Chicago: University of Chicago Press, 2012), 15; Helen Hornbeck Tanner, ed., *Atlas of Great Lakes Indian History* (Norman: University of Oklahoma Press, 1987), 65–66, 96–97. Chicago's first permanent settlers arrived in the late 1780s. They were not white Europeans but West African–French fur trader Jean Baptiste Pointe de Sable, his Potawatomi wife Catherine, and their two children.

8   *rest were taken captive and eventually ransomed or freed*   Keating, *Rising Up from Indian Country*, 164.

12   *between Beverly, Massachusetts, and Carlisle, Pennsylvania*   "Population of the 100 Largest Urban Places: 1840," table 7 in Campbell Gibson, "Population of the 100 Largest Cities and Other Urban Places in the United States: 1790–1990" (US Bureau of the Census, Population Division Working Paper No. 27, June 1998), http:// www.census.gov/population/www/documentation/twps0027/tab07.txt. This number is slightly different in other sources.

12   *By 1870 there were fourteen with populations of 100,000 or more*   For these and related statistics on Chicago in particular and urbanization in general, see Gibson, "Population of the 100 Largest Cities and Other Urban Places," http://www.census .gov/population/www/documentation/twps0027/twps0027.html.

12   *and Chicago the central stage for the enactment of modernity*   Richard Cobden, quoted in James Parton, "Chicago," *Atlantic Monthly* 19, no. 113 (March 1867): 325. The rise of Chicago in this period is the subject of many excellent studies. For the broader economic and technological developments, see William Cronon's magisterial *Nature's Metropolis: Chicago and the Great West* (New York: W. W. Norton, 1991). For a superb narrative that focuses on the people who built Chicago and the larger context of the expanding United States, see Donald L. Miller, *City of the Century: The Epic of Chicago and the Making of America* (New York: Simon and Schuster, 1996). Andreas's and Pierce's respective three-volume histories, and Harold M. Mayer and Richard C. Wade's richly illustrated *Chicago: Growth of a Metropolis* (Chicago: University of Chicago Press, 1969) are indispensable. Other outstanding surveys of the city's history are Dominic A. Pacyga, *Chicago: A Biography* (Chicago: University of Chicago Press, 2009); and Robert G. Spinney, *City of Big Shoulders: A History of Chicago* (DeKalb: Northern Illinois University Press, 2000). Perry Duis's *Challenging Chicago: Coping with Everyday Life, 1837–1920* (Urbana: University of Illinois Press, 1998) is an invaluable examination of what it was like to live in Chicago in that era.

13   *caused American wheat exports to double in volume and triple in value*   Cronon, *Nature's Metropolis*, 115.

13   *set the first formal rules for this market in futures*   Cronon, *Nature's Metropolis*, 120–24; Pierce, 2:77.

13   *and railroad cars and tracks*   On Chicago during the Civil War, see Theodore J. Karamanski, *Rally 'Round the Flag: Chicago and the Civil War* (Chicago: Nelson-Hall, 1993).

13   *as well as its own rail network, drainage system, water supply, and hotel*   Pierce, 2:93, 3:108–44; Cronon, *Nature's Metropolis*, 207–59.

13   *while lake traffic made Chicago one of the busiest ports in the country*   In spite of the fact that cold weather closed down shipping during the winter months, by 1871

more vessels stopped at Chicago than at Baltimore, Charleston, Mobile, New York, Philadelphia, and San Francisco combined, though the total tonnage of cargo was far smaller. Theodore J. Karamanski, "The People and the Port," in *EC*, http://www.encyclopedia.chicagohistory.org/pages/300010.html; Musham, 71–72; Pierce, 2:72.

13   *almost 2,100 of these in the state*   Cronon, *Nature's Metropolis*, 68; *The Forty-Third Annual Report of the Trade and Commerce of Chicago for the Year Ending December 31, 1900*, comp. George F. Stone (Chicago: J. M. W. Jones, 1901), 169.

15   *and the Union Stock Yards, on the periphery*   For an informative map, see "The Railroad System of Chicago, 1871," in Mayer and Wade, *Chicago: Growth of a Metropolis*, 43.

15   *240 freight trains arrived in or departed from Chicago every day*   Pierce, 2:72–73, 2:60, 2:55.

16   *ragged-looking space between the railroad track and the avenue*   CTrib, June 25, 1871; Pierce, 2:48–49; Colbert and Chamberlin, 131; "Michigan Avenue and Terrace Row," in *GCFWOM*, https://www.greatchicagofire.org/landmarks/michigan-avenue -and-terrace-row/.

16   *would be like an attempt to quench the stars*   Henry Brown, *The Present and Future Prospects of Chicago: An Address Delivered before the Chicago Lyceum, January 20, 1846* (Chicago: Fergus, 1876), 6.

16   *when Chicagoans knew each other much better and shared common interests*   Carl Smith, *Urban Disorder and the Shape of Belief: The Great Chicago Fire, the Haymarket Bomb, and the Model Town of Pullman*, 2nd ed. (Chicago: University of Chicago Press, 2007), 88–89.

16   *A considerably higher percentage had at least one foreign-born parent*   Skogan, 18. In 1890, 77.9 percent of the population had at least one parent born abroad; see Pierce, 3:22.

17   *There was virtually no Asian presence in prefire Chicago*   On the population statistics discussed here, see Skogan, 18–19; Pierce, 2:5–11, 2:481–82, 3:21, 3:515–16; and CTrib, April 23, 1871. On the restriction of African American civil rights, see Pierce, 3:12; and St. Clair Drake and Horace R. Cayton, *Black Metropolis: A Study of Negro Life in a Northern City* (Chicago: University of Chicago Press, 1993).

17   *were far too large to be monolithic*   "Germans" here refers to people from the German states, which were not unified into the nation of Germany until 1871.

17   *From their ranks came most of the 20 percent of Chicagoans who owned virtually all of the city's wealth*   Craig Buettinger, "Economic Inequality in Early Chicago, 1849–1850," *Journal of Social History* 11, no. 3 (Spring 1978): 413–18.

17   *as opposed to the normal ten or twelve hours, six days a week—had failed*   On the complex history of Chicago working people in this period, see John B. Jentz and Richard Schneirov's outstanding *Chicago in the Age of Capital: Class, Politics, and Democracy in the Civil War and Reconstruction* (Urbana: University of Illinois Press, 2012). See also Richard Schneirov, *Labor and Urban Politics: Class Conflict and the Origins of Modern Liberalism in Chicago, 1864–1897* (Urbana: University of Illinois Press, 1998); Hartmut Keil and John B. Jentz, eds., *German Workers in Industrial Chicago: A Comparative Perspective* (DeKalb: Northern Illinois University Press, 1983); Hartmut Keil and John B. Jentz, eds., *German Workers in Chicago: A Documentary History* (Urbana: University of Illinois Press, 1988); and Pierce, 2:150–89.

18   *then a separate city bordering Chicago on the north*   CTrib, March 18, 1871; CTrib, February 6, 1871; CTrib, May 30, 1871.

18   *and it to them*   Ellen Skerrett, "The Irish in Chicago: The Catholic Dimension," in Ellen Skerrett, Edward R. Kantowicz, and Steven M. Avella, *Catholicism, Chicago Style* (Chicago: Loyola University Press, 1993), 29–78; Thomas M. Mulkerins, *Holy Family Parish Chicago: Priests and People*, ed. Joseph J. Thompson (Chicago: Universal, 1923); Lawrence J. McCaffrey, Ellen Skerrett, and Michael F. Funchion, *The Irish in Chicago* (Urbana: University of Illinois Press, 1987). In addition to many smaller churches, the city's Catholics erected two other majestic spaces, both in the North Division. German Catholics raised St. Michael's Catholic Church, with its two-hundred-foot steeple. It was located as far to the north of the Courthouse as Holy Family was to the southwest. Holy Name Cathedral, the seat of the Archdiocese of Chicago, sat on State Street, just north of Superior, about three blocks west and slightly south of the waterworks.

19   *and ethnic politicians occupied a comparable percentage of seats on the Common Council*   CTrib, April 23, 1871, estimated the total electorate at fifty thousand, about twenty-eight thousand of whom were foreign born. See also Jentz and Schneirov, *Chicago in the Age of Capital*, 152, figure 8.

19   *only eight were from Germany*   A few weeks earlier, the paper's examination of the police force revealed that it consisted of 158 Irish and 131 "Americans," as opposed to merely 117 Germans. ISZ, May 13, 1871; ISZ, April 20, 1871.

19   *those of the entire 1847–48 fiscal year*   Pierce, 2:344.

20   *engaged in various businesses in Chicago*   Andreas, 2:51; C. H. Mottier, *Biography of Roswell B. Mason* [n.p.: n.p., 1938], mimeographed booklet in the collections of the Chicago History Museum; CTrib, January 2, 1892.

21   *protesters and police backed by local militia*   Robin Einhorn, "Lager Beer Riot," in EC, http://www.encyclopedia.chicagohistory.org/pages/703.html.

21   *a more liberal conception of the nature and commands of a Divine Providence*   CTrib, June 9, 1871.

22   *spurting a powerful stream out of its hose higher and farther than all others*   Andreas, 1:220.

22   *The boys of the volunteer department saw in its every puff a death blow to their own system*   Andreas, 1:227.

23   *Twenty thousand Chicagoans, more than one-fifth of the population, paid their respects*   CTrib, October 20, 1857; CTrib, October 22, 1857; CTrib, October 26, 1857; Andreas, 1:226–27.

23   *and with a flared brim at the rear to deflect falling water*   On the early history of firefighting in the United States, see Mark Tebeau, *Eating Smoke: Fire in Urban America, 1800–1950* (Baltimore: Johns Hopkins University Press, 2003); and Robert M. Hazen and Margaret Hindle Hazen, *Keepers of the Flame: The Role of Fire in American Culture, 1775–1925* (Princeton NJ: Princeton University Press, 1992).

24   *lengths of several hundred feet that could be attached to each other*   On the procedures of the fire department, see Musham, 75, 79–81; Bales, 207–10; and Andreas, 2:90–102.

26   *monumental project that was the Sanitary and Ship Canal in 1900*   On the construction of the waterworks, see Carl Smith, *City Water, City Life: Water and the Infrastructure of Ideas in Urbanizing Philadelphia, Boston, and Chicago* (Chicago:

University of Chicago Press, 2013), 38–52, 236–37. The precise height of the Chicago
Water Tower varies in different sources; see *CTrib*, March 26, 1867; and *CTrib*,
July 16, 1871. On the Sanitary and Ship Canal, see Ann Durkin Keating, "Sanitary
and Ship Canal," in *EC*, http://www.encyclopedia.chicagohistory.org/pages/1684.html;
and Ann Durkin Keating, "Constructing the Sanitary and Ship Canal," in *EC*, http://
www.encyclopedia.chicagohistory.org/pages/300018.html.

26   *an increase of more than $1.5 million over 1869*   *CTrib*, April 12, 1871.

26   *ornament is substituted for strength, and safety is sacrificed for cheapness*   City of
Chicago, *Report of the Board of Police in the Fire Department, to the Common Coun-
cil, of the City of Chicago, for the Year Ending March 31st, 1868* (Chicago: Illinois
Staats-Zeitung Steam Book and Job Printing Establishment, 1868), 6–7.

27   *Chicago would suffer "many devastating fires."*   City of Chicago, *Report of the Board
of Police*, 8.

27   *and that money is to be obtained by taxation*   John Blake Rice, "Mayor John Blake
Rice Inaugural Address, 1867," Chicago Public Library, https://www.chipublib.org
/mayor-john-blake-rice-inaugural-address-1867; "Rice Theatres I and II," Chicagology, https://chicagology.com/prefire/prefire117/.

27   *But, like Rice, he dodged the question of whether Chicago needed it to be larger and
better equipped*   Roswell B. Mason, "Mayor Roswell B. Mason Inaugural Address,"
Chicago Public Library, https://www.chipublib.org/mayor-roswell-b-mason-inaugural
-address-1869/.

3. *"A Regular Nest of Fire"*

29   *along with a rear barn*   For a diagram of the north side of DeKoven Street, see Andreas, 2:717; Musham, 98; and Bales, 99. Bales, 211, also provides one of both sides
of the street.

29   *Again, unbeknownst to him, the system failed*   Musham, 100. For Goll's version of
what occurred, offered in a signed affidavit prepared in 1885, see Andreas, 2:716.

30   *even if his cottage was not*   On October 2, just six days before the Great Chicago
Fire, a privately funded organization started supplementing the work of the fire department by removing valuable and flammable contents from buildings threatened
by fire. It dated to the fire of 1857, following which businesses and insurance companies formed the Citizens Fire Brigade, whose members helped save property from destruction. In 1871 Chicago insurance underwriters established the much more
substantial Chicago Fire Patrol. Like the regular firemen, it operated from stations
staffed with a trained force who wore the same kind of protective gear, though no firefighting equipment. Similar insurance patrols existed in other cities. Instead of trying to
stop the flames, they attempted the dangerous task of reducing damage by removing
possessions from harm's way in order to limit their clients' and their own losses. They
employed waterproof tarpaulins to shield property against water and smoke damage.
See Jacob Kaplan, "Fire Insurance Patrol Stations," Forgotten Chicago, https://forgot
tenchicago.com/articles/fire-insurance-patrol-stations/; and Keith M. Seafield and Michael
A. Pack, *History of the Chicago Fire Insurance Patrol, 1871–1959* ([Chicago]: n.p.,
2007). The Fire Patrol did not concern itself with small, uninsured homes like those of
William Lee and his neighbors on DeKoven Street, including the O'Learys.

31   *tried to save what they could from the burning barn*   In some places Regan's last name
is given as Ryan.

31   *finally spotted the flames*   Schaefer's name ("Matthias Schaffer" in some places) is one of many spelled differently depending on the source. This book generally follows Bales's spelling.

31   *but a mile beyond it*   Musham, 114–17, is the main source for the details of what transpired in the Courthouse. These details vary somewhat from the affidavits submitted during the fire inquiry by Brown and Schaefer, who did not concur in all respects, though they agreed that the first alarm sounded was for Box 342.

31   *they would find the right location on their way to the wrong one*   According to Musham, 101–7, this is one of several errors of perception and judgment that Schaefer and Brown made in alerting the firefighters where they should go. For unexplained reasons, Brown's sister seems to have been in his office that night, since he referred to her presence in the affidavit he submitted to the official fire inquiry. See Bales, 213–15.

32   *an actual native of Chicago*   CTrib, February 24, 1907.

32   *The facility for burning was very good*   Testimony of Michael Sullivan, in "Transcript of Inquiry into Cause of Chicago Fire and Actions of Fire Department Therein," 1:8. This is the transcript of the inquiry on the fire conducted by the Board of Police and Fire Commissioners. It is cited here for testimony not included in Bales's *The Great Chicago Fire and the Myth of Mrs. O'Leary's Cow*. To the great benefit of those interested in studying the fire, Bales prepared this four-volume typed version of the full transcript, with each witness's testimony numbered separately. It is in the Great Chicago Fire collections of the Chicago History Museum. The citation indicates the name of the witness, the volume in which the testimony appears, and the page number of the excerpt cited.

33   *a regular nest of fire*   Bales, 273.

33   *which brought out what was left of the fire department after the Saturday Night Fire*   Telegraph operator William Brown later stated that he sounded the second and third alarms on his own authority; Bales, 214.

33   *right on [its] taps*   Bales, 282.

33   *is getting ahead of me in spite of all I can do*   Bales, 274. See Williams's slightly different version of these events in CTrib, November 15, 1871.

34   *the most combustible place in the city of Chicago*   Testimony of Leo Myers, in "Transcript of Inquiry," 2:8.

34   *God only knows*   Bales, 274; CTrib, November 16, 1871.

35   *asked Swenie to give others the same treatment*   Musham, 108–9.

35   *started work as a freight agent for the Chicago and North Western Railway*   Wicker was a young man on his way up. The following June he would marry Augusta French, daughter of former Illinois governor Augustus French, and would go on to a long and successful career as a railroad executive for many lines throughout the country, from Colorado and Texas to Brooklyn and Boston.

35   *the "cataract of fire" that had engulfed their home*   Cassius Milton Wicker, letter to "Home," October 15, 1871, CHMFC, in *GCFWOM*, https://www.greatchicagofire.org /anthology-of-fire-narratives/cassius-milton-wicker/; Thomas Hoyne, fire narrative, 1871, CHMFC; Andreas, 2:737–38.

35   *was to a great extent a Protestant in practice*   In Memoriam: Sketch of the Life and Character of Thomas Hoyne, LL.D., with the Proceedings of Public Bodies on the Occasion of His Death (Chicago: Published for His Friends, 1883), 123.

35   *they wouldn't let me see it. Mean!"*   Cora Heffron Murray, fire narrative, CHMFC.

36   *and ignite frame buildings and sheds, and push their way rapidly to the northeast*   Colonel Robert R. McCormick, "Joseph Medill's Story of the Great Chicago Fire," address broadcast over WGN and the Mutual Broadcasting System, October 3, 1953, 1. A copy is in the collections of the Chicago History Museum. The address directly quotes an account by Medill. McCormick, Medill's grandson, was then near the end of his four-decade career as owner, editor, and publisher of the *Chicago Tribune*. On Medill, see also John Tebbel, *An American Dynasty: The Story of the McCormicks, Medills and Pattersons* (New York: Doubleday, 1947), 3.

37   *I'll be there in a minute*   Musham, 110; Bales, 275.

4. *"It Was Nothing but Excitement"*

39   *It was the three-story brick stable of the Parmelee Omnibus and Stage Company at Franklin and Jackson*   Just where and when the fire initially entered the South Division is one of the many details about which there has been disagreement. Some have claimed that the first place to catch fire was a roofing company on Adams Street, which still required quite a leap. See Andreas, 2:719.

39   *Another flying brand lodged on the main works of the Chicago Gas Light and Coke Company, two blocks north and one block west of Parmelee's stable*   On the conflicting versions of just what happened when the gas works caught fire, see Bales, 22–24.

41   *with painted cheeks, cursing and uttering ribald jests as they drifted along*   Andreas, 2:493–94; McIlvaine, 62.

41   *compelled it to sound its own death-knell*   Frederick Francis Cook, *Bygone Days in Chicago: Recollections of the "Garden City" of the Sixties* (Chicago: A. C. McClurg, 1910), 172; Colbert and Chamberlin, 153–54; Andreas, 2:724; Frank A. Randall, *History of the Development of Building Construction in Chicago* (Urbana: University of Illinois Press, 1949), 38.

41   *now fell in dire carnival upon the noble edifices of LaSalle Street" below the Courthouse*   CTimes, October 18, 1871.

42   *appeared to be huddled together in a solid mass, helpless and astounded*   McIlvaine, 24. See also Andreas, 2:735–36. McIlvaine identifies Frear as a member of the New York State Assembly, as well as the commissioner of public charities and a commissioner of emigration for the city of New York.

43   *and the whole city is on fire*   Mrs. Charles C. Counselman [Jennie E. Otis], "Reminiscence of the Chicago Fire and Some of My Girlhood Days," presented before the Chicago Women's Club, March 28, 1920, typescript, CHMCF, in *GCFWOM*, https://www.greatchicagofire.org/anthology-of-fire-narratives/jennie-e-otis/.

44   *"Go on and do something," he instructed*   Bales, 255–57. For a fuller description of Hildreth's actions during the fire, see Bales, 34–37.

45   *Greeley thought he felt the earth tremble*   Samuel S. Greeley, fire narrative, [1900?], CHMCF; Samuel S. Greeley, *Memories of the Great Chicago Fire of October 1871* (Chicago: Samuel S. Greeley, 1904), n.p. [3–4]. The title on this privately printed book differs from that on the memoir itself, which is "Echoes of the Great Fire." It also appeared in *Unity* 54, no. 6 (October 6, 1904): 87–93.

45   *very popular, especially with the ladies*   M. L. Ahern, *The Great Revolution: A History of the Rise and Progress of the People's Party in the City of Chicago and County of Cook, with Sketches of the Elect in Office* (Chicago: Lakeside, 1874), 152–53;

CTimes, December 3, 1871. Richard C. Lindberg, who characterizes Hickey as "a venal and dangerous police captain," discusses the shadier side of Hickey's activities in *To Serve and Collect: Chicago Politics and Police Corruption from the Lager Beer Riot to the Summerdale Scandal* (New York: Praeger, 1991), 41–42.

45 *as a horrid fear that they were to be burned alive possessed them* Andreas, 2:725.

46 *led them to a station on the North Side* Bales, 242–52. Some accounts have others—most notably, Mayor Mason—ordering the release of the prisoners. The Chicago History Museum owns a handwritten directive to this effect that is signed by Mason, but there is some doubt about its authenticity. See "Mayor Roswell Mason Note Ordering the Release of Prisoners, October 9, 1871," in "Inside the Burning City," in *GCFWOM*, https://www.greatchicagofire.org/great-conflagration/inside-burning-city/.

46 *to don their plunder and disguise themselves* Andreas, 2:725.

46 *carrying her out of the doomed building* Andreas, 2:727.

46 *"mammoth sea lions," "monster camels," and "educated dogs," performed* *CTrib*, August 6, 1871.

47 *did good service . . . and many a stranger took courage from it* Cassius Milton Wicker, fire narrative, October 15, 1871, CHMCF, in *GCFWOM*, https://www.greatchicagofire.org/anthology-of-fire-narratives/cassius-milton-wicker/.

48 *to see what aid I could give other sufferers* John G. Shortall, fire narrative, CHMCF; Joseph Kirkland, *The Story of Chicago* (Chicago: Dibble, 1892), 310–15; *CTrib*, July 24, 1908. Shortall appears to have embellished the story over the years. The first account he gave, in an interview by the *Chicago Tribune* on October 23, 1871, lacks many of the most colorful details in the 1891 version in Kirkland's book, including the story of the escaped prisoners. Later in his life Shortall became a leader of the Illinois Humane Society.

49 *He had become wealthy in law, real estate, and banking* On Scammon, see *Biographical Sketches of the Leading Men of Chicago* (Chicago: Wilson and St. Clair, 1868), 25; and *CTrib*, March 18, 1890.

50 *with a feeling of perfect security* *New-York Tribune*, October 14, 1871; Jason Emerson, *Giant in the Shadows: The Life of Robert T. Lincoln* (Carbondale: Southern Illinois University Press, 2012), 153–56. There were stories that Robert's mother, Mary Todd Lincoln, fled the house and joined other fire refugees, but they appear to be unsubstantiated.

50 *I could but cry* Jonas Hutchinson to his mother, October 9, 1871, CHMCF; Angle, 18.

50 *hurrying, pushing, scrambling, crowding, jostling, shouting, and laughing even* William Gallagher to his sister Isabel [Gallagher?], October 17, 1871, CHMCF, in *GCFWOM*, https://www.greatchicagofire.org/anthology-of-fire-narratives/william-gallagher/.

51 *the man bore a large feather bed on his back* Arthur M. Kinzie, fire narrative, 1880, CHMCF; Andreas, 2:46; McIlvaine, 114.

51 *while under the other arm she carried a piece of silk* Andreas, 2:736; McIlvaine, 31.

51 *from the evils of the credit system* Andreas, 2:734.

51 *boarded a train to Milwaukee and deposited the money in a bank there* Andreas, 2:757.

51 *For God's sake, come on," the cowed driver replied, lifting the trunk back on the wagon* Bessie Bradwell Helmer, fire narrative, 1926, CHMCF, in *GCFWOM*,

https://www.greatchicagofire.org/anthology-of-fire-narratives/bessie-bradwell/; *CTrib*, June 3, 1900; *CTrib*, November 29, 1907. For another version of the Bradwell incident, see Bales, 33–34.

52   *He was struck in the arm by a bird cage thrown from an upstairs window*   Andreas, 2:736; McIlvaine, 26–27.

52   *Rockwell repeatedly soaked his face and hands with wet cloths to protect them from the heat*   *CTrib*, October 18, 1871.

52   *The policeman decided to go on*   Helmer, fire narrative.

53   *stuffed with all sorts of cooking utensils and useful articles*   William Gallagher to Isabel [Gallagher?], October 17, 1871.

53   *Get up, get up, get up; hurry up, hurry up; it's eight o'clock*   Andreas, 2:735.

53   *Masonry will certainly be an aid at a time like this*   Helmer, fire narrative; "Myra Colby Bradwell," in *Notable American Women, 1607–1950*, ed. Edward T. James, Janet Wilson James, and Paul Samuel Boyer (Cambridge, MA: Harvard University Press, 1971), 1:268. In 1890 Myra Bradwell finally became the first woman admitted to the Illinois bar. Two years later she was the first woman admitted to practice before the US Supreme Court, which in 1873 had upheld Illinois' earlier decision to prevent her from becoming an attorney. She passed away in 1894, two days after her sixty-third birthday. Her daughter Bessie Bradwell Helmer graduated first in her class from Union College of Law (later Northwestern University Law School) in 1882 and published the *Chicago Legal News* until her death in 1925; "Helmer, Bessie Bradwell (1858–1927)," Encyclopedia.com, https://www.encyclopedia.com/women/dictionaries -thesauruses-pictures-and-press-releases/helmer-bessie-bradwell-1858-1927. When Robert T. Lincoln briefly had his mother institutionalized a few years after the fire, both James and Myra Bradwell helped win Mary Todd Lincoln's release; Emerson, *Giant in the Shadows*, 171–76.

54   *swept up the fancy shoes in a last hurried gathering of goods*   Mrs. Charles C. Counselman [Jennie E. Otis], "Reminiscence of the Chicago Fire and Some of My Girlhood Days," in *GCFWOM*, https://www.greatchicagofire.org/anthology-of-fire-narratives /jennie-e-otis/.

54   *a snow-storm lit by colored fire*   Andreas, 2:735; McIlvaine, 24.

55   *then suddenly flash up, and be gone*   Arthur M. Kinzie, fire narrative, 1880, CHMCF; Andreas, 2:746; McIlvaine, 116.

55   *whole squares vanishing as though they were gossamer*   William H. Carter to his brother, October 15, 1871, CHMCF.

55   *was a marble mantle clock*   Fanny Boggs Lester, fire narrative, October 29, 1946, CHMCF, in *GCFWOM*, https://www.greatchicagofire.org/anthology-of-fire-narratives /fanny-boggs-lester/.

55   *the hurrying fugitives gave each other notice of their approach in the pitch darkness*   George Payson, fire narrative, September 28, 1880, CHMCF; Andreas, 2:746.

56   *a grand fantastic frame-work of flames*   Andreas, 2:730.

56   *her father had to extricate her*   Mrs. A. E. [Ashleman] Sanderson, "Reminiscences," December 14, 1925, CHMCF.

56   *either wild with excitement or crazy drunk*   John R. Chapin, "Chicago in Ashes," *Harper's Weekly* 15, no. 774 (October 28, 1871): 1004, 1011.

57   *with grim enjoyment of the ominous spectacle*   Andreas, 2:728–29; McIlvaine, 8–10. Later in his career, Chamberlin became a noted Boston journalist and friend of Helen Keller. See Betsy Emerson, "Joseph E. Chamberlin: Journalist and Early Advocate of Helen Keller," American Foundation for the Blind, June 17, 2018, https://www.afb .org/blog/entry/joseph-e-chamberlin-journalist-and-early-advocate-helen-keller.

57   *The downtown to the east of the bridge was an "infernal gorge of horses, wagons, men, women, children, trunks, and plunder," Horace White wrote*   Andreas, 2:734.

57   *It was every person for himself and the fire-fiend take the hindermost," Cassius Milton Wicker recalled*   Cassius Milton Wicker, fire narrative, October 15, 1871, CHMCF, in *GCFWOM*, https://www.greatchicagofire.org/anthology-of-fire-narratives/cassius -milton-wicker/.

58   *It was nothing but excitement*   Bales, 244.

59   *unharmed but very much the worse for wear*   Andreas, 2:725.

5. "I Gave Up All Hopes of Being Able to Save Much of Anything"

63   *to sweep away cinders and keep the crib wetted down*   Bales, 253–54.

63   *we could not lift enough to quench a cooking-stove*   Horace White, "The Great Chicago Fire," letter to Murat Halstead, 1871, https://www.bartleby.com/400/prose/1863 .html. This is the full version of the letter, which appears in edited form in McIlvaine.

63   *I gave up all hopes of being able to save much of anything*   Bales, 277; *CTrib*, November 15, 1871.

64   *He especially regretted having to leave an expensive new stove behind*   Bales, 277.

64   *the businesses along the north bank of the Main Branch and Division Street*   Pine Street remained a narrow and relatively quiet roadway until the completion of the Michigan Avenue Bridge in 1920. This connected it to the avenue, and its name was changed accordingly. Much widened, it soon became the major commercial boulevard familiar to residents and visitors today.

66   *In the garden was a fountain in a pool stocked with trout*   *CTrib*, April 21, 1886; Ada (Rumsey) Campbell, fire narrative, 1924, CHMFC, in *GCFWOM*, https://www .greatchicagofire.org/anthology-of-fire-narratives/ada-rumsey/.

67   *the burning cinders falling about us*   Campbell fire narrative, 1924.

67   *the crowded procession trudging north on Clark Street*   Philena (Maxwell) R. Peabody Lloyd, fire narrative, 1924, CHMCF, in *GCFWOM*, https://www .greatchicagofire.org/souvenirs-libraries/saving-family-bible/.

67   *his library and irreplaceable collection of Lincoln memorabilia*   Andreas, 2:748.

68   *He barely closed the door to the overfilled basement by canting a trunk against it*   For Corkran's version of what happened, see Paul M. Angle, *The Chicago Historical Society, 1856–1956: An Unconventional Chronicle* (New York: Rand McNally, 1956), 63–69. For Stone's version, see Angle, *The Great Chicago Fire*, 71–79.

68   *He saved her, and permitted all his goods to burn," the Staats-Zeitung reported approvingly*   ISZ, October 14, 1871.

68   *They had been buried with everything else*   Andreas, 2:749.

69   *near the North Avenue Bridge*   Mary Kehoe to Gladys K. Peters, January 21, 1942, CHMCF, in *GCFWOM*, https://www.greatchicagofire.org/anthology-of-fire-narratives /mary-kehoe/.

69   *set the mattress—and the money—on fire*   *CTrib*, October 12, 1871.

69   *The Sands' unsavory reputation persisted*   Pierce, 2:433–34; John J. Flinn, *History of the Chicago Police from the Settlement of the Community to the Present Time* (Chicago: Chicago Police Book Fund, 1887), 82–83.

70   *they could only recover one of the trunks*   Justin Butterfield to Chum [Philip Prescott], October 1871, CHMCF; "Saving the Goat," in "A Visual Record," in *GCFWOM*, https://www.greatchicagofire.org/eyewitnesses/visual-record.

72   *to avoid the waves of heat*   Lambert Tree, fire narrative, CHMFC; Andreas, 2:743–45; McIlvaine, 94–104.

72   *the largest public space in the North Division*   North Avenue now ends farther east to Lake Shore Drive, which is built on landfill.

72   *carrying the "noxious compounds" of decaying bodies into the public water supply*   John H. Rauch, *Intramural Interments in Populous Cities, and Their Influence upon Health and Epidemics* (Chicago: Tribune Company, 1866), 54. Lincoln Park eventually expanded northward, mainly on filled land, until by the middle of the twentieth century it reached its current northern border at Hollywood Avenue, about five miles above North Avenue.

72   *what became the Gold Coast neighborhood*   For a lively, detailed, and resourceful study of the city cemetery, see Pamela Bannos, *Hidden Truths: The Chicago City Cemetery & Lincoln Park* (n.p.: Northwestern University, 2019), http://hiddentruths.northwestern.edu/home.html.

73   *the graves of the impoverished and forgotten*   For this and related images, see "The Refugees," in *GCFWOM*, https://www.greatchicagofire.org/great-conflagration/refugees/.

74   *to drop in their tracks and wait for they knew not what*   A. S. Chapman, "Boy's Recollections of the Chicago Fire," 1910, in the collections of the Chicago History Museum.

74   *no houses to burn*   Patrick Webb, fire narrative, in Andreas, 2:749.

75   *the newcomers were a woman and her little boy*   Julia Wyszynski Lemos, fire narrative, CHMFC, in *GCFWOM*, http://greatchicagofire.org/anthology-of-fire-narratives/julia-lemos; Julia Lemos, *Memories of the Chicago Fire* (oil painting), in "A Visual Record," in *GCFWOM*, https://www.greatchicagofire.org/eyewitnesses/visual-record/.

75   *the number that died that night from hunger, exhaustion and the cold*   William Gallagher to his sister Isabel [Gallagher?], October 17, 1871, CHMFC, in *GCFWOM*, https://www.greatchicagofire.org/anthology-of-fire-narratives/william-gallagher/.

76   *there had been five hundred deliveries on the prairie on Monday*   Amelia [?] to sister Nan, October 1871, CHMFC.

76   *died in the midst of a mixed crowd of men, women, and children*   Andreas, 2:744; McIlvaine, 102–3.

76   *The poor helped the rich, and the rich helped the poor (if anybody could be called rich at such a time), to get on with their loads*   McIlvaine, 69.

76   *Life was the only question then*   Emma Lander Hambleton to Mrs. W. H. Lander, October 11, 1871, CHMFC.

76   *James W. Milner wrote to a friend four days after the fire*   James W. Milner to Bannister, October 14, 1871, CHMFC, in *GCFWOM*, https://www.greatchicagofire.org/anthology-of-fire-narratives/james-w-milner/.

76   *the same grim hoping against hope*   Andreas, 2:756.

77   *The brutality and horror of the scene made it sickening*   Andreas, 2:736.

77   *presenting pictures of squalid misery most pitiable," the* Chicago Times *observed*   CTimes, October 18, 1871.

77   *every now and then a woman, wild with grief, would run in and out among the alleys, and cry aloud her grief," presumably over a missing child*   CTrib, October 11, 1871.

77   *and is required to lament less*   Colbert and Chamberlin, 223–24.

78   *By Tuesday evening, October 10, the family was reunited*   Isaac N. Arnold, fire narrative, Isaac N. Arnold Papers, Chicago History Museum; Andreas, 2:748–49. Less than two years later, Arthur Arnold would drown in a boating accident in view of his father, who tried to save him but failed. See *In Memoriam: Isaac Newton Arnold, Nov. 30, 1813–Apr. 24, 1884. Arthur Mason Arnold, May 13, 1858–Apr. 26, 1873* (Chicago: Fergus Printing Company, 1885).

79   *who housed them and treated their injuries*   McIlvaine, 96–110.

79   *Two brought wagons to help carry things away*   Thomas Hoyne, fire narrative, 1871, CHMFC; Andreas, 2:738.

79   *the townspeople helped to make articles to replenish our wardrobe*   Ada (Rumsey) Campbell, fire narrative, 1924, CHMFC, in *GCFWOM*, https://www.greatchicagofire.org/anthology-of-fire-narratives/ada-rumsey/.

80   *the means of escape from the devouring element*   Colbert and Chamberlin, 253.

80   *they had only fourteen inmates in tow*   CTrib, October 20, 1871.

6. Endgame

81   *Chicago was handling more mail than any other US city besides New York*   Andreas, 2:389–90.

81   *"bounded through the hall" to the customs offices*   Francis William Test to his mother, October 13, 1871, CHMFC, in *GCFWOM*, https://www.greatchicagofire.org/anthology-of-fire-narratives/francis-william-test/.

82   *It reminded Medill of descriptions of the Battle of Waterloo*   Colonel Robert R. McCormick, "Joseph Medill's Story of the Great Chicago Fire," address broadcast over WGN and the Mutual Broadcasting System, October 3, 1953, 2–7. As noted earlier, a copy of this transcript is in the collections of the Chicago History Museum. On the fate of the *Chicago Tribune* and other papers, see Colbert and Chamberlin, chap. 21, "The Newspapers and the Fire," 374–87.

82   *and uncanny ability to "outflank" them*   Chicago Evening Post, October 17, 1871.

83   *It was all "too vast, too swift, too full of smoke, too full of danger" to take in, let alone process*   McIlvaine, 60.

83   *recalled Joseph Edgar Chamberlin*   McIlvaine, 8.

83   *thought the day of judgment had come*   Aurelia R. King to "My Dear Friends All," October 21, 1871, CHMCF.

83   *he asked her if this was "the Last Day"*   Julia Lemos, fire narrative, CHMFC, in *GCFWOM*, https://www.greatchicagofire.org/anthology-of-fire-narratives/julia-lemos/.

83   *My God, when will it end*   Jonas Hutchinson to his mother, October 9, 1871, in Angle, 17.

83   *implying that the devil himself was behind it*   Angle, 38.

83   *bounding from one to another*   McIlvaine, 8, 62.

83   *All sit here and write whatever comes into your heads!"*   John McGovern, *Daniel Trentworthy: A Tale of the Great Fire of Chicago* (Chicago: Rand, McNally, 1889), 191.

84   *drawn into the maw of the fiery hell*   *Chicago Evening Post*, October 18, 1871. For a discussion of language in the accounts of the fire, see Carl Smith, *Urban Disorder and the Shape of Belief: The Great Chicago Fire, the Haymarket Bomb, and the Model Town of Pullman*, 2nd ed., 22–29.

84   *Medill now thought it resembled a volcano*   McCormick, "Joseph Medill's Story," 7.

86   *shooting him through the heart in a Randolph Street saloon in September 1866*   Perry Duis, *Challenging Chicago: Coping with Everyday Life, 1837–1920* (Urbana: University of Illinois Press, 1998), 206; *CTrib*, October 19, 1871; Richard C. Lindberg, *The Gambler King of Clark Street: Michael C. McDonald and the Rise of Chicago's Democratic Machine* (Carbondale: Southern Illinois University Press, 2009), 16–17. While Mollie Trussell took George's name, they evidently never married. She briefly served time for the murder before being pardoned.

86   *an orchestral performance conducted by German maestro Theodore Thomas, for Monday evening, October 9*   "The Opera House," in James W. Sheahan, *Chicago Illustrated* (Chicago: Church, Goodman, and Donnelley, 1866–67), n.p. This was originally published, with visually arresting color illustrations, by the firm of Jevne and Almini, which also painted the frescoes on the wall of Crosby's Opera House. See also "Crosby's Opera House," in *GCFWOM*, https://www.greatchicagofire.org/landmarks/crosbys-opera-house/.

87   *One fiddled away while his Rome was burning, and the other roamed away while his fiddles were burning*   William Gallagher to his sister Isabel [Gallagher?], October 17, 1871, CHMFC, in *GCFWOM*, https://www.greatchicagofire.org/anthology-of-fire-narratives/william-gallagher/.

87   *streetcar tracks at the corner of State and Randolph*   Dominic A. Pacyga, *Chicago: A Biography* (Chicago: University of Chicago Press, 2009), 73.

88   *you might as well have them as to let them burn*   *Biographical Sketches of the Leading Men of Chicago* (Chicago: Wilson and St. Clair, 1868), 35–46; Andreas, 2:733; McIlvaine, 78, 84.

89   *a trip Bross made after the Civil War*   Aurelia R. King to "My Dear Friends All," October 21, 1871; Angle, 41.

89   *one of the most splendid blocks in Chicago*   Andreas, 2:733; McIlvaine, 85.

89   *the White Stockings easily defeated an amateur squad in spite of having only eight players, two of whom covered the entire outfield*   Pierce, 2:470n143; *CTrib*, October 8, 1871; "Chicago White Stockings," Baseball Reference, n.d., https://www.baseball-reference.com/teams/CNA/index.shtml.

89   *enabling Horace White and his family to pass through*   Andreas, 2:735.

89   *strong enough to blow a chair left alone clear across the park*   Cassius Milton Wicker to "Home," October 15, 1871, CHMFC, in *GCFWOM*, https://www.greatchicagofire.org/anthology-of-fire-narratives/cassius-milton-wicker/.

90   *to keep from burning up*   Bessie Bradwell Helmer, fire narrative, 1926, CHMFC, in *GCFWOM*, https://www.greatchicagofire.org/anthology-of-fire-narratives/bessie-bradwell/.

90   *lay the lowly and the proud*   Cassius Milton Wicker to "Home," October 15, 1871.

90   *the South Division fires finally ended late Monday afternoon*   Bales, 260. Hildreth was, for obvious reasons, the person who made the greatest claims for the effectiveness of the gunpowder. Musham (134) is the most skeptical: "Attempts to demolish buildings had no effect whatsoever as it took at least an hour of preparation before the powder could be touched off and the buildings burned before this could be done." Musham comments further, "Nor did tearing down the smaller ones have any effect, as very little could be done before the fire was upon them and because the wrecked material remained on the ground and burned."

92   *Jeffersonville, Indiana, and Omaha, Nebraska, for tents and troops*   Philip H. Sheridan, *Report to the Honorable W. W. Belknap, Chicago, December 20, 1871* ([Chicago], n.p., 1871), 1–3; "General Sheridan in Command," in *GCFWOM*, https://www.greatchicagofire.org/rescue-and-relief/general-sheridan-command/; "Military Rule in Chicago," in *GCFWOM*, https://www.greatchicagofire.org/rescue-and-relief-library/military-rule-chicago/.

92   *had already stopped the fire*   Bales, 34–37, 259.

92   *its owner that it would not. Drake won the bet*   Andreas, 2:508–9; Frank A. Randall, *History of the Development of Building Construction in Chicago* (Urbana: University of Illinois Press, 1949), 53.

7. "Pray for Me"

93   *Close to eighteen thousand buildings were gone*   City of Chicago, *Eleventh Annual Report of the Board of Public Works to the Common Council of the City of Chicago, for the Municipal Fiscal Year ending March 31st, 1872* ([Chicago]: D. and C. H. Blakely, 1872), 41, 4, 7. As with other details, different sources offer varying figures on the losses. Some sources calculate the extent of the Burnt District as much as one-third higher than did the Board of Public Works. For summaries, see Andreas, 2:760–61; Colbert and Chamberlin, 285–303; Chicago Relief and Aid Society, *Report of the Chicago Relief and Aid Society of Disbursement of Contributions for the Sufferers by the Fire* (Chicago: Riverside, 1874), 9–13. Attempting to translate 1871 figures into current costs reveals the complexity of finding some simple equivalent. According to the website Measuring Worth, the comparative price of $200 million in valuation loss measured by the change in the Consumer Price Index would be (such calculations are necessarily imprecise) about $4,240,000,000. But in relation to the overall economy, it would be far greater—$537,000,000,000. This latter figure may seem too high, but an equivalent cost of between $4 billion and $5 billion is too low, since it does not take into account such things as lost wages and profits, the expense of relief efforts discussed in the following chapters, and the fact that destroyed buildings were generally replaced with bigger and more costly ones. For calculators and explanations of these and other measures of worth, see "Seven Ways to Compute the Relative Value of a U.S. Dollar Amount—1790 to Present" (web calculator), Measuring Worth, https://www.measuringworth.com/calculators/uscompare/index.php.

93   *Pray for me*   Charles Shanabruch, *Chicago's Catholics: The Evolution of an American Identity* (Notre Dame, IN: University of Notre Dame Press, 1981), 17.

94   *Mollie Trussell's silver-plated pistol*   CTrib, October 19, 1871.

94   *emitting a terrible stench*   CTrib, October 12, 1871.

95   *Dearborn Street between Ohio and Ontario Streets*   McIlvaine, 107; Andreas, 2:745.

95   *retrieved from the river below the bridge*   Mary Kehoe to Gladys K. Peters, October 21, 1942, CHMCF, in *GCFWOM*, https://www.greatchicagofire.org/anthology-of -fire-narratives/mary-kehoe/.

95   *bodies that were never accounted for*   The number of fatalities is another of the many details that differ depending on the source, but virtually all estimates fall in this range. There does not seem to be a reliable listing of nonfatal injuries.

95   *to this day the worst loss of life to fire in American history*   Richard N. Current, *The History of Wisconsin*, vol. 2, *The Civil War Era, 1848–1873* (Madison: State Historical Society of Wisconsin, 1976), 475–76; "Peshtigo Fire," Wisconsin Historical Society, https://www.wisconsinhistory.org/Records/Article/CS1750.

95   *In many the extent of their calamity completely obliterated ambition, affection, sensibility*   CRepub, October 12, 1871.

96   *No other spot will seem like it to me*   William H. Carter to his brother, October 15, 1871, CHMFC, in *GCFWOM*, https://www.greatchicagofire.org/conflagration-library /william-h-carter-tells-his-brother-sad-news/.

96   *In short, the day seemed a* dies non*—a day burnt out of the history of the city*   Colbert and Chamberlin, 278.

96   *his burial in Springfield, Illinois*   Lincoln's body lay in a half-open casket atop a catafalque in the center of the Courthouse rotunda, as well over a hundred thousand mourners streamed around it. They waited for hours, sometimes five or six abreast, in a line twenty blocks long. It had rained steadily the week before, so the catafalque negotiated the muddy streets between the lakefront, where the train had stopped, and the Courthouse only with great difficulty. *CTrib*, May 1, 1865; *CTrib*, May 2, 1865.

96   *Francis William Test told his mother*   Francis William Test to his mother, October 13, 1871, CHMCF, in *GCFWOM*, www.greatchicagofire.org/anthology-of-fire-narratives /francis-william-test/.

96   *lost among the streets that contain not a house for miles," Cassius Milton Wicker remarked*   Cassius Milton Wicker to "Home," October 15, 1871, CHMFC, in *GCF-WOM*, https://www.greatchicagofire.org/anthology-of-fire-narratives/cassius-milton -wicker/.

96   *the preserves were "burnt to a crisp."*   George M. Higginson, fire narrative, June 1879, CHMCF; Andreas, 2:754.

96   *like an apparition, when he thought it far away," Colbert and Chamberlin wrote*   Colbert and Chamberlin, 390.

97   *what struck A. S. Chapman as "great bows."*   A. S. Chapman, "A Boy's Recollections of the Chicago Fire," 1910, CHMFC.

97   *they soaked the house directly*   Andreas, 2:759.

97   *than a tribute to either stout construction or staunch defense*   Frank A. Randall, *History of the Development of Building Construction in Chicago* (Urbana: University of Illinois Press, 1949), 61. Musham, 139, states that a few other scattered buildings survived the fire. On Tuesday morning, October 10, a North Side resident named Stephen L. Robinson, who worked as a telegraph operator, took a long walk to sur-

vey the damage, which he marked on a Chicago street map that he carried with him. For the story of Robinson and his map, see "Mr. Robinson Assesses the Damage," in "The Burnt District," in *GCFWOM*, https://www.greatchicagofire.org/ruined-city /burnt-district/.

97   *If a man wants his mind impressed with what the end of the world will be, let him come here* James W. Milner to Bannister, October 14, 1871, CHMFC, in *GCFWOM*, https://www.greatchicagofire.org/anthology-of-fire-narratives/james-w-milner/.

99   *creatures who lurk among the ruined tombs and devour the belated wanderers there* James W. Sheahan and George P. Upton, *The Great Conflagration* (Chicago: Union, 1871), 255–57.

101   *find their counterpart in the fire-built ruins of last week's palaces* Rev. E. J. Good-speed, *The Great Fires in Chicago and the West* (Chicago: J. W. Goodspeed, 1871), 56–57. It is probable that Goodspeed had considerable editorial assistance in preparing his fire histories.

103   *against their deadlines, the* Tribune *observed* New-York Tribune, October 13, 1871; *New-York Tribune*, October 14, 1871.

104   *there was not enough space to lie down* Mary Kehoe to Gladys K. Peters, October 21, 1942, CHMCF, in *GCFWOM*, https://www.greatchicagofire.org/anthology-of-fire -narratives/mary-kehoe/.

105   *they have no stoves to keep them warm and are obliged to lie on the ground* Amelia [?] to sister Nan, November 5, 1871, CHMCF.

105   *who had not had any food in almost twenty-four hours* Andreas, 2:749.

105   *whose occupants washed themselves in its small pond* CRepub, October 12, 1871.

105   *she carted that great heavy* Legal News *subscription book for nine hours* Bessie Bradwell Helmer, fire narrative, October 7, 1926, CHMCF, in *GCFWOM*, https://www .greatchicagofire.org/anthology-of-fire-narratives/bessie-bradwell/.

105   *Payson remained dressed in the same clothes and barely slept the entire week following the fire* George Payson, fire narrative, September 28, 1880, CHMFC; Andreas, 2:746–48.

106   *baleful influence over lives that, up to then, were vigorous, healthful and sound* Andreas, 2:755–56.

106   *heart sick to go through the ruins* Francis William Test to his mother, October 13, 1871, CHMCF, in *GCFWOM*, www.greatchicagofire.org/anthology-of-fire-narratives /francis-william-test/.

106   *were burned away* ISZ, October 14, 1871.

106   *forever running from fires* Aurelia R. King to "My Dear Friends All," October 21, 1871, CHMCF; Angle, 41.

106   *with no way to recover from this setback* Andreas, 2:748.

106   *he confessed to his mother* Jonas Hutchinson to his mother, October 9–10, 1871, CHMCF; Angle, 18.

107   *towns of Aurora, Bloomington, Freeport, Quincy, and Springfield* City of Chicago, *Report of the Board of Police, in the Fire Department, to the Common Council of the City of Chicago, for the Year Ending March 31, 1872* (Chicago: Hazlitt and Reed, 1872), 15; Pierce, 3:7.

107   *HELP, HELP, HELP* "Emergency Measures," in *GCFWOM*, https://www.great chicagofire.org/rescue-and-relief/emergency-measures/; "Organizing the Relief," in *GCFWOM*, https://www.greatchicagofire.org/rescue-and-relief-library/organizing -relief/.

107   *for the relief of your suffering people* Chicago Relief and Aid Society, *Report of the Chicago Relief and Aid Society*, 26; Andreas, 2:767. The *Report* contains a compendium of such messages.

107   *some had little room for anything else* Andreas, 2:765–66.

108   *stayed to help distribute them* Andreas, 2:768.

109   *The Peekskill, New York, Mutual Stove Works shipped twenty-five stoves* The fullest summary of contributions and disbursements, from which these examples are drawn, is in Chicago Relief and Aid Society, *Report of the Chicago Relief and Aid Society*, 295–440.

109   *from a designated regular or special performance* CTrib, October 22, 1871.

109   *for the benefit of her new home* CTrib, October 12, 1871.

109   *a money-raising exhibition* CTimes, October 19, 1871.

110   *but this is all I could raise from my schoolmates at this time* Chicago Relief and Aid Society, *Report of the Chicago Relief and Aid Society*, 68.

110   *people tossed on additional bundles of food and goods* "The Relief and Aid Society Takes Over," in *GCFWOM*, https://www.greatchicagofire.org/rescue-and-relief/relief -and-aid-society-takes-over/.

110   *FOR THE BENEFIT SUFFERERS CHICAGO* Harper's Weekly 15, no. 775 (November 4, 1871): 1035.

111   *and the wonder of the world* Colbert and Chamberlin, 9.

112   *"Chicago Outdone by Wisconsin Terrors," read a headline* Chicago Evening Mail, October 11, 1871.

112   *to "reconstruct that fortress" and resupply the garrison* Edward Everett Hale, quoted in Sheahan and Upton, *The Great Conflagration*, 295.

113   *his four reporters' running account of Chicago under siege* Richard A. Schwarzlose, *The Nation's Newsbrokers*, vol. 2, *The Rush to Institution, from 1865 to 1920* (Evanston, IL: Northwestern University Press, 1990), 70–71.

113   *Other leading Chicago papers owned four-cylinder models* Colbert and Chamberlin, 383–84; CTrib, October 12, 1871.

114   *and the Western News Company in Chicago* Harper's Weekly 15, no. 775 (November 4, 1871): 1027.

115   *hungry for information* New York Herald, October 10, 1871.

115   *from measured and carefully detailed to wild and woolly* See "Stage, Story, and Song," in *GCFWOM*, https://www.greatchicagofire.org/fanning-flames/stage-story-and -song/; and "Fanning the Flames Library," in *GCFWOM*, https://www.greatchicagofire .org/fanning-flames/fanning-flames-library/.

116   *In tears of pity died the flame!* For the full text of the poem, see John Greenleaf Whittier, "Chicago," 1871, Bartleby.com, https://www.bartleby.com/270/13/550.html. The *Chicago Tribune* published the poem on its front page of November 19, 1871. It also appeared in multiple other newspapers, magazines, and contemporary histories of the fire.

116   *an event already in the public mind*   For the Harte poem, see " 'Chicago,' by Bret Harte," in *GCFWOM*, https://www.greatchicagofire.org/fanning-flames-library /chicago-bret-harte/.

Whittier and Harte's poems, while undistinguished, were the best of the mostly terrible poetry the fire inspired. Popular poet Julia Moore, the syntax-challenged "Sweet Singer of Michigan," devoted eight excruciating stanzas to Chicago's deadly trial. Across the ocean in Dublin, a street poet named Jeremiah Cronan published in very irregular typesetting, meter, and rhyme a broadside titled *Lines Written on the Most Dreadful Fire That Broke Out in Chicago in America*. Given its origin, its sympathy with the suffering of Chicago's Irish and those they left behind is not surprising, but that makes it exceptional among the popular literature of the fire. See Julia A. Moore, "The Great Chicago Fire," in *The Sweet Singer of Michigan: Poems by Mrs. Julia A. Moore*, ed. Walter Blair (Chicago: Pascal Covici, 1928), 148–49; Jeremiah Cronan, *Lines Written on the Most Dreadful Fire That Broke Out in Chicago in America* (Dublin: P. Brereton [1871]), in *GCFWOM*, https://www.greatchicagofire.org/fanning -flames-library/"lines-written-most-dreadful-fire-broke-out-chicago-america" -jeremiah-cronan/.

116   *One-fifth of the proceeds were to go to the sufferers*   *CRepub*, November 5, 1871.

117   *that is, "with fire."*   George F. Root, "Passing Through the Fire" (Chicago: Root & Cady, 1871), Lester S. Levy Sheet Music Collection, Johns Hopkins University, https://levysheetmusic.mse.jhu.edu/collection/179/101; see also " 'Passing Through the Fire,' by George F. Root," *GCFWOM*, https://www.greatchicagofire.org/fanning-flames -library/"passing-through-fire"-george-f-root/. At the *GCFWOM* website, one can hear the song performed by Patrice Michaels, soprano. The Levy Sheet Music Collection is one of several that are online. A Library of Congress collection holds multiple other songs on the fire; see Library of Congress, "Music for the Nation: American Sheet Music, ca. 1870–1885," https://www.loc.gov/collections/american-sheet-music -1870-to-1885/.

117   *the Field, Leiter & Company store*   See the stereograph viewer and stereographs at "Arresting Images," in *GCFWOM*, https://www.greatchicagofire.org/media-event /arresting-images/. The stereographs here are viewable in 3-D with anaglyph lenses. On the popularity of stereograph fire images, see Robert M. Hazen and Margaret Hindle Hazen, *Keepers of the Flame: The Role of Fire in American Culture, 1775–1925* (Princeton, NJ: Princeton University Press, 1992), 227–28.

117   *The fire also inspired much fiction*   See "Stage, Story, and Song," in *GCFWOM*, https://www.greatchicagofire.org/fanning-flames/stage-story-and-song/.

119   Success with Small Fruits   E. P. Roe, "My First Novel," *The Cosmopolitan* 5, no. 3 (July 1887): 327; Edward P. Roe, "A Native Author Called Roe," *Lippincott's Monthly Magazine* 42 (October 1888): 479–97; Glenn O. Carey, *Edward Payson Roe* (Boston: Twayne, 1984); John W. Tebbel, *A History of Book Publishing in the United States*, vol. 2, *The Expansion of an Industry 1865–1919* (New York: R. R. Bowker, 1975), 170–71; James D. Hart, *The Popular Book: A History of America's Literary Taste* (New York: Oxford University Press, 1950), 121, 169; Frank Luther Mott, *Golden Multitudes: The Story of Best Sellers in the United States* (New York: Macmillan, 1947), 147–48, 309.

120   *Well, now I can almost say, Praise God for the fire*   Rev. Edward P. Roe, *Barriers Burned Away* (New York: Dodd, Mead, 1873), 285, 401, 408, 446; for an excerpted chapter, see Rev. Edward P. Roe, "Barriers Burned Away," in *GCFWOM*, https://www .greatchicagofire.org/fanning-flames-library/barriers-burned-away/.

120   *a riveting moment of national unity and reaffirmation*   See especially John J. Pauly's insightful essay "The Great Chicago Fire as a National Event," *American Quarterly* 36 (1984): 668–83. On the importance of the fire in establishing the visibility of Chicago, see Lisa Krissoff Boehm, *Popular Culture and the Enduring Myth of Chicago, 1871–1968* (New York: Routledge, 2004), esp. chap. 1, " 'Do You Wonder Chicago Burned?': The Great Chicago Fire and the Launching of Chicago's National Reputation," 25–44.

8. *"Chicago Shall Rise Again"*

122   *the two young Norwegian women who kept house for them*   *Album of Genealogy and Biography, Cook County, Illinois: With Portraits* (Chicago: Calumet Book and Engraving, 1897), 419–21; Andreas, 2:772–73. Information on Holden's income, family, and servants is from the 1870 census.

124   *some half dozen of the city's forty aldermen were also present*   For Holden's account, on which this summary is based, see Andreas, 2:761–72. In some places Moore's first name is spelled Orrin.

124   *the preservation of order and relief of suffering*   For the text of this and other proclamations and orders, see "Official Actions," in *GCFWOM*, https://www.greatchicagofire.org/rescue-and-relief-library/official-actions/; and Chicago Relief and Aid Society, *Report of the Chicago Relief and Aid Society of Disbursement of Contributions for the Sufferers by the Fire* (Chicago: Riverside, 1874), 14–19.

127   *set in glass containers so she could surround the candles with water*   Fanny Boggs Lester to Joseph Cudahy, October 29, 1946, CHMFC, in *GCFWOM*, https://www.greatchicagofire.org/anthology-of-fire-narratives/fanny-boggs-lester/.

127   *had to abide by regular prefire rates*   For these rates, see Richard Edwards, *Fourteenth Annual Directory of the Inhabitants, Institutions, Incorporated Companies and Manufacturing Establishments of the City of Chicago, Embracing a Complete Business Directory for 1871* (Chicago: Richard Edwards, 1871), 36.

128   *a desire to keep hoping*   CTrib, October 11, 1871; CTrib, October 12, 1871.

129   *with no unpleasant taste or effects*   McIlvaine, 72.

129   *gastric irritation*   CRepub, October 17, 1871; CTrib, October 19, 1871.

129   *fetching water from artesian wells*   Harper's Weekly 15, no. 775 (November 4, 1871): 1028.

129   *gas pipes, laths, and baseball bats*   CRepub, October 12, 1871.

129   *put them on duty watching over the vault*   Mrs. Charles C. Counselman [Jennie E. Otis], "Reminiscence of the Chicago Fire and Some of My Girlhood Days," presented before the Chicago Women's Club, March 28, 1920, typescript, CHMCF, in *GCFWOM*, https://www.greatchicagofire.org/anthology-of-fire-narratives/jennie-e-otis/.

129   *but Death shall be their fate*   A copy of the broadside is in the collections of the Chicago History Museum. See "Thieves and Burglars!," in "Emergency Measures," in *GCFWOM*, https://www.greatchicagofire.org/rescue-and-relief/emergency-measures/.

129   *he printed the words "Police" or "Special Police" with his hobby press*   For an image of one of these badges, worn by F. A. Winchell, see "Badge Used by Special Police," in *GCFWOM*, https://www.greatchicagofire.org/rescue-and-relief/emergency-measures/. The badge is in the collections of the Chicago History Museum.

130   *to put every incendiary to instant death*   McIlvaine, 71.

130   *the fire victims would also get clothing and food*   William Gallagher to his sister Isabel [Gallagher?], October 17, 1871, CHMFC, in *GCFWOM*, https://www.greatchicagofire.org/anthology-of-fire-narratives/william-gallagher/.

130   *the person could proceed to the next patrol*   Eben Matthews, fire narrative, CHMFC, in *GCFWOM*, https://www.greatchicagofire.org/anthology-of-fire-narratives/eben-matthews/.

130   *as it was on that fearful Monday and the few succeeding days*   Andreas, 2:764.

131   *one-third of Chicagoans outside the Burnt District hosted fire fugitives*   Andreas, 2:765.

131   *some thirty thousand people boarded outbound trains*   Andreas, 2:767. Andreas claims this many left on Monday and Tuesday, but it may have taken a few days longer. For images of railroad passes, see Andreas, 2:767; and "Railroad Pass for Eliza Talbot," in "Emergency Measures," in *GCFWOM*, https://www.greatchicagofire.org/rescue-and-relief/emergency-measures/.

131   *The trains were so crowded that some men and boys rode atop the cars*   Andreas, 2:765.

131   *but we came through it all right*   "Experience of Mrs. Mary [Maria Lindsten] Schweiding in the Great Chicago Fire," January 20, 1942, CHMFC.

131   *"We were too scared to go there," Kehoe admitted*   Mary Kehoe, fire narrative, 1942, CHMFC, in *GCFWOM*, https://www.greatchicagofire.org/anthology-of-fire-narratives/mary-kehoe/.

132   *Lemos said she could not remember his name*   Julia Lemos, fire narrative, CHMFC, in *GCFWOM*, https://www.greatchicagofire.org/anthology-of-fire-narratives/julia-lemos/.

133   *a boiler big enough to power the machine*   Colonel Robert R. McCormick, "Joseph Medill's Story of the Great Chicago Fire," address broadcast over WGN and the Mutual Broadcasting System, October 3, 1953, 8–10. As previously noted, a copy of the transcript is in the collections of the Chicago History Museum.

133   *four other dailies had ten thousand or more*   *Geo P. Rowell & Co's American Newspaper Directory* (New York: Geo. P. Rowell, 1871), 27–30.

134   *in no sense to be human beings*   Justin E. Walsh, *To Print the News and Raise Hell! A Biography of Wilbur F. Storey* (Chapel Hill: University of North Carolina Press, 1968); Franc B. Wilkie, *Personal Reminiscences of Thirty-Five Years of Journalism* (Chicago: F. J. Schulte, 1891), 112, 114, 130–31, 193–96.

134   *several other leading dailies*   *ISZ*, October 12, 1871; *ISZ*, October 13, 1871; *ISZ*, October 14, 1871.

134   *and hope the supply did not run out*   Colbert and Chamberlin, 384.

135   *HENRY W. DARLING (formerly of Montreal), Hamilton, Ontario*   *CTrib*, October 12, 1871; *CTrib*, October 17, 1871. Colbert and Chamberlin, 384, state there was no charge for listings of missing persons.

137   *Chicago's "manifest destiny"*   *New-York Tribune*, October 14, 1871; *New-York Tribune*, October 17, 1871; William Bross, "The Great Chicago Fire," in *History of Chicago* (Chicago: Jansen, McClurg, 1876), 95–98.

137   *at the corner of Kinzie and Clark Streets*   *CTrib*, October 14, 1871.

137   *they would meet all their obligations*   *CTrib*, October 13, 1871.

138   *had just lost its major printing facilities*   *CTrib*, October 11, 1871.

138   *the world's greatest recovery*   CTrib, October 11, 1871.

138   *a day so full of promise*   CRepub, October 12, 1871.

138   *as if naught save victory had ever perched on our banners*   CTimes, October 18, 1871.

138   *to invest a little money out here?"*   Joel Bigelow to S. and O. Bigelow, October 10, 1871, CHMCF, in *GCFWOM*, https://www.greatchicagofire.org/anthology-of-fire -narratives/joel-bigelow/.

9. Controversy and Control

139   *to surrender its responsibilities and resources to the Relief and Aid Society and then immediately disband*   For documents cited here and throughout the chapter relating to the appointment of Sheridan and the Chicago Relief and Society, see "Military Rule in Chicago," in *GCFWOM*, https://www.greatchicagofire.org/rescue-and-relief-library /military-rule-chicago/; "Organizing the Relief," in *GCFWOM*, https://www.great chicagofire.org/rescue-and-relief-library/organizing-relief/; Philip H. Sheridan, *Report to the Honorable W. W. Belknap, Chicago, December 20, 1871* ([Chicago: n.p., 1871]); and "Action of the City Authorities," in Chicago Relief and Aid Society, *Report of the Chicago Relief and Aid Society of Disbursement of Contributions for the Sufferers by the Fire* (Chicago: Riverside, 1874), 14–23. The best discussion of Chicago under military authority and during the administration of relief by the society is Sawislak. See also Carl Smith, *Urban Disorder and the Shape of Belief: The Great Chicago Fire, the Haymarket Bomb, and the Model Town of Pullman*, 2nd ed. (Chicago: University of Chicago Press, 2007), 64–87.

140   *until public confidence could again be restored*   Sheridan, *Report to the Honorable W. W. Belknap*, 2.

140   *They were commanded by Colonel Hubert Dilger and armed with a thousand muskets*   Message of Governor John M. Palmer, to the Adjourned Session of the Twenty-Seventh General Assembly, May 15, 1871, also (Annexed) the Report of Adjutant-General Dilger (Springfield: Illinois State Journal Printing Office, 1871). This pamphlet, which contains Dilger's report, lacks unified pagination, and the cover mistakenly reads "May" rather than "November."

140   *to do so with safety*   This is a reprint of the paper from the day before, with some supplementary material.

141   *consequent on the appalling catastrophe*   New-York Tribune, October 13, 1871.

141   *forced to endure the leering of the vile*   Andreas, 2:754–55; Smith, *Urban Disorder and the Shape of Belief*, 69–71.

141   *plundering & trying to set new fires*   Jonas Hutchinson to his mother, October 9 and 10, 1871, CHMFC; Angle, 22.

142   *murders and the like*   Eben Matthews, fire narrative, CHMCF, in *GCFWOM*, https:// www.greatchicagofire.org/anthology-of-fire-narratives/eben-matthews/.

142   *sleeps in the valley*   Chicago Evening Journal—Extra, October 10, 1871.

142   *The station houses are filled with prisoners*   St. Louis Dispatch, October 11, 1871.

142   *such as setting new fires and stealing*   Phillip C. Morgan to his parents, October 11, 1871, CHMFC.

142   *seven men who were trying to torch a church*   Cassius Milton Wicker to his family, October 15, 1871, CHMFC, in *GCFWOM*, https://www.greatchicagofire.org /anthology-of-fire-narratives/cassius-milton-wicker/.

142   *the moment he was spotted setting a fire*   CTrib, October 14, 1871.

144   *thus preventing an actual crime*   Bales, 246–47. When the man stepped into an alley to relieve himself, the mob apparently thought he was setting a fire.

144   *inclined to accept these statements with some degree of allowance*   Joel Bigelow to his brothers, October 10, 1871, CHMFC, in *GCFWOM*, https://www.greatchicagofire.org /anthology-of-fire-narratives/joel-bigelow/. The only known murder that took place during the fire was a gruesome double homicide Monday afternoon, October 9, in the West Side saloon of Gregory Peri, when Peri stabbed two men in a dispute over a broken window. The crime was an isolated incident that evidently had nothing to do with the fire. *CTrib*, December 19, 1871. Peri was hanged for the murders in 1873.

144   *the very heart of the Garden City of the West*   Chicago Evening Post, October 18, 1871.

144   *the reports of the proceedings of the late Paris Commune*   CTrib, June 9, 1871.

145   *With a scourge for the Queen of the West?*   "Paris and Chicago," quoted in James W. Sheahan and George P. Upton, *The Great Conflagration* (Chicago: Union, 1871), 367. For a brief discussion of the fire and the Paris Commune, see Smith, *Urban Disorder and the Shape of Belief*, 49–50, 301–2nn35–37.

145   *the great conflagration was several simultaneous fires, not just one*   CTimes, October 23, 1871. The *Illinois Staats-Zeitung* ridiculed the "confession," especially the notion that it came from an American worker who claimed to be enthusiastic about the Paris Commune, observing that if radicals marked any city for destruction, "a far more 'representative' place might have been found, than Chicago particularly, where the opposition between capital and labor has not by any length developed to the same acuteness as in London and Manchester, England." *ISZ*, October 24, 1871.

145   *in the midst of her calamity*   Every Saturday 4, no. 97 (November 4, 1871): 439–40.

147   *bring the city through its troubles*   Sheridan, *Report to the Honorable W. W. Belknap*, 7–8; "Military Rule in Chicago," in *GCFWOM*, https://www.greatchicagofire.org /rescue-and-relief-library/military-rule-chicago/.

147   *give him sole command or lose him entirely*   Report of the Select Committee on Governor J. M. Palmer's Messages of Nov. 15 and Dec. 9, 1871. Including, also, The Evidence Taken before the Committee, and Resolutions Recommended. Submitted to the House, January 6, 1872 (Springfield: Illinois State Journal Printing Office, 1872), 20.

148   *where the White Stockings had so recently played baseball and local residents had fled from the fire*   CTrib, October 12, 1871; Andreas, 2:775.

148   *smokes a cigar in the street after nightfall*   Francis William Test to his mother, October 13, 1871, CHMFC, in *GCFWOM*, https://www.greatchicagofire.org/anthology-of -fire-narratives/francis-william-test/.

148   *he made decisions requiring someone to back them up*   These orders are in the Chicago Fire Guards Collection, CHMFC; "The Mayor Shuts Two Saloons," in "Sheridan in Command," in *GCFWOM*, https://www.greatchicagofire.org/rescue-and-relief /general-sheridan-command/.

148   *needed written permission after dark*   Sawislak, 56–57.

148   *giving us the much needed security*   Matthews, fire narrative.

149   *citizens going about their business*   This and Waud's other drawings of Chicago during and right after the fire are in the collections of the Chicago History Museum; for a selection, see "The Waud Drawings," in *GCFWOM*, https://www.greatchicagofire .org/eyewitnesses/waud-drawings/.

149   *drove him from the city*   Francis William Test to his mother, October 13, 1871.

149   *the agitated public mood was settling down*   Philip H. Sheridan to Roswell Mason, October 12 and 17, 1871, in *GCFWOM*, https://www.greatchicagofire.org/rescue-and -relief-library/military-rule-chicago/; Sheridan, *Report to the Honorable W. W. Belknap*, 15–16; "Military Rule in Chicago."

149   *he informed his mother*   Francis William Test to his mother, October 13, 1871.

149   *makes every precaution advisable*   James W. Milner to Bannister, October 14, 1871, CHMFC, in *GCFWOM*, https://www.greatchicagofire.org/anthology-of-fire-narratives /james-w-milner/.

150   *but they were evidently intoxicated*   Both documents are in the Chicago Fire Guards Collection, CHMFC.

151   *flocked here like vultures from every point of the compass*   William Bross, "The Great Chicago Fire," in *History of Chicago* (Chicago: Jansen, McClurg, 1876), 94.

151   *there was to be no end to the world's charity*   Andreas, 2:768.

151   *of right, ought to be turned over to them*   Andreas, 2:769. Holden claimed after the fact that one reason he had decided to act while the city was burning on Monday was because the Chicago Relief and Aid Society had not stepped in right away. He recalled asking himself, "Where was the Chicago Relief and Aid Society?"; Andreas, 2:762.

152   *indicating that he was prematurely bald*   CTrib, May 19, 1890; Edward T. Blair, *A History of the Chicago Club* (Chicago: [Chicago Club], 1898), 16.

152   *screen applicants, often in their homes*   For two contrasting evaluations of the society, see Otto M. Nelson, "The Chicago Relief and Aid Society, 1850–1874," *Journal of the Illinois State Historical Society* 59, no. 1 (Spring 1966): 48–66; and Timothy J. Naylor, "Responding to the Fire: The Work of the Chicago Relief and Aid Society," *Science and Society* 39, no. 4 (Winter 1975–76): 450–64. For another assessment, see Emily C. Skarbek, "The Chicago Fire of 1871: A Bottom-Up Approach to Disaster Relief," *Public Choice*, 160, nos. 1–2 (July 2015): 155–80. On the context of the rise of "scientific" philanthropy, see Kathleen D. McCarthy, *Noblesse Oblige: Charity and Cultural Philanthropy in Chicago, 1849–1929* (Chicago: University of Chicago Press, 1982), 53–72. The Chicago History Museum holds the archives of the Chicago Relief and Aid Society in its United Charities of Chicago Collection.

153   *from slipping into "permanent pauperism*   Chicago Relief and Aid Society, *Report of the Chicago Relief and Aid Society*, 122.

154   *"possessed all the paraphernalia and facilities" now needed*   Andreas, 2:769.

155   *added to the directory of said Society*   Andreas, 2:769. An announcement published in the newspapers on Wednesday, October 12, stated that Relief and Aid Society directors were requested to meet the mayor and Common Council at ten o'clock that morning at the Relief Headquarters in the First Congregational Church. How this related to the meeting described by Holden, including whether it is the same one, is not clear.

156   *your best men*   Andreas, 2:769. For a study of the meaning of the term "best men" at the time, and to whom it applied, see John G. Sproat, *"The Best Men": Liberal Reformers in the Gilded Age* (New York: Oxford University Press, 1968).

156   *it had assisted about seventy thousand Chicagoans*   Chicago Relief and Aid Society, *Report of the Chicago Relief and Aid Society*, 119.

157   *accepted legal liability for its actions in this capacity*   CTrib, November 4, 1871.

157   *well known nationally for their integrity*   New York Times, October 14, 1871.

158   *Chicago women were turning them down in the expectation they could obtain aid even if they remained idle*   CTrib, October 16, 1871.

10. "More Strength and Greater Hope"

159   *also on the West Side, until early in 1872*   City of Chicago, *Proceedings of the Common Council of the City of Chicago, for the Municipal Year 1870–71* (Chicago: J. S. Thompson, [1872]), 326; Andreas, 3:143–45.

159   *leaking service pipes needed repair or replacement*   Andreas, 3:132; CTrib, October 19, 1871.

160   *It predicted revenge in future elections*   ISZ, October 31, 1871; ISZ, November 7, 1871.

160   *charging riders half fare*   CTrib, October 18, 1871.

160   *though many had been buried beneath bricks and stones*   Francis William Test to his mother, October 13, 1871, CHMCF, in GCFWOM, https://www.greatchicagofire .org/anthology-of-fire-narratives/francis-william-test/.

161   *my vault stood the fire*   John S. Goff, *Robert Todd Lincoln: A Man in His Own Right* (Norman: University of Oklahoma Press, 1969), 156.

161   *to a spot beyond the fire*   Cassius Milton Wicker to his family, October 15, 1871, CHMFC, in GCFWOM, https://www.greatchicagofire.org/anthology-of-fire-nar ratives/cassius-milton-wicker/.

161   *as rolls of bills crumble at its touch*   A. S. Chapman, "Boy's Recollections of the Chicago Fire," 1910, CHMFC, in GCFWOM, https://www.greatchicagofire.org/anthology -of-fire-narratives/chapman/.

161   *pouring water from a bucket on an overturned safe to cool it*   "Cooling a Safe amid the Ruins," in "Among the Ruins," in GCFWOM, https://www.greatchicagofire.org /ruined-city/among-ruins/.

161   *years after the fact*   Mrs. A. E. [Ashleman] Sanderson, "Reminiscences," December 14, 1925, CHMCF.

161   *and the insurance proved up*   Eben Matthews, fire narrative, CHMFC, in GCFWOM, https://www.greatchicagofire.org/anthology-of-fire-narratives/eben-matthews/.

161   *"Writing Perfectly Restored," it promised*   Advertisement of J. Morris & Company, CTrib, December 3, 1871.

162   *the new Palmer House hotel under construction at State and Monroe*   CTrib, October 14, 1871; CTrib, October 20, 1871.

163   *I will pile it up on a piece of ground worth $100,000 and Mortgage to secure it*   Jared Bassett to D.E.B., October 21, 1871, CHMFC.

163   *will rise phoenix like from the ashes*   William H. Carter to his brother, October 15, 1871, CHMCF, in GCFWOM, https://www.greatchicagofire.org/conflagration-library /william-h-carter-tells-his-brother-sad-news/.

163   *wheat fields near the Mississippi River*   Jack Harpster, *The Railroad Tycoon Who Built Chicago: A Biography of William D. Ogden* (Carbondale: Southern Illinois University Press, 2009); Andreas, 2:564.

164   *ever seeing the past literally restored*   Harpster, *The Railroad Tycoon Who Built Chicago*, 226–48; Anna Sheldon Ogden West, "Reminiscences," CHMFC. West quotes letters from Ogden to Wheeler.

165   *the expectation that the city would recover*   Pierce, 3:13–14.

165   *which might otherwise follow this severe trial*   *Chicago Weekly Post*, October 26, 1871.

165   *our National Wheel of Commerce*   John S. Wright, *Chicago: Past, Present, Future. Relations to the Great Interior, and to the Continent*, 2nd ed. (Chicago: John S. Wright, 1870), ii.

166   *than she would have had without the fire*   John Stephen Wright, quoted in Harold M. Mayer and Richard C. Wade, *Chicago: Growth of a Metropolis* (Chicago: University of Chicago Press, 1969), 117. Wright used this quotation in the promotional literature for some of his postfire projects. See the booklet *The Chicago Fire Will Help Wright's Washington Heights' Enterprise* ([Boston]: n.p., [1871]), a copy of which is in the collections of the Chicago History Museum.

166   *to erect temporary one-story wooden buildings on their property*   *CTrib*, October 13, 1871.

167   *obligated to tear down what they had built and move out*   Some delayed in giving up their spots. See *CTrib*, January 4, 1872.

167   *Mayhon, Daly & Company*   See "Temporary Buildings on Michigan Avenue," in "Back in Business," in *GCFWOM*, https://www.greatchicagofire.org/queen-of-west-once-more/back-business/.

167   *breezy atmosphere of hope and energy*   *New-York Tribune*, October 14, 1871; Pierce, 3:11.

167   *Old Prices*   For an image of Schock, Bigford & Company's stand, see "First Store in the Burnt District," in "Back in Business," in *GCFWOM*, https://www.greatchicagofire.org/queen-of-west-once-more/back-business/.

168   *CHILDREN and ENERGY*   Andreas, 3:61; *CTrib*, January 6, 1918.

169   *as the Courthouse had been before the fire*   Andreas, 3:61–62.

169   *upon every unprotected point of picturesque ruin*   *New-York Tribune*, October 19, 1871.

171   *and I won't see them ruins—!"*   James W. Sheahan and George P. Upton, *The Great Conflagration* (Chicago: Union, 1871), 262–63.

171   *ten thousand men working amid the South Division ruins*   *CRepub*, October 27, 1871.

171   *in spite of the fire*   *CTrib*, October 20, 1871.

171   *and the Trees*   *CTrib*, January 26, 1906.

171   *Tremont House hotel*   *CTrib*, October 20, 1871.

171   *Unlike stone, bricks could be reused*   On brick recycling, see architect John M. Van Osdel's comments in a letter to the *Chicago Tribune*, January 3, 1872.

172   *less than 40 percent of the amount claimed had been disbursed*   Pierce, 3:12–13; *The Chicago Fire and the Insurance Companies. An Exhibit of the Capital, Assets and Losses of the Companies, Together with a Graphic Account of the Great Disaster* (New York: J. H. and C. M. Goodsell, 1871).

172   *the Staats-Zeitung boasted*   *ISZ*, October 13, 1871.

172   *running again*   *CTimes*, December 14, 1871.

172   *the classrooms of the Sunday school*   Andreas, 2:390; *CTrib*, November 21, 1871.

172   *Hay reported*   *New-York Tribune*, October 14, 1871.

172   *a fashionable brick mansion*   Samuel S. Greeley, fire narrative, [1900?], CHMFC.

173   *whether he could spell or not*   W. A. Croffut, "Reconstruction," in *The Lakeside Memorial of the Burning of Chicago, A.D. 1871* (Chicago: University Publishing, 1872), 54–55; *New York Times*, August 2, 1915.

173   *These booklets often contained a brief account of the disaster*   *CTrib*, October 20, 1871. See, for example, the directory distributed by the New Tremont House, *Full Account of the Great Fire and New Business Directory of Leading Houses* (Chicago: Northwestern, [1871 or 1872]), https://catalog.hathitrust.org/Record/100698939, and in "Instant History," in *GFCWOM*, https://www.greatchicagofire.org/media-event/instant-history/.

174   *reserve their orders for me until my return*   John G. Ashleman, "I have been obliged . . . to move my quarters," October 20, 1871, CHMFC, in "Back in Business," in *GFCWOM*, https://www.greatchicagofire.org/queen-of-west-once-more/back-business/.

174   *gloves near the State Street door*   Lloyd Wendt and Herman Kogan, *Give the Lady What She Wants! The Story of Marshall Field & Company* (Chicago: Rand McNally, 1952), 114–15; *CTrib*, November 7, 1871.

174   *offered hospitality to a disconsolate horse*   Croffut, "Reconstruction," 55.

175   *Ogden underestimated that number by 325,000*   *CTrib*, October 16, 1871.

175   *shared Zion Congregation's choir*   Sinai Congregation, board of directors minutes, November 5, 1871, in "Foreign Language Press Survey," Newberry Library, https://flps.newberry.org/article/5423972_11_0199.

175   *clearly human-instigated violence like wars and riots*   For a recent discussion of this phenomenon, see Rebecca Solnit, *A Paradise Built in Hell: The Extraordinary Communities that Arise in Disaster* (New York: Viking, 2009).

175   *on Tuesday, October 17*   *CRepub*, October 17, 1871.

175   *A week is enough time for Chicago to plume herself for a new flight*   *CTrib*, October 18, 1871.

175   *it counseled*   *ISZ*, November 4, 1871.

175   *I have seen only one complainer and that was a millionaire*   Aurelia R. King to "My Dear Friends All," October 21, 1871, CHMFC; Angle, 45.

175   *Men are full of excitement now & hope*   Anna E. [Tyng] Higginson to Mrs. Mark Skinner, November 10, 1871, CHMFC, in *GCFWOM*, https://www.greatchicagofire.org/anthology-of-fire-narratives/anna-e-tyng-higginson/; Angle, 47.

175   *would make residents all the stronger*   James W. Milner to Bannister, October 14, 1871, CHMFC, in *GCFWOM*, https://www.greatchicagofire.org/anthology-of-fire-narratives/james-w-milner/.

176   *you see that eyes have moistened*   Frederick Law Olmsted, "Chicago in Distress," *Nation* 13, no. 332 (November 9, 1871): 303. Best known for their 1858 plan for New York's Central Park, Olmsted and Calvert Vaux had also prepared designs for what would become Chicago's ring of parks. Olmsted had in addition recently laid out the streets of the western suburb of Riverside, one of the few places in the Chicago area not built along an orthogonal grid.

176   *assisting tens of thousands of people a day*   *CTrib*, October 19, 1871.

176   *two doors away from the Lester home*   John J. Healy, *A Little Bit of the Old North Side* ([Chicago]: n.p., [1947]); Fanny Boggs Lester, fire narrative, October 29, 1946,

CHMFC, in *GCFWOM*, https://www.greatchicagofire.org/anthology-of-fire-narra tives/fanny-boggs-lester/.

177 *while giving out coffee instead of tea cost an extra seventeen cents* Chicago Relief and Aid Society, *Report of the Chicago Relief and Aid Society of Disbursement of Contributions for the Sufferers by the Fire* (Chicago: Riverside, 1874), 150–51.

177 *and rascals have no mercy shown them* CTrib, October 18, 1871.

177 *Only then might they receive help* Chicago Relief and Aid Society, *Report of the Chicago Relief and Aid Society*, 197–98.

178 *at least as good as what the occupants had known before the fire* Chicago Relief and Aid Society, *Report of the Chicago Relief and Aid Society*, 189.

178 *so we were [not] the worse for our awful experience* Mary Kehoe to Gladys K. Peters, January 21, 1942, CHMFC, in *GCFWOM*, https://www.greatchicagofire.org /anthology-of-fire-narratives/mary-kehoe/.

179 *idleness, disorder, and vice* Chicago Relief and Aid Society, *Report of the Chicago Relief and Aid Society*, 215, 184.

179 *with their house watched day & night by policemen* Anna E. [Tyng] Higginson to Mrs. Mark Skinner, November 10, 1871; Angle, 53.

179 *all the lip service about sympathy* ISZ, October 17, 1871.

180 *and thus keeping those wages down* Chicago Relief and Aid Society, *Report of the Chicago Relief and Aid Society*, 158.

180 *on which Chicago's future depended* Chicago Relief and Aid Society, *Report of the Chicago Relief and Aid Society*, 184.

181 *a spot on which to put them* Chicago Relief and Aid Society, *Report of the Chicago Relief and Aid Society*, 185–89; "House with One Room," in "The Relief and Aid Society Takes Over," in *GCFWOM*, https://www.greatchicagofire.org/rescue-and-relief /relief-and-aid-society-takes-over/.

181 *to keep the very flammable building from catching fire* Healy, *A Little Bit of the Old North Side*.

182 *which conveys his sense of how minimal it was* Andreas, 2:750. Virtually all of these shelter homes disappeared over time, as intended.

182 *any further application for assistance* Chicago Relief and Aid Society, *Report of the Chicago Relief and Aid Society*, 201.

182 *they were not the kind of people to resort to imposition* Chicago Relief and Aid Society, *Report of the Chicago Relief and Aid Society*, 198.

182 *as quickly and "delicately" as possible* CTrib, November 17, 1871.

182 *for their friends to come forward* Ellis S. Chesbrough to Ellis S. Chesbrough Jr., October 21, 1871, CHMFC.

183 *Higginson commented sharply* Anna E. (Tyng) Higginson to Mrs. Mark Skinner, November 10, 1871; Angle, 52.

183 *let alone at prefire wages* CTrib, December 17, 1871.

183 *suspicion that characterized the society's procedures* Sawislak, 114–17.

183 *it could be done only by kindness* CTrib, October 20, 1871.

184 *of a character unfit for food* CRepub, October 27, 1871.

184 *the society provided no translators for non-English speakers* ISZ, October 18, 1871.

184   *These women spoke from personal experience ministering to fire sufferers*   On the role of women in charitable efforts during this period, see Lori D. Ginzberg, *Women and the Work of Benevolence: Morality, Politics, and Class in the Nineteenth-Century United States* (New Haven, CT: Yale University Press, 1990), esp. chap. 6, "The Moral Eye of the State," 174–213; and Maureen A. Flanagan, *Seeing with Their Hearts: Chicago Women and the Vision of the Good City* (Princeton, NJ: Princeton University Press 2002), esp. chap. 1, "'The Whole Work Has Been Committed to the Hands of Women': Women Respond to the Fire of 1871," 13–30. On the considerable fire relief work done by women, and on disputes between different women's groups, see Sawislak, 110–14.

184   *boxes of clothing to be distributed in violation of all general rules*   Sawislak, 110; Flanagan, *Seeing with Their Hearts*, 16.

185   *She divulged that even her husband agreed with her*   Aurelia R. King to "My Dear Friends All," October 21, 1871; Angle, 45.

186   *knowing nothing at all about firearms*   *CTrib*, October 22, 1871.

186   *"old soldiers" rather than college students*   *Message of Governor John M. Palmer to the Adjourned Session of the Twenty-Seventh General Assembly, May 15, 1871, also (Annexed) the Report of Adjutant-General Dilger* (Springfield: Illinois State Journal Printing Office, 1871), 10. As already noted, this pamphlet lacks unified pagination, and the cover mistakenly reads "May" rather than "November."

186   *in violation of law*   *Message of Governor John M. Palmer*, 12; Andreas, 2:776.

186   *the emergency required me to take the step that I did*   *Message of Governor John M. Palmer*, 13; Andreas, 2:776.

187   *this anomalous state of things*   Andreas, 2:776.

187   *is one of enumerated and limited powers*   John M. Palmer, *Personal Recollections of John M. Palmer: The Story of an Earnest Life* (Cincinnati: Robert Clarke, 1901), 287.

187   *profoundly ignorant of everything outside their own profession*   George Thomas Palmer, *A Conscientious Turncoat: The Story of John M. Palmer* (New Haven, CT: Yale University Press, 1941), 80. On the constitutional issues raised by the occupation, see Andrew L. Slap, "'The Strong Arm of the Military of the United States': The Chicago Fire, the Constitution, and Reconstruction," *Civil War History* 47, no. 2 (June 2001): 146–63.

188   *he told Townsend*   Andreas, 2:777.

188   *they would be right at hand if needed*   *Report of the Select Committee on Governor J. M. Palmer's Messages of Nov. 15 and Dec. 9, 1871. Including, also, The Evidence Taken before the Committee, and Resolutions Recommended. Submitted to the House, January 6, 1872* (Springfield: Illinois State Journal Printing Office, 1872), 11; Sawislak, 60–61.

188   *are now sending their charities here to relieve the distressed*   Sheridan, *Report to the Honorable W. W. Belknap*, 20.

11. The Triumph of the Fire-Proof Ticket

189   *"professional thieves and jobbers" on the Common Council*   *CTrib*, October 17, 1871.

190   *in the Ku Klux districts of the south*   *CTimes*, October 22, 1871; *CTimes*, October 23, 1871; *CTimes*, November 3, 1871; *CTimes*, November 6, 1871.

190   *proposed William B. Ogden to succeed Mason*   *CTimes*, October 20, 1871.

190   *he still kept his home in the Chicago (which had been burned in the fire) and voted there*   CTrib, August 4, 1877.

190   *as we often find in a mortal frame*   Biographical Sketches of the Leading Men of Chicago (Chicago: Wilson & St. Clair, 1868), 260.

191   *were born there after he arrived*   CTrib, October 21, 1871.

192   *to fund Chicago's recovery*   CTrib, October 24, 1871.

192   *and unquestionable integrity*   CTimes, October 25, 1871.

193   *to brand him "Chief Caucus Packer" Holden*   CTrib, November 6, 1871.

193   *widows and orphans went cold and hungry*   CTrib, November 4, 1871.

194   *the projects in which affluent Chicago businessmen were heavily invested*   CTrib, November 1, 1871.

194   *the* Tribune's *opposition to some national Republican Party policies*   This advocacy of orthodox Republicanism persisted through several changes of owners and editors. See Elmer Geertz, "Charles A. Dana and 'The Chicago Republican,'" *Journal of the Illinois State Historical Society* 45, no. 2 (1952): 124–35; *Cincinnati Daily Enquirer*, July 23, 1866; *New-York Tribune*, August 8, 1866; *Watertown* (WI) *News*, November 23, 1870; Sawislak, 305n61.

194   *for their own selfish interests*   CRepub, October 30, 1871; CRepub, October 31, 1871.

194   *the venal sin of heavy lying*   CRepub, November 1, 1871; CRepub, November 2, 1871; CRepub, November 3, 1871; CRepub, November 4, 1871; CRepub, November 5, 1871; CRepub, November 6, 1871.

195   *candidates who would oust the crooks from office*   CTimes, October 19, 1871.

195   *make sure the bummers did not pull any dirty tricks*   CTrib, November 7, 1871.

195   *and vote the right ticket*   CTrib, November 7, 1871.

195   *no liquor could be sold or given away during the voting*   CTrib, November 5, 1871.

196   *which has been common*   CTimes, November 8, 1871.

196   *a majority of almost 73 percent*   "Chicago Mayors, 1837–2007," in EC, http://www.encyclopedia.chicagohistory.org/pages/1443.html.

196   *the* Tribune *shouted in triumph*   CTrib, November 8, 1871.

196   *early and often*   CRepub, November 8, 1871.

196   *that would bring the city the continuing financial support it needed*   ISZ, November 7, 1871.

197   *redound to the best interests of the city*   Workingman's Advocate, November 11, 1871.

197   *his backing of Medill reveals how weak the opposition was*   John B. Jentz and Richard Schneirov, *Chicago in the Age of Capital: Class, Politics, and Democracy during the Civil War and Reconstruction* (Urbana: University of Illinois Press, 2012), 134.

198   *our beloved city now rising from its ruins*   CTrib, November 8, 1871.

198   *very timid or very wicked*   Report of the Select Committee on Governor J. M. Palmer's Messages of Nov. 15 and Dec. 9, 1871. Including, also, The Evidence Taken before the Committee, and Resolutions Recommended. Submitted to the House, January 6, 1872 (Springfield: Illinois State Journal Printing Office, 1872), 22–23.

199   *at a very unreasonable hour*   CTrib, November 21, 1871; Carl Smith, *Urban Disorder and the Shape of Belief: The Great Chicago Fire, the Haymarket Bomb, and the Model Town of Pullman*, 2nd ed. (Chicago: University of Chicago Press, 2007), 71.

199   *the basin was virtually gone*   Andreas, 3:59; Sawislak, 168; CTrib, November 27, 1871.

200   *he had his old anvil mounted in the church*   For more on Collyer and the anvil, including an illustration of the latter, see Moncure D. Conway, "Ilkley," *Harper's New Monthly Magazine* 48, no. 288 (May 1873): 821–30.

200   *as any blacksmith in Chicago*   Harper's Weekly 15, no. 775 (November 4, 1871): 1027; Colbert and Chamberlin, 268, 404–5; Smith, *Urban Disorder and the Shape of Belief*, 40.

200   *knocked down and carted away*   Andreas, 3:59; *Harper's Weekly* 15, no. 775 (November 4, 1871): 1025; "Cover of *Harper's Weekly*, November 4, 1871," in "Body and Soul," in *GCFWOM*, https://www.greatchicagofire.org/queen-of-west-once-more /body-and-soul/. It is not clear how to reconcile this first cornerstone story with one reporting that on the evening of December 7, a day short of two months after the fire, one Jim Egan laid the first brick in the downtown Burnt District. It was the start of his building on Madison near Franklin, a few blocks southwest of Courthouse Square. Speeches, recitations, and reminiscences marked the occasion, which was followed by "a sumptuous repast." CRepub, December 8, 1871.

200   *the area was ripe for redevelopment*   Christine Meisner Rosen, *The Limits of Power: Great Fires and the Process of City Growth in America* (Cambridge: Cambridge University Press, 1986), 113.

202   *to purchase inventory for his postfire business*   CTrib, October 12, 1871; CTrib, October 20, 1871; A. S. Chapman, "A Boy's Recollections of the Chicago Fire," 1910, CHMFC, in *GCFWOM*, https://www.greatchicagofire.org/anthology-of-fire-narra tives/chapman/.

202   *warm biscuits and cold water*   New-York Tribune, October 26, 1871.

203   *he raises his hands, perhaps in benediction*   Frank Luzerne, *The Lost City! Drama of the Fire Fiend!* (New York: Wells, 1872), 165; "The Wedding Amid the Ruins," in "Body and Soul," in *GCFWOM*, https://www.greatchicagofire.org/item/ICHi -02931/.

204   *a fielder's choice in a 4–1 loss*   CTrib, November 3, 1871.

204   *as did Bertha, the Sewing Machine Girl for DeBar*   CTrib, November 2, 1871; CTrib, November 28, 1871.

204   *as part of the Star Lecture course*   CTrib, November 9, 1871; CTrib, December 3, 1871; CTrib, December 13, 1871.

204   *the woman who glories in her dirty ideas*   CTimes, November 26, 1871; CTrib, November 26, 1871.

204   *white folks that had come together to hear him have his say*   CTimes, December 30, 1871.

205   *Chicagoans filled the 2,500 seats in the auditorium*   CTrib, November 28, 1871; CTrib, November 29, 1871; CTrib, December 3, 1871. On the Emerson family's unhappiness with this trip, which ruined their Thanksgiving, see Joel Myerson, ed., *The Collected Works of Ralph Waldo Emerson*, vol. 8, *Letters and Social Aims* (Cambridge, MA: Belknap, 2010), cxxvi–cxvix.

205   *that put him at once* en rapport *with an audience*   CTrib, December 20, 1871. See
        also Trygve Thoreson, "Mark Twain's Chicago," *Journal of the Illinois State Histori-
        cal Society* 73, no. 4 (Winter 1980): 277–90; Mark Twain, *Mark Twain's Letters*, vol. 4,
        1870–1871, ed. Victor Fischer and Michael B. Frank (Berkeley: University of Califor-
        nia Press, 1995), 519.

205   *discolored and out of shape*   CRepub, October 12, 1871.

205   *signs of what they had been though*   "Touched by Fire," in GCFWOM, https://www
        .greatchicagofire.org/souvenirs/touched-fire/.

205   *gone with the flames*   "Alive, if Not Still Ticking," in "Pieces of the Past," in GCF-
        WOM, https://www.greatchicagofire.org/souvenirs/pieces-of-past/.

205   *the ceramic head of a favorite doll survived without a crack, even if it had been black-
        ened and its cloth body burned away*   Mrs. A. E. [Ashleman] Sanderson, "Reminis-
        cences," December 14, 1925, CHMCF; see also "Childhood's End; Porcelain Doll
        Bust," in "Pieces of the Past," in GCFWOM, https://www.greatchicagofire.org
        /souvenirs/pieces-of-past/.

206   *fragments of the burned city that he had collected*   Charles R. Lott, fire narrative,
        October 7, 1926, CHMFC.

206   *Wedged in the rubble next to the safe is a business relocation sign*   Rev. E. J. Good-
        speed, *The Great Fires in Chicago and the West* (New York: H. S. Goodspeed, 1871),
        627. "Enterprising Young Merchant Disposing of Relics Opposite the Ruins of the
        Sherman House," in "Selling History," in GCFWOM, https://www.greatchicagofire
        .org/souvenirs/selling-history/.

206   *cluttered with pieces of Chicago touched by the fire*   See Robert M. Hazen and Mar-
        garet Hindle Hazen, *Keepers of the Flame: The Role of Fire in American Culture,
        1775–1925* (Princeton, NJ: Princeton University Press, 1992), 39.

208   *doll's heads, and iron toys*   "Relic House," in GCFWOM, https://www.greatchicagofire
        .org/item/ICHi-51044/.

208   *for anything that might be valuable*   "View of the Courthouse Bell after the Fire, Shaw
        Photographer, Stereograph, 1871," in "Among the Ruins," in GCFWOM, https://www
        .greatchicagofire.org/item/ICHi-64280/.

208   *signed by members of the city's Board of Public Works*   "Selling History," in GCF-
        WOM, https://www.greatchicagofire.org/souvenirs/selling-history/.

208   *extremely apocryphal*   CTimes, November 19, 1871.

12. Who Started the Great Chicago Fire?

209   *a stable in which a woman was milking*   Chicago Evening Journal—Extra, October 9,
        1871; "The Great Calamity of the Age!," in "Front Page News," in GCFWOM, https://
        www.greatchicagofire.org/media-event/front-page-news/.

209   *to find confirmation*   Sawislak, 44, notes that "it is important to recognize that the
        tale of Mrs. O'Leary's cow, while on one level merely a picaresque media creation, at
        the time represented a vilification fraught with specific meaning: in much of the
        English-language press, Mrs. O'Leary became an easy target for anti-Irish, antiwork-
        ing class, and antiwoman invective."

210   *she remained guilty in the court of public opinion*   See an obviously bogus photo-
        graph supposedly of Mrs. O'Leary and her cow in Sawislak, 45.

210   *the vermin which haunt our streets*   CTimes, October 18, 1871.

210 *as the lamp goes flying* For examples, see "A Star is Born," in *GCFWOM*, https://www.greatchicagofire.org/oleary-legend/star-born/; and "The Saga Continues," in *GCFWOM*, https://www.greatchicagofire.org/oleary-legend/saga-continues/.

212 *sat at the window, knitting* *New-York Tribune*, October 17, 1871. The reprint in the *Chicago Times* appeared on October 30, 1871.

212 *the many friends who threw water on its walls and roof* CTrib, October 19, 1871.

213 *the love of plunder, Divine wrath, etc* CTrib, October 20, 1871; Andreas, 2:708–9; Bales, 64, 201–3; Kerby A. Miller, *Ireland and Irish America: Culture, Class, and Transatlantic Migration* (Dublin: Field Day in Association with the Keough-Naughton Institute for Irish Studies at the University of Notre Dame, 2008), 33–34.

213 *its profusion of theaters, brothels, and "gambling-hells"* Rev. E. J. Goodspeed, *The Great Fires in Chicago and the West* (Chicago: J. W. Goodspeed, 1871), 81.

214 *its worship to the Golden Calf* Granville Moody, quoted in Colbert and Chamberlin, 522.

214 *were intended to lead our minds* The text of Mayor Mason's proclamation is in "Official Actions," in *GCFWOM*, https://www.greatchicagofire.org/rescue-and-relief-library/official-actions/.

215 *they responded with $5,000 in pledges* Henry Ward Beecher, "Lessons from the Great Chicago Fire," in *The Sermons of Henry Ward Beecher in Plymouth Church, Brooklyn. From Verbatim Reports by T. J. Ellinwood, "Plymouth Pulpit," Seventh Series: September 1871–March 1872* (New York: J. B. Ford, 1872), 99–114.

216 *Relief for the Sufferers of Chicago* "Relief for the Sufferers of Chicago," in "Blazing Visions," in *GCFWOM*, https://www.greatchicagofire.org/fanning-flames/blazing-visions/.

218 *Chicago's lap is discreetly draped* In Memory of the Great Fire at Chicago, in "Blazing Visions," in *GCFWOM*, https://www.greatchicagofire.org/fanning-flames/blazing-visions/; Andreas, 2:frontispiece.

218 *Frear wrote* Andreas, 2:735; McIlvaine, 24.

218 *the rescue of their properties* Bales, 139–41. Bales refers to the brief period of praise as the "Fireman's Honeymoon."

218 *the quality of the firefighters' defense* Bales, 140–41.

219 *because they were so poorly equipped* CTrib, November 15, 1871; CTrib, November 16, 1871; CTrib, November 17, 1871; CTrib, November 18, 1871; CTrib, November 19, 1871.

219 *the only chair in the room with a cushion* CTimes, December 3, 1871.

219 *The full transcript totals about 1,170 foolscap pages* Bales, 204–7, 144. The commissioners themselves put the number at nine hundred; CTrib, December 12, 1871.

220 *drew nourishment from immense reservoirs* CTimes, December 3, 1871.

220 *upon my word I worked hard for them* Bales, 217–21.

220 *the stenographer's inability to keep up with his runaway brogue* CTimes, December 3, 1871.

220 *I don't know who done it* Bales, 235.

220 *Commissioner Thomas B. Brown at one point instructed him to stick to the fire* CTimes, December 3, 1871.

221   *like drugstore owner Bruno Goll, did not testify*   Musham (70) notes that while the report "disclosed considerable information of value," it "ignored many pertinent facts" because of the board's desire to evade responsibility itself or blame anyone else. Bales (155) describes the inquiry as a "farce" whose real intention was to exonerate the department rather than evaluate it. In 1885, fourteen years after the fire, Bruno Goll offered his recollection of the evening in a signed affidavit; see Andreas, 2:716.

221   *which was nothing unusual at the time*   Testimony of William Mullin, in "Transcript of Inquiry into Cause of Chicago Fire and Actions of Fire Department Therein," CHMFC, 1:11–13.

221   *the request of any individual for personal gain for himself*   Testimony of Leo Myers, in "Transcript of Inquiry," 2:17.

221   *I was working under orders*   Testimony of Michael Sullivan, in "Transcript of Inquiry," 1:11.

222   *I don't think it could have been prevented*   Bales, 281.

222   *their December 11 semiweekly meeting*   It was signed by only three of the commissioners, Thomas B. Brown, Mark Sheridan, and J. E. Chadwick. The fourth, Frederick Gund, had been replaced in the recent election and was by this time out of office.

223   *greater portion of the wooden city which now remains*   Bales, 295–97. Bales reproduces verbatim the version that appeared in the *Evening Journal*. As he indicates, it was published in several Chicago papers, with minor variations. See Bales, 294, 297n1.

226   *whose destruction had been its own fault*   Frederick Law Olmsted, "Chicago in Distress," *Nation* 13, no. 332 (November 9, 1871): 303, 305.

13. The Limits of Limits

227   *or abrogating any of its powers*   CTrib, December 5, 1871.

228   *are odious in a republican country*   Joseph Medill, "Mayor Joseph Medill Inaugural Address," Chicago Public Library, https://www.chipublib.org/mayor-joseph-medill-inaugural-address-1871/.

229   *bay windows, and other projections*   CTrib, November 17, 1871.

229   *close to forty thousand people*   Chicago Relief and Aid Society, *Report of the Chicago Relief and Aid Society of Disbursement of Contributions for the Sufferers by the Fire* (Chicago: Riverside, 1874), 183–89.

229   *homes of their own choosing*   ISZ, November 9, 1871.

230   *uncrowded parts of the city*   ISZ, January 16, 1872; see Ogden's letter on this subject, CTrib, December 3, 1871.

230   *the charges against them were eventually dropped*   CTrib, December 30, 1871; CTrib, December 31, 1871; Pierce, 2:299.

230   *a major snowstorm was followed by sleet and rain*   CTrib, November 10, 1871; CTrib, December 24, 1871.

231   *under construction in the South Division*   Andreas, 3:59.

232   *Soon the Cook County Circuit and Superior Courts also moved there*   Andreas, 3:104; CRepub, October 27, 1871; CTrib, October 18, 1871; CTrib, December 19, 1871; "Temporary City Hall," in "Temporary City Hall and Public Library," in GCF-WOM, https://www.greatchicagofire.org/landmarks/temporary-city-hall-and-public-library/.

232　　*stay on the job after dark*　"Working at Night on Palmer's Grand Hotel, by Calcium Light," in "Palmer House," in *GCFWOM*, https://www.greatchicagofire.org/landmarks /palmer-house/.

232　　*the smallest possible regard for stability*　CTrib, December 24, 1871; Frank A. Randall, *History of the Development of Building Construction in Chicago* (Urbana: University of Illinois Press, 1949), 67.

232　　*it completed in one hundred days*　CTrib, November 2, 1871; CTrib, December 31, 1871.

232　　*nepotism, thievery, and fraud*　CRepub, November 23, 1871; CTrib, December 2, 1871; CTrib, December 4, 1871; CTrib, December 6, 1871; CTrib, December 7, 1871; CTrib, December 13, 1871; CTrib, December 16, 1871; CTrib, December 23, 1871; CTrib, December 25, 1871.

233　　*which the officers of the society are as anxious to correct as anyone in the community can be*　CTrib, November 24, 1871.

233　　*to gain the confidence of the residents of the district*　CTrib, December 24, 1871.

234　　*the reporter concluded*　CTrib, November 21, 1871.

234　　*an appealing and decent home for themselves*　CTrib, November 24, 1871.

235　　*to retrieve their overwhelming misfortunes*　CTrib, December 27, 1871.

235　　*lumber, iron, and merchandise*　CTrib, December 31, 1871.

236　　*barrels ready for shipment*　CTrib, January 3, 1872.

236　　*the grand duke told them*　CTrib, January 3, 1872.

236　　*orphan asylums and foundling homes*　CTrib, January 5, 1872.

237　　*the* Illinois Staats-Zeitung *reported*　ISZ, January 15, 1872.

237　　*the grey old scoundrel*　ISZ, January 20, 1872; ISZ, January 22, 1872.

238　　*had committed this act*　ISZ, January 16, 1872.

238　　*the same period in England*　CTrib, January 16, 1872.

239　　*were drained in quick succession*　CTimes, January 16, 1872.

239　　*the just demands of the workers and small-plot owners*　ISZ, January 19, 1872. Hesing said that the *Chicago Mail*, a small evening paper, was the only exception.

239　　*The Star-Spangled Banner*　CRepub, January 16, 1872.

239　　*the* makers of *capital*　ISZ, January 18, 1872.

240　　*are the people of Chicago*　ISZ, January 23, 1872.

241　　*The new measure said little about improved enforcement*　CTrib, February 13, 1872.

14. New Chicago

243　　*published in Myra Bradwell's* Chicago Legal News　CTrib, December 16, 1871; Richard F. Bales, "Title Insurance Records and the Great Chicago Fire," *Probate and Property* 18, no. 1 (January–February 2004): 46–49; Chicago Title and Trust Company, "160 Years and Beyond" (webpage, section titled "Burnt Records Act"), https:// www.ctic.com/history2.aspx; Illinois General Assembly, "(765ILCS45/) Destroyed Property Records Act," http://www.ilga.gov/legislation/ilcs/ilcs3.asp?ActID=2145& ChapterID=62; Mary L. Volcansek, "Myra Bradwell," in *Women in Law: A Bio-bibliographical Sourcebook*, ed. Rebecca Mae Salokar and Mary L. Volcansek (Westport, CT: Greenwood, 1996), 47.

243   *which sometimes swayed from party orthodoxy*   Andreas, 3:698. The *Tribune* would
        oppose Ulysses S. Grant's reelection and endorse the candidacy of Horace
        Greeley.

243   *The stone structure he lost was four stories, the replacement six*   Frank A. Randall,
        History of the Development of Building Construction in Chicago (Urbana: Univer-
        sity of Illinois Press, 1949), 79; "The Rebuilding of the Marine Building," in "Bricks
        and Mortar," in *GCFWOM*, https://www.greatchicagofire.org/queen-of-west-once
        -more/bricks-and-mortar/.

243   *plus another $600,000 for furnishings*   Andreas, 3:63; *CTrib*, January 28, 1872.

243   *only thoroughly fireproof hotel in the United States*   Palmer House, "About Our
        Hotel," https://www.palmerhousehiltonhotel.com/about-our-hotel/; "Palmer House,
        Chicago," in "Palmer House," in *GCFWOM*, https://www.greatchicagofire.org/landmarks
        /palmer-house/; "Palmer House II and III, Chicagology, https://chicagology.com
        /rebuilding/rebuilding001/.

244   *the largest theater in Chicago*   Andreas, 3:666.

244   *Auld Lang Syne*   *CTrib*, October 10, 1872; "Finishing the Roof of the Chamber of
        Commerce," in "Bricks and Mortar," in *GCFWOM*, https://www.greatchicagofire.org
        /queen-of-west-once-more/bricks-and-mortar/.

244   *a female figure holding a torch*   See Ross Miller, *American Apocalypse: The Great
        Fire and the Myth of Chicago* (Chicago: University of Chicago Press, 1990), 148–49.
        This book was reprinted in 2000 by the University of Illinois Press with the title *The
        Great Chicago Fire*. Jenney's 1884 Home Insurance Building, considered the first build-
        ing with a load-bearing steel frame, made way for the modern skyscraper, with which
        Chicago is so closely associated.

245   *a description of Chicago a year after the fire*   Chicago Inter-Ocean, October 28, 1872;
        Chicago Inter-Ocean, October 31, 1872; *CTrib*, October 31, 1872; "William LeBaron
        Jenney, Proposed Fire Monument," in "Resurrexit!," in *GCFWOM*, https://www
        .greatchicagofire.org/commemorating-catastrophe/resurrexit/.

245   *increased property values*   "The Silver Lining of the Cloud," *Harper's Weekly* 15,
        no. 774 (October 28, 1871): 1002; *CTimes*, October 9, 1872.

246   *the progress was unmistakable*   [*Chicago Times*,] *New Chicago: A Full Review of the
        Work of Reconstruction for the Year, Embracing a Mention of Every Structure Built
        and Being Built in the City* (Chicago: Horton and Leonard, 1872), 19, 25. "Map of
        the Rebuilt Downtown," in "The New City," in *GCFWOM*, https://www
        .greatchicagofire.org/queen-of-west-once-more/new-city/.

246   *the metropolis of America!*   *Chicago Illustrated: One Year from the Fire* (Chicago:
        J. M. Wing, 1872), 2; "One Year from the Fire," in "The New City," in *GCFWOM*,
        https://www.greatchicagofire.org/queen-of-west-once-more/new-city/. Wing pub-
        lished a sequel on the second anniversary of the fire.

247   *an indication of extraordinary science and skill in our farmers*   E. O. Haven, "Reli-
        gious and Educational Institutions," in *Lakeside Memorial of the Burning of Chicago,
        A.D. 1871* (Chicago: University Publishing, 1872), 72–75. The volume was a reprint,
        with supplementary material, of the January 1872 edition of the *Lakeside Monthly*.

247   *were well worth considering*   D. H. Wheeler, "Political Economy of the Fire," in *Lake-
        side Memorial of the Burning of Chicago*, 100. Olmsted expressed similar concerns
        about the cultural costs of the fire; see Frederick Law Olmsted, "Chicago in Distress,"
        Nation 13, no. 332 (November 9, 1871): 305.

248   *which were further supplemented by gifts from dozens of Americans* CTrib, December 7, 1871; "CPL History 1871," Chicago Public Library, https://www.chipublib .org/cpl-history/.

249   *anyone who wished to browse the collection* CTrib, March 16, 1871; CTrib, September 17, 1871; CTrib, November 23, 1871; CTrib, January 7, 1872; CTrib, January 9, 1872; CTrib, January 14, 1872; CTrib, January 16, 1872; CTrib, January 21, 1872; Andreas, 3:414–16; Daniel Hautzinger, "Out of the Ashes: The Birth of the Chicago Public Library," WTTW, https://interactive.wttw.com/playlist/2017/01/09/out -ashes-birth-chicago-public-library; "Temporary City Hall and Public Library," in GCF-WOM, https://www.greatchicagofire.org/landmarks/temporary-city-hall-and-public -library/. See also Thomas Hoyne, *Historical Sketch of the Origin and Foundation of the Chicago Public Library* (Chicago: Beach, Barnard, 1877).

249   *the downtown before the fire* See the maps in Christine Meisner Rosen, *The Limits of Power: Great Fires and the Process of City Growth in America* (Cambridge: Cambridge University Press, 1986), 110, 141–43.

251   *and in every way it was noted for its hospitality* Ada [Rumsey] Campbell, fire narrative, 1924, CHMFC, in GCFWOM, https://www.greatchicagofire.org/anthology-of -fire-narratives/ada-rumsey/.

251   *and for restoration to home* In Memoriam: Isaac Newton Arnold, Nov. 30, 1813– Apr. 24, 1884. Arthur Mason Arnold, May 13, 1858–Apr. 26, 1873 (Chicago: Fergus Printing Company, 1885), 10.

252   *and by 1873 nearly 100,000* Homer Hoyt, *One Hundred Years of Land Values in Chicago: The Relationship of the Growth of Chicago to the Rise of Its Land Values, 1830–1933* (Chicago: University of Chicago Press, 1933), 109. See also Rosen, *The Limits of Power*, 101–77; and Dendy Macaulay, "The Importance of Neighborhood Ties: Relocation Decisions after the Chicago Fire of 1871" (PhD dissertation, University of Chicago, 2007).

252   *to help see Chicagoans through the winter* Chicago Relief and Aid Society, *Report of the Chicago Relief and Aid Society of Disbursement of Contributions for the Sufferers by the Fire* (Chicago: Riverside, 1874), 92–94; CTrib, January 26, 1872.

252   *willing and industrious* CTrib, March 4, 1872; CTrib, March 14, 1872.

252   *but it was almost certainly in the low millions of dollars* Individual cash donations the society administered, like the one from A. T. Stewart, plus interest on money deposited, brought the total financial contributions to $4,996,782.74. See Chicago Relief and Aid Society, *Report of the Chicago Relief and Aid Society*, 295–440; the summation of figures is on 439–40.

253   *the overall mortality rate was the same as in nonexceptional times* Chicago Relief and Aid Society, *Report of the Chicago Relief and Aid Society*, 146, 201–2, 440, 221.

253   *worthy of the highest praise* See Emily C. Skarbek, "The Chicago Fire of 1871: A Bottom-Up Approach to Disaster Relief," *Public Choice* 160, nos. 1–2 (July 2015): 155–80.

254   *defined the terms in this self-serving way* CTrib, March 21, 1872.

254   *put their own profits ahead of Chicago's needs* CTrib, February 14, 1872.

255   *temporary suspension of tariff duties* "Petition of Citizens of Chicago, Praying the Passage of the Bill to Allow a Drawback of the Duties Paid on Materials Used in the Construction and Repair of Buildings in the Burned District of that City," February 19, 1872, 42nd Cong., 2nd Sess., Misc. Doc 78; CTrib, February 17, 1872.

255   *well calculated to rebuke selfishness*   CTrib, February 17, 1872.

255   *proved of little actual economic benefit*   CTrib, February 18, 1872; CRepub, February 17, 1872; CRepub, February 19, 1872; CRepub, March 29, 1872; Pierce, 3:16–17.

255   *praised the generosity of their sister city*   Pierce, 3:7–8.

256   *following sacred Christian duty in opposing the soup-houses*   CTrib, January 26, 1872.

257   *deciding what to do with its remaining resources*   CTrib, February 1, 1872; CTrib, February 2, 1872; CTrib, February 3, 1872; CTrib, February 4, 1872; CTrib, February 5, 1872; CTrib, February 6, 1872; CTrib, February 7, 1872; CTrib, February 8, 1872.

257   *with modesty and good temper*   CTrib, February 1, 1872.

257   *the disgraceful charges alluded to above*   CTrib, February 6, 1872.

257   *and far less need for them*   CTrib, February 12, 1872; Sawislak, 4–5; CRepub, February 8, 1872.

258   *in an honorable and impartial manner*   Chicago Inter-Ocean, April 11, 1872.

259   *self-knowledge and a sense of humor*   A Chicago Lady, *Relief: A Humorous Drama* (Chicago: University Publishing, 1872); CTrib, February 25, 1871.

259   *fifty thousand men were employed in rebuilding the city*   John B. Jentz and Richard Schneirov, *Chicago in the Age of Capital: Class, Politics, and Democracy during the Civil War and Reconstruction* (Urbana: University of Illinois Press, 2012), 141.

259   *Chicago's workers were true patriotic Americans*   CTrib, May 16, 1872; Workingman's Advocate, May 18, 1872.

259   *similarly working together to keep those wages down*   CTimes, May 4, 1872.

260   *but their families had to eat*   Workingman's Advocate, May 11, 1872.

260   *the rebuilding of the city*   Workingman's Advocate, May 18, 1872.

260   *those who did the work lived poorly*   Workingman's Advocate, May 18, 1872; Sawislak, 192–99.

261   *the rebuilding of the Burnt District*   CTimes, May 16, 1872; CTimes, May 17, 1872; Workingman's Advocate, May 18, 1872.

261   *without putting him to a penny's extra cost*   Sawislak, 210–13; Workingman's Advocate, October 12, 1872.

262   *the Lager Beer Riot of 1855*   Robin Einhorn, "Lager Beer Riot," in EC, http://encyclopedia.chicagohistory.org/pages/703.html.

262   *say 3,000 in all*   M. H. Ahern, *The Great Revolution: A History of the Rise and Progress of the People's Party in the City of Chicago and County of Cook, with Sketches of the Elect in Office* (Chicago: Lakeside, 1874), 31.

263   *the majority he needed*   CTrib, August 19, 1873.

263   *He would eventually be convicted of the crime*   Ahern, *The Great Revolution*, 46; Andreas, 3:860.

264   *they kept their doors closed and windows covered*   CTrib, March 10, 1874.

264   *a huge practical joke*   CTrib, November 5, 1873.

264   *many Colvin supporters had voted illegally*   Chicago Inter-Ocean, November 5, 1873; Chicago Inter-Ocean, November 6, 1873.

264 *the Lord is generally on the side which casts the most votes* CTimes, November 6, 1873.

15. City on Fire

265 *more recently, residential buildings dominated* CTrib, October 9, 1873.

265 *When Johnny Comes Marching Home* In 1869 Gilmore mounted a National Peace Jubilee in Boston, during which he had one hundred Boston firemen each strike an anvil with a hammer during a performance of the "Anvil Chorus" from Guiseppe Verdi's *Il Trovatore*; Robert M. Hazen and Margaret Hindle Hazen, *Keepers of the Flame: The Role of Fire in American Culture, 1775–1925* (Princeton, NJ: Princeton University Press, 1992), 143–44.

266 *magnificent in the rapidity and grandeur of her resurrection* These out-of-town newspapers are cited in *CTrib*, June 11, 1873.

266 *and measured sixty feet across* The Inter-State Exposition Souvenir (Chicago: Van Arsdale and Massie, 1873), 37–41; "Interstate Exposition Building," Chicagology, https://chicagology.com/rebuilding/rebuilding016/.

267 *the most valuable contribution to the great exposition* Inter-State Exposition Souvenir, 242.

268 *industrial production, wages, and employment* Homer Hoyt, *One Hundred Years of Land Values in Chicago: The Relationship of the Growth of Chicago to the Rise of Its Land Values, 1830–1933* (Chicago: University of Chicago Press, 1933), 117–19.

268 *which he had mortgaged at 10 percent* CTrib, March 18, 1890.

269 *of the COMMUNISTIC UPRISINGS in Europe* CTimes, December 22, 1873.

269 *there was good order* CTimes, December 23, 1873.

269 *When men were hungry they did not think of politics or religion* CTimes, December 24, 1873; CTrib, December 24, 1873; Sawislak, 261–78.

269 *but this was still a substantial sum* Chicago Relief and Aid Society, *Report of the Chicago Relief and Aid Society of Disbursement of Contributions for the Sufferers by the Fire* (Chicago: Riverside, 1874), 440.

270 *Our Communists* CTrib, December 25, 1873.

271 *accept the charity of those who cheat and swindle them* CTrib, December 28, 1873.

271 *the Fireman's Fund insurance company* CTrib, January 1, 1874; CTrib, January 2, 1874; CTrib, January 3, 1874; CTrib, January 4, 1874; CTrib, January 5, 1874; CTrib, January 6, 1874; CTrib, January 7, 1874.

272 *the annoyance and delay of applying in person* Chicago Relief and Aid Society, Minutes of Executive Committee meeting of January 2, 1874, United Charities of Chicago Records, Chicago History Museum; CTrib, January 4, 1874.

272 *a mile southwest of where the 1871 fire had begun* Chicago Inter-Ocean, September 18, 1873; CTrib, September 18, 1873.

273 *the main torrent was sweeping northward* Report of the Board of Police, in the Fire Department to the Common Council of the City of Chicago, for the Year Ending March 31, 1875 (Chicago: Hazlitt and Reed, 1875), 159; Andreas, 3:461–62.

273 *he didn't want Wilbur Storey and the* Chicago Times *after him again* CTrib, July 15, 1874.

274 *She claimed that she had dreamed this would happen* CTrib, July 15, 1874.

274   *this latest trial by fire*   Mrs. A. E. [Ashleman] Sanderson, "Reminiscences," December 14, 1925, CHMFC.

274   *hampered its efficiency and effectiveness*   Andreas, 3:461.

274   *the department promoted Third Assistant Marshal Mathias Benner up to Schank's position*   CTimes, February 11, 1872; CTimes, February 13, 1872; CTimes, February 17, 1872; CRepub, February 17, 1872.

275   *Williams never came through with any payment*   CTrib, August 2, 1873. The name is spelled Halleck in some sources. Isaac Hallock was the driver for Hook and Ladder Company No. 4.

275   *Then she sent a letter to the press that denied the denial*   CTrib, August 5, 1873.

275   *to keep a tinder-box and an oil factory where it suits him best*   CTrib, July 15, 1874.

276   *Chicago needed to find comprehensive fire prevention solutions and reform the fire department*   CTrib, July 19, 1874.

276   *the removal of all lumber yards from built-up areas*   New-York Tribune, July 28, 1874; Harry Chase Brearley, *The History of the National Board of Fire Underwriters: Fifty Years of a Civilizing Force* (New York: Frederick A. Stokes, 1916), 41–45.

276   *a more ample water supply*   CTrib, July 21, 1874.

277   *they would withdraw from Chicago*   New York Times, September 30, 1874; Andreas, 3:462.

277   *and improved trade*   CTrib, July 26, 1874.

278   *such a metropolitan moral exemplar as Boston*   CTrib, November 12, 1872.

278   *this proportion rose to one-half*   Brearley, *The History of the National Board of Fire Underwriters*, v.

279   *though the presidential proclamations make no mention of it*   Hazen and Hazen, *Keepers of the Flame*, 114–15; "Proclamation 1746: Designation the Week beginning Sunday, October 4, 1925, as National Fire Prevention Week," Wikisource, https://en.wikisource.org/wiki/Proclamation_1746; "Don't Let It Happen Again," in "Enduring Symbol," in GCFWOM, https://www.greatchicagofire.org/commemorating-catastrophe/enduring-symbol/.

280   *the Great Fire of 1871*   Everett Marshall, *The Great Chicago Theater Disaster* (Chicago: Publishers Union of America, 1904); Nat Brandt, *Chicago Death Trap: The Iroquois Theater Fire of 1903* (Carbondale: Southern Illinois University Press, 2003); Anthony P. Hatch, *Tinder Box: The Iroquois Theater Disaster, 1903* (Chicago: Academy Chicago, 2003). Far more people—almost three thousand—perished when the two main buildings in New York's World Trade Center burned and collapsed on September 11, 2001, though the fact that this was caused by terrorists purposely crashing commercial airliners into the buildings puts it into a category of disaster all its own.

281   *He resigned the following year and passed away in 1907*   CTrib, February 24, 1907. William Musham's son H. A. Musham's carefully researched 1940 account of the fire, which praises the work of the firefighters (and scorns William Hildreth and his gunpowder), is a form of tribute to his father.
       The Chicago Union Stock Yards, which escaped the great fire, suffered an appalling blaze on December 22–23, 1910. Three civilians and twenty-one firemen perished. One of the firemen was Chicago Fire Chief James J. Horan, killed when a burning building collapsed. In 2004 a monument to these firefighters by S. Thomas Scarff, since expanded in purpose to honor all members of the department who have

died in the line of duty, was placed behind the stone entrance gate designed by the architectural firm formed in 1873 by Daniel H. Burnham and John Wellborn Root. By that time, the Burnham and Root gate was virtually all that remained of the stock yards. The statue depicts three firemen in the midst of a battle to the death with the flames.

In 1864, seven years before Chicago's great fire, a memorial statue by noted sculptor Leonard Volk was raised in Rosehill Cemetery, four miles north of the city in Lakeview, to honor volunteer firemen. A handsome and fit young volunteer, helmet resting on his curls, strikes a confident pose, his right hand upraised and the left holding a speaking trumpet at his side. He stands atop a tall Doric column with coiled fire hose at its base, at whose corners are four fire hydrants. Fifteen men who perished defending Chicago against fire rest nearby.

16. Celebrating Destruction

283   *making it the nation's second largest metropolis after New York*   Skogan, 18–20; Ann Durkin Keating, "Annexations and Editions to the City of Chicago," in *EC*, http://www.encyclopedia.chicagohistory.org/pages/3716.html. Chicago's population would peak at just over 3.6 million in the early 1950s. Los Angeles became the country's second largest city shortly after 1980.

283   *The cornerstone and its short-lived time capsule were removed in 1882*   Ross Miller, *American Apocalypse: The Great Fire and the Myth of Chicago* (Chicago: University of Chicago Press, 1990), 148–49.

284   *the grass will grow in the streets of every city in the country*   William Jennings Bryan, "Bryan's 'Cross of Gold' Speech: Mesmerizing the Masses," History Matters, http://historymatters.gmu.edu/d/5354/; this webpage includes a sound recording of the speech. The source of the text is *Official Proceedings of the Democratic National Convention Held in Chicago, Illinois, July 7, 8, 9, 10, and 11, 1896* (Logansport, IN: Wilson, Humphreys and Company, 1896), 226–34, reprinted in *The Annals of America*, vol. 12, *1895–1904: Populism, Imperialism, and Reform* (Chicago: Encyclopedia Britannica, 1968), 100–105. The Coliseum, where Bryan was nominated, stood at Sixty-Third Street and Stony Island Avenue. It was the second of three buildings in the city with that name. The first was erected downtown in the 1860s, the third in 1899 at 1513 South Wabash Avenue. See Robert Pruter, "Chicago's Other Coliseum," *Chicago History* 38, no. 1 (Spring 2012): 44–65.

284   *which no doubt owed its prosperity to Republican fiscal policy*   *CTrib*, October 9, 1896; G. W. Steevens, "The Biggest Parade on Earth," in *The Land of the Dollar* (Edinburgh: William Blackwood and Sons, 1897), 185–94.

284   *the recovery*   "Origin of the 'I Will' Woman," Chicagology, https://chicagology.com/columbiaexpo/fair081/.

285   *the Most Significant and Grandest Spectacle of Modern Times*   Rossiter Johnson, ed., *A History of the World's Columbian Exposition, Held in Chicago in 1893*, vol. 1 (New York: D. Appleton, 1897), 453; "The Most Significant and Grandest Spectacle of Modern Times," in "Columbian Carnival," in *GCFWOM*, https://www.greatchicagofire.org/commemorating-catastrophe/columbian-carnival/.

The fair, which had trumpeted the city's resurrection from the ashes, fell prey to fire fiends of its own. On July 10, 1893, when the World's Columbian Exposition was in full swing, twelve firefighters and three civilians died in a terrible blaze in the Cold Storage Building, where perishable items were kept refrigerated. In January 1894 a fire that killed another fireman burned a portion of the Court of Honor, by this time emptied of its exhibits. The rest of the main exhibition buildings were lost to flames six months later. Carl Smith, *Urban Disorder and the Shape of Belief: The Great Chicago Fire, the Haymarket Bomb, and the Model Town of Pullman*, 2nd ed. (Chicago: University of Chicago Press, 2007), 268–69.

287   *It is easy to think that photographs of the paintings are of the actual fire*   David Swing, *A Story of the Chicago Fire* ([Chicago]: H. H. Gross, 1893); "Advertisement for Chicago Fire Cyclorama," in "Blazing Visions," in *GCFWOM*, https://www.greatchicagofire .org/fanning-flames/blazing-visions/. "Blazing Visions" also includes images of five scenes from the Chicago Fire Cyclorama. Visiting a cyclorama was a more immersive experience than viewing a panorama. The former was a long scroll on which an artist or artists painted scenes of the fire that could be unrolled before spectators' eyes. In the late 1870s, audiences could witness a 1,600-foot panoramic retelling of the Chicago disaster, more than twice the length of the panorama executed by H. H. Cross immediately after the fire. As the oversized scroll was unfurled, they beheld the most gripping moments of Chicago's struggle. An 1878 advertising poster excerpts scenes of firemen training water on the flames, the rush for life over the Randolph Street Bridge, a shooting in a saloon, and the lynching of an arsonist from a lamppost. See "Stage, Story, and Song," in *GCFWOM*, https://www.greatchicagofire.org/fanning-flames/stage-story-and -song/.

287   *White City, the amusement park at Sixty-Third Street and South Park*   Freedomland, located in the Bronx on the current site of the mammoth housing complex Co-op City, had a brief life in the early 1960s as the Northeast's unsuccessful answer to Disneyland. Visitors (including the author) assisted firemen in period costume in operating hand-pumped engines (already obsolete in 1871) that rushed to combat the flames preying on a steel-and-asbestos model of Chicago. See Fighting the Great Chicago Fire in the Bronx, https://www.youtube.com/watch?v=beDmmvxqWP0.

    Reenactments of armed conflicts and disasters enjoyed a long partnership with world's fairs and the amusement parks. *Buffalo Bill's Wild West*, which ran through the summer of 1893 a few blocks from the Columbian Exposition, employed Native Americans to do battle with performers playing settlers. The 1901 Pan American Exposition in Buffalo, New York, at which President William McKinley was shot by an assassin, featured a staged skirmish between soldiers and Indians on horseback; for a video of the performance in Buffalo, see "Sham Battle at the Pan-American Exposition," Library of Congress, https://www.loc.gov/item/00694341/. At the 1904 World's Fair in St. Louis, one could see a re-creation of the Galveston, Texas, flood of 1900.

288   *wrapped in fire and mantled luridly with smoke*   CTrib, September 26, 1903; CTrib, September 27, 1903. This event took place not on the anniversary of the fire but as part of the centennial commemoration of the original construction of Fort Dearborn in 1803. Delegations from the Chippewa, Fox, Menominee, Potawatomi, Sac, and Winnebago nations, whose ancestors had been removed from the Chicago region, camped in an "Indian Village" in Lincoln Park.

289   *the drama of the rising glory of Chicago*   [Chicago Association of Commerce], *Semi-Centennial Observance of the Chicago Fire*, [1921], pamphlets in the collections of the Chicago History Museum. One of the pamphlets is a "preliminary announcement," while the other, with the epigraph "Undaunted—We Build," is the formal announcement. Other documents include "Report: Semi-Centennial Observance of Chicago Fire," October 20, 1921. See also "Festival Play," in *GCFWOM*, https://www

.greatchicagofire.org/commemorating-catastrophe-library/festival-play/; "The Seven Fires," in *GCFWOM*, https://www.greatchicagofire.org/commemorating-catastrophe-library/seven-fires/; and *Chicago Commerce*, August 13, 1921.

290   *battled the great conflagration sixty-three years earlier*   CTrib, October 8, 1934.

290   *The fire department sold a stamp created for the occasion*   CTrib, October 8, 1971; *Chicago Sun-Times*, February 23, 1971; *Chicago Sun-Times*, October 9, 1971; *Chicago Sun-Times*, October 10, 1971; "Centennial Fire Medal," in "Tending the Fire," in *GCF-WOM*, https://www.greatchicagofire.org/commemorating-catastrophe/tending-fire/.

291   *Handel's* Music for the Royal Fireworks   "Official Dinner Commemorating the 100th Anniversary of the Chicago Fire, Sponsored by Mayor Richard J. Daley and the Members of the City Council," combined menu and program, October 8, 1871, collections of the Chicago History Museum. See also "Medium Rare, Please," in "Onward to the Centennial," in *GCFWOM*, https://www.greatchicagofire.org/commemorating-catastrophe/onward-centennial/.

291   *This is an epic failure*   CTrib, October 14, 2014.

292   *when Market Street was widened and became North Wacker Drive*   Frank A. Randall, *History of the Development of Building Construction in Chicago* (Urbana: University of Illinois Press, 1949), 61, 44.

292   *that honors a longtime employee*   CTrib, August 19, 1994.

293   *nearly a billion gallons of water a day*   City of Chicago, "Water Management," https://www.chicago.gov/city/en/depts/water.html.

293   The Great Fire*, an original production that offered a reimagined version of the disaster*   Lookingglass Theatre Company, "The Great Fire," https://lookingglasstheatre.org/event/the-great-fire-2011/.

293   *taken from a burned-out hardware store after the fire*   Jennifer Billock, "Five Places Where You Can Still See Remnants of the Great Chicago Fire," *Smithsonian*, January 24, 2018, https://www.smithsonianmag.com/travel/remnants-great-chicago-fire-180967918/.

294   *wood fragments purportedly from her barn*   "Pieces of the Past," in *GCFWOM*, https://www.greatchicagofire.org/souvenirs/pieces-of-past/.

294   *but it has been closed to all traffic since 1939*   "LaSalle Street Tunnel," in *GCFWOM*, https://www.greatchicagofire.org/landmarks/lasalle-street-tunnel/.

295   *There is no sign on or near it to inform the possibly curious passerby of this*   "Courthouse Finial," in "Living Memory," in *GCFWOM*, https://www.greatchicagofire.org/souvenirs/living-memory/.

295   *now almost lost among much larger buildings*   "Washington Block," in *GCFWOM*, https://www.greatchicagofire.org/landmarks/washington-block/.

295   *Since 2011 it has been a Chicago landmark*   Commission on Chicago Landmarks, *Landmark Designation Report: Holden Block* (Chicago: Commission on Chicago Landmarks, 2011), https://www.chicago.gov/content/dam/city/depts/zlup/Historic_Preservation/Publications/Holden_Block.pdf.

296   *in his memoir of the period*   Frederick Francis Cook, *Bygone Days in Chicago: Recollections of the "Garden City" of the Sixties* (Chicago: A. C. McClurg, 1910), 189.

296   *the construction of the Art Institute of Chicago*   When it opened in 1893, the building was temporarily called the World's Congress Auxiliary of the World's Columbian Exposition. Under this name it hosted over two hundred "congresses" on issues ranging

from religion to women's progress to agriculture. Chicago Public Library, "World's Congress Auxiliary Pre-Publications, Programs and Circulars Collection," https://www.chipublib.org/fa-worlds-congress-auxiliary-pre-publications-programs-and-circulars-collection/.

297   *In 1913 they were sold as scrap for two dollars*   *CTrib*, April 9, 1913.

297   *she is still in the milk business*   *Chicago Daily News*, October 8, 1886.

298   *the Chicago that she so heedlessly destroyed*   Colbert and Chamberlin, 202.

298   *lamp of the kind that Dushek supposedly found*   Andreas, 2:708, 2:714, 2:715; "Lamp Found in O'Leary's Barn," in "A Star Is Born," in *GCFWOM*, https://greatchicago fire.org/oleary-legend/star-born/. In 1909 insurance man Robert J. Critchell stated improbably in a self-published memoir that Mrs. O'Leary had confessed to him shortly after the event that she had started it. "I never saw the cow," he wrote, "but I did interview the old lady and was informed by her in rather an ungracious way that the story was true." Robert S. Critchell, *Recollections of a Fire Insurance Man, Including His Experience in U.S. Navy (Mississippi Squadron) during the Civil War* (Chicago: Robert S. Critchell, 1909), 81. See also Bales, 62.

298   *questionable information supposedly collected by Andreas*   Musham, 96–97.

298   *The four kept mum when their joke ended up burning the city down*   *CTrib*, September 26, 1903.

299   *one of them knocked over the lamp*   *CTrib*, October 8, 1997.

299   *that he could not do it himself*   *CTrib*, January 21, 1915; John Kelly to Patrick O'Leary, March 2, 1927, CHMFC.

299   *before I left the house*   *CTrib*, May 25, 1894.

300   *There'll Be a Hot Time in the Old Town Tonight*   *CTrib*, October 8, 1933.

300   *There'll be a hot time in the old town tonight!*   "Hot Time in the Old Town Tonight," ScoutSongs.com, https://www.scoutsongs.com/lyrics/hot-time-in-the-old-town-tonight.html.

300   *a monumental fake*   *CTrib*, January 23, 1925; *CTrib*, January 27, 1925; *CTrib*, January 31, 1925.

300   *which supposedly explains their simultaneity*   Mel Waskin, *Mrs. O'Leary's Comet* (Chicago: Academy Chicago, 1985).

300   *before rushing to awaken the O'Learys*   Bales, 112–38.

301   *as charged sixty-three years ago*   "Mrs. O'Leary and Her Cow" and "Justice Has at Last Caught Up with Her," in *GCFWOM*, https://www.greatchicagofire.org/oleary-legend/saga-continues/; *CTrib*, October 9, 1934.

302   *who wants to look at the rear end of a cow for 12 months?"*   "Mrs. Catherine O'Leary Milking Daisy," in "The Saga Continues," in *GCFWOM*, https://www.greatchicagofire.org/oleary-legend/saga-continues/; *New York Times*, January 1, 1991.

302   *It won the grand prize*   *Chicago Sun-Times*, January 2, 1960. A film of the parade, including the Chicago float, is viewable online. See 1960 Rose Parade Pasadena California Wisconsin vs. Washington 79804, https://www.youtube.com/watch?v=rSgpqT9ASFE/.

302   *and Extended to Lincoln Park*   In 1890 Michael Suchy, also from Bohemia, bought the home from Kohler for $8,000. Four years later the city paved the alley between DeKoven and Taylor Streets. It also raised the level a few feet, so that Suchy had to

climb up three steps from his yard to get to the alley. *CTrib*, May 25, 1894; "Sacred Site," in "The Saga Continues," https://www.greatchicagofire.org/oleary-legend/saga-continues/.

303   *clearing the block for urban renewal*   To view a newsreel of the burning of the house then on the O'Leary lot, see "City Gets Revenge on Mrs. O'Leary," in "The O'Learys on Film," in *GCFWOM*, https://www.greatchicagofire.org/oleary-legend/olearys-film/.

304   *where the Great Chicago Fire began*   "Chicago Fire Monument," in "Enduring Symbol," in *GCFWOM*, https://www.greatchicagofire.org/commemorating-catastrophe/enduring-symbol/. Bales, 174, includes a photograph of the emblem marking the "exact spot."

305   *all blame in regard to the Great Chicago Fire of 1871*   Committee on Police and Fire, *Exoneration of Mrs. O'Leary and Her Cow from All Blame in Regard to Great Chicago Fire of 1871* (Chicago: Committee on Police and Fire, October 6, 1997), https://d4804za1f1gw.cloudfront.net/wp-content/uploads/sites/3/2014/09/28111030/council journal10281997.pdf.

INDEX